DATE DUE

Islam and Politics in Central Asia

Islam and Politics in Central Asia

Mehrdad Haghayeghi

St. Martin's Press
New York

ISBN 0-312-09622-4

Library of Congress Cataloging-in-Publication Data

Haghayeghi, Merdad.
    Islam and politics in Central Asia / Mehrdad Haghayeghi.
        p.   cm.
    Includes bibliographical references (p.   ) and index.
    ISBN 0-312-09622-4
    1. Islam and politics—Asia, Central. 2. Asia, Central—Politics
and government—1991- 3. Islam—Asia, Central—History—20th
century. 4. Asia, Central—Ethnic relations.   I. Title.
DK859.5.H34 1995
320.958—dc20   94-30960
                                                       CIP

First Edition May 1995:
10 9 8 7 6 5 4 3 2 1

Interior Design by Digital Type & Design

For Arthur Kaye,
whose standards of dignity and decency
have forever changed my life.

❧ ☙

CONTENTS

LIST OF TABLES

LIST OF FIGURES

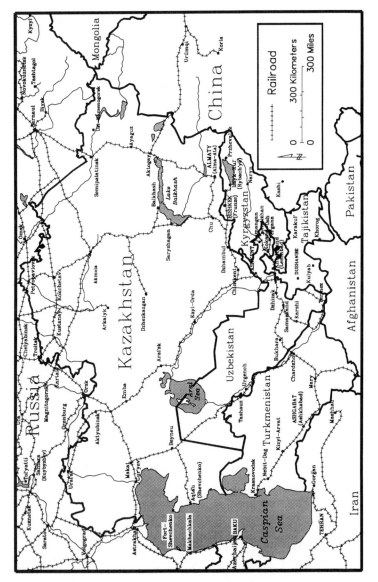

Central Asian States

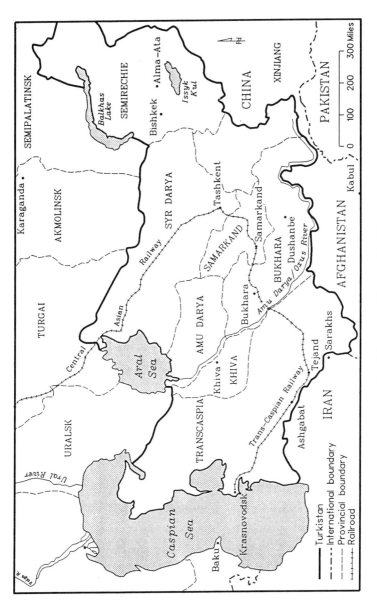

Turkistan Circa 1917

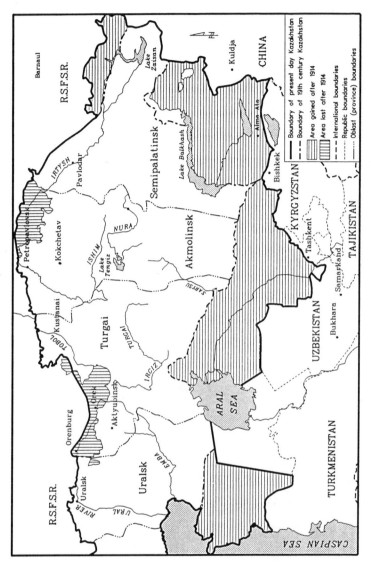

Nineteenth-Century Kazakhstan

NOTE ON TRANSLITERATION

Given the present state of flux in the spelling of Central Asian names, both of individuals and places, I have tried to use the closest possible transliteration to the actual pronunciation in the languages of the region, rather than utilizing translations of the same names from the Russian into English. As such, I have refrained from the use of Russified versions of the Central Asian names and places, unless such versions are still widely employed in the media and academic pieces. Where needed, I have used two versions to avoid confusion. The transliteration of the Russian names and places are based on the style recommended by the Library of Congress with some modifications, for instance, endings such as (ii) or (ev) have been changed to (i) and (yev). Spellings in quotations, however, may not follow the consistent pattern used in the text, as I have avoided alterations for the sake of authenticity.

PREFACE

THIS BOOK GREW out of an article I drafted in the summer of 1992 to satisfy a personal interest about the future political prospects of the newly-independent Central Asian republics of Kazakhstan, Kyrgyzstan, Tajikistan, Turkmenistan, and Uzbekistan. What began as simple curiosity, however, turned into an intense passion for the history and the cultures of a region that is now plagued with enormous economic and political problems not experienced, to the same degree, by any other postcolonial region in the world. What sets apart the Central Asian republics, and for that matter the other former Soviet successor states, is the Communist experience that, for all practical purposes, defined the very nature of society and its highest political expression, the Soviet state. As the antithesis to capitalism and liberal democracy, Communism has left behind the least-hospitable environment for post-independence economic and political restructuring. These republics have also been faced with a crisis of identity, the resolution of which will ultimately determine the future structural nature and functional scope of the governments in the region. In this process, Islam, democracy, and ethnicity are the principal players in the Central Asian drama, whose script has yet to assume its final shape. My visits to the region have only confirmed the enormity of the problems that will have to be endured in the years to come before the region can experience some semblance of prosperity. But there may be light at the end of the tunnel.

I owe a debt of gratitude to a number of individuals and institutions on both sides of the Atlantic that rewarded my enthusiasm for this project with approbation and support. Sincere thanks to the chair of my department at Southwest Missouri State University, Denny Pilant, who saw the potential in my project and thus facilitated my efforts toward its completion in every way he could. In addition, I would like to thank Dean Bernice Warren, Dr. Frank Einhellig, and Dean Curtis Lawrence, whose generous financial support in the form of research grants and a summer fellowship made my trips to the region and stay in Washington, D.C., a reality.

My heartfelt appreciation to the senior editor of BBC Monitoring, Shahrzad Ghorashian, whose uncompromising material and emotional support played a critical role in my decision to pursue this research. I am also grateful to the Finance Director of the Royal Institute of International Affairs, David Weller, and the library staff of the institute for facilitating the completion of this project. Arthur Kaye deserves my deepest appreciation for his untiring support throughout the drafting of the manuscript. I also benefited from the insightful remarks of Dr. C. B. Holman in designing the conceptual framework of this study. Also worthy of mention is the staff of the Research and Information Division of BBC Monitoring, and the staff of the Slavic, Baltic, and Eurasian Archives of Radio Liberty in Munich for their valuable assistance in compiling data for various chapters.

Special thanks to Pauline Woods for her incisive editorial remarks, the interlibrary loan staff of the Southwest Missouri State University, whose impeccable professionalism expedited the completion of this project, Rick Havel for his brilliant cartography, and Valeri Pavlov for his translation of a handful of Russian sources used in this work.

This publication was prepared in part under a grant from the Kennan Institute for Advanced Russian Studies of the Woodrow Wilson International Center for Scholars in Washington, D.C. The center played an instrumental role in my intellectual and academic development. One can only hope that in this era of shrinking budgets, the financial well-being of such inspiring institutions are not compromised. Research for this publication was also supported by two grants from the International Research & Exchanges Board, with funds provided by the National Endowment for the Humanities and the Andrew W. Mellon Foundation. None of these organizations are, however, responsible for the views expressed in this book.

Lastly, I must pay tribute to the late V. V. Barthold; H. A. R. Gibb; Robert Pierce; Geoffery Wheeler; Alexandre Bennigsen; Marie Broxup; Helene Carrere d'Encausse; Edward Allworth; Martha Olcott; Barnet Rubin; Michael Rywkin; Yaacov Ro'i; William Fierman; James Critchlow; Boris Rumer; Muriel Atkin; Shirin Akiner; Bess Brown; Azade-Ayse Rorlich; Nancy Lubin; Teresa Rakowska-Harmstone; and Shahrbanou Tadjbakhsh, whose pioneering work enlightened and inspired me to carry on.

WASHINGTON, D.C.
DECEMBER 7, 1994

INTRODUCTION

We Central Asians are seeing ourselves more and more distinctly against the panorama of the former Soviet Union, the panorama of the contemporary East, and the panorama of the modern West. It is this consciousness that will help shape our national and regional identities in the years to come. By drawing on our sublime past, while constructing our future, we are destined to find our deserved place in history.

—MUHAMMAD SADIQ MUHAMMAD YUSUF,
FORMER HEAD, MUSLIM RELIGIOUS BOARD
OF CENTRAL ASIA AND KAZAKHSTAN

Nearly a decade has passed since the Gorbachev revolution fundamentally altered the political chemistry of the Soviet Union and subsequently propelled a largely well-defined bipolar world into a period of relative uncertainty. Despite the available explanations, it is not at all clear why Gorbachev followed the path he initiated, which in essence brought about the demise of the last great colonial empire. Some observers have pointed to the sobering realization, on the part of the Gorbachev team, that if proper structural reforms had not been undertaken, the Communist bloc would have entirely missed the second industrial revolution championed by the West and, in particular, by the United States. To Gorbachev's disappointment, however, the cure has proven to be much more difficult than the diagnosis. Other observers, on the other hand, have offered an ideological rather than a technological interpretation, stressing the inherent weaknesses of Marxist-Leninism as a paradigm capable of guiding man, and thus society, toward achieving its full potential. Gorbachev is said to have grappled with this ideological deficiency and hoped merely to redefine Marxism, not abandon it altogether. Yet, others have argued that the Soviet philosophy of progress was designed, above all, to impress the West rather than to address its urgent domestic needs. Gorbachev's policies, as are well known, failed to salvage the remnants of decades of structural neglect.

Leaving aside its causes, the inevitable consequence of the collapse of the Soviet Union has been the emergence of 15 independent republics with indeterminate political and economic futures. Decidedly unprepared to cope with the vacuum created by the death of Marxism, these republics have become a lively forum for a multiplicity of ideological trends, of which Islam has become a major source of preoccupation for the West, particularly in the context of the Central Asian republics where Islam has exhibited considerable vigor after 70 years of Soviet antireligious repression.[1] Clearly, there is legitimate room for concern given the twentieth-century radical and fundamentalist interpretations of Islam and the practical implications of such interpretations that have, among other things, given rise to the Islamic Republic of Iran and other forms of extremism elsewhere in the world.[2] It is the availability of such Islamic doctrines to the Central Asian republics that has greatly contributed to an overall uncertainty with regard to the future political development of these newly independent states.

This study is an attempt to put into comparative perspective the principle dynamics of Islamic revival in Central Asia. It should be pointed out that while there has been a general consensus on a set of conceptual parameters believed to be capable of having a definite qualitative impact on the process of Islamic revival, very few observers seem to agree on the relative weight and significance of these parameters vis-à-vis one another and thus in relation to the subject under investigation. Some scholars, for instance, have emphasized internal economic factors as the primary force with the potential to push Islam in a more radical direction in the near future.[3] Interestingly enough, however, the continuing economic decline in the region has for the most part strengthened the status of the die-hard Communists and ultra-nationalists rather than Islamic forces.[4] As such, this study will not concern itself with the economic determinants of Islamic revival. Others, focusing on the role of Iran and Afghanistan in Tajik affairs in recent years, have been compelled to assign considerable importance to external pressures exerted from the Middle East when evaluating the patterns of Islamization.[5] Although the significance of the Middle Eastern influence can hardly be contested, this book will focus primarily on domestic factors, which are considered here to be more critical in shaping the Islamic orientation of the Central Asian republics in the foreseeable future.[6]

CONCEPTUAL PARAMETERS

The nature, scope, intensity, and speed of the Islamic revival are intimately related to two sets of factors. The specific factors that address the unique characteristics of Islam in Central Asia include the general regional proclivity toward Islam, which is seen here as a function of the method by which Islam was introduced into the sedentary and tribal societies of Central Asia, the nature of the dominant Islamic doctrine, and the prevailing doctrinal diversity. This Islamic proclivity is influenced, in turn, by the organizational reach and mobilization capacities of the Islamic forces operating in the region. The general factors that are equally significant in shaping the overall pattern of Islamization include the strengths or weaknesses of the nascent democratic forces and their ability to institute an inclusive rather than exclusive method of governance, the nature of the republican governments' policies toward Islam, as well as their ability or willingness to institute genuine political reforms, and finally the ethnic makeup and orientation of each republic.

Despite the obvious inter- and intrarepublican variations in Islamic disposition, the overall religious orientation of the Central Asian republics can not be described as the firebrand variety generally associated with Shi'i or Sunni fundamentalism in the Middle East. Three historical factors, among others, may largely be responsible for the development of an essentially moderate Islamic framework in the region. The first factor has to do with the manner in which Islam made its way into the region. Conversion to Islam was carried out in two phases. The first phase, which mostly took the forms of conquest and subjugation, lasted for a relatively short period of time beginning in the mid-seventh century and effectively ending early in the eighth century, subsequent to the death of Qutayba ibn Muslim, who was in reality responsible for the successful Arab infiltration into Central Asia. The second phase of conversion was made possible by Muslim merchants and, later, by missionaries who exposed the local population to Islam along the trade routes, in particular the famous Silk Road. It was during this peaceful expansionist phase from the ninth to the twelfth century that Islam made its lasting imprint on the population of Central Asia, not so much as a religious ideology, but as a way of life.[7] This development, as will be detailed later, strengthened the cultural rather than the religious dimensions of Islam among the local inhabitants, thereby creating a qualitatively different Islamic orientation than that which had taken root in the Arab world.

The second factor that contributed to the liberal nature of Islam, involves the milieu within which it gained widespread acceptance. This was, of course, determined essentially by the geographical conditions of Central Asia, which had given birth to two rather distinct, yet interactive societies: the sedentary populations of the oases enclaves of Merv, Balkh, Bukhara, Samarkand, Fergana, and so on, and the tribal populations of the Steppe and the surrounding regions. Conversion to Islam was more effective in the case of the former societies but lacked depth and substance in relation to the latter. The enormous size and remoteness of the Steppe, the lack of adequate military manpower, the political instability at the heart of the Arab empire, and the absence of missionaries early on to spread Islam among the pastoral population have been partially responsible for Islam's relatively poor performance in the tribal regions of Central Asia. As such, Kazakhstan, Kyrgyzstan, and Turkmenistan have developed a mild proclivity toward Islam compared to Tajikistan and Uzbekistan, which have been more thoroughly exposed to its tenets.

The third factor is closely related to the essential characteristics of the dominant Islamic doctrine on the one hand, and the Islamic doctrinal diversity on the other hand. With an estimated population of 54 million, Central Asian inhabitants are predominantly Sunni Muslims of the Hanafi school, noted for its liberal theological orientation. Abu Hanifeh al-Numan ibn Thabit ibn Zuta (699–767 A.D.), the founder of the school, is claimed to have placed heavy emphasis on analogy *(qyias)*, public consensus *(jima)*, and private opinion *(ra'y)*, in the administration and interpretation of Islamic principles, the use of which have been altogether condemned or severely restricted by the less liberal Islamic schools. There is also considerable sub-doctrinal diversity that offers a less promising environment for the growth of radical Islam, which requires a high degree of doctrinal consensus if it is to succeed in capturing power. There is, for instance, a variety of Sufi sects in Central Asia with rather exclusive membership rights. In addition, there are a few Shi'i minority groups represented in some regions, most noticeably the Ismailis of the Gorno-Badakhshan and the Twelvers of the Samarkand and Bukhara.

The overall Islamic orientation of the region has also been influenced by the organizational reach and mobilization capacity of the Islamic forces active in the region. As will be discussed in considerable detail later, the Islamic forces lack sufficient organizational networks in Kazakhstan, Kyrgyzstan, and Turkmenistan, and have lost their legal status in Tajikistan and Uzbekistan where they have been well-organized and capable of reaching the public through an ever-increasing network of mosques and traditional Islamic schools. So far, however, the Islamic organizations and movements—with the exception of the largely misunderstood case of Tajikistan—have in principle exhibited moderate tendencies as, for instance, electoral methods of political competition and power-sharing rather than violence and force have been advocated.

The dynamics of Islamic revival will be further conditioned by the strengths or weaknesses of the newly emerging democratic forces in Central Asia. It will be argued that as an essentially imported ideology, democracy has a difficult task ahead, but the popular principles it espouses are undoubtedly the most powerful alternative to those sponsored by the Islamic forces in any future electoral competition for power. It is noteworthy that with the exception of Turkmenistan, which has displayed both weak Islamic and democratic tendencies, the democratic process has been most successful in those republics where the Islamic forces have had a considerably smaller following. This has placed Kazakhstan and Kyrgyzstan at the top of the most likely republics to complete the transition to democracy. In Turkmenistan, Tajikistan, and Uzbekistan, the democratic drive has been arrested by those in power, dimming the prospects for its normal evolutionary expansion in the near future.

The Central Asian governments' general political orientation, as well as their attitude toward Islam, constitute the third conceptual parameter of this work. As had been anticipated, the present republican leaders have demonstrated a marked reluctance to carry out substantive political reforms with the objective of including the newly emerging democratic and Islamic forces in the political discourse. This has been most noticeable in Tajikistan, Uzbekistan, and Turkmenistan where repression has been the preferred method of political control, and less apparent in Kazakhstan and Kyrgyzstan where a respectable degree of political tolerance has been displayed by Presidents Askar Akayev and Nursultan Nazarbayev. The problem is due to the fact that Central Asian independence did not substantially alter the nature of the power structure, leaving intact Communist personnel whose authority is being slowly challenged by the very nature of the reforms they are obligated to institute if they are to shed their Communist reputation. This has also been true with respect to the governments' approach to Islam, which, in essence, is a skillfully disguised continuation of what was commonplace under Soviet rule: an official religious structure closely tied to, and monitored by, the top leadership in each republic. In the light of ongoing repression and strict political control over the official Islamic structures, Islam forces may move in a more radical direction in the years to come.

The ethnic makeup and orientation of each republic is also considered a major determining factor influencing, in the long term, the very essence of the process under scrutiny. The estimated 7.2 million Kazakhs, for instance, are a minority in their own republic, with nearly as many non-Muslim Slavs residing there.[8] Yet the Uzbeks constitute 72 percent of the population, with less than 20 percent non-Muslim citizens in the republic. Such pronounced ethnic disparities offer a powerful explanatory parameter in understanding the patterns of Islamic revival in Central Asia. But, in addition, the Central Asian republics have witnessed the emergence of two ethnic currents with the potential to influence the Islamic drive in the future. The first, and the weaker of the two, is pan-Turkism, which has been a secular-liberal trend conceived in the late-nineteenth century in response to the decline of the Ottoman empire and the Turkic civilization. The second, identified here as "ethnic separatism" refers to the ongoing process of ethnic self-assertion. Reinforced by the age-old regional, subregional, and local exclusivist tendencies, ethnic separatism has the potential to severely curtail the scope and speed of Islamic revival, as each dominant ethnic group within the multiethnic republics strives to maintain its supremacy.

ORGANIZATION OF THE BOOK

The next six chapters are intended both to offer some background information and to address the mentioned conceptual parameters. The first chapter provides an overview of Islam under Communism. Organized into five sections, it presents the crux of the Marxist discourse on religion that helped shape Soviet policies on Islam between the 1920s and the 1980s. It then chronicles the Soviet antireligious design in Central Asia during the Leninist, Stalinist, and post-Stalinist eras. Each era is in turn broken down with respect to the particular set of strategies utilized to deal with active and passive Islamic resistance to Soviet repression. It is concluded that the antireligious campaign in Central Asia succeeded only in suppressing the rituals and not the spiritual power of Islam, and for that matter other religions.

Chapter 2 addresses the Gorbachev era and the changing nature of the Soviet policies toward religion in general and Islam in particular. Having outlined the sequence of events that led to the rise of Gorbachev to power, the chapter presents a discussion of perestroika and glasnost in Central Asia and the region's response to Gorbachev's reformist platform. It is argued that Gorbachev's Islamic policies were largely in line with his predecessors during his first three years in office. What led to his decision to entirely abandon the decades-old antireligious campaign in the Soviet Union was a matter of necessity rather than choice, as it was concluded that economic reforms could not succeed without substantive political and ideological reforms, of which religion was a key policy issue. As expected, it was Christianity and not Islam that became the early beneficiary of Soviet policies. In due course, Islam, too, was offered its freedom.

Chapter 3 presents an overview of the Islamic revival in post-Communist Central Asia. Organized into four sections, it details the various factors that have contributed to the emergence of a mild Islamic proclivity in the region, in particular as it pertains to the manner in which Islam was introduced to the Central Asian population and the nature of the dominant Islamic school of jurisprudence adhered to by the majority. The contemporary Islamic organizations and movements and their overall political orientation and agenda constitute the third section of the chapter. Finally, a discussion of the quantitative dimensions of Islamic revival with respect to the number of mosques, Islamic schools, and the observance of Islamic rituals have been presented.

The nature and scope of the democratic movements in Central Asia is the subject of chapter 4. Having traced the evolution of the Central Asian nationalist movements and their eventual transformation into democratic organizations, this chapter provides a classification of the newly emerging liberal democratic and national democratic parties as well as the revamped Communist and presidential parties in the region. While far from monolithic, the democratic movement in Central Asia has had a generally promising beginning in all republics, and given the opportunity, it could transform the political makeup of some of the republics under examination in the future. The chapter is designed to provide a basis for a comparative assessment of the strength of democracy versus Islam.

Chapter 5 outlines the Central Asian governments' response to the ongoing Islamic revival. It first puts into perspective the Communist heritage of the present power elite as a factor in slowing the progress of reform in the region. A discussion of the Tajik catastrophe, as it relates to the power struggle between the old Communist *nomenklatura* and the emerging Islamic and democratic forces in that republic, constitutes the backbone of this section. This is followed by an overview of the post-independence role of the so-called official Islam in the region. This section provides an analysis of the emerging patterns of response, by the "official" clergy, to the continuing government intervention in the religious affairs of the republics. This chapter focuses some attention on the potentially destabilizing effects of the governments' repressive policies toward the Islamic forces, which have further legitimized these forces in the eyes of the public at large.

Chapter 6 addresses the ethnic parameters of Central Asia. A discussion of the ethnic lineage makes up the introductory section of the chapter. Here a synopsis of the impact of Stalin's national territorial delimitation program on the ethnic chemistry of the region is presented. This is followed by some demographic and ethnographic data related to the subject of this study. The contemporary ethnic currents of pan-Turkism and ethnic separatism are discussed next. This section outlines the central Asian ethnic dilemmas caused primarily by the presence of a relatively large non-Muslim Slavic population, and the subtle resurgence of hegemonic tendencies, of which the subtle Uzbek drive for dominance over the other ethnic groups has been highlighted. The chapter attempts to underscore the centrifugal force of ethnic, regional, subregional, and local exclusivist tendencies as a powerful counterpoise to the intrinsically unifying forces of radical and populist versions of Islam.

As a final thought, it is hoped that this book will further stimulate debate and discussion on Central Asia, a region with a dignified past that has once again found itself at a difficult crossroads in history. One can only wish that this time destiny will bring peace and prosperity for its peoples.

CHAPTER 1

Islam Under Communism

Religion is like a nail; the more you hit it, the deeper it goes in.

—ANATOLI VASILYEVICH LUNACHARSKI

The Marxist-Leninist revolution that swept through Russia in 1917 aspired to transform the czarist empire into a socialist state whose ideological orientation necessitated, among other things, a comprehensive eradication of all religions. Having survived the late nineteenth-century cultural tidal wave of the czars nearly intact, Central Asia became one of the most significant ideological battlegrounds where the Soviet authorities challenged Islam and put to test a multiplicity of antireligious strategies and tactics to spread their culture of atheism among the population. The outcome of this process, as will be demonstrated in this chapter, was one of humiliating defeat for socialism, as Islam and the other great religions in the Soviet Union managed to adapt to the changing circumstances and to endure nearly seven decades of unabated oppression. In the end, the Soviet efforts could merely suppress the rituals and not the spiritual power of Islam.

CENTRAL ASIA AND THE CZARIST LEGACY

The conquest of Turkistan that began in 1860 and ended in 1887 was in retrospect the final expansionist phase of an ailing empire intent on the wholesale colonization of Central Asia. Almost four decades earlier (1822 to 1854) Russia had managed to gradually transform its titular control into actual sovereignty over the vast Kazakh Steppe where the three Hordes of "Small," "Middle," and "Greater" had coexisted since the mid-sixteenth century. In line with their imperial policies in that region, the czarist rulers set out to first dominate and then to incorporate Turkistan into the empire. The two regions of Turkistan and the Kazakh Steppe, however, were largely governed by two distinct traditional social systems with which the Russian colonial administrators were only marginally familiar.

The first sizable Russian encounter in Central Asia involved the pastoral nomadic societies that sparsely populated a wide range of territories from the Kazakh Steppe to the Turkmen grasslands near the eastern border of the Caspian Sea. The socioeconomic foundation of these societies was characterized as patriarchal, predicated on a strict seniority system. Extended families constituted the smallest building blocks of the nomadic tribes, and in the case of the Kazakh Hordes formed the basis of tribal villages, *aul,* which ranged from two to more than one hundred tents, *yurts.* The Kazakhs' structure of political authority was two-tiered with khans and sultans operating at the *inter-aul* level, and *beys* and clan elders managing the *intra-aul* affairs. Economically self-sufficient, the nomadic tribes of Central Asia depended upon vast herds of livestock for whose grazing needs well-thought-out migratory routes were followed annually throughout the region.[1]

The conquest of Central Asia also brought under the czarist dominion a relatively large sedentary population, which had evolved into a far more complex social system than that of the Kazakh Steppe and the Turkmen regions.[2] On the eve of the Russian advances in 1860, these densely inhabited oases were largely under the jurisdiction of the two khanates of Khiva and Kokand, and the emirate of Bukhara in Turkistan. The political structure of the three principalities was despotic with roughly similar administrative subdivisions, *velayat,* governed by representatives of the emir or the khan known as *hakim* or *beg (bey).* The economic infrastructure of the cities and surrounding villages was based on agricultural production undertaken with the aid of a network of artificial irrigation channels, the construction of which had been completed over many generations. Despite the apparent nuances, the prevailing land tenure structure was similar in substance if not form to that of other neighboring Muslim communities bordering to the south. In principle, all land belonged to the emir or the khan, who could loan out parcels in perpetuity. As such, the allocated lands fell under four broad categories. First, state land, which included the *miri* or land belonging to the khan or the emir, uncultivated land, and *mawat* or wasteland. Second, private land, *mulk,* held in hereditary ownership theoretically subject to the khan's tacit approval. Third, land allocated on a temporary basis to close relatives or associates of the khan. Finally, the *waqf* or religious endowment land parceled out by wealthy individuals or the khan, to be used for the maintenance of religious schools or mosques and the sustenance of the clergy.[3] The sharecropping arrangements, though subject to seasonal and local variations, usually left as little as one-fifth but on occasions as much as one-half of the harvest to peasant families. The exploitative nature of tax and surplus expropriation on the one hand and the absence of well-defined borders among the three principalities on the other hand, left the majority of the peasant population destitute and the region in a semi-permanent state of conflict.[4] Against this backdrop Russia embarked upon the colonization of the whole of Central Asia. The general strategy was motivated, above all, by three broad objectives: political, economic, and cultural. Much like other European colonial strategies of the nineteenth century, the czarist political aim was first to undermine the power of the traditional political authority at the highest level, though not dismantle it altogether, and second to extend its own political and administrative authority, already in place elsewhere in the empire, into that region.

Between 1822 and 1854, through the use of force and at times diplomacy, and despite widespread revolt, the Kazakh Hordes of the Steppe region were coerced to shift their allegiance to St. Petersburg and to accept the Russian hegemony. The conquest of Turkistan then followed shortly along the Syrdarya River toward the Kyrgyz mountains. In 1860 Tokmak and Pishpek, in 1861 Julek (Djulek) and Yani-Kurgan, and in 1865 Chimkent and Tashkent were conquered.[5] By 1868 Zeravshan and Samarkand were captured, forcing Bukhara to accept the Russian protectorate. Khiva was subjected to the same fate in 1873. In August and September of that year the khan of Khiva and the emir of Bukhara signed treaties under which territorial and commercial concessions were granted to the Russian authorities.[6] Kokand was incorporated in 1876 and the Turkmen region was enveloped by 1884–85.

In conjunction with Russian efforts to partially dismantle the region's traditional political structure, the task of devising a plan for the Russian administrative division of Central Asia was given to the Steppe Commission established in 1865, and two years later to a special committee headed by the minister of war. A proposal was finally presented to the czar that among other things included the following: First, the separation of Turkistan from the Orenburg governor-general territory and the subsequent creation of the Turkistan governor-general composed of the two oblasts of Semirechie and Syrdarya, which would also incorporate the southern part of the Semipalatinsk oblast—hitherto a part of west Siberia—into the Semirechie oblast. Second, the formation of an independent military district in Turkistan. Third, the consolidation of the military and civilian authority in the position of the governor-general. Finally, the plan set forth a hands-off policy by the colonial administrators in all local affairs devoid of political significance.[7]

The great executive of the Russian eastern design was General Konstantine Von Kaufman who, prior to his death in 1882, succeeded in extending the czarist administrative control over most of the Turkistan territories. Within a year of his appointment as the governor-general of Turkistan in 1866, Kaufman had made substantial headway in establishing the new administrative division in his two oblasts. The next step was to explain to the local population the specifics of the plan and the concomitant responsibilities to be shouldered by the people. Therefore, the Russian military set out to spread the message and to count the nomadic population of northern Turkistan for taxation and other administrative purposes. A more difficult endeavor was to conduct a survey on the settled population of Turkistan where Kaufman encountered opposition and hostility by the religious establishment and the former officials of the khan whose livelihood was severely undercut by the new arrangement. Consequently, in a series of military and diplomatic maneuvering, Kaufman delivered a speech to the members of the Tashkent elite in which he demanded obedience and granted protection against the despotic rule of the khan. Hence, by 1868, he had managed to establish administrative control over his native subjects.

The Kazakh Steppe was also subjected to a similar administrative scheme by the Russian government under the auspices of the Steppe Commission. In 1868 the region was divided into the three oblasts of Uralsk, Turgai, and Akmolinsk. Subsequently, the administrative officials began the implementation of more or less similar provisions carried out in northern Turkistan, which required a census of the tribal households and possessions to assess the tax ratio and to determine the appropriate jurisdiction of *uezds* (subdivisions of oblast) and *volosts* (subdivisions of *uezd* comprised of several *auls).* Quite predictably, the plan met with selective resistance from the Kazakh tribes and it was not until the end of 1869 that opposition was crushed and administrative control was effectively extended to the entire region. In the years prior to and following General Kaufman's death, several administrative reorganizations were introduced to streamline the colonial operations and to incorporate the newly conquered land into the administrative structure. For instance, in 1876 and in 1886, Kokand, renamed Fergana, was added to the Turkistan governor-general jurisdiction. In 1882, subsequent to a major reorganization, the Semirechie oblast was annexed from Turkistan and went under the jurisdiction of the Steppe governor-general. Later in 1886 Turkmenistan was incorporated into the Turkistan region. Despite widespread resentment, passive resistance, and frequent rebellion, the Russian political reorganization of Central Asia achieved its objectives: it divided the population along artificial lines, thus weakening the much cherished tribal cohesion, undermined the khan's political and financial authority, extended the coercive arm of the colonial government into the far reaches of the land, and helped pave the way for further financial exploitation of the population.

Russia's second colonial objective was economic in nature. In retrospect, three overarching needs defined the parameters of Russian interests in this regard. First, the expanding Russian textile industries found in the region—particularly in the fertile Fergana Valley—an economically suitable supplier of cotton whose productivity was to be substantially improved by the introduction of American varieties in the early 1880s.[8] The Russian pricing, transportation, and tariff policies with respect to cotton production helped increase the output from 873,000 poods in 1888 to 2,673,000 poods in 1890; and land under cultivation from 13,200 hectares in 1886 to 597,200 hectares by 1914.[9] A number of irrigation projects were also carried out to help expand cultivation and further increase productivity on the existing land. The impressive Nicholas I Canal, which was completed in 1898, provided sufficient irrigation for some fifty square miles in Khiva. By the end of the nineteenth century Russia not only had diversified its agricultural efforts in Turkistan by encouraging the production of fruits and silk, but it had also introduced, upon the recommendation of Kaufman, grapevines of the French and Spanish varieties for commercial production.[10] Some Steppe land had also been brought under cultivation subsequent to a series of land surveys conducted apparently to ensure that adequate pastures remained available to the Kazakh herds. In addition, the czars managed to exploit the mineral resources of the region that included, among others things, such important items as coal, copper, and oil.[11]

Russia's other economic interest was the Central Asian market, which presented a somewhat lucrative opportunity for the growing industrial base of the empire. The completion of the Trans-Caspian, Trans-Siberian, and Orenburg-Tashkent railroads helped increase the import-export volume of trade with Central Asia. But even before such transportation networks were in place, Russia had managed to increase the value of its export to the region threefold between 1863 and 1867.[12] By 1894, Russia had managed to effectively block out the Indian commodity trade, which was considered the only sizable competition in the region.[13] This virtual trade monopoly further increased St. Petersburg's profit margins and helped accelerate production of Russian consumer goods. The main commodities that found their way into Central Asian markets were cotton fabrics, metal wares, tobacco, sugar, and spirits.

Finally, the Russian colonizers hoped to generate enough tax revenue to sustain their military-bureaucratic machinery in the region, and to turn over a surplus to the empire's treasury. Quite predictably, separate plans were devised to address this issue within the context of the two socioeconomic systems in Turkistan and the Kazakh Steppe. In the case of the former, the plan involved a systematic disruption of the land-tenure arrangement that began by the nominal transfer of land ownership to the cultivators, thus effectively curtailing the financial control of the landlords on the peasants. The *waqf* land was excluded from the provisions of this plan. Consequently, the new land reform measure accorded a greater role to the colonial agents who could then pursue a tax reform policy believed to be necessary to improve the quality of revenue administration, and hence the quantity of surplus generated. A two-phase reform of the traditional tax system was thus implemented in earnest. During the first phase, the existing tax codes on land that included harvest tax (*kheraj*), land tax (*tanap*), and other taxes such as religious income tax (*zekat*), were simplified, among other things, through the introduction of uniform tax ratios. The second phase began in 1870 and combined the two traditional agrarian taxes of *kheraj* and *tanap* into a single land tax based on the yield of the 1869 harvest season. Later, in 1875, the *zekat* tax was abolished. The new tax code eliminated the burden and expenses of local tax collectors who had traditionally pocketed a substantial sum of the revenue generated each year. The colonial administrators were thus empowered, in most cases, to levy taxes directly on the population of the region.

As for the Kazakh Steppe where pastoral life prevailed, a new land policy was implemented subsequent to the 1867–68 legislation that laid claim to all tribal pastures—hitherto the property of the Hordes—held in common. This legislation also empowered the colonial administrators to determine the Hordes' migratory paths for winter and summer grazing. Furthermore, a new uniform tax of two and three-quarter rubles were imposed on every household (*kibtika*), to be paid in a lump sum by the *volost*. The Kazakhs were also subjected to *zemski,* a local tax for the maintenance and upkeep of the infrastructure and buildings, and a cart tax, all of which were raised several times between 1872 and 1892 without regard to the financial ability of the Kazakhs to pay.

Despite the comprehensive nature of the economic and administrative reforms, the czarist agents failed to accomplish the objective of transforming Central Asia into a lucrative source of tax revenue for the empire. Corruption and bureaucratic mismanagement played an important role in this regard. Numerous reports indicated cases of overtaxation and illegal expropriation of funds by colonial agents who, instead of channeling the funds to St. Petersburg, used them for personal gain. Pierce, for instance, has pointed out that "most of the *uezd* commandants approached the problem of arrears by levying taxes on the natives, usually to a degree that not only covered the normal expenses but enabled them to live in luxury."[14] In the final analysis, however, the czarist reforms helped generate enough revenue to sustain the bulk of the colonial personnel in both Turkistan and the Steppe region.

Russia's third colonial objective was the cultural infiltration and eventual Russification (*russifikatsia*), of the Central Asian population. Although, here too, a somewhat different strategy was used in Turkistan as compared to the Kazakh Steppe, the czarist cultural plan was based on two principles. First, the traditional religious and cultural patterns were not to be disrupted by the Russian authorities. This principle was adopted not out of choice but sheer necessity: czarist earlier attempts to curb Islamic rituals and practices had been met with fierce and uncompromising opposition, which invariably had led to the strengthening of the Islamic faith and not vice versa. Second, the native population was to be exposed to the great Russian cultural and linguistic patterns. Such an exposure through physical contact, as well as education taught in the native language, was believed to be sufficient in raising the inhabitants' awareness of the superiority of the Russian culture, and hence the desire for assimilation.

Even though the czarist declared policy toward Islam in Turkistan was noninterventionist in character, it was subjected to various interpretations by the Russian authorities involved in its on-sight implementation. General Kaufman, for instance, completely ignored Islam and its rituals performed by the believers, but consistently attacked the structure of religious authority and its apex, as in the position of the grand kazi, which he eventually succeeded in dismantling.[15] Kaufman also barred the activities of the Russian Orthodox Church as he did not wish to offend the local population, arguing that "we must introduce Christian civilization in Turkistan but we must not try to propound the Orthodox faith to the native population."[16] In contrast, his successors went so far as to attempt to infiltrate the highly secretive Sufi sects in order to better understand Islam's modus operandi in places where Sufism was prevalent, and to uncover the privately expressed Muslim attitudes toward the Russian colonizers. In the Steppe region, the Russian principle of cultural and religious nonintervention was less seriously upheld, as the Kazakhs' proclivity toward Islam had been generally weak. For centuries, the widespread tribal lifestyle had prevented not only Islam, but also other established religions to take root and flourish in the region. In fact, during the reign of Catherine II attempts were made to strengthen Islamic institutions in the Steppe. She believed that such a strategy would restore trust in the Kazakhs and thus expedite her colonial efforts. And to this end, Tatar Muslim preachers were dispatched to the region.[17] However, as victims of Russian religious persecutions in the past, the Tatar Muslims instead conducted anticolonial propaganda and portrayed Islam as a powerful ideological weapon to be used against Russian intentions. Catherine's policy toward Islam was abandoned during the reign of Alexander II, who found merit in the superficiality of Islam among the Kazakhs, making Russian Westernization of the region a more likely possibility.

The czarist cultural policies were carried out, for the most part, with the aid of Russian education in Central Asia. The aim was twofold: one was to expose the population to the Russian culture, and the other was to train the indigenous population for service in various low-level bureaucratic positions to aid in the administration of the region. In the Steppe, Russian education was selectively introduced in the various oblasts as early as the mid-nineteenth century. The Russian initiative was welcomed by some Kazakh intellectuals who had found such cultural influence generally beneficial. Between 1879 and 1883 four elementary schools were founded in each of the *uezds* of the Turgai oblast for the joint education of the Kazakhs and the Russians. A teacher-training center was also established to remedy shortages. Later, *aul* schools were developed to extend education into the tribal format. By 1897, 71 schools with 2,000 students were in place in the Tugrai oblast alone. The adopted school curriculum in the Steppe was identical to those used in schools elsewhere in the empire, which heavily emphasized and thoroughly glorified Russian culture and civilization, and that had very little practical relevance to the daily lives of Kazakh youth. Nevertheless, the plan produced a number of trained officials for various minor administrative posts, and created a suitable breeding ground for the small but expanding Kazakh intelligentsia.

In Turkistan, where Islamic education had been an established part of the cultural landscape, the Russian educational plans were met with resistance. In 1911, there were a respectable 6,000 traditional elementary schools (*maktabs*), and 328 secondary schools (*madrasehs*), with a total student enrollment of more than 100,000.[18] Determined to spread the Russian cultural influence in the region, attempts were made to establish schools that would enroll both Russian and indigenous students. Various financial incentives were offered to those native parents who would send their children to these schools. The plan, however, failed to attract enough Muslim students. A more successful school system was masterminded by the renowned Orientalist, Nikolai Ilminski, in which curriculum was taught in the native language at the elementary level and Russian at the advanced level.[19] By 1909, an estimated 89 Russo-native schools with 2,552 Muslim students had been established.[20] Between 1879 and 1886 two Russian high schools and fourteen Russian elementary schools were also established in Tashkent to serve the growing needs of the migrant population and to increase the level of Russian cultural exposure in Turkistan.

In the closing years of the nineteenth century a new Islamic educational trend inspired by the *jadid* movement began to make its appearance in Turkistan. The movement was an essentially Tatar phenomenon, led by Ismael Gasprinski and others who wished to modernize the teachings of Islam. Its main objective was to rid Islam of its archaic dimensions and to modernize Islamic culture primarily through education, for which an estimated 5,000 reformist schools had been established mainly in Kazan, Crimea, and Azerbaijan by 1905.[21] In Central Asia these newly created schools, which combined Islamic as well as modern scientific subjects, threatened the relative success of the Russo-native schools. The Russian strategy was to defeat the movement by supporting the traditional clergy who were adamantly against the reformist tendencies of the *jadid* movement. The logic of the czarist action stemmed from the overriding principle that any meaningful cultural change should be in the direction of Russification rather than a modification of the existing Islamic culture. It was thus not surprising that the *jadids* of Central Asia who were despised by the Russians lent their support to the Bolsheviks after the October Revolution.

By the early years of the twentieth century, the czarist colonization of Central Asia had undoubtedly produced noticeable results, particularly in the economic and political spheres. In a period of less than three decades, Russia had transformed the region into a supplier of raw materials, with the devastating consequence of the loss of self-sufficiency in food production in Turkistan. Equally devastating was the Russian settlement policy in the Kazakh Steppe, and to some extent in Turkistan, which significantly contributed to the economic decline of the native population.[22] Politically, the structure of the traditional authority was severely weakened and subordinated to the Russian military-bureaucratic machinery, thus paving the way for its eventual dissolution under Communist rule. The Central Asian response to these developments generally followed two distinct patterns. The first was outright rebellion, which became an increasingly frequent method used against the Russian colonization after the Andijan uprising of 1898.[23] The most serious incident of widespread rebellion occurred in 1916. Triggered by the czarist decree of June 25, 1916, that required labor services to the empire by the Muslim population, as well as by the misguided land policies in the Steppe, the rebellion engulfed almost the entire region leaving behind a large number of dead and wounded. The clerical establishment had played a leading role in this and many other rebellions and riots that swept through Turkistan. Although suppressed expeditiously, the rebellion clearly politicized the population and intensified the anti-Russian sentiments. Nevertheless, the rebellion sent a clear signal to St. Petersburg as to the volatility of the situation and the necessity to reformulate the Central Asian policy: Islam had once again proven to be a potent anti-colonial instrument. This realization, as will been seen later, was passed on to the Bolsheviks who, at least initially, adopted a more cautious and reconciliatory approach to the region than their czarist predecessors.

Reformist in character, the second Central Asian pattern of response involved the adoption of liberal ideas that had come of age during the reign of Alexander II in Russia, and continued to flourish throughout the empire despite the unfavorable political atmosphere following his assassination in 1881. Though discouraged by the Russians, the growth of the *jadid* movement was an Islamic articulation of liberal tendencies to which many Muslims had been introduced through frequent intellectual encounters with the West. The increasing physical contact with the Russians created yet another liberal trend among some members of the Central Asian upper class who wished to modernize their political culture along Russian lines.[24] Subsequent to the revolution of 1905, such tendencies found meaningful local expressions, particularly in terms of active collaboration by some natives with the Russian Social Democrats, and participation in Muslim congresses by others.[25]

Despite growing liberal trends, the Russian cultural impact on the region—be it inadvertent or otherwise—was much more circumscribed in nature than its economic and political effects. Whether out of fear or negligence, the czarist cultural strategy did not include the wholesale destruction of the Islamic tradition. Instead, it aimed at projecting a positive image of the Russian culture, assuming that over time the "inferior" and archaic Islam would wither away.[26] This policy, however, was to be radically challenged in the aftermath of the October Revolution of 1917 by the victorious Bolsheviks who believed that religion in general and Islam in particular would not wither away on its own, but must be dealt with swiftly and systematically if socialism was to succeed in Central Asia. Quite predictably, Marxist-Leninism was to provide the philosophical justification and the practical methods in the fight against Islam.

THE RELIGION OF COMMUNISM

As the spiritual father of Communism, Marx (1818–1883) left behind a powerful antireligious legacy unrivaled by his contemporaries. After all, Marx, and to the same degree Engels, had taken it upon themselves to create a new intellectual paradigm inexorably antithetical to capitalist society and its material and metaphysical manifestations, of which private property and religion played the most pivotal roles. Marx had abandoned his religious beliefs long before he was enrolled at the Berlin University in 1836 where he began to follow in the footsteps of such great German commentators on religion as Hegel and Feuerbach. But, in borrowing Hegel's method of analysis (dialectics) and Feuerbach's theoretical approach to religion (alienation), Marx transcended both philosophers, offering his own antireligious framework, which not only emphasized the unquestionably mundane origin and essence of religion but also its exploitative function throughout most of the history of mankind. "For Germany," Marx wrote, "the criticism of religion is in the main complete, and the criticism of religion is the premise of all criticism."[27]

Marx and Engels argued that religion was an historical phenomenon characteristic of a particular phase in man's socioeconomic development: "Religion arose in very primitive times from erroneous, primitive conceptions of men about their own nature and external nature surrounding them."[28] Thus, it was man's inability to master the environment and to comprehend the powerful forces of nature—during the early stages of his development—that compelled him to rely upon self-made illusory notions and conceptions in order to overcome his fears and anxieties. In *Anti-Duhring,* Engels once again reaffirmed this belief arguing that "All religion is nothing but the fantastic reflection in men's minds of those external forces which control their daily life, a reflection in which the terrestrial forces assume the form of supernatural forces."[29] Marx went on to argue that with the advancement of the forces of production in the later stages of history, man gradually learned to control his environment, thus transforming his deification of nature into a more abstract metaphysical and largely monotheistic entity. Yet, the very same forces of production that made man the master of his environment brought about new socioeconomic relations of domination and exploitation, hence of alienation, forcing him to further immerse himself in the psychological comfort of religion. As such, Marx believed that religion was but a mythical expression of social frustration and of the dehumanizing conditions of society. The essence of Marx's perception of religion is captured in a passage from *Contribution to the Critique of Hegel's Philosophy of Law:*

> Religion is the general theory of that world, its encyclopedic compendium, its logic in a popular form, its spiritualistic *point d'honneur,* its enthusiasm, its moral sanction, its solemn complement, its universal source of consolation and justification. It is the fantastic realization of the human essence because the human essence has no reality. The struggle against religion is therefore indirectly the fight against the world of which religion is the spiritual aroma. Religious distress is at the same time the expression of real distress and also a protest against real distress. Religion is the sigh of the oppressed

creature, the heart of a heartless world, just as it is the spirit of spiritless conditions. It is the opium of the people.[30]

Both Marx and Engels believed that religion was bound to wither away when the society from which it had emanated was completely transformed through class struggle, and by means of the great proletarian revolution. The validity of this theoretical assumption, however, was questioned by Lenin and others who did not find substantial evidence as to the disappearance of Christianity or Islam in Russia, even though the October Revolution of 1917 had supposedly brought about the type of social transformation that Marx and Engels had envisioned.

Although the debate over the origin, function, and the future role of religion in Russia was essentially dominated by Lenin after the October Revolution, not all Russian revolutionaries supported his position that irrefutably condemned all religions. The disagreements had both philosophical and practical underpinnings with clear political ramifications for postrevolutionary Russia.[31] The most significant philosophical disagreement occurred between Lenin and Anatoli Vasilyevich Lunacharski. The latter was a leader of the left wing of a Bolshevik faction who was appointed by Lenin to the post of the People's Commissar of Education after the revolution until 1929 when he was removed by Stalin. Lunacharski was one of the main proponents of the Russian philosophical school of god-building *(bogostroitelstvo),* which advocated the creation of an atheistic and secular religion based on the principles of materialism, centered on man. In his book *Religion and Socialism,* he argued that although religion was in essence a form of false consciousness, it was the manifestation of genuine desires and feelings of man in his quest to discover the meaning and purpose of life. Socialism, he argued, should therefore take over, guide, and dignify such human expressions, not eradicate them. The essence of his proposed new religion of socialism was based on the glorification of man and his potential to assume the characteristics that he has attributed to God. His views on this are expressed in the following passage: "The faith of the active human being is a faith in future mankind; his religion is an aggregate of those feelings and thoughts which make him a co-participator in the life of mankind, a link in the chain which stretches toward . . . a beautiful and powerful creature, a perfected organism."[32] Lunacharski believed that Marxism was in fact a religion because it was based on a system of values. And since its purpose was to build man's "Godlike future," it was the "most religious of all religions."[33]

Lenin, of course, was vehemently opposed to the idea of god-building and categorically denied the distinction that had been made between the atheistic religion of god-building and the monotheistic religion of god-seeking, arguing that both religious types were instruments of oppression and should not be allowed to flourish under a socialist framework. Lenin's own philosophical views on the origin and function of religion did not differ much from those expressed by Marx and Engels. But he was an opportunistic politician with a keen awareness of the volatility of the sociopolitical environment within which he hoped to bring about the sweeping changes that was to become his own brand of Russian socialism. Therefore, he modified and toned down his attack on religion early on. In fact, the position he expressed in a draft program of the Russian Social-democratic Party in 1902 could hardly be considered antireligious, as he declared his support for freedom of conscience. Lenin's liberal position, however, slowly gave way to his hard-line Marxist stance as he began to solidify his position within the Russian revolutionary movement. In line with Marx and Engels, Lenin connected the fight against religion to the contemporary class struggle against capitalism and exploitation in Russia:

> Religion is one of the forms of spiritual oppression which everywhere weighs down heavily upon the masses of the people, overburdened by their perpetual work for others, by want and isolation. Impotence of the exploited classes in their struggle against the exploiters just as inevitably gives rise to the belief in a better life after death as impotence of the savage in his battle with nature gives rise to belief in gods, devils, miracles and the like. Those who toil and live in want all their lives are taught by religion to be submissive and patient while on earth, and to take comfort in the hope of a heavenly reward. . . . Religion is the opium for the people. Religion is a sort of spiritual booze in which the slaves of capital drown their human image, their demand for a life more or less worthy of man.[34]

In addition to his philosophical differences with Lunacharski, Lenin stood in sharp contrast to Georgi Valentinovich Plekhanov—his onetime philosophical mentor—over the practical means of combating religion in Russia.[35] Plekhanov believed that antireligious propaganda should not be abusive and offensive. Rather, it should aim at expanding the knowledge of the believer as to the true essence of religion and its mundane origin. Religion, he wrote, would disappear when the Russian masses were adequately informed and enlightened. The cure for the persistence of religion in Russia, Plekhanov asserted, was to be found in atheistic education, public lectures, and mass production and circulation of atheistic literature by such philosophers as Marx, Engels, Diderot, Voltaire, and so on. Lenin, however, did not believe that atheistic education alone was capable of combating religion in Russia and warned against Plekhanov-style antireligious methods based entirely on "abstract, idealistic formulation of the religious question by 'reason' apart from class struggle."[36] Lenin, instead, advocated a more hostile and aggressive stance toward religion in which atheistic education constituted only a part and not all of the antireligious design in Russia. Lenin's overall orientation on the question of religion is summarized in the following passage:

> Marxism is materialism. As such it is as relentlessly hostile to religion as was the materialism of the eighteenth-century Encyclopaedists or the materialism of Feuerbach. This is beyond doubt. But the dialectical materialism of Marx and Engels goes further . . . for it applies the materialist philosophy to the domain of history, to the domain of social sciences. We must combat religion—that is the ABC of *all* materialism, and consequently of Marxism. But Marxism in not a materialism which has stopped at the ABC. Marxism goes further and says: We must know how to combat religion; and in order to do so we must explain the source of faith and religion among the masses in a materialist way. The combating of religion cannot be confined to abstract ideological preaching . . . it must be linked up with the concrete practice of the class movement, which aims at eliminating the social roots of religion.[37]

Lenin thus pursued a two-pronged religious strategy that not only called for a comprehensive program of atheistic education, but also a plan for a systematic attack on the religious establishment.

The success of the October Revolution, coupled with the death of Plekhanov in 1918, and Lunacharski's shifting orientation in favor of a Leninist stance, further strengthened and legitimized Lenin's philosophical and practical approach to religion. His two-pronged antireligious strategy, however, was primarily concentrated on the Russian Orthodox Church, which had exhibited open hostility toward the Bolshevik cause. Islam, too, became the target of some verbal criticism after the revolutionary takeover. But, for a variety of strategic and tactical considerations, efforts to undermine Islam proceeded more slowly, and with the exception of the civil war period from 1917 to 1920, assumed a more forgiving and complex character when compared to the treatment of the other faiths. Five factors seem to have contributed to the development of this uniquely anti-Islamic policy. First, the memory of the 1916 uprising in Central Asia was still fresh in Lenin's mind. The uprising had left behind a devastating anti-Russian legacy from which there was no easy escape. Second, War Communism (civil war) was, for the most part, being fought on the periphery of Russia, including Central Asia. Any attempt to religiously antagonize the Muslim population would have had far-reaching consequences insofar as the consolidation of the power of the Communist regime was concerned. Third, Lenin did not have enough trained cadres in Central Asia to carry out his policies. This lack of personnel eventually forced him to rely upon Muslim Communist sympathizers to spread socialist ideas in Central Asia. As such, he could not have possibly engaged such fledgling forces in anti-Islamic activities right at the outset. Fourth, Lenin was preoccupied with more pertinent political and economic issues intimately related to the success of the revolutionary regime at the center of the Russian empire. Islam and Central Asia did not rank prominently on Lenin's immediate postrevolutionary agenda. Last but not least, Lenin was cognizant of Islam's modus operandi and the tremendous power the clergy enjoyed over the believers. Therefore, it was essential to adopt a more cautious approach toward Islam as opposed to Christianity per se. However, in the years following the October Revolution, Islam was also subjected to the same iron-fist policy that other religions had faced only a little earlier.

It is argued that while the scope and intensity of the anti-Islamic campaign was primarily a function of preference and style for Soviet leaders and thus varied, they all, more or less, built upon Lenin's two-pronged strategy, which was designed to combat Islam both directly and through indirect mechanisms. As for the former, Soviet policies were targeted against the outward attributes of Islam, the formal religious training and education of the believers, and the clerical organization and power structure. In the case of the latter, the Soviet regime pursued two separate policies. One was to carry out a comprehensive Marxist education and atheistic indoctrination of the Central Asian population. The other was designed to co-opt and assimilate the Muslim Communist sympathizers into the party structure through a system of sanctions and incentives. Far from consistent, the Soviet anti-Islamic strategy up until the Gorbachev era has followed a number of phases, each characterized by the application of a particular mix of the above policy components emphasized by the various Soviet leaders.[38]

THE LENINIST ERA

The foundation of the Soviet anti-Islamic strategy was laid out in considerable detail during the reign of Lenin, and no qualitative shift in its direction was introduced until 1927–28, three years after his death. As a practical politician, Lenin proceeded to actualize his plan primarily through legal and constitutional measures as well as institutional innovations that were to be built upon and reinforced by his successors. The decade under investigation may adequately be divided into two phases. The first phase corresponded to War

Communism, which ended in 1920. It was characterized on the one hand by the resurgence of Muslim religious nationalism in search of autonomy, and on the other hand by frequent raids on Muslim religious institutions and property by local Bolshevik supporters who had been largely cut off from the capital. This was followed by the second phase lasting through 1927 when Lenin engaged Islam in a tug of war, gradually and peacefully gaining ground to the cultural detriment of the region.

1917 to 1920

The October Revolution did not physically or emotionally engross the indigenous population of Central Asia. The majority were oblivious to the events that shook the foundation of the czarist empire, and even more had a very shallow understanding of Bolshevik philosophy and policies, except for its well-advertised liberal stance on the nationality question prior to 1917. Lenin was fully aware of the significance of non-Russian nationalities in the battle for power, and as early as 1913 he had recognized the right of the nationalities to secede from Russia if they so desired. In 1917, to further strengthen their position, the Bolshevik tacticians issued a decree granting a number of political concessions that included such rights as equality and sovereignty of all people, the right of self-determination, and even secession. At the same time a special written appeal was made to the Muslims, bearing the signature of Lenin and Stalin: "Muslims of Russia, Tatars of the Volga and Crimea, Kirgiz and Sarts of Siberia and Turkistan, Turks and Tatars of Transcaucasia, Chechens and Mountain Peoples of the Caucasus, and all you whose mosques and prayer houses have been destroyed, whose beliefs and customs have been trampled upon by the Tsars and oppressors of Russia: Your beliefs and usages, your national and cultural institutions are forever free and inviolate. Know that your rights, like those of all peoples of Russia, are under the mighty protection of the Revolution and its organs, the Soviet of Workers, Soldiers and Peasants."[39] Shortly thereafter, as a gesture of goodwill the Koran of Usman, which had been confiscated at the time of the czarist conquest of Samarkand, was returned to the Muslims. Such deliberate maneuvers were designed to galvanize the native Muslim population in favor of the revolution, but instead it further intensified the old aspirations for cultural independence and political autonomy, for which a number of congresses and Muslim organizations had been convened and established as early as 1905.[40] To remedy the problem, Stalin appealed to the Muslim leaders to support the Bolshevik cause. Although successful among Tatar and Kazan Muslims, Stalin's design failed to bring about the anticipated result, particularly in Turkistan, and to some extent in the Kazakh Steppe, where distrust of the Russians was deep-rooted.

Consequently, the main Turkistani Muslim organizations, the Shora-i Islami-ya, supported by the *jadid* liberal reformist clergy, and the Ulema Jama'ati, dominated by the traditional conservative clergy, later united to create Ittifaq-al Muslimin (Union of Muslims) and declared national autonomy in late November 1917.[41] Similarly, the Alash Orda of the Steppe—founded in March 1917—led by the Russian-educated Kazakh intelligentsia, declared their autonomy in mid-December.

Two interrelated factors seem to have exacerbated Soviet nationality policies in Central Asia. First, in September the local Russian supporters of the revolution, who eventually established the Tashkent Soviet, ordered the arrest of administrators and members of the Provisional Government with which many Muslims organizations had close ties. Later, the situation was made even worse when the Tashkent Soviet refused to include local Muslims in their organization, despite the willingness of some members of the Ulema Jama'ati—headed by Sher Ali liapin—to form a coalition with the Bolsheviks.[42] These actions antagonized and alienated both the conservative and liberal factions of the clerical establishment in charge of the Muslim organizations, effectively removing any possibility for Muslim support of the Bolsheviks, at least in the immediate postrevolutionary period. Second, the Leninist directives, which were supposedly issued to avoid harsh treatments of the Muslims, were never fully implemented due to a virtual cutoff of communication between Petrograd and Central Asia.

There is very little doubt, however, that by early 1918, the Bolsheviks had reversed their liberal position on the nationalities question, and set out to dismantle all Muslim nationalist organizations in Turkistan, the Kazakh Steppe, and elsewhere.[43] As a result, a military unit under the leadership of the Tashkent Soviet was dispatched, successfully defeating the Muslim resistance in Kokand, where the main anti-Soviet clerical organization had moved to escape the persecution of the local Soviets. Until November 1919, when the road to Tashkent was finally secured by the Red Army, leading to the resumption of the central command and communications to the region, the local Russians were left free to conduct antireligious campaigns during which mosques were profaned, clergy shot, religious endowment land confiscated, Shariah courts closed, and religious schools were demolished.

The most devastating consequence of the Soviet mistreatment of the Muslims in Turkistan was the Basmachi revolt that began in 1918, and although largely contained by 1924, continued in the Fergana Valley until 1928.[44] The term *basmachilik* means highway banditry, but it signified the brave Central Asian warriors who took up arms in defense of their Islamic and national heritage, which had been threatened by the Soviets and the reform-minded *jadids*. The roots of the revolt have been traced back to the 1916 uprising, the massacre of the Muslim population of eastern Fergana by the Russians, the dismantling of the Kokand autonomy, the famine of 1917 and 1918, and the exclusion of Muslims from the Tashkent Soviet. The Basmachi activities were for the most part concentrated in four areas of Turkistan: the Fergana Valley, the Lokay region, Bukhara, and the Turkmen Steppes near Khiva. In 1922, at the height of the battle against the Red Army, an estimated 18,000 rebels were involved in the revolt. In 1921, with the arrival of Enver Pasha, a leader of the defunct Young Turkish Government of Turkey, the Basmachi revolt assumed, albeit temporarily, a unified leadership, only to become polycephalic again upon his death a year later. For Lenin, the Basmachi movement was: ". . . a form of class struggle which after the overthrow of capitalist rule, after the destruction of bourgeois state, after the establishment of the dictatorship of proletariat does not disappear . . . but merely changes form and in many respects becomes fiercer."[45] To subvert the activities of the Basmachi, Lenin relied upon force as well as diplomacy, granting concessions to the clerical leaders who had been dealt a severe political and economic blow by the operations of the Tashkent Soviet. But a number of other factors may be identified as the underlying causes of the eventual Soviet success over the Basmachis. First, the movement lacked a unified command structure, and was plagued by personal rivalries and feuds. This translated into synchronous military expeditions, hardly capable of producing sizable victories. Second, in 1923 the Red Army succeeded in inflicting heavy casualties on the Basmachi forces in a series of engagements in the Turkmen Steppe and Lokay, substantially reducing the movement's capacity to regroup. Third, the already fragile Muslim unity was broken by the assimilation of Muslims into the Red Army, many of whom were Basmachi defectors. Fourth, with an estimated force of 160,000, the Soviet military force under the command of General Frunze decisively outmatched the poorly equipped and disorganized Basmachi units. Frunze had also managed to reduce outside assistance to the movement coming from Afghanistan. Finally, the peasant population of the region, which had provided logistical support to the Basmachis amid deteriorating economic conditions, could no longer sustain the forces. By 1924 the Basmachi struggle had been pushed into the remote mountains of the Fergana Valley posing no serious threat to the security of the Soviet government.

1921 to 1927

Despite the heavy military and bureaucratic burden of War Communism, Lenin managed to develop a comprehensive legislative and institutional framework to meet the Islamic challenge ahead. But given the unmistakable blunders of the Tashkent Soviet, the Basmachi episode, and the recommendation of some prominent Muslim nationalists-turned-Communist—namely Mir Said Sultan Galiyev—it was decided to postpone the application of the anti-Islamic framework until 1923–24.[46] Instead, every effort was made to restore trust among the clerical establishment by returning the confiscated *waqf* property, reopening mosques and Islamic schools, and resuming the practice of the Shariah laws. In conjunction with this policy, serious attempts were made to reverse the earlier Tashkent Soviet attitude toward the admission of Muslims into the party. The primary instrument of assimilation was the Central Muslim Commissariat (Muskom), which was established in January 1918 as an auxiliary organ under the auspices of the Commissariat of Nationality Affairs (Narkomnats), headed by Stalin since November 1917.[47] It was through Narkomnats and later Muskom that Stalin succeeded in recruiting a number of well-known Muslims who had decided to cooperate with the Communists either out of a deep conviction for Marxism or for mere political survival. To expedite the assimilation process, Stalin bestowed a considerable degree of functional autonomy on Muskom that proved successful, but it also led to the renewal of demand for Muslim autonomy within a Communist framework. Consequently, in 1920 the Commissariat of Nationality Affairs was restructured and Muskom was altogether abolished by Stalin. In Central Asia, where Marxism was the least popular among the Muslims, the Soviets were less discriminatory in their selection of recruits for the party. As with most other Muslim regions of the Soviet Union, the local *jadids* dominated the party in Turkistan and controlled various other institutions such as the Commissariat for National Education.[48] One outcome of Stalin's assimilation policy was a steady rise in the number of Muslim administrative staff needed to carry out the Soviet policies in the region. Most, however, remained partial to Islam and continued with the fundamental practices of their religion. In this connection, it has been documented that during the first years of the regional Central Asian party conferences, the meetings were interrupted at prayer time.[49] Despite serious warnings, this practice was continued, albeit less obtrusively, by Muslim party members who individually walked out of meetings in order to pray privately.

Once the assimilation process had ensured some degree of Muslim support in Central Asia, Lenin began to apply his two-pronged anti-Islamic strategy in earnest. The immediate targets were the legal Islamic institutions charged with the application of the Shariah laws and customs (*adat*), presided over by the clergy. As one of the main pillars of clerical power and prestige, the Islamic courts were sure to rank high on Lenin's Islamic agenda. This was accomplished through the implementation of a series of new decrees as well as old legislation not yet enforced in the region. In 1923, for instance, two decrees were issued to limit both the authority and the caseload of the Islamic courts. The first decree extended the jurisdiction of the Soviet courts over civil suits, hitherto litigated in the Muslim courts, conditioned upon the objection of one of the parties to the verdict rendered by the kazi. The decree, in reality, made the decision of the Shariah court absolutely voluntary. The second decree imposed a fee on Shariah courts, thus making it less affordable for Muslims to use such institutions for dispute settlements. In 1924, the Islamic courts were prohibited from reviewing both civil and criminal cases in excess of 25 rubles. In October of that year, subsequent to the enactment of the Soviet Criminal Code, the practice of many Muslim customs such as polygamy and bride price (kalym), were outlawed.[50] In 1925–26, in line with the policy to undermine Shariah courts, the registration of births, deaths, and marriages were ordered to be undertaken by the Soviet civil authorities.[51] The final blow to the Islamic court system came in 1927 when the Central Executive Committee of the Soviet Union issued a decree "On Shariah and Adat Courts" invalidating the legal status of all such entities in Central Asia. The decree also prohibited the establishment of new Islamic courts anywhere in the Soviet Union, discontinued the financial aid disbursed to the courts by the local governments, and declared the verdicts of the kazi invalid.

In conjunction with the eradication of the Islamic courts, Lenin set out to destroy the financial autonomy of the clerical establishment by confiscating the *waqf* property, which had been returned to the clergy subsequent to two 1922 decrees of the Central Executive Committee of Turkistan. The return of *waqf*, however, had not been unconditional as, for instance, some proceeds from the *waqf* land were to be given to the peasant cultivators beyond that which were given to them as part of the sharecropping agreements. Major restrictions had also been placed on the establishment of new *waqf*. The preparation for the final assault on the financial independence of the clergy came in 1924–25 when the Soviet land-reform program was extended to Central Asia, deliberately raising legal questions as to the ownership rights of the *waqf* property. Thus, from 1925 to 1927, local Soviet governments in Kyrgyzstan, Turkmenistan, and Uzbekistan issued a series of decrees authorizing the confiscation of the *waqf* land. In Uzbekistan, however, only the rural *waqf* located outside the city limits, with the exception of orchards and vineyards, were claimed by the Commissariat for Agriculture. Nevertheless, by 1930 the institution of *waqf* had been effectively, and with minimal opposition, dismantled.

The final dimension of Lenin's strategy to dismantle the clerical power structure involved the Islamic education and training of the Central Asian population, which had been monopolized by the clergy for decades. Lenin was cognizant of the power of education and its capacity to perpetuate religious ideology. Consequently, in 1918, he had laid the groundwork for the wholesale secularization of education in the Soviet Union by what may be referred to as the single most important piece of antireligious legislation drafted while he was at the helm. Entitled "Separation of the Church from the State and the Schools from the Church," this 13-item legislation prohibited the teachings of religious doctrines in public schools.[52] Originally designed to paralyze the Russian Orthodox Church, the law was not officially carried out in Central Asia until much later.

Muslim education was traditionally conducted at two levels. At the elementary level the traditional *maktabs* were the prevailing institutions, though a number of *jadid* schools with a more modern curriculum had also been operating in the region since the late 1880s. The *madrasehs* were the primary institutions for advanced Islamic learning. In addition to these schools, there were a number of Russian schools that had been set up under the czarist rule prior to the revolution. The Muslim schools enjoyed an impressive network, covering the entire region with an estimated 6,000 *maktabs,* 300 *madrasehs,* and a 100,000 student enrollment. The first attempts to implement the 1918 law in Central Asia came in 1922, but upon the urging of some members of the Turkistan Commissariat of Education, the matter was postponed, due to the fear that Muslim parents might refuse to send their children to schools with a secular curriculum. Only a year later, and despite the local government's warning, the Executive Office of the Turkistan Communist Party proposed a three-stage plan for the secular conversion of the traditional Muslim schools. The plan called for the introduction of modern scientific subjects, replacement of religious subjects with ethics, and the substitution of clergy with modern-educated teachers. By 1924, the modern Soviet schools had outstripped their Islamic counterparts, and only three years later the public clerical control of the Islamic schools for the most part had been undermined. In 1927 only 250 of these schools were in operation in Central Asia.[53]

Lenin's two-pronged anti-Islamic strategy included yet another qualitative dimension that was characteristically in line with Plekhanov's advice to carry out a massive campaign of atheistic education and propaganda. The idea received its full legal expression in the 1918 Constitution of the Soviet Union, which permitted the freedom of religious as well as antireligious propaganda. This, however, did not translate into reality until 1919, subsequent to the formulation of a broad-based policy of scientific and educational propaganda at the Eighth Party Congress of the Soviet Union. A year later, the Agitation and Propaganda Department of the Communist Party Central Committee was established to coordinate the early antireligious activities. The Communist Party's policy was given further legitimacy by the 1922 publication of Lenin's article "On the Significance of Militant Materialism" wherein he urged an aggressive yet cautious approach to antireligious propaganda.[54]

At the Twelfth Party Congress, convened in 1923, some preliminary resolutions were prepared, giving the antireligious propaganda an organizational backbone as well as a functional direction. The following resolution was targeted specifically at Islam: "Taking into account the fact that the thirty million Muslims of the USSR have so far preserved almost intact their numerous medieval prejudices connected with religion, which are being utilized for counterrevolutionary purposes, it is necessary to develop forms and methods for the liquidation of these prejudices, while making allowances for the characteristics of the various nationalities."[55] Among the first institutional arms of the campaign was the eighth division of the Commissariat of Justice. Its responsibilities included organizing debates, lectures, and facilitating the production of literature on the subject. Other organizations such as the Red Army and the Peoples Commissariat of Education also became involved in similar activities immediately. Later, other institutions were called upon to engage in scientific, educational, and antireligious propaganda, among which the Communist Youth League (Komsomol) ranked prominently. As early as December 1922 the Soviet regime began publication of the weekly *Bezbozhnik* (The Atheist), devoted entirely to antireligious propaganda. The architect of Lenin's propaganda design was Emilien Yaroslavski who created the notorious League of the Militant Godless in 1925. The league became the dominant coordinating body in charge of all antireligious propaganda in the country, adding to its arsenal yet another publication entitled *antireligioznik,* a "scientific" review for antireligious activities. In conjunction with *Bezbozhnik* and other publications from Moscow, a number of branch organizations with similar publications and functions, including Allah-syzlar, Khoda-syzlar, and Din-syzlar, began to operate in Central Asia and other Muslim regions, each carrying articles that attacked Islam and the clerical establishment.[56] In the pages of such publications Islam was frequently depicted as an antisocial, antifeminist, intolerant, and xenophobic religion with barbaric and unhealthy customs. Despite the vigor of the campaign in Central Asia, the league failed to substantially reduce the influence of Islam among the population at large. This failure was later acknowledged by Lunacharski, who stated that "Religion is like a nail; the more you hit it, the deeper it goes in." It was not until Stalin's era that the activities of the league and the overall strategy for antireligious propaganda were given a new lease on life.

THE STALINIST ERA

Although comprehensive in character, Lenin's anti-Islamic policies were most successful in weakening the clerical power structure and eradicating public Islamic education and training. Stalin, therefore, concentrated his efforts more heavily on the third and final target of the master plan, that is, the elimination of the outward attributes of Islam. This, however, did not mean that the anti-clerical policies initiated by Lenin were altogether abandoned or even eased.

The Stalinist treatment of Islam may be adequately organized into two phases. The first phase lasted through 1938 and was characterized by the intensification of the Soviet efforts to undermine all religions, including Islam. The second phase corresponded to the outbreak of World War II and ended upon Stalin's death in 1953, during which a somewhat permanent relaxation of religious policies were pursued. Two factors seem to have been responsible for such a qualitative shift in policy orientation in the latter phase. First, World War II had exacted a heavy toll on Stalin's military manpower, making the Muslim communities of the Soviet East highly desirable recruitment targets. The obvious price to enlist the Muslims for military service was to abandon the war on Islam. The second factor had to do with the Soviet Union's post-World War II rise in global status and its subsequent foreign policy attempt to expand its sphere of influence among the Muslim nations in the Third World, particularly in the Middle East.

1928 to 1938

Stalin's antireligious drive coincided with the First Five-Year Plan (1928–1935) in the Soviet Union. The well-publicized plan was to become a vehicle for achievement of socialism in all spheres of the Soviet life. This naturally included the cultural sphere and hence the justification for Stalin's stepped-up efforts to combat Islam. Among the first steps taken was the large-scale closure of mosques and prayer houses whose numbers were drastically reduced from an estimated 26,279 in the prerevolutionary period to 1,312 by 1942. In Central Asia alone some 14,000 mosques and religious schools were closed. The clergy, too, became the target of persecution as their numbers were sharply reduced from 45,339 to a mere 8,872 for the entire Soviet Union. Another estimate puts the numbers of persecuted clergy at 50,000.[57] In 1929, as a show of force, open trials for clergy were held in Tashkent and many were subjected to heavy taxation to further limit their financial autonomy.

By far the most significant aspect of Stalin's antireligious crusade was his constitutional reforms and legislative initiatives. The most sweeping reform was a 1929 amendment to the Constitution that abolished the right to proselytize by any religious establishment. Under article four of the old Constitution, the freedom of religious and antireligious propaganda was granted to all citizens. The amended version omitted the right to religious propaganda, leaving intact the right to antireligious indoctrination. This new development permanently restricted religious practices and seriously threatened the public survival of religion as was hitherto known. The solution, as will be discussed later in this chapter, was to go underground in order to escape extinction or persecution.

Equally devastating was Stalin's legislative initiatives—the most significant of which was the 1929 "Law on Religious Associations." It established strict functional guidelines for organized religion, thus authorizing the state to control and supervise religious activities. As with most other related legislation, this law was chiefly designed to paralyze the Russian Orthodox Church, but it did have serious ramifications for Central Asia, as it further empowered the Soviet authorities to move against Islam as well. In particular, six dimensions of the law seem to have substantially strengthened government control. First, religious associations were required to obtain government-approved registration in order to operate. Second, the law prohibited charitable, economic, and recreational activities by religious associations, allowing only those functions that were necessary for the common spiritual needs of their members. Third, the law defined the basic procedures by which any religious association was to conduct its affairs, limiting, for instance, the membership age to eighteen and older. Fourth, the locations for religious functions were specified and restricted. Fifth, the law denied the right of juridical person from all religious institutions, thus effectively preventing the capacity to generate revenue. Finally, the Soviet government was empowered to liquidate any religious association that violated the letter of the law, for which clear guidelines were established. In October, the People's Commissariat of Internal Affairs was instructed to enforce the law immediately.[58]

In conjunction with the direct assault on Islam that continued throughout the pre-World War II period, Stalin set out to simultaneously revitalize the antireligious propaganda campaign introduced under Lenin, and to cleanse the Communist Party from the vestiges of the so-called national deviationists, people like Sultan Galiyev of Tatarstan and Akmal Ikramov of Uzbekistan, who had posed a threat to the Soviet domination of the Muslim regions. In relation to the former objective, Soviet antireligious publications were flooded with articles designed to discredit Islam and its rituals. A number of prominent Soviet scholars such as Lucian I. Klimovich actively participated in government-sponsored Islam-bashing through widely advertised books and articles written on the subject. Among the most influential publications was *The*

Contents of the Koran, published in 1928. It heavily criticized the ulterior motives of those whom Klimovich considered to have drafted the Koran in the interest of the wealthy classes of the Mecca. In yet another piece, he went so far as to altogether deny the existence of the Prophet Muhammad. Apart from scholarly publications of this nature, the *Bezbozhnik* undertook the printing of a number of articles with such antagonistic titles as "Hajj, the Vampire of Islam" and "Against the Uraza" (fasting).[59]

In addition to printed propaganda, the League of Militant Godless, under the leadership of Yaroslavski, embarked upon a sizable recruitment drive in Central Asia. In Uzbekistan, for instance, membership rose from a mere 13,115 in 1930 to 60,000 in 1931 and 90,000 in 1932.[60] The success, however, was short-lived as in the ensuing years the numbers dropped considerably, leaving legitimate doubts as to the long-term effectiveness of atheist propaganda in Central Asia. In a 1940 report, for instance, an estimated 1,200 branches of the league operating in the Central Asian region had only 27,000 members. The weakness of the propaganda campaign was also evident in various reports on underground religious activities. For example, the Soviet authorities in Kazakhstan were informed of an underground mobilization drive to re-open the mosques. In another report, compiled in 1938, Yaroslavski himself indicated that an estimated 106 mosques existed in Kyrgyzstan despite the government restrictions and widespread closures of such institutions. And in the Pamir region of Tajikistan, disturbing news on religious unrest was communicated to Moscow in 1939–40.

From the outset, Stalin put the blame for such utter failures not on the weakness of the propaganda campaign, but on the Muslim leaders who, under the guise of Communism, had succeeded in dominating the state bureaucratic and propaganda machinery, acting leniently toward Islamic culture and religion. For Stalin, the most potent remedy was the ruthless purging of top Central Asian party officials and the subsequent recruitment of new cadres, who would give absolute obedience to their Soviet masters. Quite expectedly, the systematic arrests of the Muslim leaders began in Tatarstan in 1928 and almost simultaneously was carried out in Kazakhstan. But it was not until 1932 that the rest of Central Asia was consumed by Stalin's brutal purges, culminating in the 1937–38 arrests and executions of prominent Muslim Communist leaders, some of whom were later proven to be falsely indicted. The list included such high-ranking officials as the presidents of Tajikistan, N. Maksum and Shotemar, the prime ministers of Tajikistan, Khojoyev and Rahimboboyev, prime ministers of Kazakhstan, U. Kulambetov and U. Isayev, the prime minister of Kyrgyzstan, Y. Abdulrahmanov, the first secretary of the Communist Party of Uzbekistan, Akmal Ikramov, chairman of the Turkmen Central

Executive Committee, N. Aytakov, and secretaries of the Turkmen Central Committee, Chary Velikov, and Khan Atamyshev. In 1937, 55.7 percent of the party members in key party organizations and 70.8 percent in district party committees were replaced by new cadres. The clergy, too, were accused of collaboration with nationalist leaders and savagely punished by Soviet authorities.[61] Some high-ranking clergy were arraigned on charges of espionage for the Japanese and other counterrevolutionary activities, while the low-ranking clergy were denounced for sabotaging the collectivization campaign in agriculture and practicing the ritual of circumcision, which was identified as criminal mutilation.

1939 to 1953

With the outbreak of the "Great Patriotic War" Stalin was forced to reconsider his domestic political agenda if the nation were to survive the onslaught of the German army. Insofar as the Central Asian question was concerned, this required a qualitative shift in policy orientation, characterized by a firm but conciliatory gesture toward Muslim believers. As indicated earlier, Stalin's decision in this regard was primarily motivated by his need for military manpower. To expedite the recruitment drive in Central Asia and other Muslim-inhabited regions of the Soviet Union, Stalin decided to create an official Islamic power structure whose ranks would be filled by those clergy willing to support the Soviet policies. Given his Central Asian legacy of the 1930s, Stalin was convinced that the instinct for religious survival would help his new Islamic design to succeed in attracting the believers. Thus, in 1941 the Soviet government established four Muslim Spiritual Directorates covering Central Asia and Kazakhstan, European Russia and Siberia, northern Caucasus and Daghestan, and Transcaucasia. As legally sanctioned entities, each directorate exercised its jurisdiction through a Religious Board whose membership was tightly controlled by the authorities. In 1944 the Spiritual Directorates came under the supervision of the newly created Council for the Affairs of Religious Cults, itself directly connected with and accountable to the all-powerful Council of Ministers of the Soviet Union. To strengthen the position of the Spiritual Directorates, Stalin was forced to issue a decree in January 1946, reversing an important provision of the "Law on Religious Associations," which denied the right of juridical person from religious organizations. This helped revitalize religious activities as it allowed, for instance, the manufacturing and sale of religious items, or the acquisition of buildings and means of transportation.

Among the first official clergy to engage the Muslim population in war-related sermons was Abdul Ramhman Rasulayev of Ufa. Referred to as the

"Chief of the Central Council of Islamic Religious Centers in the USSR," Rasulayev began his patriotic propaganda in 1941, calling upon the Muslims to support the Soviet war efforts. Lacking sufficient authority in Central Asia, he was later joined by the Ishan Babakhan Ibn al-Majid Khan and Zia al-Din Babakhanov, the Mufti and the vice-chairman of the Muslim Religious Board of Central Asia and Kazakhstan, to mobilize the population. Despite the propaganda efforts of the directorate, the general negative attitude toward the Soviet government did not substantially change, making the recruitment drive a less-than- successful endeavor in the end. The war estimates indicated that almost half of the 1,600,000 Muslim draftees eventually defected to the Germans. When the war ended, some 600,000 Muslim—almost all from outside Central Asia—were accused of treachery by the Soviet government and subsequently deported to Siberia.

The allied victory brought to the Soviet Union a new found global status, and therefore a chance to increase its political influence among the Third World nations, some of which had acquired an ideological taste for Marxism. Stalin sought to capitalize on this new development, particularly in connection to the Middle East and other Muslim nations of Africa and Asia. The obvious prerequisite for success was to project a more receptive and positive image of the Soviet domestic treatment of Islam. This took a variety of forms ranging from sending official clergy on propaganda tours to other countries to receiving religious dignitaries from Muslim nations, to a limited and sufficiently controlled toleration of formal Islamic educational training and rituals.

Among the most significant policy revisions of the post–World War II Stalinist era was a restricted resumption of public theological training in Central Asia. The Mir Arab *madraseh,* founded in 1535 in Bukhara, was permitted to reopen in 1952.[62] As the only formally functioning school, it provided Islamic training to a mere 100 students enrolled in a five-year program. Of a total of 12,081 hours of schooling, 4,392 were devoted to the study of Arabic and Persian. And, despite the Islamic orientation of the school, the pupils were required to learn the Soviet Constitution for a period of two hours per week.[63] According to Bennigsen, the *madraseh* neither could extend adequate training at the level necessary to graduate Muslim jurists, or ulema, nor could it replenish the shrinking pool of the clergy. Islamic literature, though legally prohibited, were also permitted to be carried out on a small scale under the supervision of the Spiritual Directorates. The publications, however, were largely limited to such items as the Koran—first permitted to be reprinted in 1948—and Islamic calendars.[64]

As part of the overall shift in policy orientation, a number of previously banned Islamic rituals were allowed to be practiced. For instance, the pilgrimage to Mecca *(hajj)*, was resumed on a selective basis as early as 1944. This was the most successful method of propaganda for the authorities to demonstrate to the Muslim world the freedom enjoyed by Soviet Muslims. Other Islamic rituals such as the Islamic income tax *(zekat)*, the Ramadan fast, and public prayer *(salat)*, were to some extent allowed to be observed in the postwar period. To further accommodate the Muslims, the number of legally sanctioned mosques was gradually increased to approximately 3,000, some 1,700 more than the official estimate for the prewar decade.[65] A 1954 report indicated that up to 3,000 believers participated in traditional Friday prayers held at the main Tashkent mosque.

In conjunction with the softening of the Soviet attitude toward Islam, Stalin practically abandoned the government-sponsored antireligious propaganda activities by dissolving the notorious League of Militant Godless and suspending the publication of *Bezbozhnik* and *Antireligioznik* in 1941. But with the allied victory in sight, the Party Central Committee issued a decree in the fall of 1944 authorizing the resumption of antireligious activities throughout the Soviet Union. By 1947, Stalin had brought the Soviet anti-religious activities under the institutional control of the "All-Union Society for the Dissemination of Political and Scientific Knowledge," *Znanie*, or Knowledge for short. Stalin saw no contradiction in pursuing an antireligious propaganda policy on one hand, and allowing a limited government-sponsored Islamic revival on the other hand. After all, he was chiefly motivated by his foreign policy concerns in the Muslim world, for which his Spiritual Directorates and official clergy seemed to have erected a somewhat perfect facade to mask the realities of Soviet religious life. And by 1948, a number of branch organizations under the auspices of *Znanie*, had been put in place all across Central Asia, utilizing a wide range of propaganda techniques such as lectures, films, literature, posters, radio programs, and so on. In Kazakhstan, for instance, 15 regional branches with 209 chapters delivered an astonishing 23,000 lectures for the 1946–48 period.[66] If not for the effective-ness of its propaganda campaign, *Znanie* achieved an almost overnight suc-cess for its membership drive, which rose from 1,414 in 1947 to 130,000 by 1950.[67] Despite the more comprehensive and systematic character of *Znanie* activities, it did not seem to have succeeded any more than its predecessor the League of Militant Godless in combating Islam, or for that matter, other reli-gions in the Soviet Union. In 1953, after two and a half decades of brutal purges, innovative organizational schemes, and massive propaganda cam-paigns, Stalin took to his grave the harsh reality of his less-than-successful war on religion.

THE POST-STALINIST ERA

With the departure of Stalin and the eventual consolidation of power by Khrushchev, it was almost certain that a new stage in the treatment of religion would commence. But with the exception of the 1960–64 period, during which a hard-line approach reminiscent of the 1930s was followed, the antireligious drive in the post-Stalinist period lost some of its steam, only to be reinvigorated in the aftermath of Iran's Islamic Revolution of 1979 and the perceived threat it posed to the Soviet Muslim republics.

Khrushchev was fully aware that the persistence of religion in the Soviet Union had been manipulated by the West to delegitimize the ideological claims of socialism. Therefore, he felt obligated to at least intensify, if not the actual attack on religion, the state's antireligious rhetoric upon assuming power. It is interesting to note that in addition to the ideological justifications set forth by his predecessors, Khrushchev brought to light an economic rationalization to further legitimize his antireligious position, arguing that certain rituals such as pilgrimage to holy places during the summer harvest as well as fasting had an adverse effect on agricultural production.[68] For a period of five years, however, he limited his activities only to direct or indirect verbal condemnations. A number of factors seem to have delayed plans to carry out a frontal attack on religion right from the outset. First, there seemed to have been sharp political divisions within the top ranks of the Communist Party as to what constituted the most appropriate antireligious course of action. This was evident in two somewhat contradictory party resolutions publicized within a few months of each other in 1954. The July resolution criticized the Stalinist policy that was claimed to have caused an increase in the number of believers, and called upon the Ministry of Education and Komsomol to step up antireligious activities. It included twelve concrete provisions. The most important items were as follows: first, the Department of Agitation and Propaganda of the Party Central Committee was to conduct a series of lectures on the subject in Marxist-Leninist universities. Second, in cooperation with *Znanie,* the Ministers of Culture in all republics were to draft proposals with the objective of improving the atheistic propaganda by 1956. Third, *Znanie* was to publish a monthly journal, Science and Religion (*Nauka i religiia)*, with an initial circulation of 75,000 issues. Finally, the state publishing houses, the publishing house of the Academy of Sciences, and the national and local media were to step up their propaganda activities. This resolution marked the beginning of the so-called Hundred Days antireligious campaign that came to an abrupt halt after nearly four months with the announcement of the second resolution in November. Entitled "On Errors in the Conduct of Scientific-Atheistic Propaganda Among the People," it emphasized the need to rely primarily upon scientific explanations of nature and society, criticizing the arbitrary character of enforcement of religious laws, mistreatment of the clergy and the believers, and the insulting nature of antireligious campaigns in the past.[69] The former resolution bore the signature of Khrushchev, while the latter did not, which seems to point to the existence of factionalism within the party's Central Committee. The second cause of delay in the intensification of the antireligious campaign was intimately related to Soviet foreign policy concerns. Khrushchev was faced with the same predicament that forced Stalin to modify his antireligious orientation, at least with respect to Islam. The Muslim Middle East had become a vital strategic region subsequent to the Soviet reversal of support for Israel, and particularly since the rise of Gamal Abdel Naser to power in Egypt. The Soviet government was intent on expanding its sphere of influence, which required the adoption of a conciliatory gesture toward the Islamic faith. Third, Khrushchev was preoccupied with other more pressing domestic policy matters such as bureaucratic reorganization, urgently needed to politically neutralize the Stalinist hold on Soviet society. This, in combination with pressing economic problems, led to a temporary break in the application of religious policies. Finally, the tenacity of religion forced Khrushchev to call for a comprehensive reassessment of the theoretical and practical dimensions of the Soviet antireligious policy before any further action could be taken.

Between 1954 and 1959 the Soviet government continued its efforts to study the problems facing the antireligious campaign. To expedite the process, a number of atheistic conferences were held throughout the Soviet Union to engage the participants in active diagnostic debates. In 1956, for instance, two sizable interrepublican conferences were held in Baku and Tashkent to discuss the fate of the atheistic movement with respect to Islam. But the primary task for the study of the atheistic propaganda was given to Bonch Bruevich as the new director of the Coordinating Committee in the Presidium of the Academy of Sciences for atheistic research. The preliminary conclusions reached by the academy and other institutions involved in the process encompassed both quantitative and qualitative dimensions. As for the former, it was considered necessary to rapidly increase the volume of scientific and atheistic propaganda literature. By 1955 a 20-volume collection of atheistic sources was compiled by Bruevich. In a separate project, 143 titles by 116 authors were also compiled.[70] By 1957, the academy had put together the first *Yearbook of the Museum of History of Religion and Atheism*. In addition to the academy's work, a number of classic books on the subject were reprinted on a large scale as a tribute to the atheistic movement and its contributors in the Soviet Union, the most noteworthy of which was *On Religion* drafted by Yaroslavski.[71]

Particular attention was also given to the early prevention of religious assimilation. In 1956, for instance, a Turkmen-language book entitled *Atheistic Education of Children* was published to guide party activists in this area. In conjunction with the expansion of literature, it was decided that lectures and other commonly used propaganda methods were inadequate in combating Islam, and therefore, the establishment of permanent atheistic institutions capable of continuous action at the republican level were deemed necessary. Consequently, a variety of such institutions were established in Central Asia. In Alma-Ata (Almaty), for instance, a so-called House of the Atheist was founded. In Ashkhabad (Ashgabat), a "University of Scientific Atheism" was constructed. In Tashkent, an antireligious museum was set up to help the Soviet propaganda machine. A host of other institutions, such as atheistic clubs, were also given special attention by the Komsomol and the Communist Party to facilitate the campaign.

As for the qualitative shortcomings of the antireligious campaign, three problem areas were given serious consideration. First, it was concluded that the content of the antireligious propaganda was partially obsolete, and thus generally ineffective. The main argument revolved around the inability to connect with the believers through the use of such abstract and outdated material, often written in a dry and technical language. Thus, it was decided to modernize the process and to rely more extensively upon individualized methods that could go beyond the impersonal approach hitherto utilized in atheistic propaganda. One such method was the house-to-house agitation that had been utilized in the past, but on a limited scale.[72] The method was based on a two-step process. First the believer would be exposed to secular literature. Then the agitator would gradually raise the level of skepticism in his mind so as to prove the falsehood of religion.[73] The second qualitative problem had to do with the weak ideological commitment of individuals charged with the dissemination of atheistic propaganda. It is noteworthy that only two decades earlier Stalin had to reckon with the same reality, which brought about the brutal purges of party officials. However, under Khrushchev it was decided, at least in the beginning, only to impose a stricter screening of those involved in the atheistic campaign, rather than repeating the Stalinist policy.[74] Finally, it was argued that Marxism lacked adequate symbolism, and therefore could not compete with such colorful ritualistic religious ideologies as Judaism, Christianity, and Islam. This rather sobering conclusion led to the renewal of the old debate over the merit of god-building based on the socialist belief system, advocated by Lunacharski and others earlier on. As a result, suggestions were made to develop secular Marxist rituals for such events as births, marriages, funerals, and so on. To fulfill the vacuum created by the gradual disappearance of religion. Khrushchev, however, found such ideas in utter violation of Leninist philosophy and did not pursue the matter seriously.[75] The 1954–59 period saw qualitative improvements in the methods of the antireligious campaign as well as a steady rise in the quantity of propaganda available in all Soviet republics. The number of lectures on atheistic themes was increased from 120,000 in 1954 to 400,000 in 1959. Despite their relatively new appearance in some republics, the antireligious museums attracted an estimated 465,000 visitors in 1959. The membership of *Znanie* was reported at 850,000 for the same year, an eightfold increase since 1950. It also began publication of *Nauka i religiia* in 1959 with a circulation of 100,000 issues. The quantity of atheistic literature was also increased substantially during this period, making available to the agitators a wider range of material for their individual house-to-house contact with the believers.

The year 1960 marked the official beginning of Khrushchev's new offensive on religion, first publicized in the form of a Central Committee resolution entitled "On the Tasks of Party Propaganda in Present Conditions." Quite expectedly, it called for an intensification of attacks on religion. In January of that year, as a show of support for the new policy, *Znanie* held an antireligious conference that was attended by a number of top party officials including Brezhnev, Kosygin, Mikoyan, Suslov, Ignatiyev, and Polianski. Shortly thereafter, orders were sent out to high-ranking republican party leaders to prepare the ground for the implementation of the new party resolution. This, quite predictably, manifested itself in the form of a series of public acknowledgments of the past policy failures, designed to set the stage for the resumption of hardline attacks on religion. For instance, the first secretary of the Kyrgyz Party Central Committee, Razzakov stated: "One of the harmful survivals of the past is religious ideology. . . . Party organizations are not taking the necessary measures for developing an aggressive scientific-atheistic propaganda, and the work that is being done in this field does not reach the faithful, does not draw them away from religion."[76] Similar statements were also made by the second secretary of the Turkmen Party, Grishaenkov.

Contrary to the Leninist and Stalinist eras, no new legislation or constitutional reforms were introduced by Khrushchev to reorient the antireligious drive. He, instead, focused on the law enforcement aspects of the Soviet antireligious campaign for which the Soviet Council of Ministers issued a decree entitled "On the Strict Observance of the Laws on Religious Cults" in March 1961. The overall strategy was threefold. First, a direct attack was to be launched against the clergy as well as the external attributes of religion. Second, the existing laws were to be thoroughly implemented. Third, the penalties for religious offenses were to be made more severe. By 1962 the

Russian Criminal Code had been revised to reflect the new strategy of the Soviet government, setting an example for the other republics to follow.[77] The code included a number of specific articles designed to address religious offenses. Article 142 made violations of the law on Separation of Church from State and State from Schools punishable by up to one year of corrective work or a fine of up to 50 rubles. Article 143 reduced the punishment for interference with religious ceremonies, giving the state more freedom to limit religious activities. Article 227 introduced a sentence of up to five years imprisonment or exile for practicing religious rituals considered harmful to one's health. In addition to these, a number of other articles were frequently invoked to punish the believers such as article 70, which designated severe punishment for involvement in anti-government activities and the like. In 1962 several amendments were secretly introduced to the 1929 "Law on Religious Associations" to further limit religious activities. While the content of the amendments were not publicized, oral directives were issued to carry out the law. Presumably the changes had been made to simply give legal appearance to government actions.

By 1963 the severity of Khrushchev's antireligious campaign had reached new heights. The number of operating mosques that had seen a slight rise in the postwar era was sharply reduced to an estimated 400 for the entire Soviet Union. The number of registered clergy was also reduced to between 2,000 to 3,000, forcing many to operate through illegal channels. Apart from persecution and imprisonment, the Soviet government relied upon other harsh methods to discredit Muslim clergy. For instance, Pir Niyaz Khodzha (Khoja), a reputed *Seyyed*—a direct descendent of the Prophet Muhammad—was used by the local Communist officials to openly denounce several clergy, calling them parasites and adventurers. In another case, the spiritual righteousness of a Kyrgyz clergyman, who had been found guilty of a minor crime, was publicly called into question by the authorities in order to ruin the reputation of the clergy as a whole. The internal pilgrimage by Muslims to various holy sites was also prohibited by the government to further restrict Islamic rituals. Despite all these efforts, Khrushchev's hard-line approach of the 1960–64 period did very little to change the overall picture of religious life in the Soviet Union. With his demotion in October 1964, the antireligious campaign assumed a less hostile character. A month later, a party resolution similar to that of the November 1954 acknowledged the mistakes that had been made on the antireligious front, once again condemning the mistreatment of the clergy and the believers. Such public announcements, however, did not result in a return to the pre-1959 arrangements since the mass closure of the mosques remained in effect and none of the official clergy were apparently reinstated, though some were released from prisons.

Similar to Khrushchev, Brezhnev focused on the law enforcement aspects of the antireligious drive, while at the same time he called for a comprehensive study of the believers' religious proclivity so as to devise more effective policies. One of the most significant findings of the study underscored the sobering reality that a sizable portion of the younger generation, born after the October Revolution, exhibited strong religious tendencies. This finding repudiated the generational argument so frequently resorted to by the Soviet authorities that stated that only the older generations were religious. By 1965–66, a number of proposals were introduced, none of which were essentially new or differed from what had been discussed for nearly five decades. The only change under Brezhnev involved the reordering of priorities in the fight against religion. At the general level, it was decided to focus more heavily on socialist and atheistic education, rather than attacking religion directly. At a more specific level, it was argued that: ". . . the basic efforts should be concentrated on the steady reduction of the reproduction of religiousness among the new generation of Soviet society. This is why it is necessary to improve in every way the atheist education in family and in school, show special attention to children from religious families, and seek the most lively, emotion-packed and aesthetical forms of anti-religious propaganda among children, teenagers and young people."[78] The implementation of the new approach was signaled by the removal of Leonid Il'ichev, the head of the Department of Propaganda and Agitation of the Central Committee (1958–61), and the Communist Party secretary for Ideological Affairs (1961–65), who masterminded the hard-line antireligious policies of the Khrushchev years. In the ensuing years until 1979, Brezhnev continued his efforts to strengthen the legal and constitutional aspects of church-state relations. The basic philosophy was to deal swiftly with the violators of the existing religious laws. In 1966 three new laws were introduced to help clarify the position of the state vis-à-vis religion. The first law (ordinance) was designed to elucidate the types of offenses that were punishable under article 142 of the Criminal Code. It identified six categories of offenses including collection of taxes for religious purposes, dissemination of information to encourage violation of the religious laws, and incitement of religious superstition among the masses. The second law also involved the execution of article 142. It addressed cases involving recidivism and repeat offenses, making them punishable by up to three years of imprisonment. The third law dealt with administrative penalties for violations of rules governing various religious matters, such as registration of religious associations and gatherings.[79] Moreover, in an effort to further streamline the application of the Soviet religious laws and to remove legal ambiguities, Brezhnev introduced a series of amendments to the 1929 "Law on Religious Associations" in 1975. The amendments effectively centralized the state control over religious activities and strengthened the administrative authority of the Council for Religious Affairs.[80] Two years later, the Brezhnev Constitution introduced additional amendments that reflected an increasingly less belligerent government attitude toward religion. Article 52, for instance, replaced the phrase "freedom of antireligious propaganda" with "freedom of atheistic propaganda." Although insignificant to most believers, the change in the constitutional language signaled the resumption of a modus vivendi similar to the postwar Stalinist era.[81] As far as Islam was concerned, the Soviet government went even one step further by moderating its traditional position which depicted it as a reactionary instrument used for the spiritual oppression of the peoples of the East. Islam under Brezhnev was assigned a progressive character and praised as an anticolonial ideology. It was further admitted that some social principles of Islam were essentially compatible with Marxism. Such a drastic change in interpretation was, of course, designed for foreign policy purposes and did not bring about a significant shift in the manner in which Islam was treated domestically. In addition to the changing Soviet position on Islam, the government encouraged a limited and tightly controlled interaction between its official clergy and the Muslim world. The Muslim Religious Board of Central Asia and Kazakhstan thus became the staging ground for the Soviet propaganda activities. Since 1969 the board had been given permission to publish the *Muslims of the Soviet East* in the Uzbek and Arabic languages to further legitimize its operations.

The outbreak of Iran's Islamic revolution in 1978–79 put an end to a decade of relatively stable relations between the Soviet authorities and Islam. But at the same time it strengthened, albeit temporarily, the resolve of the Central Asian population, particularly in Tajikistan and Uzbekistan, but also in Kazakhstan and Kyrgyzstan, to demand religious liberty.[82] The news of the Islamic revolutionary success in Iran seemed to have helped trigger a series of anti-Soviet demonstrations and riots in Dushanbe, Alma-Ata, and other cities. Although not all disturbances had religious causes, Islamic ideology played a role in inciting the masses. In March 1979, for instance, the Persian New Year celebrations were used by the clergy to politicize the young. Reports from Kyrgyzstan also indicated renewed efforts to illegally reopen mosques and resume religious training. The Soviet response to the events in Iran and Central Asia followed three distinct and somewhat contradictory patterns. The first was to implicitly welcome the revolutionary change in Iran, and as a defensive strategy, to glorify Islam. The Islamic Revolution was characterized as an anti-imperialist movement, and thus progressive in nature. Moreover, in 1979 and 1980, three well-publicized Islamic conferences were held to demonstrate the accommodating orientation of the Soviet regime with respect to Islam. The first 1979 conference was attended by 12 Muslim nations (including Iran) and celebrated the tenth anniversary of the publication of *Muslims of the Soviet East.* In a written declaration the conference participants unanimously condemned Israel, the United States, South Africa, and China for their imperialist policies. In an attempt to ideologically pacify Iran, a Persian version of the journal was allowed to be published shortly thereafter. The second conference in 1979 was designed to commemorate the "contribution of the Muslims of Central Asia, of the Volga, and of the Caucasus to the development of Islamic thought, to the cause of peace, and social progress." It was attended by 30 Muslim countries. The 1980 conference was organized to celebrate "the 15th century of the Higra," as the century of peace and international friendship. The conference called for the establishment of a permanent exposition on the subject of Islam in the Soviet Union. In addition to such high-profile activities, the Soviet government officially acknowledged Sufism in Turkmenistan in an effort to preempt an ideological offensive by the Islamic fundamentalists in Iran to infiltrate the highly secretive Sufi orders.

The second pattern of response corresponded to the strengthening of security and law-enforcement aspects in the Muslim republics. The close proximity to Iran, quite expectedly, caused serious concern over the possibility of foreign ideological subversion destabilizing the region. The head of the Turkmenistan KGB, Major General Z. Yusef Zade, went so far as to blame the United States for "trying to exploit the Islamic religion—especially in areas where the Muslim population lives—as one factor in influencing the political situation in our country." The first secretary of the Turkmen Communist Party, Gapurov, is quoted to have warned the central authorities of the foreign propaganda activities being conducted by some individuals who had exhibited pan-Turkish or Pan-Islamic tendencies. He went on to say: "Muslim pseudo-confessors, champions of old, reactionary principles and rites, operating wilfully in the so called 'holy places,' are trying to kindle religious fanaticism, fuel feelings of national narrow-mindedness and instill in family relations harmful feudal survivals and rituals."[83] Consequently, extra security measures were taken along the southern borders with Iran and Afghanistan, and the KGB's presence was substantially increased in the Muslim republics. This policy continued until the mid-1980s.

Finally, the Soviet government intensified its propaganda activities across the board in Central Asia. In 1979–80 a series of articles appeared in *Nauka i religiia* and in *Pravda Vostoka,* a daily Uzbek publication, attacking Islam and its reactionary orientation—a far cry from the Soviet foreign policy position on Islam alluded to earlier. Similar articles also appeared in *Kommunist*

Tadzhikistana, criticizing both Islam and the ineffectiveness of atheistic education and antireligious propaganda in the republic. Although there are no accurate statistics available as to the extent of the antireligious propaganda in the region, the scope of such activities seems to have been expanded since the Islamic revolution. For instance, in 1981 the Soviet government published 24 anti-Islamic books. The numbers were raised to 37 and 72 titles for the years 1982 and 1983 respectively. The quantity of antireligious lectures also seems to have risen in Central Asia. In the city of Namangan in Uzbekistan's Fergana Valley, an astonishing 11,000 lectures were delivered in 1979. Similar unofficial estimates had been reported for the three succeeding years.

With the exclusion of the extra security measures, taken to ensure stability in the region, the Soviet response failed either to substantially reduce the influence of Islam on the believers, or to convince the outside world of the good intentions of the central government. Far from successful, the end result was the containment of the Islamic sentiments of the Central Asian population—a familiar process that dominated the Soviet struggle against religion since its beginning.

CONCLUSION

Although in retrospect the Soviet campaign against Islam was proven to be an utter failure, it did have some residual impact on the Central Asian population. While it is impossible to discern a general pattern as to the socioeconomic background of the nonbelievers, the majority seems to have belonged to the urban educated class of technocrats who had been sufficiently modernized and Westernized through extra-cultural contact over the last few decades. Reliable statistics on the degree of religiosity among the Muslims in the region are neither comprehensive nor reliable. The most frequently cited study of the subject was conducted in Karakalpak in northwestern Uzbekistan in the early 1970s. It put the estimates of nonbelievers at 23 percent for males and 20 percent for females. Of the remaining 77 percent male believers and 80 percent female believers, on average 11.1 percent were identified as devout Muslims and the rest declared some degree of affiliation with the Muslim religion.[84] As far as the observance of the major Islamic rituals were concerned the non-Soviet estimates for daily prayer (*salat*), range from 20 to 40 percent of the adult population. The figure stood at 50 percent for fasting, and observed for only three days instead of a month.

This apparent failure may be attributed to a number of factors most of which had been acknowledged and frequently discussed by the authorities since the inception of the Soviet antireligious campaign. The first, and perhaps the most significant factor, was the lack of a genuine ideological commitment to socialism on the part of those intimately involved in the conduct of antireligious campaign. Most party members, Komsomol, and *Znanie* were sympathetic to the Islamic and nationalist causes and thus reluctant to vigorously pursue their task. Several explanations account for such tendencies. For instance, many high-ranking officials saw no contradiction between Islam and Communism. Also, the Central Asian population was generally distrustful of the Russians, a legacy that was inherited from their czarist predecessors. And finally, the Soviet government failed to disrupt the reproductive cycle of Islamic ideology at the family level.[85] Thus the family environment consistently neutralized the Soviet educational efforts to inculcate socialist ideology in the minds of the younger generation. Second, the antireligious campaign was plagued by organizational inefficiency as many institutions duplicated one another's functions, or pursued contradictory policies. Such practices introduced confusion into the process and adversely affected the attitude of the cadres involved in the campaign. Third, the Soviet government had no accurate measurement technique to ascertain the extent to which its antireligious strategies were effective. The surveyed believers, more often than not, misinformed the authorities as to their true religious propensity. Fourth, the subject of antireligious propaganda repeatedly took on alien forms, thus effectively reducing the agitators' capacity to relate to the daily lives of the Muslim believers. As early as the 1960s, the Party Central Committee had admitted that the propaganda was detached from life, had no bearing on Communist construction, lacked purpose and cohesion, and above all was abstract and intangible in nature. Fifth, although the Soviet government succeeded in dismantling the clerical power structure, many continued their religious practices illegally or in private. The survival of this underground network of clergy was guaranteed by the secret donations of the believers throughout the years, particularly in the rural areas of Tajikistan and Uzbekistan, keeping alive the Islamic rituals whose public practice had been severely restricted by the authorities. Sixth, the frequent violence and coercion involved in the conduct of antireligious propaganda almost invariably helped strengthen Islamic tendencies as it galvanized the population in support of the victims of religious persecutions. This was especially noticeable during the Stalinist purges of the 1930s and later during the 1960–64 period. Seventh, the generally rural character of the Central Asian region posed an insurmountable challenge to the implementation of the Soviet antireligious propaganda. The difficulty in reaching the remote villages meant less frequent exposure to atheistic propaganda. But more importantly, the effect of such propaganda activities was often offset by subsequent sermons offered by rural clergy.

Eighth, despite continued pressure and periodic outbursts of coercion and violence against Islam, the Soviet foreign policy concerns in the Middle East helped guarantee its unobtrusive existence in Central Asia throughout the post–World War II era. And last but not least, the nature of Islam made the Soviet Propaganda objective an almost unattainable dream. Islam was, and still is, a way of life that culturally defined every facet of the believer's existence. To destroy Islam, therefore, meant to destroy the centuries-old identity of the Central Asian believer. Socialism as a relatively young and conclusively foreign ideology was proven to be no match for such a culturally well-embedded religion like Islam.

In the final analysis, the fate of the anti-Islamic campaign under Brezhnev was no brighter than that of his three predecessors. With the invasion of Afghanistan in 1979, Brezhnev further delegitimized his stance toward Islam. Clearly, he could not deny the existence of an armed Muslim opposition to his supposedly progressive revolution in Afghanistan, nor could he justify this aggression among the Central Asian Muslims. His departure in 1982 temporarily disrupted the struggle against Islam as the Soviet government was consumed by a leadership succession crisis that eventually brought Mikhail Gorbachev to the forefront of the political scene. It was under his leadership that socialism itself and not religion withered away.

CHAPTER 2

The Gorbachev Era

*We need spiritual values, we need a revolution of the mind.
This is the only way toward a new culture and new politics
that can meet the challenge of our time. We have changed our
attitude toward some matters such as religion. Now, we not
only proceed from the assumption that no one should interfere in matters of the individual's conscience; we also say that
the moral values that religion generated and embodied for
centuries can help in the work of renewal in our country, too.*

—MIKHAIL GORBACHEV

On March 10, 1985, Mikhail Sergeyevich Gorbachev succeeded Konstantin Chernenko as the first Soviet leader from the post-Brezhnev generation. In the ensuing years, until his resignation in 1991, Gorbachev set out to transform Soviet society through his well-advertised policies of perestroika (restructuring), and glasnost (openness). Though intended to remedy an entirely different set of socioeconomic and political ills in the country, Gorbachev's glasnost became an official vehicle for the expression of ethnic, linguistic, cultural, environmental, and religious grievances that had not been addressed openly in recent decades. An inevitable by-product of this process, as will be discussed in the following pages, was a gradual revival of religion, including Islam in Central Asia. It is noteworthy, however, that

Gorbachev followed his predecessors' policies on religion during the first three years at the helm. Nor did he or his reform-minded colleagues remotely anticipate the magnitude of responses that brought about the eventual dissolution of the Soviet empire. Thus, the subsequent adoption of a tolerant religious policy toward Islam was a matter of necessity rather than choice, as it was concluded that reform in the economic infrastructure would not succeed unless accompanied by similar initiatives in the ideological superstructure and because the government hoped to regain some of its lost popularity due to failed economic policies. Leaving aside the consequences of Gorbachev's reform initiative, its origin and underlying causes must be sought in the last years of the Brezhnev era.

THE POLITICS OF TRANSITION

Governed by rigid bureaucratic principles rather than flexible market mechanisms, the Soviet economy of the late 1970s was marred by pronounced contradictions to which Brezhnev and his provincial governors had chosen to turn a blind eye. During his long tenure in office (1964–82), Brezhnev had managed to create what in essence may be referred to as a neopatrimonial system in which the relative material well-being of the population was guaranteed by the top leadership in return for general political acquiescence and loyalty.[1] The outcome of this arrangement, which had been made possible primarily by way of massive state subsidies and price controls, was a gradual depletion of the Soviet financial power to the point where it could no longer maintain an adequate productive momentum. So, on the one hand, while the standard of living of the average Soviet citizen had been raised, his real income more than doubled, and his educational opportunities substantially improved,[2] on the other hand, most macroeconomic indices painted a grim picture of a stagnant society, slowly collapsing under its own weight. According to one estimate, the rate of economic growth, measured in terms of national income, dropped from 7.8 percent in 1966–70 to 5.7 percent in 1971–75, to 3.6 percent in 1981–85.[3] The rate of growth in labor productivity also declined substantially and chronic labor shortages became a permanent feature of the Soviet economy in the 1970s and early 1980s. And, despite its tremendous potential and costly investment drives under Brezhnev, the agricultural sector consistently failed to reduce the Soviet grain dependency on the outside world. In fact, agricultural output had declined from 237 million tons in 1978 to 158 million tons in 1981.[4] But more important, it was the technological stagnation that put the Soviet economic landscape into its proper perspective.[5] Apart from its advances in military hardware, the Soviet competitive edge in technology had become virtually nonexistent by the late 1970s, as exemplified by its inability to produce high-technology products such as personal computers. The Soviet sociopolitical environment was no more promising than its economic conditions. The lack of discipline in the workplace, excessive alcohol consumption, and widespread corruption at all levels of the state apparatus had become norms rather than exceptions throughout the Soviet Union. A 1982 report, for example, indicated an astonishing 30 percent absenteeism among the workers surveyed at any given time. A similar survey of 800 Moscow factories reported that in some instances only 10 percent of the workforce were present before the closing hour.[6] Alcohol consumption, which was later identified as one of the root causes of Soviet social problems, doubled during the 1960–80 period, and the number of alcoholics and heavy drinkers in some age categories increased by 35 to 37 percent during the latter part of the Brezhnev era. But, perhaps the most devastating consequence of Brezhnev's neopatrimonial rule was the rampant corruption that it had harbored. The local party bosses were given relative autonomy in return for political allegiance and obedience. This arrangement had, of course, opened multiple avenues of opportunity for various industrial and agricultural embezzlement schemes of unprecedented proportions. One of the most elaborate schemes is quoted to have been masterminded by the first secretary of the Uzbek Communist Party, Sharaf Rashidov, who was elected in 1959. In an effort to draw himself closer to Brezhnev, Rashidov attempted to triple the cotton production, promising him to deliver five million tons of cotton and more every year, to which Brezhnev replied, "Make it six million, my little Sharaf."[7] As a result, millions of rubles were skimmed by Rashidov and his aides as they fabricated phony production quotas and covered up the short falls by bribing the firms involved in the delivery of cotton. While Rashidov's illegal dealings were common knowledge, he was protected by Brezhnev who apparently had working knowledge of this operation through his son-in-law, Yori Churbanov, who was the deputy minister of the interior and directly involved in the bribe-taking from Uzbekistan.

Given his deteriorating health and declining legitimacy, Brezhnev failed to secure the election of his protégé, Konstantin Chernenko, to the position of Central Committee secretary for ideological affairs before his death in November 1982. Instead, Yori Andropov, who had earlier resigned his post as the head of the KGB, was chosen for the position in May. Quite expectedly, his rise to power produced a sigh of relief among those cadres who had been disenchanted with Brezhnev's management of the body politic. By June 1983, nearly seven months after becoming the General Secretary, Andropov had consolidated his power, adding the chairmanship of the Presidium of the USSR Supreme Soviet to the list of positions he occupied. In his first major speech, on November 22nd, Andropov presented a less rosy and thus more realistic account of the economic state of the Soviet Union, outlining in broad strokes the need for greater efficiency, energy conservation, technological innovation, and targeted funding for major economic projects.[8] There is very little doubt that Andropov was intent on altering Brezhnev's modus vivendi by introducing reform measures. As the former head of the KGB, he knew more than any other high-ranking official the extent of the economic decline and political decay in the country. But Andropov did not seem to have a comprehensive and long-term program of reform of the sort that was eventually instigated by Gorbachev. Nevertheless, it was Andropov who sowed the seeds of change. His primary concern was to put the economy back on the right track and to revitalize the Soviet social structure through disciplinary action. Thus, within days of his ascendancy to power, Andropov embarked upon a tough anti-corruption and anti-alcohol campaign to improve the morale and productivity of the workforce. He also called for a number of exploratory research projects to investigate the nature of the Soviet economic problems.

On the political front he spoke of glasnost as a strategy to restore the trust of the people in government and the Communist Party. Andropov went so far as to set a date of January 1985 for the official commencement of his reform initiatives. But his plans were cut short when he became critically ill in August 1983 and passed away in February of the following year. Prior to his departure, however, Andropov succeeded in paving the way for Gorbachev's assimilation into the core leadership structure. It is plausible to argue that without Andropov, Gorbachev might never have reached the top in such a short period of time, if at all.

Gorbachev had joined the Communist Party in 1952, rising through the ranks until he was appointed the first secretary of Stavropol in 1970.[9] It was during this period that Andropov, who frequently vacationed in the Caucasus, developed an interest in Gorbachev as an effective and innovative manager, leading to his eventual election to the party's Central Committee. Although powerful, Andropov was not a part of the Brezhnev's inner circle. But Gorbachev's effective agricultural strategies in Stavropol, and more important, in Ipatovo had left a lasting impression on Brezhnev and his associates as well.[10] With the 1978 death of Feiodor Kulakov, the Central Committee secretary in charge of agricultural affairs—Gorbachev's first mentor in Stavropol—Andropov was provided with a timely occasion to recommend Gorbachev for the position. In September of that year, subsequent to a meeting between Brezhnev, Chernenko, Andropov, and Gorbachev in Mineralnie Vody station, Gorbachev was given the opportunity of a lifetime.[11] He was now a Central Committee secretary and a member of the Politburo, intimately involved in the politics of power. And later, with Andropov's ailing health, Gorbachev was granted yet another opportunity to assume informally the responsibilities of the General Secretary, as well as to play the role of an intermediary between him and the rest of the Politburo.

Andropov's political lobbying before his death, in favor of Gorbachev's succession, was undermined by the weary conservative leadership who felt more secure with Konstantin Chernenko at the helm. Born in Siberia, Chernenko had been a party member since 1931 when Gorbachev was born. His rise to power was the result of his close association with Brezhnev, which dated back to the early 1950s. He had become Central Committee secretary in 1976 and a Politburo member in 1978, finally assuming the top rank at the age of seventy-two without any substantive accomplishments to his name. As the product of the Brezhnev era, Chernenko largely abandoned the reform measures undertaken by his predecessor. In his first major speech as the general secretary, he presented an optimistic account of the economy, leaving a definite impression of his overall satisfaction with the status quo. During his short tenure in office, he participated in two Central Committee Plenums neither of which, as expected, carried reformist tones of the sort that highlighted the Andropov era. He was, however, interested in three projects, one educational in nature and the other two agrarian. Chernenko was supportive of a school reform program that had been designed to improve the existing system. The agricultural schemes were related to the diversion of Russian rivers and a large-scale land reclamation project to expand production rather than productivity per unit of cultivation. Both projects were, of course, unrealistic and were thus disregarded altogether.[12]

Chernenko was last seen in public in December of 1984 and the news of his death was made public in March 1985. Gorbachev, who had remained as the de facto second secretary with substantial power, was now in an ideal position to become the next Soviet leader. Within hours of Chernenko's death the Politburo selected Gorbachev as the top man of the Kremlin. Andre Gromyko, a highly respected veteran of Soviet foreign affairs, was instrumental in strengthening Gorbachev's position and helped sway the vote in his favor in a rather evenly divided Politburo.[13] With his election, the generational transition of power was completed. But Gorbachev was far from secure in his new position. It was thus necessary to weaken and eventually eliminate the old Brezhnev sympathizers from the Soviet power structure through the recruitment of relatively young and reform-minded technocrats for high positions. From the outset, it was clear that Gorbachev's consolidation of power did not follow the traditional pattern in one respect: contrary to his predecessors, he concentrated his efforts more heavily on the apex of the leadership structure rather than on the lower levels of the party and bureaucracy. Altogether five Communist Party Plenums were held during Gorbachev's first year in power as the new general secretary, during which 23 top-ranking members of the Central Committee and the Politburo changed or lost their positions. At the April 1985 Plenum, the KGB head, Viktor Chebrikov, an Andropov appointee, was promoted to a full member of the Politburo. Yegor Ligachev and Nikolai Ryzhkov, also Andropov appointees to the Secretariat, became full members. During the July Plenum Lev Zaikov and Boris Yeltsin joined the Secretariat. Grigori Romanov, Gorbachev's main rival retired from the Politburo and the secretariat. Edward Shevardnadze, who had been a candidate member since 1978, became a full member. In the September Plenum, the eighty-year-old Nikolai Tikhonov, prime minister since 1980, resigned and was replaced by Ryzhkov. In October Nikolai Baibakov who had been the head of Gosplan since 1965 was removed and succeeded by Nikolai Talyzen. The following year, two other Brezhnev supporters, Viktor Grishin and Konstantin Rusakov, retired from the Politburo and the Secretariat. Further personnel changes took place at the 27th Party Congress in February 1986. Anatoli Dobrynin, the tenured ambassador to the United States, and Alexander Yakovlev, an associate of Gorbachev and the former ambassador to Canada, were appointed to the secretariat. Also appointed, were Vadim Medvedev, Georgii Razumovski, and Alexandra Biryukova all of whom were more or less in tandem with Gorbachev's line of thinking. According to Stephen White, by the end of 1986, 52 percent of the Central Committee members were newly appointed, "a rate of turnover much higher than the Brezhnev years of 'stability of cadres.'"[14] The Council of Ministers experienced similar changes as 48 of its 134 members were replaced within a year of Gorbachev's assumption of power. In the same time span, approximately 30 percent of the republican and regional leaders were also pushed aside. During the next four years, Gorbachev continued his "bloodless" purge of the cadres at the lower levels, a process that he believed to be intimately related to the success of his reform initiatives.

PERESTROIKA AND GLASNOST IN CENTRAL ASIA

Although Gorbachev was fully aware of the magnitude of the socioeconomic and political problems facing the Soviet Union, he did not push for a radical reformist agenda during his first year in office. Obviously, he had to build a team and a consensus before he could translate his abstract ideas into concrete reality. In fact, in his inaugural speech in April 1985, Gorbachev simply reaffirmed the leadership commitment to the strategy of *uskorenie,* "acceleration" of the socioeconomic development, formulated during the 26th Party Congress

(1981) and the subsequent Central Committee Plenum. It is clear, therefore, that at least at this stage Gorbachev seemed to have been satisfied with this strategy, which did not call for fundamental structural reforms. But to those closely involved in Soviet political affairs, Gorbachev had been known for having far more radical ideas than what he had initially prescribed. As early as 1984, Gorbachev's overall philosophy had been made public in speeches in which he emphasized the merits of economic self-management, social justice, "commodity-money relation" (a Marxist substitute for market mechanisms), and glasnost, described as an inseparable part of socialist democracy.[15]

Quite expectedly, Gorbachev's support for *uskorenie* quickly waned as he became more aware of its limitations, and as his base of support within the party became stronger. Bialer has identified three sets of internal factors that seems to have compelled Gorbachev to abandon *uskorenie* in favor of more radical reforms: "First, the domestic performance of the Soviet system during the Brezhnev era; second, the new and necessary conditions of Soviet economic growth under contemporary circumstances; and third, the changed nature of Soviet society and the conditions of its stability."[16] The earliest official sign of a qualitative shift in reform strategy came at the 27th Party Congress in February 1986 when Gorbachev skillfully outlined his vision of perestroika as a natural outgrowth of *uskorenie,* only more comprehensive in character:

> How do we interpret the word acceleration [*uskorenie*]? Above all, it means increasing the rates of economic growth. But that's not all. Its essence is a new quality of growth: the all around intensification of production . . . the restructuring of the economy, and effective forms of management, of organizing labor and providing incentives . . . acceleration is not confined to transformations in the economic field. It envisages the implementation of an active social policy and the consistent affirmation of the principle of social justice . . . improvement of social relations, the updating of the forms and methods of the work of political and ideological institutions, the deepening of socialist democracy.[17]

Gorbachev further defined perestroika as a revolutionary process that "rests on the living creativity of the masses, it seeks the manifold development of democracy and socialist self-management, it encourages private initiative, independent action, a strengthening of discipline and order, more widespread openness (glasnost), criticism and self-criticism in every area, it means a deeper respect for the value and dignity of human beings."[18] At the concrete level, perestroika was intended to accomplish, among other things, four primary objectives.[19] First, was the modernization of the Soviet technological infrastructure that had clearly lagged behind by Western standards. Second, was the modernization of the organization of production and concomitant decentralization of the management structure. Third, was the elimination of waste and inefficiency in both production and extraction of raw material.[20] Finally, was the democratization of the social and political spheres through glasnost.

For Gorbachev, as for Andropov, the average citizen was to be drawn back into the active sphere of Soviet political life, a process that necessitated, above all, the regaining of the people's trust by means of accurate and open dissemination of information about past and present Soviet conditions:

> We want more openness about public affairs in every sphere of life. People should know what is good, and what is bad, too. . . . Truth is the main thing . . . which makes it possible for people to understand better what happened to us in the past, what is taking place now, what we are striving for. . . . The people should know life with all its contradictions and complexities. . . . We regard the development of *glasnost* as a way of accumulating the various diverse views and ideas which reflect the interests of all strata, of all trades and professions in the Soviet society. . . . We need *glasnost* as we need air.[21]

Leaving aside its theoretically constructive dimensions, glasnost was in essence a strategy adopted by Gorbachev for political and bureaucratic housecleaning. It was to allow public criticism of officials and policies throughout the Soviet Union so as to expose corruption and inefficiency at all administrative levels. Given the prevailing dissatisfaction with the Communist Party and the Soviet government, glasnost was to help Gorbachev expand his popular base of support, hence improving the odds for a successful implementation of his reform program.

As universal and all-encompassing as they were officially portrayed, glasnost and perestroika, at first, neither encompassed Central Asia nor Islam, as if Gorbachev had designed his program of reform primarily with an Slavic audience in mind. Slowly, however, reforms made their way into the region. The application and subsequent impact of perestroika and glasnost on Central Asia in general, and on Islam in particular, may be adequately organized into two phases. The first phase began in 1985 when Gorbachev assumed power, and ended in 1988. This period was marked by a massive anti-corruption campaign as Gorbachev attempted to reestablish tighter control over Central Asia. This was largely accomplished by a large-scale purge of the cadres, which had already begun under Andropov, and that ran through the fabric of the regional party structures. The Soviet policy toward Islam during this phase differed very little from the previous eras outlined in chapter 1. In fact, Gorbachev blamed Islamic culture for the wide-spread corruption in Central Asia. The second phase corresponded to the 1988–91 period during which glasnost was permitted to be practiced relatively freely on a scale similar to other republics in the Soviet Union. It is noteworthy that although the immediate reaction to glasnost varied from republic to republic, in Central Asia the overall pattern reflected the ethnic, linguistic, cultural, and environmental sentiments more heavily than the religious aspirations. Rapidly, however, religious concerns began to be heard frequently in all of the republics. The seeds of Islamic revival were cultivated during these few years. This phase triumphantly ended in the declarations of independence by the Central Asian republics and the eventual dissolution of the Soviet empire in the aftermath of the failed August 1991 coup.

First Phase: 1985 to 1988

Measured in both scope and intensity, no other region in the Soviet Union experienced the same anti-corruption campaign and party purges than were conducted in Central Asia by the authorities. The region was already well under fire by the time Gorbachev assumed power. In fact, party shake-ups had begun almost immediately after the death of Brezhnev who had apparently sheltered the republican party leaders from criminal investigation. Of the five neopatrimonial leaders in Central Asia, two escaped embarrassment and possible prosecution due to their deaths. Jabar Rasulov of Tajikistan died in April 1982 after 22 years of service to the party apparatus—he was succeeded by Rahman Nabiyev. Next to go, at an early age (sixty-five) in 1983, was Sharaf Rashidov of Uzbekistan who is believed to have died of a heart attack, seemingly caused by the news of an impending investigation into what later became known as the "cotton affair." A 24-year veteran of Uzbek politics, he had held an alternate membership position in the Politburo. During the 1983 and 1984 period, the Uzbekistan party structure became the target of an open and unprecedented anti-corruption campaign in which many regional party leaders, local party managers, and law-enforcement officers were replaced in almost all regions of the republic. In addition to the purges within the strict party hierarchy, some of the republican cabinet ministers were also replaced, including the ministers of Justice, Education, Cotton Processing, and the Interior. Later, in an effort to strengthen bureaucratic control in Uzbekistan, a number of structural reforms were initiated, among which the merger of the ministry of cotton processing and agriculture ranked prominently.[22]

The other three republican leaders of Central Asia were replaced in the aftermath of Gorbachev's reform program. Cognizant of his shaky future, Turdiakun Usulbaliyev of Kyrgyzstan opted for an early retirement in 1985.

To save his position, however, Usulbaliyev at first took the initiative to replace corrupt party officials, but to no avail. His departure coincided with a large-scale housecleaning by the central authorities of the sort that was carried out in Uzbekistan and to some extent in Kazakhstan.[23] Upon assumption of power, his successor Absamat Masaliyev removed the second party secretary and two of the four oblast secretaries. Faced with the same predicament as Usulbaliyev, the head of the Turkmenistan party, Muhammadnazar Gapurov, also quietly retired at the age of sixty-three after 15 years of active party membership. He had also occupied such critical positions as the head of the Turkmen KGB. The last of the old guards, Dinmuhammad Kunayev, was replaced by Gorbachev in 1986.

Disillusioned by the extent of corruption and wrongdoing, Gorbachev openly criticized Uzbekistan, Kyrgyzstan, and Kazakhstan in his address to the 27th party Congress in February 1986, setting the stage for a further tightening of control in Central Asia: "Negative processes caused by an absence of criticism and self-criticism were manifested in their most acute form, perhaps, in Uzbekistan. . . . Discipline became lax in the republic Party organization, and those who received favor were persons whose only principles were lack of principle. . . . All this could not help but affect the state of affairs. The situation in the economy and in the social sphere deteriorated sharply, all sorts of shady deals, embezzlement and bribery became widespread and socialist legality was flagrantly violated." He went on to say that: "We incur considerable losses because some Communists behave unworthily and commit disreputable acts. Recently, a number of executives have been relieved of their posts and expelled from the Party for various abuses. Criminal charges have been brought against them. Such instances have occurred in particular, in Alma Ata and Chimkent and certain other provinces and republics."[24] In conjunction with the purges, and upon the recommendation of Ligachev, the Central Committee secretary in charge of cadres, an interrepublican exchange policy was adopted to fill the ranks of the Central Asian Communist Party with outside members. Ligachev, much like Gorbachev, saw the rampant corruption in the region as a by-product of native culture and religion, and he believed imported cadres could rectify the problem. Although the policy was clearly unpopular, some republican party leaders praised Ligachev for his proposal.[25] Yet, the Alma-Ata riots of December 1986 which were brought on by the replacement of Kunayev, a native Kazakh, with Genady Kolbin, clearly demonstrated the difficulties involved in the actual administration of Ligachev's policy. The ramifications of this and other ethnic disturbances will be discussed in detail later on in chapter 6. Suffice it to say that this incident was a grim testimony to the leadership's lack of understanding of nationality problems in the Soviet Union, which eventually led to the 1991 disintegration of the socialist empire.

By 1986, the purges had significantly altered the composition of the party and bureaucracy in the Central Asian republics. According to Inamjon Usmankhojayev, who succeeded Rashidov, more than half of the Uzbek Central Committee and *nomenklatura* (the party elite), had been replaced between 1983 and 1986. In 1986 alone, he reportedly had replaced 750 individuals in leadership ranks, and more than 2,000 had received reprimands. Similarly, by 1986 more than 82 percent of the Kyrgyz secretaries at the raion (oblast subdivision), and city party committees had been replaced.[26] Despite the apparent variations, the Central Asian corruption charges may be adequately organized into two interrelated categories. The first may be referred to as illegal activities for personal gain. The second was unlawful activities whose ultimate aim was to strengthen the network of patronage among the local party cadres; this included violations of Soviet laws, party rules, and bureaucratic discipline. Of the two categories, the former by far outstripped the significance of the latter and clearly contributed to its scope.

The Cotton Scandal

The most widely publicized dimension of corruption in Central Asia involved the production and delivery of cotton, mainly in Uzbekistan, but also in Kyrgyzstan and Tajikistan as well.[27] Cotton constituted the only valuable local agricultural commodity that had been produced on a large scale for use by the center for decades. It practically defined, without exaggeration, the very nature of the Uzbek economy and livelihood. "There is not one person in the republic of Uzbekistan," Islam Karimov indicated, "who is not anxious about the price of cotton." The price of cotton "determines literally everything."[28] As the only purchaser of Central Asian cotton the Soviet government was the sole determinant of the annual price of cotton, calculated by Gosplan officials on the basis of a formula that supposedly took into account the production costs. In reality, however, the designated prices, were deliberately set at artificially low levels, hence creating the initial impetus for embezzlement. It was precisely the unfair pricing of cotton that had forced the farmers and local managers to contemplate ways in which they could increase their share of what they perceived to be their just entitlement. The most common method of embezzlement was fictitious delivery reports of cotton to the procurement agencies. Given the extensive network of production, storage, and transportation, almost every official involved in the process was drawn into the scheme as each lower layer bribed the higher layers, all the way to Moscow.

Oftentimes spoilage and theft were used as justifications for uncovered discrepancies between the reported and actual deliveries.

This rather large and elaborate scheme was discovered perhaps as early as the late 1970s, and maybe earlier by Andropov who, at the time, was the head of the KGB and intimately involved in the domestic surveillance of cadres' activities at various levels. But as long as Brezhnev, who had working knowledge of this particular case, was alive, Andropov had no choice but to put his plans on hold. The move against Uzbek officials finally began in 1983 when Andropov ordered the transfer of the second party secretary and removed the minister of internal affairs as well as the republican head of the KGB. Party secretary Rashidov died later that year just as an investigative team headed by Telman Gdlyan and Nikoli Ivanov from the General Prosecutors office were dispatched to the republic. In 1984, based on the evidence gathered by Gdlyan, a criminal case was filed against the chairman and two ministers of the Uzbek Council of Ministers, four secretaries of the Central Committee, and six regional secretaries. The investigation found that an estimated four billion rubles were embezzled in the cotton scandal. According to one report the fictitious production figures between 1976 and 1985 amounted to approximately six million metric tons. The initial targets of investigation were Abduvakhit Karimov, the first secretary of the Bukhara oblast, Ruzmat Gaipov, and Akhmadjan Adylov, the manager of the Papski agricultural complex in Fergana Valley. Adylov had apparently created a principality complete with border guards, jail, harem, stables, and elaborate personal facilities presumably constructed by embezzled funds and forced labor. He had established absolute control over the town of Gurumsari and adjacent areas. It is reported that an estimated 30,000 people were under his command. The following is an account of his oversight:

> The autocrat conducted himself with the dignity of a born sovereign. His favorite place was a granite podium alongside a fountain, beneath a shadow of a tree; there stood his desk with a multitude of phones (one of which was a direct line to Rashidov). . . . Adylov loved to hold meetings here in the open air; it was here that he gave orders, issued reprimands, and, depending on his mood, scourged his subjects with the lash. It was here that they brought the outsiders . . . doused them with cold water in the winter (they called this method of interrogation *Karbyshevka*) until they confessed why they were there and who had sent them. . . . That is how the master governs a population of many thousands in the name of Soviet authority.[29]

Adylov was arrested in August 1984 on criminal and other charges, Gaipov attempted to commit suicide at the time of his arrest, and Karimov along with Vakhobjan Usmanov, the minister of cotton processing, were later sentenced to death. Those others involved at the local level such as Petr Gegelman, the former minister of interior and Nuin Nurov, the chief of police in Tashkent were sentenced to nine years in prison. Many local police officers and bureaucrats were given jail sentences. The investigation also revealed the active involvement of Brezhnev family members and his close associates in Moscow. Yori Churbanov, Brezhnev's son-in-law, was finally arrested in 1987 after it was proven that he had accepted as much as $150,000 in bribes in connection with the cotton scandal.

Later, those arrested provided shocking testimony as to how the network operated through a system of sanctions and incentives to assimilate the new cadres and keep silent those involved in the massive operation:

> They made me the director of the regional sector for agricultural machinery. For two years I fought a useless battle. No way to get machinery or spare parts. What could I do? My assistant, who knew the score, said "grease this and that person's palm." I did it, for the first time in my life. Everything suddenly changed, like a fairy tale: it started raining spare parts.

Another detainee revealed:

> No one has the right to refuse a bribe. A refusal is taken as a betrayal. Refusal to grease a palm is a 100 per cent betrayal. They hound you out of your job, expel you from the Party, they could kill you. . . . We had a strict rule. Never appoint anyone but your own to a responsible position.[30]

It is interesting to note that the domestic public perception on corruption and the concomitant charges leveled against the Central Asian elite and party members stood in stark contrast to that of the authorities in Moscow. The Uzbeks, as Critchlow has correctly pointed out, considered themselves as the beneficiaries of their supposedly corrupt system. In fact, some of the illegal activities carried out did not have any personal material motive and were conducted to help the community at large. For instance, funds were diverted for local construction, renovation, and maintenance of public facilities. Furthermore, Critchlow argued that the Uzbeks benefited from these illegal activities in two ways. First, the network provided goods and services that had been scarce or simply unavailable. Second, it carved out avenues of upward mobility for the locals who would have otherwise become victims of the system's discriminatory policies.[31] On the whole, the Central Asians considered the purges and corruption charges as colonial acts of oppression and exploitation designed to worsen the socioeconomic conditions of the population. Gorbachev's assault on Central Asia continued unabated until 1988. But, as other, seemingly more significant economic and political issues confronted the Soviet leader, the scope of purges subsided and the corruption investigations lost their tempo. In the final analysis, perestroika in Central Asia did not go far beyond what was discussed above during the first three years of Gorbachev's experimentation. As far as the economic aspects of restructuring were concerned, some pressure was put on the local authorities; in Uzbekistan, for instance, Gorbachev had expressed dissatisfaction with the levels of production of nonferrous metals, cotton, and other local industrial products.[32] As for the social policies of the Soviet government, perestroika was even less meaningful in nature than the economic restructuring in the region.

Islam and Gorbachev

Gorbachev was perhaps the only Soviet leader in recent decades who did not have a well-publicized antireligious agenda of the sort that was discussed in chapter 1. It was the economy that became his main preoccupation and the target of his overall planning during his tenure in office. He chose, however, not to abandon the antireligious policies that had already been in place prior to his accession to power. Nor did he object to Ligachev—the central committee secretary for cadres and ideological affairs—who was in favor of the continuation of the atheistic campaign that had been somewhat reinvigorated during the Andropov-Chernenko period.[33] Gorbachev's first direct reference to religion came two weeks after the 27th Party Congress was held in late February 1986, when he reiterated the all-too-familiar Brezhnevian antireligious view, which emphasized indirect scientific propaganda methods rather than direct attacks on religion: "The Party will use all forms of ideological influence for the wider propagation of a scientific understanding of the world, for the overcoming of religious prejudices without permitting any violation of believer's feelings."[34] Yet Gorbachev opted for a discriminatory and selective application of this view, as Muslim, and to some extent, the Uniate, Baptist, and Catholic believers were subjected to rather harsh treatments. It is safe to assume that Ligachev was clearly behind the decision since he had frequently expressed his contempt for religion, and in particular the latter three mentioned above. In a speech delivered to a group of social scientists in October 1986 he made the following remarks:

> Sometimes when certain people encounter violations of socialist morality they begin to talk about the advisability of showing toler-

ance for religious ideas and of returning to religious morality. In doing so they forget the Marxist truism that religion can never be the source of man's moral principles. . . . Sometimes nationalism disguises itself in religion. This is clearly apparent, for example, in the reactionary elements of the Islamic, Uniate and Catholic clergy. We must continue to search for new approaches, for new ways and means of atheist propaganda.[35]

For Gorbachev, however, the battle against Islam was more than a battle against a reactionary religion. As Olcott has accurately pointed out, "The prevalence of Islam is viewed [by Gorbachev] as troublesome insofar as it undermines the regime's reform program."[36] This general perception became Gorbachev's driving force in Central Asia. In fact, the first and perhaps the only public denunciation of any religion by Gorbachev was delivered in Tashkent in November 1986 when, during a stopover on the way to India, he underscored the errors that had been committed by the local authorities. He further expressed concern about the religious situation in the region, demanding "an uncompromising battle against all religious phenomena."[37] To this end, Gorbachev called for an immediate intensification of the antireligious campaign and a stricter enforcement of religious laws. Shortly thereafter, in a reversal of Brezhnev's official party line, Islam was declared incompatible with socialism.

It should be noted, however, that as early as 1985, and in connection with the ongoing anti-corruption campaign in Central Asia, efforts had been made to draw attention to the deficiencies of ideological work at various republican levels. As a result, numerous articles had appeared in native-language newspapers as well as the Soviet papers, condemning Islam and Islamic practices.[38] By 1986, the local party plenums had become the primary platforms from which to launch direct attacks on Islam and to mobilize support for the intensification of atheistic propaganda. It was generally concluded that Islam's stubborn hold on society was due in part to the absence of a genuine antireligious campaign, and the insincere actions of the institutions involved in the process. As such, the third plenum of the Uzbek Communist Party, convened in October 1986, called for a unified plan of action whereby not only the ideological cadres, but all party members would join forces in battling religious influence. The plenum also demanded a frontal assault on the celebration of Islamic festivals. Finally, the Ministry of Education and Culture, Academy of Science, the first party organizations for education and other scientific institutions were called upon to study the problems of atheistic education as it specifically related to Islam. In a similar vein, B. Bekkulueva, the secretary of the Kirovski region in Kyrgyzstan, held the local party officials responsible for their lenient attitude toward the practice of Islamic rituals. To combat the problem, disciplinary action was taken to punish the local authorities. Moreover, schools were provided with "appropriate" antireligious guidelines, and additional ideological clubs were established in various oblasts. The same was true of the April 1986 plenum of the Tajikistan Communist Party when it was concluded that "the republic has relaxed its struggle to overcome religious prejudices and introduce new customs and is not exercising proper control over the enforcement of legislation on religious cults. . . . Atheist work lacks aggressiveness and concertedness."[39]

In the ensuing months, hundreds of full-time ideological cadres were dispatched to the rural areas in Central Asia to conduct atheistic campaigns. Moscow also sponsored an "Atheism month" in the region to demonstrate its resolve in combating Islam. In this connection, top party officials were asked to introduce new interpretations of history so as to highlight the negative impact of the Arab conquest of Central Asia. Moreover, concerted efforts were made to depict Islam as a reactionary ideology.[40] But, as indicated earlier, the Soviet regime did not limit its activities to an indirect atheism campaign or direct ideological attacks on Islam. Coercion was also used to control and to curb the spread of Islam. Many so-called unofficial clergy were arrested and sentenced to jail during the period under investigation. Abdullah (Abdolo) Mir Saidov of the Vakhsh Valley of Tajikistan was arrested in August 1986 for his religious activities. He had allegedly denounced the Tajik government and called for the establishment of an Islamic state. His arrest caused riots and protests from his supporters that were quickly put down by the authorities. He was charged with anti-Soviet slander and sentenced to six years in prison in 1987. Kambar Ibrahimov and Kurbankhuja Tabarov, from the village of Bustunkala, Tajikistan, were arrested for operating an illegal Koranic school. Negmatollah Inoyatov, from Kulyab, and his associate Abdulrakhim Karimov were convicted of possessing illegal literature and training children in the Islamic tradition. Imomali Isoyev, Kurbanov Azim, Hamid Kaiumov, Hafiz Hadimov, and Asomiddin Arbobov were charged for listening to religious radio broadcasts into Tajikistan from Iran and Pakistan. Arrests and persecution of Muslims were also reported in Uzbekistan and Turkmenistan. In Namangan, Budanov and Sultanov were arrested for the sale of religious literature, swindling, and speculating in religious objects. A. Bakhirov, N. Alayev, Z. Akhmedov, M. Rajabov, U. Baimirzayov, and I. Umarov were sentenced to various jail terms in the Samarkand region. Aqberdi Eshqulov, who had been previously sentenced to six years in jail for conducting religious activities, was sentenced again for healing practices through Koranic recitation.[41]

Despite the government's iron-fist policy, religious activities among the different age groups in Central Asia demonstrated a steady upward trend that even the officials could no longer deny. Although statistics vary according to the region, the period in which it had been conducted, and the subjective biases of the surveyor, the overall picture presented a humiliating defeat for the Soviet officials. In Lenin Raion of Tajikistan, a sample of 160 inhabitants were surveyed by the philosophy department of the Tajik Academy of Sciences. Only an estimated 6.7 percent considered themselves atheists. Other related statistics also provided convincing evidence as to the growth of Islamic tendencies. In Kurgan-Tyube of Tajikistan, for instance, the mosques' income had risen 150 percent in the period between 1981 and 1985. In Osh region of Kyrgyzstan the number of unregistered Islamic groups and mosques had risen at an alarming rate. Reports also indicated a rise in the number of women who conducted religious activities as clergy in Tajikistan's Isfariski and Kaniabadski regions near Dushanbe.[42] Similar observations regarding the rise in religious activity in Uzbekistan and Turkmenistan were also reported. Be as it may, the anti-Islamic campaign continued throughout the 1985–88 period. In fact, some republican leaders took the liberty of interpreting Gorbachev's perestroika as an attempt to destroy the vestiges of religion. One such interpretation was presented by Ghahar Makkhamov in an interview given to *Nauka i religiia* in early 1987, in which he characterized perestroika "as a struggle for a new type of human being who is free of any kind of prejudices, superstitions, and survivals of the past," in particular those prejudices associated with religion.[43]

The Soviet policies toward Islam, and for that matter other religions, began to show signs of positive change in 1988. At about the same time, Gorbachev's reform initiatives, in particular glasnost, began to generate a slow and cautious response in Central Asia. The underlying reason for this rather belated reaction to glasnost was, of course, the unpopular legacy of Gorbachev's anti-corruption campaign that devastated the local power structure and scarred the political psyche of the population. Most found it hard to believe that the government, after years of absolute oppressive intolerance, would welcome criticism of its conduct and even lend an ear to the grievances of the ordinary people. Therefore, it was not until glasnost was successfully put to the test in other republics that the Central Asian intelligentsia began to trust Gorbachev's intentions.

As indicated earlier, despite noticeable republican variations, the overall pattern of response to glasnost reflected more heavily the ethnic, linguistic, cultural, and environmental sentiments than religious aspirations. However, concern over religious rights and practices began to be widely expressed in all republics. In Central Asia, as elsewhere in the Soviet Union, glasnost brought about the formation of informal groups and associations with location-specific agendas and highly energetic but limited followings. Some of these organizations were later evolved into political parties and movements. A detailed breakdown of the origins, political orientation, objectives, and relative significance of these organizations will be presented in chapter 4. Suffice it to say that the overwhelming majority of these associations were organized by the local intelligentsia. Most were secular in orientation, issue-specific, and pursued—at least until the disintegration of the Soviet Union—what in essence may be referred to as anticolonial nonreligious agendas.

Second Phase: 1988–1990

What helped bring about a change in Gorbachev's policy orientation toward religion was a combination of three factors. First, and perhaps the most critical, was the decisive defeat of the conservative faction of the Politburo, led by Gorbachev's archenemy Ligachev in early 1988.[44] Ligachev's eventual demotion paved the way for more far-reaching reforms, including religious reforms, which could not have otherwise been implemented. The friction between the Gorbachev and Ligachev camps became rather pronounced in September 1987 when the latter personally demanded the resignation of Yakovlev for his seemingly reactionary non-Marxist predilections. The factional fighting reached its climax in March 1988 when Ligachev made an orchestrated attempt to derail Gorbachev's reform initiatives.[45] In much the same Soviet tradition, the timing of the conservative attack coincided with the absence from Moscow of some major opposition personalities: Gorbachev was on an official visit to Yugoslavia, Yakovlev was in Mongolia, and the defense minister, General Dmitri Yazov was in Geneva. The plot began by the publication of an anti-perestroika article in *Sovyetskaya Rossiya,* the official newspaper of the Russian Republic, drafted by Nina Andreyeva, a university lecturer. The article challenged the socialist credentials of the reformers and called attention to perestroika's corrosive effect on the principles of Marxist-Leninism. It further criticized the reformers for their utterly negative portrayal of the Soviet past, in particular the Stalinist era. It was later discovered that the letter was thoroughly edited by Ligachev supporters at the newspaper's headquarters and indeed reflected his overall views on perestroika and glasnost. Shortly after the publication of the article, as the acting General Secretary, Ligachev convened a meeting of the Soviet editors to redefine the party policy. He urged the reprinting of the Andreyeva article, which was later taken up by 43 newspapers. Of the two leading papers *Pravda* sided with Ligachev and *Izvestia* remained loyal to the reformists' cause. Ligachev's attempt to organize support in the media seemed to have been designed to reinforce the conservative sentiments among the Soviet population and thus force a change in the official party line, or perhaps bring the removal of Gorbachev closer to reality. But, he had clearly overestimated both the impact of his strategy and the size of active conservative support.

Upon his return, four days after the publication of Andreyeva's article, Gorbachev and Yakovlev mobilized a counteroffensive that repeated the very same steps taken by Ligachev. The process began when Ligachev departed for the Volodga region. Subsequently, Yakovlev called a meeting of the editors to reestablish the reform agenda set by Gorbachev. It was decided at the meeting that *Pravda* would publish a definitive rebuttal to the Andreyeva article to be drafted by Yakovlev. But, at the time of the article's delivery to *Pravda* headquarters, the building was deliberately left empty: a clear sign that Gorbachev's authority was being passively challenged. In a political gamble, Gorbachev put his career on the line and threatened to resign if the high-ranking members of the party and the Politburo did not lend an unequivocal support to him and his policies. Later, in a Politburo meeting he reexamined Ligachev's involvement in the Andreyeva plot and demanded the publication of Yakovlev's article in *Pravda*. Although it is not clear as to what went on in the meeting, the Politburo decided to support Gorbachev. Yakovlev's article under the title of "Principles of Perestroika: Revolutionary Nature of Thinking and Acting," finally appeared in the April 5 issue of *Pravda*. With this high profile battle, Ligachev and his camp suffered a serious setback. Three months later Gorbachev managed to capitalize on his victory during the 19th All-Union Party Conference when a number of major superstructural reforms were unanimously adopted.[46] Gorbachev also used the occasion to announce the government's reconciliatory stance on religion, which was to be guided by a new law on freedom of conscience. In September-October 1988 Ligachev formally lost his ideological portfolio and five other conservative members of the Politburo were forced to retire. There is little doubt that Gorbachev's victory over the conservative faction of the Politburo was a key factor in preparing the way for further reforms that eventually altered the very nature of the Soviet ideological orientation. There is also little doubt that Ligachev, as the secretary in charge of ideological affairs, was instrumental in limiting the parameters of Gorbachev's reforms to the economic sphere. In fact, in 1987 Ligachev had expressed his opposition to the way in which glasnost was chipping away at the political legitimacy of the Soviet system and the party structure. Rightly so, glasnost had assumed a qualitatively new dimension in which not only the policies of the Soviet state came under scrutiny, but the legitimacy of the Soviet government became the subject of glasnost discussions. This was clearly unacceptable to Ligachev and his colleagues who were well aware of the outcome of the zero-sum game Gorbachev had initiated with his conservative counterparts.

The second factor that led to a change in Soviet policy toward religion was the realization on the part of Gorbachev and his confidants, that reform in the economic infrastructure would not be successful unless it was accompanied by reforms in the ideological superstructure. This was generally interpreted as political reforms, but it also included religious reforms as well. Yet given the strength of the conservative opposition prior to their major defeat in 1988, such reforms could not have been proposed openly, let alone implemented. One of the main advocates of the politico-ideological reforms was Alexander Yakovlev, who persuaded Gorbachev that the cure for the pressing Soviet problems was more democratization. In an interview with Bailer in 1989, Yakovlev spelled out the crux of his reasoning for democratization:

> We believe that without democratization there can be no *perestroika* at all, either in the economic basis of the society, as we say, or in the superstructure, that is in the spiritual sphere. Today the superstructure is democratization itself, it is the action of the superstructure, the dynamic of it . . . there were attempts to improve state management of the economy in the middle of the 1950s and at the end of the 1960s. But they were not accompanied by democratic transformations. they were attempts to improve and make the economy function more effectively, but the human factor, that which can guarantee deep economic reform and democratization, was missing.[47]

What seemed to have motivated Yakovlev and persuaded Gorbachev to go beyond economic reforms was the government's desperate need to broaden its popular base of support, which had been slowly weakening due to the deteriorating living conditions and unfulfilled economic promises. This was to be achieved primarily through two measures. The first was to dismantle the party's monopoly over decision making, and facilitate the assimilation of the newly emerging social forces that had been denied access to the political process by the party apparatchiks. The adoption of secret ballots, and multi-candidate elections were undoubtedly designed to expedite the application of this measure. Populist in character, Gorbachev was sure to gain considerable political capital from such initiatives. The second was to offer more freedom, in particular religious freedom, which was perceived to be an effective strategy in revitalizing popular support for Gorbachev's reform program.

Third, there was the increasing pressure exerted from below by the believers, the clerical leadership, and some segments of the intelligentsia who wanted to see the application of glasnost and perestroika extended to the spiritual realm of the Soviet life. The discourse on religion and morality began in 1986 with the publication of articles and literary pieces that either implicitly defended religion or passively criticized the Soviet religious policies. For instance, Yevgeny Yevtushenko, a well-known poet, criticized state-sponsored atheism in an article that appeared in the widely respected hard-line newspaper *Komsomolskaya pravda,* arguing that:

> The source of morality is culture. But religion cannot be dismissed from the historical experience—both positive and negative—of morality, for its history is inseparable from history as such. . . . In our country church and state are separate, and that is as it should be. But nowhere in our laws is it written that atheism and state are inseparable. . . . Atheism in itself is not a source of morality. The source of morality is culture.[48]

Authors such as Viktor Astaf'ev, Vasili Bykov, and Chingiz Aitmatov were also on the forefront of the debate on the value and significance of spiritual existence in the early stages of glasnost. Aitmatov's highly controversial *Plakha* (The Executioner's Block) glorified the life and the eventual death of a deeply religious man in the hands of a gang leader who was obsessively driven by Stalinist convictions. Aitmatov's work was heavily criticized by a prominent atheist scholar, Dr. Ivon Kryvelev, for flirting with the idea of God and religion: "To reject principled, consistent atheism is to reject the very foundations of a scientific and materialistic worldview. And to leave morality to the domain of religion—isn't that a form of flirting with God?"[49]

The clergy and seminary teachers also partook in the debate on the status of religion in the Soviet Union. Quite expectedly, the tone of these early clerical reflections was passive, nonantagonistic, and reconciliatory in nature. Nevertheless, from the outset, the laws governing the religious institutions became the primary targets of criticism. For instance, in a unique interview with the Metropolitan of Leningrad and Novgorod, published in *Moskovskie Novosti,* Mr. Alexi stated:

> We ought to note that the Decree on Religious Associations that regulates church-state relation dates from 1929 and underwent only insignificant changes in 1975. It was adopted when the course of the revolution and ensuing events were still fresh in people's memories: a time, that is, when believers and church representatives were far from consistent in adopting the proper attitude. This was reflected in the laws promulgated. The real course of church-state relations has outgrown this framework, a point that is brought up in the publications of this subject.[50]

Attempts were even made to appeal directly to Gorbachev as Patriarch Pimen did in a letter he wrote in April 1987:

> After seventy years of state atheism, constant pressure and even perse-
> cution, believers are still both a dynamic and a growing force in Soviet
> society. They are a major sector of the workforce. They do not want to
> overthrow: they want to construct something better from within. . . .
> They were of course grieved when, last year in Tashkent, you called for
> renewed and more effective measures to combat religion. However,
> were you to give a lead in a new direction, doubtless they would be
> ready to support you as academician Sakharov has already done.[51]

Despite the appearance of an inviting atmosphere for debate and discussion
on religion, the government policy remained more or less unchanged. But
Gorbachev seemed to have become increasingly concerned about the issue.
Given the government's emphasis on the all-encompassing nature of glasnost
and perestroika, Gorbachev was faced with a major policy inconsistency in
regard to religion. One that was frequently brought to his attention since his
program of reform was introduced. With the conservative opposition effectively checkmated early in 1988, Gorbachev resolved his policy contradiction,
by granting religious concessions that culminated in the officially sanctioned
celebration of the millennium of Christianity: hence the opening of a new
chapter in church and state relations.

Religious Revival in the Soviet Union

The first clear sign of a qualitative shift in the orientation of the Soviet government toward religion came on April 29, 1988, when Gorbachev agreed to
meet with the head of the Russian Orthodox Church, Patriarch Pimen. The
meeting was presumably arranged at the request of the patriarch to discuss the
upcoming millennium celebrations. It was the first of its kind since 1943, when
Stalin summoned the Metropolitan Sergi to ask for his support in the war
efforts against German aggression. Gorbachev, too, was in need of support in
his struggle for perestroika that, up until then, had only increased the economic
pain and suffering of the Soviet population, hence the declining popularity of
Gorbachev and his reform initiatives. The promise of religious freedom, it was
believed, could provide some spiritual relief at a time of material deprivation,
and thus restore trust in the general direction of Gorbachev's reform program.
In short, Gorbachev needed to boost his dwindling popularity or suffer a
severe setback with grave political repercussions.

At the April 29 meeting with the patriarch, Gorbachev delivered a sincere
and forthright speech, setting the tone for things to come, including a new law
on freedom of conscience:

> Not everything has been easy and simple in the sphere of church-
> state relations. Religious organizations were not free from being

affected by the tragic developments that occurred in the period of the cult of personality. The mistakes that were made in the treatment of the church and the believers in the 1930s and the subsequent years are being rectified. . . . More active participation of religious leaders in the work of public [charities] like the Culture Fund, the Lenin Children's Fund, the Motherland Society, and others has become possible. . . . The new law of freedom of conscience that is being drafted will reflect the interests of religious organizations. All these things are the real fruits of new approaches to state-church relations in conditions of *perestroika* and democratization of Soviet society. . . . Believers are Soviet people, workers, patriots, and they have the full right to express their convictions with dignity. *Perestroika,* democratization and openness concern them as well—in full measure and without restrictions.[52]

According to Michael Bourdeaux, Gorbachev used the new law on freedom of conscience as a diplomatic tool to reward the believers in return for their backing of glasnost and perestroika. Of course, Gorbachev was provided with a verbal assurance at the meeting by Patriarch Pimen who "pledged the unconditional support of believers for the 'architect of perestroika.'" Two months after the historic meeting, the millennium of the introduction of Christianity to Russia was celebrated with official approbation from the 5th to the 17th of June. The government went so far as to facilitate the celebrations by making available the Bolshoi Theater and other sites, as well as radio and television broadcasts of the events. As a gesture of goodwill, 100,000 Bibles had been printed domestically and some 500,000 were to be imported from the West.[53] There were also signs of easing restrictions on the opening of churches throughout much of the Soviet Union.

The subject of church-state relations was once again brought up by Gorbachev at the 19th All-Union Party Conference in June to demonstrate his commitment to religious reform:

I want to deal with important question of freedom of conscience. Attention to this matter is currently at a high point because of the millennial anniversary of the introduction of Christianity into Russia. We do not hide our opinion that the religious worldview is nonmaterialistic and nonscientific. But this is no reason to show disrespect for the spiritual world of believing people, and it certainly is no justification for the use of any administrative pressure in order to confirm materialistic views. Lenin's decree on the separation of church and state and school from the church, which was adopted seventy years ago, created new bases for a relationship among these institutions. It is well known that these relations have not always worked

out in a normal way. . . . The draft of the law on freedom of conscience, which is now being prepared will be based on Leninist
principles and will take into account the realities of the present.[54]

Gorbachev's remarks included two basic policy directives that were to be
implemented in the ensuing months. First was the easing of administrative
pressure on the religious institutions and practices within the limits of the existing laws. This meant less harassment of the believers and the clergy, the
adoption of a nonantagonistic government attitude toward religion, and a significant slowdown of the atheistic campaign. Consequently, more churches
were permitted to engage in charitable work and volunteer activities at hos-
pitals. Second, the drafting of the new law was to remain, at least in principle,
within the confines of Lenin's decree on separation of church from state and
school from church. Explanations abound as to the reasons for Gorbachev's
decision to abide by the basic Leninist principles in this regard. The most plausible of these explanations point to opposing directions. First, it was suggested
that Gorbachev's reference to Lenin was symbolic, and that he had every
intention of abandoning the much-revered Leninist principles on religion in
the near future. The advocates of this view called attention to the fact that
every step of the way in his struggle for reform, Gorbachev was obligated to
reaffirm his commitment to socialist ideology to ensure his political survival
during the transition stage. Second, it was argued that Gorbachev was simply
satisfied with the broad outline of Lenin's decree and wished to basically modernize its outdated dimensions. In retrospect, however, the former explanation
was proven to be closer to the reality as the legislation paid only lip service
to Lenin's basic religious principles.

Whatever the justification for the drafting of a new law on religion, the
responsibility for carrying out Gorbachev's directives fell on the chairman of
the Council for Religious Affairs, Konstantin Karachev.[55] It took approximately two years of controversial debates at the highest government levels and
several drafts before the final version was enacted into law in the fall of
1990.[56] According to Karachev, the Council for Religious Affairs, the
Ministries of Foreign Affairs and Justice, the Soviet Academy of Sciences, and
the Judiciary of the Supreme Soviet were all involved in the drafting process.
Karachev was also instructed to consult with influential religious organizations. It is interesting to note that almost all major religious organizations
including the Russian Orthodox Church, Seventh-Day Adventist, All Union
Council of Evangelical Christian Baptist, Muslim Board for the European Part
of the USSR and Siberia, and the Catholic Church of Lithuania were asked for
their views on the draft law except for the Muslim Board of Central Asia and

Kazakhstan. It is not known whether the board was contacted, and chose not to deliver a response or if it was simply excluded from having any substantive input into the drafting process.[57] Altogether, three preliminary drafts were made public at the time. According to Boiter, the 1988 official draft was the most conservative and provided the narrowest parameters for religious freedom.[58] For instance, the draft had a vague reference to the right of clergy to provide religious education to children. But it did include some critical provisions such as the extension of legal status to religious organizations. The most liberal draft, within the confines of the existing Soviet ideology, was prepared by Dr. Yuri Rosenbaum from the Soviet Institute of State and Law. Rosenbaum's draft was based on the premise that the freedom of conscience was an absolute right of every citizen. As such, the purpose of the legislation was to establish "observance and uniform practice of the principles of freedom of conscience on the whole territory of the USSR, and also to realize the right of citizens to enjoy this freedom." The third and final official draft was publicized in 1989 subsequent to the signing of the Document of the Conference on Security and Cooperation in Europe (CSCE) by the Soviet Union in Vienna. Article 16 of the document included certain provisions on religious freedom that obligated the Soviet Union to further liberalize its domestic attitude toward religion if it was to abide by the CSCE agreement.[59] In legal preparation for the enactment of the new law on freedom of conscience, the Council for Religious Affairs passed a special resolution abolishing all normative documents adopted by the Council from 1961 to 1983, such as the banning of charitable work by religious organizations.[60] The council's action, however, was symbolic in that Gorbachev had informally removed such restrictions.

The law was officially approved on October 1, 1990. It included 31 articles among which the following were of particular significance. Article 3 professed the right to freedom of conscience, placing "only those restrictions that are necessary for protecting public safety and order, life, health and morality, as well as the rights and liberties of other citizens." Article 5 addressed the separation of church and state, specifying that the state must not finance the activity of religious organizations or engage in promotion of atheism. This provision put an end to 70 years of almost unabated, and at times violent, pursuit of atheism by the Soviet government. It also banned religious organizations from participating in the activities of political parties, creating parties, or in financially assisting political parties. Article 11 provided guidelines for the establishment of religious educational institutions. Article 13 extended legal status to religious organizations, thus granting the right to purchase property, and other ownership rights, to such organizations. Article 14 significantly eased restrictions on registration of religious charters and organizations by allowing as few as ten people to file applications for registration. Articles 17 and 18 restored property rights to religious organizations. Article 19 provided a legal framework within which religious organizations were permitted to engage in profitable economic activities.[61]

Although as early as 1988 the fruits of Gorbachev's new religious policy were enjoyed by most Christian and Jewish believers, Muslims, quite typically, were not awarded the same benefits until later. In fact, it was approximately a year after the conclusion of the millennium celebrations that Islam was granted similar concessions, and only after public protests made it clear to the authorities that Central Asia demanded its share of religious freedom. It is simply astonishing that in 1988, at about the same time that Russian Orthodox Church was given assurance of a more open spiritual environment in the near future, the first secretary of the Uzbek Communist Party, Rafiq Nishanov, was still engaged in Islam bashing:

> Withdrawn from struggle with Islam and other religions, with attempts to pass off religious patriarchal customs as national traditions. . . . Even for many Communists, the Muslim "science of life" is more authoritative than the party rules and norms of socialist morality. . . . The former first secretary of Samarkand district party, M. Sherkulov, personally took part in the construction and organization of the so-called holy place, while the former deputy chairman of the Samarkand regional *Soviet, I.* Kurandykov, illegally redirected considerable material resources to the construction of a mosque.[62]

The first series of religious protests in Central Asia occurred in December 1988 when spontaneous demonstrations by Uzbek students broke out in Tashkent. Although the focus of the demonstration was the restoration of the Uzbek language and culture, according to Critchlow some participants waved green banners—a symbol of the Islamic faith—and read Koranic verses during the demonstration.[63] Two months later, a second public protest was carried out by Muslims in Tashkent to demand the resignation of the head Mufti of the Religious Board of Central Asia and Kazakhstan, Shamsuddin Babakhanov ibn Zeyudin. The campaign was apparently masterminded by an organization named Islam and Democracy whose declared objective was to "cleanse Islam in the Soviet Union." Babakhanov was accused of gross violations of Islamic codes of behavior and conduct. He was forced to resign sometime after the demonstrations subsided.[64]

The Babakhanov affair caused serious concern among the local party leaders as well as the members of the Council for Religious Affairs. This was perhaps the first and only direct public attack on the legitimacy of the official clerical establishment in Central Asia. The Muslim Religious Board of Central Asia and Kazakhstan had been established as one of the four "spiritual directorates" in 1941 to oversee the religious affairs of the Soviet Union. The membership and recruitment policies of the Board were tightly controlled by the central authority. Its responsibilities included the appointment of the Mufti of Uzbekistan, Kyrgyzstan, and Kazakhstan as well as the Kazi of Tajikistan and Turkmenistan. It was no secret that to move up the ranks, members of the board were to support, albeit tacitly, the official policies of the Soviet government. As such, the Board at best represented an adumbrated version of Islam, devoid of any political or ideological substance. Given the board's pro-Soviet track record, such an attack, in the era of glasnost, was not only possible, but quite probable. To prevent further chaos and disorder, Karachev decided to participate in the Fourth Kurultay of the Muslim Religious Board of Central Asia in March 1989 and formally announce the new Soviet religious orientation as it related to Islam. He repeated the famous 1917 passage in which Lenin and Stalin promised to restore religious and cultural rights to the Central Asian population and put an end to the czarist exploitation of the region. Furthermore, as a gesture of goodwill, the Koran of Usman was transferred from the Tashkent museum where it had been displayed since 1918 to the Religious Board, to be kept in its library.[65] In the light of changing church-state relations, the Kurultay was also called upon to draw up a new charter for its future religious activities, and elect new muftis for the vacant positions. Apparently, the resignation of Babakhanov had triggered a chain reaction, causing the resignation of a number of other muftis whose spiritual legitimacy had been questioned by the believers. The Kurultay elected the rector of the Tashkent Islamic Institute, Muhammad Sadiq Mamayusupov (Muhammad Yusuf), to replace Babakhanov. In an interview, shortly after assuming office, the new head mufti made the following remarks: "At first, Muslims were rather passive and did not react quickly to what was happening elsewhere in the country. Now we are demanding the same privileges accorded to other religions. For Moscow the assertion of Muslim power first on ethnic and then on religious grounds is a challenge to reckon with."[66] Thanks to grassroots pressure, by early 1989 Islam had joined the ranks of other free religions in the Soviet Union, and by December most local party plenums had included a discussion on freedom of religion in their agendas. In Uzbekistan for instance, the following announcement was made: "The republican Party organization is actively in favor of *freedom of religion and the legal rights of believers,* and for co-operation with religious. . . . Believers are entitled to all opportunities for participation in the public political and cultural life of the Republic."[67] The most visible manifestation of an Islamic revival in Central Asia was the enthusiastic reopening of old mosques and holy shrines, whose numbers had been drastically reduced by the Soviet authorities since the 1920s. In July 1989 the foundation of an elaborate mosque was completed in the capital of Turkmenistan, Ashkhabad, which had been without a functioning mosque since 1948 when an earthquake severely damaged its only government-authorized mosque. In February and March 1989 alone, 25 mosques were opened in Uzbekistan, 6 in Tajikistan, and 3 in Turkmenistan. In a report published in *Pravda,* the number of mosques in the Soviet Union had been more than doubled between 1985 and 1990 reaching an all-time high of 751. In addition to the opening of mosques, a number of religious educational institutions were permitted to begin operations in Uzbekistan. Moreover, the Uzbek Commission for Religious Affairs increased the funding and enrollment capacity of the Mir Arab and Barak Khan *madrasehs.* Under the new policy, Muslim religious associations were granted expeditious registration permits. According to government statistics, during the January 1985 and July 1990 the numbers of such associations had been increased from 392 to 1,103, comprising the third fastest-growing associations after the Russian and Georgian Orthodox churches.[68] Although the formation of religious parties were prohibited under the new law on Freedom of Conscience, individual clergy were allowed to participate in the political process. The greater Muslim political participation received an enthusiastic response in Central Asia. Among the first to take advantage of the new opportunity was Muhammad Yusuf, who won a seat in the Congress of the people's deputies in Spring of 1989.[69]

In the final analysis, Communism was proven to be no match for such a culturally well-embedded religion like Islam. Sadly, it took the Soviet Union seven long decades to reckon with the powerful reality of man's spiritual tenor. For those Muslim believers who endured the suffering and humiliation, the long-awaited victory was celebrated by collective participation in Friday prayers, religious festivals, and pilgrimage to holy places in Central Asia. The tenacity of Islam had indeed paid off.

CONCLUSION

In his opening speech to the 19th All-Union Congress in June 1988, Gorbachev stressed the need to make the process of perestroika irreversible by reforming the political system. With that remark, Soviet society started a peaceful revolutionary transformation—the eventual outcome of which was the rapid disintegration of the Soviet Union. It began with reforms such as the dismantling of the party control over the political process that inadvertently increased the vigor of national independence movements in the Baltic republics and elsewhere in the country, with no prospects for reaching a meaningful compromise with the central authority. Gorbachev had but himself to blame, for he had utterly failed to understand the simple truth that the Soviet Union was an artificial entity held together by force or threat of violence since its inception. Democratization, in particular the introduction of secret ballots and multi-member candidates, also provided the necessary mechanisms for the nationalist elements to first reassert their dominance and later, under the protection of glasnost, to question entirely the legitimacy of the Soviet rule over their republics. By 1990 the pace of reform had accelerated beyond the Kremlin's control, threatening the very existence of a largely delegitimized system of governance. In clear violation of the Soviet law, Turkmenistan, Tajikistan, Kazakhstan, and Kyrgyzstan declared their legislative sovereignty between August and October of that year. Similar declarations were also adopted by other republics.

In an effort to reestablish his authority, Gorbachev began to redefine his role by resorting to unprecedented legal as well as extra-legal measures. On December 25, 1990, Gorbachev forced through the congress a constitutional amendment that granted him extended presidential powers. Shortly thereafter, as a show of authority, and to maintain law and order amidst widespread instability, he ordered the military to patrol the streets in major cities and towns throughout the country. It was later discovered that Gorbachev had acted under pressure from the conservative elements within the party, the armed forces, and the military-industrial complex who wished to prevent the imminent breakup of the Soviet Union. However, in a series of maneuvers, Gorbachev abandoned his promises to the conservative forces in March and April when, in pursuit of his liberal reforms, he proposed the so-called Nine-Plus-One Agreement to the republics. A natural outgrowth of the Union Treaty first publicized in December 1990, the agreement effectively recognized the right of the six republics of Lithuania, Latvia, Estonia, Moldovia, Georgia, and Armenia to secede from the Soviet Union. The rest of the republics were to be included in a loose federation with extensive political and economic autonomy. On July 25, Gorbachev announced that a compromise had been reached on the substance of the Union Treaty to be signed on August 20. Two days after the announcement, at the Central Committee plenum Gorbachev carried out his final offensive against the ideological integrity of the Soviet Union when he introduced a new program for total eradication of Marxist-Leninism. These radical policies, once again, brought Gorbachev into almost open confrontation with the conservative hard-liners who later masterminded the August 18 coup to restore Leninist rule over the Soviet Union. Fortunately, the coup collapsed three days later, but in the process the supremacy of the Union and the preeminence of Gorbachev had been lost. Consequently, in a momentous series of decrees that further revolutionized the politics of the Soviet Union, Gorbachev resigned as the general secretary, demanded that the Central Committee disband itself, and nationalized party assets and property.

By October 1991, Uzbekistan, Tajikistan, Kyrgyzstan, Turkmenistan, and Kazakhstan had declared their full independence and later joined the newly-established Commonwealth of Independent States which was composed of eleven former republics of the Soviet Union. As with most postcolonial societies, the Central Asian republics have been faced with serious political uncertainties that have been brought about by the clash of the old Communist power structure, reorganized under a nationalist disguise, and the emerging new Islamic and democratic forces in each republic. In the following chapters an attempt will be made to put into perspective the essential dynamics of post-independence politics in the region.

CHAPTER 3

Islamic Revival in Central Asia

*With our people, the notion of democracy means no restrictions.
. . . It would not be a one party state; the franchise would be
universal; the rights of ethnic and religious minorities would
be protected; and private property would be honored.*

—ABDULLAH YUSUF, FIRST DEPUTY OF THE
ISLAMIC REVIVAL PARTY, UZBEKISTAN

The year 1991 marked the beginning of a new chapter in the history of the Central Asian republics when the dream of national independence was quickly transformed into a political reality. Interestingly enough, the Central Asian population as a whole played a marginal or, at best, an indirect role in the realization of that dream. Rather, it was the breakdown of Soviet central authority that provided an almost effortless opportunity for independence. Unfortunately, the rapidity with which political freedom was brought to bear left these republics ill-prepared to fill the ideological void created by the collapse of Marxism, leading to the proliferation of a variety of ideological trends, the roots of which were inadvertently nurtured by Gorbachev's policy of glasnost. Of these, only the Islamic trends seem to have attracted considerable attention. There are, of course, grounds for concern, especially when one considers the radical manifestations of Islam in the twentieth century and their practical implications, which have, among other things, given rise to the

Islamic Republic of Iran and other forms of Islamic extremism elsewhere in the world. It is the availability of such Islamic doctrines to the Central Asian republics that has greatly contributed to the overall uncertainty with regard to the future political development of these newly emerging states. Yet so far, with the exception of the largely misunderstood case of Tajikistan, which will be addressed in chapter 5, the Islamic revival in Central Asia has demonstrated an overall moderate character. It has been moderate because violence as a method of political struggle has been ruled out by the Islamic forces, at least in principle, and no widespread anti-Western sentiments have been expressed by such forces. An equally significant dimension of the ongoing Islamization is that it has not been a monolithic phenomenon with uniform interrepublican sociopolitical manifestations. Quite the contrary, proclivity toward Islam varies considerably from republic to republic with Kazakhstan and Kyrgyzstan having the weakest and Uzbekistan and Tajikistan having the strongest tendencies. Sizable variations also exist at the intrarepublican level.

As indicated in the introduction, the nature, scope, intensity, and speed of Islamic revival are intimately related to two sets of factors. The general factors that will be presented in the following chapters include: the strength or weakness of the nascent democratic forces and their capacity to institute an inclusive rather than exclusive method of governance; the ethnic orientation and makeup of each republic; and the nature of the governments' Islamic and political reform policies. The specific factors that are equally capable of having a qualitative impact on the pattern of Islamization include the general Islamic proclivity in Central Asia and the organizational reach and mobilization capacities of the Islamic forces operating in the region. It is within this framework that an attempt will be made to put into perspective the dynamics of Islamic revival in the region.

ISLAMIC PROCLIVITY

Despite the apparent inter- and intrarepublican variations in Islamic propensity, the overall religious orientation of the Central Asian population has not been characterized as the firebrand type routinely associated with Shi'i or Sunni fundamentalism in the Middle East and North Africa. The available literature on this subject, however, is haphazard and lacks sufficient detail. Nevertheless, it provides the platform from which to introduce some possible explanations that could strengthen the argument in favor of the above generalization. While it is beyond the scope of this study to produce a comprehensive set of historical, geographic, cultural, ethnic, and social justifications, it is possible to focus on two such explanations that are intimately related, first to the broad nature of the Central Asian societies within which Islam gained widespread acceptance, and second, to the essential characteristics of the dominant Islamic doctrine in the region. It must be emphasized that these explanations are not intended to portray Islam as a static phenomenon. To the contrary, Islam, much like other great religions of the world, has exhibited considerable resiliency and adaptive vigor since its genesis. In fact, the sizable doctrinal differentiation of Islam over the past millennia is a strong indication of its dynamic character. Such dynamism may well move Islam in a more radical and anti-Western direction in the future, the preconditions of which will be discussed in the following chapters.

Sedentary Versus Tribal Societies

The early conversion to Islam of the Central Asian population may be adequately categorized into two phases. The first phase began with the Arab invasion of the region under Usman in 649 A.D. and ended in 715 A.D. subsequent to the death of Qutayba ibn Muslim who was in essence responsible for the successful establishment of Arab rule in the area.[1] The second phase, during which Islam was propagated by peaceful means, followed shortly after, until the middle of tenth century, when it finally assumed the dominant status among the religions of the region, though conversion continued as late as the nineteenth century. The environment within which Islam was to take root was largely defined by the geographic conditions of Central Asia, which had given birth to two rather distinct yet interactive societies: the sedentary populations of the oases enclaves of Merv, Balkh, Bukhara, Samarkand, Fergana, and so on, and the tribal populations of the Steppe and the surrounding areas. Conversion to Islam was more effective in the case of the former societies but lacked depth and substance in relation to the latter. Explanations as to the causes of Islam's relatively poor performance in the tribal areas range from the enormous size and the remoteness of the Steppe, to the lack of adequate military manpower to secure such vast regions once conquered, to the frequent political instability at the heart of the Arab empire, and to the lack of Islamic missionaries to spread Islam among the pastoral populations at that stage. In the final analysis, the success or failure of religious indoctrination was a function of Islam's ability to transform the social structures of the Central Asian societies. This, of course, was more achievable in the context of the settled communities of the oases where Arab, and later converted Iranian and Turkish rulers, introduced and maintained Islamic polities.

The Arab conquest of Central Asia was conducted on two separate fronts, following the decisive defeat of the Persian royal army at the battle of Nahavand in 642, which led to the escape of the last Sasanian king, Yazdgerd III.

Although small-scale resistance by the Persians continued, the Arab armies proceeded from a northerly direction through Hamadan and Ray toward Khorasan. This flank was led by the governor of Kufa, Sa'id ibn al-As. The second flank was headed by the governor of Basra, Abdullah ibn Amir, advancing through Fars, Kerman, Tabas, and onto Nishabour and Merv. The latter forces made it to Khorasan first and established temporary control over the region. From there, for a period of a decade, the Arabs conducted raids into the nearby Central Asian towns and villages until 656, when political instability hit the heart of the Arab empire during the caliphate of Ali, leading to the withdrawal of Arab forces from Khorasan. Later, Abdullah ibn Amir recaptured Khorasan and further brought under Arab rule Badghis, Herat, and Balkh despite fierce opposition.[2]

Under Ziad ibn Abi Sufiyan (664), the successor to Abdullah ibn Amir, the Arab conquests were systematically expanded to the north of the Oxus into Chaghanian and lower Tukharistan and Khorezm. It was at this time that an effective centralized administrative system over Khorasan was established, paving the way for the long-term control of the Central Asian territories. To further strengthen the Arab and Islamic hold on the region, fifty thousand families from Basra and Kufa were sent to colonize Khorasan.[3] Although, by 674, the Arab armies had marched into Bukhara through Paykand and raided the neighboring regions, the successful domination of the major Central Asian oases took place under Qutayba ibn Muslim subsequent to his arrival in Merv, the capital of Khorasan, around the year 704. Qutayba's expeditions resulted in the recapturing of lower Tukharistan in 705, the conquest of Bukhara and the submission of the ruler of Samarkand between 706 and 709, the consolidation of Arab reign in the Oxus valley by 712, and substantial gains in the Jaxartes provinces, as far as Shash and Fergana, by the year 715.[4] Although the departure of Qutayba brought about considerable setbacks to Arab power in the region, the basic territorial outline established by him was more or less maintained until the overthrow of the Ummayad caliphate in 750. Under the Arab rule, the financial and military-bureaucratic control of the region was entrusted to the walis or the representatives of the Arab governor of Khorasan. However, the local "dynastic houses were everywhere maintained as the representative of the conquered peoples and the vehicle of civil administration."[5]

Details as to the methods of conversion to Islam are inadequate and thus inclusive. But the general patterns of conversion in other Arab territories could be applied to Central Asia. In conjunction with forced conversion, many areas accepted the new faith to avoid violence, as was the case in parts of Khorasan. Heavy taxation of the conquered people in the form of *jaziyah* also brought about conversions to reduce the financial burden, since Muslims were subjected to a much lighter tax expropriation under Islamic law. There were also financial rewards extended for those who adopted Islam. Qutayba, for instance, is reported to have offered two *dirhams* to every person who attended the Friday prayer session in the great mosque of Bukhara.[6] Finally, some peasants embraced the faith of the conquerors to escape overexploitation by the local rulers. Whatever the methods of conversion may have been, the sedentary population of Central Asian oases were influenced by Islam, whose presence was gradually reinforced under the Qutayba's rule through the introduction of Muslim religious and educational institutions and by the presence of Arab settlers.

The second phase of conversion was made possible by the Muslim merchants and, later, missionaries, who exposed the Central Asian population to Islam along the trade routes, in particular the great Silk Road. By the beginning of the thirteenth century, which coincided with the Mongol invasion of Central Asia, substantial progress had been made in the Steppe region and Kyrgyz mountains. It was during this peaceful expansion—the ninth through twelfth century—that Islam made its lasting imprint on the sedentary population of Central Asia, not so much as a religious ideology, but as a way of life. Geoffery Wheeler, for instance, has indicated that "Islamic culture and civilization were spread by Muslim traders who, during the eighth century, penetrated as far as Khorezm and thence to the banks of the Volga. These traders propagated Islam more as a way of life than a creed." In support of this thesis, he further pointed out that ". . . in many parts of the Steppe Region, where the Arabs never penetrated, Islamic canon law (the *shariah*) and customary law (*adat*) and even the limited use of Arabic script, came into vogue among peoples who still retained shamanistic rites and religious beliefs."[7] Barthold goes one step further by arguing that no direct propagation was carried out by the Arab settlers and merchants.[8] The conversions thus took place as a result of observation and causal contact with the Arab elements and the converted Iranians. This development strengthened the cultural rather than religious aspects of Islam among the population, thereby creating a qualitatively different Islamic orientation in Central Asia as compared to the rest of the Arab world. Also significant in shaping the general Islamic proclivity of the region was the colonial attitude of the Abbasid caliphate who abandoned the direct Arab rule, paving the way for the emergence of the non-Arab dynasties of Iranian and Turkish origin in Central Asia. This policy facilitated the amalgamation of Islamic and non-Islamic traditions that modified the latter's ideological character. Linguistic and cultural innovations, such as those carried out under the Tahirid dynasty (820–70) and later by other Muslim non-Arab rulers of Central Asia, undoubtedly helped ameliorate Islam, giving it an overall mild character.[9] By the tenth century the Central Asian oases of Bukhara and Samarkand had become the main centers of Islamic civilization, powerful enough to culturally withstand, and subsequently assimilate, the various tribal conquerors of Turkish and Mongol origin throughout the next few centuries until the advent of Russian imperialism in the sixteenth century. While Islam made a lasting cultural and religious impact on the sedentary population of Central Asia early on, the tribal population of the Steppe and the surrounding regions were converted to Islam much later. The Islamization process also failed to significantly alter the basis of social organization of the tribes, leaving behind a shallow imprint that has been carried over to the present. Alexandre Bennigsen has provided perhaps the most concise account of the conversion to Islam of the tribal populations in Central Asia.[10]

Of the three main tribal regions of Central Asia, the southern section of the Kazakh Steppe, most noticeably Chimkent, bordering the present-day Uzbekistan, was first exposed to Islam in the ninth century. As a predominantly semisedentary region of the Kazakh Steppe, located in close proximity to the already converted Central Asian oases, Islam found its way into Chimkent with relative ease. As for the western, central, and northern Steppe, it was not until the early fourteenth century that Islam gained acceptance, first among the ruling elite who practiced the faith and, later, among other segments of the tribal societies. The majority, however, remained attached to their tradition of shamanism and demonstrated only a superficial interest in Islam. In the fifteenth and sixteenth centuries, a second attempt at conversion was carried out by the Sufi missionaries of the Yasawi and Naqshbandi orders. Ironically, the most successful drive to spread the faith among the Kazakh tribes was led not by Muslims but by Russians in the late eighteenth and early nineteenth centuries, mainly during the reign of the Catherine II, who relied upon Tatar clergy to carry out missionary work in the region. Toward the end of the czarist rule, yet another attempt at Islamization was made by the Uzbek merchants of Bukhara and Kokand that was effectively offset by the growing popularity of secular trends sponsored by influential Kazakh intellectuals, such as Chokan Valikhanov (1835–65), Ibrahim Altynsarin (1841–89), and Abai Kunanbai Uli (1845–1904).[11]

A demographically similar pattern of conversion also introduced Islam first to the sedentary and semisedentary populations of Kyrgyzstan in the late sixteenth and early seventeenth centuries through the Fergana Valley, with the heaviest concentration of activities in the Osh and Jalalabad regions. The mountainous regions of central and northern Kyrgyzstan were exposed to Islam in the early eighteenth century. Conversions, however, continued as late as the early twentieth century. The Islamization of the Kyrgyz was carried out almost exclusively by the Sufi missionaries who had found a convenient passageway to Kyrgyzstan through the Fergana Valley. The most prominent Sufi orders who succeeded in the region were the Naqshbandi from Bukhara, Qadiri from Fergana, Yasawi from southern Kazakhstan, and Kubrawi from Khorezm. In the late nineteenth and early twentieth centuries, two branches of Yasawi— the Lachi and Hairy Ishans—made an entry on the religious scene in Fergana. The former order made its initial impact on the Kyrgyz after the Russian domination of the region under the guidance of sheikh Babajan-Khalfa Rahmanquluv, who settled in eastern Fergana and spread his faith among the members of the Jookesek clan who inhabited the Frunze district of the Osh region. The latter order, Hairy Ishan, gained a reputation for its anti-Soviet orientation, conducting much of its religious activities in complete secrecy.

The Turkmen tribes were exposed to the Islamic faith between the twelfth and fourteenth centuries, which is considerably earlier than the Kyrgyz and Kazakh tribes, though here, too, the Sufi orders were primarily responsible for the conversion of the population. In particular, three orders found relatively widespread acceptance. The Yasawi that made its way from the city of Turkistan in southern Kazakhstan, the Kubrawi established by the Najmuddin Kubra in the Tashauz oblast of present-day Turkmenistan in the thirteenth century, and the Naqshbandi with its center in Bukhara appearing in the Turkmen territory in the nineteenth century. The latter succeeded in absorbing the Yasawi, which had gathered a considerable following in all the Turkmen territory. The Kubrawi followers were also assimilated into the Naqshbandi subsequent to its penetration into the region, this time from Khorezm.[12] However, according to Bennigsen: "Turkmen Sufism is marked by the persistence of purely shamanistic practices, condemned by orthodox establishment but deeply rooted in popular beliefs. By a curious process of inter-penetration, the shamanistic practices, rites, and rituals have acquired during the Soviet period an external appearance of Islam, while the Sufi adepts, especially those of Kubrawi *tariqa,* often behave like shamans."[13]

Bennigsen's characterization of Turkmen Islam is more or less true of other tribal regions where the shamanistic traditions were retained by the population long after Islam was accepted as the dominant religion in the region. Moreover, the basic tribal and clan structures of these societies were only marginally affected by Islam, thus leaving a considerably weaker religious imprint as compared to the sedentary regions of Central Asia. The combination of Islam's relatively late entry into the Kazakh Steppe, the Kyrgyz mountains, and the Turkmen grasslands and the survival of the tribal social structures have produced an Islamic landscape with mild ideological colorings that have continued to survive until today. Although the broad parameters of Islamic proclivity are defined by the sedentary versus tribal structural dichotomy of the Central Asian societies, within each of the five republics there exists considerable regional diversity, which has so far been an obstacle to the wholesale radicalization of Islam in the region. It is interesting to note that the strength of Islamic proclivity in all of the Central Asian republics is closely related to the presence of the Uzbek population.

Of Kazakhstan's 18 oblasts, Chimkent bordering northern Uzbekistan is the most religious, with Muslims constituting approximately 75 percent of its nearly 2 million inhabitants. A relatively large rural Uzbek population resides in Chimkent. The city of Turkistan, which has been home to a number of famous clerics, is located in this region. The adjacent Kyzyl Orda oblast, though less religious, has the second highest concentration of Muslim residents, with nearly 80 percent of its total estimated population of a quarter of a million adhering to Islam. Uzbeks are also present in this oblast. The remaining 16 oblasts of Kazakhstan have a considerably weaker Islamic proclivity than Chimkent and Kyzyl Orda and the usual visible signs of Islam such as mosques, Islamic schools, and so on are noticeably absent in those regions.

In Kyrgyzstan, the Islamic strongholds are in the Osh and Jalalabad oblasts, located in or near the Fergana Valley that stretches into Uzbekistan with almost entirely Muslim residents. Although a high percentage of the believers in these two oblasts are of Uzbek origin, the Kyrgyz inhabitants have traditionally exhibited a relatively strong adherence to Islam. More than 50 percent of the 4.2 million population of Kyrgyzstan live in the Osh and Jalalabad regions. In the Issyk-Kul, Chu, and Talas regions, Islam has a weak following and its presence has assumed symbolic dimensions as manifested in the observance of the rituals of circumcision, marriage, burial, and celebration of religious holidays. These regions also represent a much higher percentage of non-Muslim Kyrgyz.

While the pattern of Islamic proclivity at the intrarepublican level in Kazakhstan and Kyrgyzstan follow oblast divisions, in Turkmenistan the Islamic propensity is strongest near the holy places that are scattered throughout the republic. A large concentration of such holy places is found in the Tashauz oblast in northern Turkmenistan and the Krasnovodsk oblast in western Turkmenistan. The Islamic proclivity also increases in areas where Turkmenistan borders Uzbekistan. For instance, in parts of the Charjow oblast where a high percentage of Uzbek population resides, the practice of basic principles of Islam is much more strictly observed than elsewhere. The Uzbek clerics have been instrumental in strengthening the Islamic hold on the Turkmen population of the oblast. The most common religious activity among the Turkmens is the pilgrimage to various tombs of revered ancestral heroes and religious saints and personalities.

In Tajikistan, where Islamic tendencies are, on the whole, stronger than the three republics discussed earlier, sizable variations still exist. These variations do not follow either the Kazakh/Kyrgyz or the Turkmen patterns. Five areas may be identified as more Islamic than the rest of the republic. First, the area known as Gharm (Garm or Gharatakin) located in the former Kulab (Kulyab) oblast. Second, the city of Ghorghan Tepeh (Kurgan Tyube) and the surrounding villages. The most religious inhabitants of this area have common roots with the people of Gharm, many of whom were relocated to the Ghorghan Tepeh area in the 1930s to foster economic development. Third, the population of the city of Dushanbe and the immediate surroundings, whose role in the spring 1992 demonstrations against the Nabiyev government was instrumental in forcing the creation of a coalitional government that included members of the Islamic-democratic opposition. Fourth, the sparsely populated mountainous region of Gorno Badakhshan whose Shi'ite population have doctrinal disagreements with the predominantly Sunni Tajikistan. Finally, there are pockets of Islamic strongholds in the Khojend oblast, namely the Maschah and Ura Tepeh whose residents also enjoy a common linguistic and cultural heritage with the people of Gharm.

Of all the Central Asian republics, Uzbekistan is more uniformly religious than any other republic, and is where Islamic culture has had the most profound impact on the population.[14] Here too, however, there are marked regional variations. The most religious regions of Uzbekistan are located in the opposite ends of the republic. The Fergana Valley, particularly the cities of Namangan and Andijan (Andizhan), is considered the bastion of Islamic activism in the whole of Central Asia. As the most densely populated region of Uzbekistan, the valley has historically espoused various religious trends that have spread into other parts of Central Asia. The most recent of these trends, which will be addressed in the following pages, is Wahhabism. It is slowly spreading into the Osh and Jalalabad regions of Kyrgyzstan. The Karakalpak region in the northern part of Uzbekistan is perhaps the second most religious part of the republic. Karakalpak has also been one of the main centers of Sufi activism in Central Asia where the three main *tariqa* of Naqshbandi, Yasawi, and Kubrawi have strong roots. In addition, the Kalendari *tariqa* is particularly popular among Karakalpaks. Besides these two regions, the cities of Samarkand and Bukhara have been the main cradles of culture and civilization, with a long-standing Islamic tradition.

The second critical element shaping the parameters of Islamic proclivity in Central Asia is intimately related, on the one hand, to the nature of the dominant Islamic doctrine, and on the other hand, to the prevailing doctrinal diversity at the republican level. The combination of these two factors, as will be discussed later, have so far helped bring about a mild Islamic revival, curtailing the activities of fundamentalist Islam to a few isolated pockets of influence.

Doctrinal Orientation and Diversity

With an estimated population of a little more than 54 million, Central Asian inhabitants are predominantly Sunni Muslims of the Hanafi school, which is noted for its liberal religious orientation. There are also Sunni Muslims who adhere to Sufism common to all republics, but most prevalent in Turkmenistan. In addition, there are the Shi'ite minorities represented in some regions, most noticeably, the Ismaili Shi'ites of the mountainous region of Gorno Badakhshan and the Twelver Shi'ites of the Samarkand and Bukhara. Finally, there are the Wahhabis of Fergana, a small but growing fundamentalist sect known as the puritans of Islam.

Founded by Abu Hanifah al Numan ibn Thabit ibn Zuta ibn Mah (d. 767) in Kufa, the Hanafi school assumed prominence during the Abbasid caliphs. It later spread eastward into Khorasan and Transoxania. According to Barthold, a branch of the Hanafi school of theology was established in Bukhara in the early ninth century, attracting Islamic scholars and followers. In fact, a number of well-known representatives of the school came from Central Asia. For instance, Abu-Hafs, who died in 832, was a famous Hanafi Bukharan referred to as "the teacher of scholars of Mawarannahr."[15] The Hanafi school wielded considerable political influence in Bukhara from the eleventh century until well into the Mongol era under the Banu Maza family, as the hereditary chiefs (*ra'ees*), of the Hanafis. It also became the preferred doctrine of the Seljuk rulers and of the Ottoman Turks, maintaining its high status until the present.

Two attributes of the Hanafi school made it particularly appealing to the Central Asian population. First, Abu Hanifah was of non-Arab but Ajam origin. His grandfather, Numan, was a Persian who adopted Islam voluntarily.[16] The non-Arab identity of Abu Hanifah created a positive psychological impression on the population of the region, which had been under the umbrella of Persian culture and civilization for centuries. Second, the liberal orientation of the school allowed for the incorporation of the pre-Islamic traditions of Central Asia. This would not have been possible under the more theologically rigid schools of Hanbali, Shafi'i, or Maliki, prevalent elsewhere in the Muslim world.

Several Hanafi principles have been instrumental in providing a flexible framework for the practice of Islam, hence offering more freedom to the Central Asian believer. First, and perhaps the most critical aspect, is the qualitative distinction that has been made between faith (*iman*), and work or practice (*amal*). The Hanafis argue that if a Muslim wholeheartedly believes in God and the prophethood of Muhammad, but is negligent in performing his religious duties, he is not an infidel. Abu Hanifah illustrated this point in a letter to Usman Batti in which he stated "You can give the title of *Mu'min* to a person who is unaware of duties: such a person is ignorant so far as duties are concerned, but all the same, a believer in respect to affirmation. . . . Would you equate a person who refuses to acknowledge God and his apostle with one who, though a believer, is ignorant of practical duties." He further indicated that "He who has faith but omits to act is certainly a Muslim, but a sinful one. It is up to God to punish or forgive him."[17] This interpretation clearly reduces the religious significance of duties performed in connection with one's faith, thus providing a more tolerant belief system. Second, the Hanafis place heavy emphasis upon the expediency and the beneficiality of Islamic jurisprudence, thus refraining from the so-called devotional interpretation of Islam based on absolute obedience, a characteristic associated with the fundamentalist practice of Islam. Abu Hanifah argued that the underlying purpose of all Islamic precepts can be understood through rational construction. In connection with the act of prayer, for instance, he presented yet another critical distinction between the form and the substance or essence of prayer, indicating that the manner in which the prayer is carried out is subordinate to the object of prayer, which is the achievement of spiritual salvation for the believer. Seen in this light, the Hanafi school permits the conduct of prayer in languages other than Arabic. It also provides freedom of choice in selection of the Koranic ingredients of prayer.[18] Third, the principle of socioeconomic necessity overrides the need for religious orthodoxy. Abu Hanifah advocated the view that the conduct of religious affairs may be postponed or altered to accommodate the needs of the believer. This aspect of the Hanafi school is based on the realization that socioeconomic change is inevitable and some degree of flexibility is required if religion itself is to survive. As such, the role of private opinion *(r'ay)*, analogy *(qiyas)*, critical scrutiny *(derayat)*, and public consensus *(jima)*, in administration and interpretation of Islamic principles have been greatly emphasized. Fourth, the Hanafi school has provided a more tolerant view of matters concerning civil and criminal punishment, divorce, and almsgiving. For instance, as far as the rules governing divorce are concerned, Hanafis have offered a much more favorable position to women than any other school of Islamic jurisprudence. Finally, it is argued that "difference of opinion in the community is a token of divine mercy."[19] The principle embodied in this statement unequivocally places the Hanafi school farthest away from the conservative or dogmatic understandings of Islam.

The combination of these aspects has given the Hanafi school its relatively nonbinding character, thus facilitating its rapid spread in the non-Arab regions of the Middle East. While there is a widespread consensus that only a small portion of the Central Asian population is adequately familiar with the fundamental tenets of the Hanafi school, its general liberal orientation has been undoubtedly internalized by a wide cross section of the population since the early introduction of the faith.

The prevalence of Sufism in parts of Central Asia, most notably in Turkmenistan, has been yet another significant contributory factor in limiting the scope of fundamentalist Islam in the region.[20] First, the most popular Sufi sect, the Naqshbandi, has a liberal orientation. The order was founded by Muhammad ibn Muhammad Bahaudin Naqshband (1317–89) in Bukhara. It penetrated the Kyrgyz region through Kashgar in the eighteenth century. The Turkmen tribes were exposed to the order in the seventeenth and eighteenth centuries leading to the gradual replacement of the Yasawi order. Khorezm was introduced to the Naqshbandi order in the nineteenth century where it succeeded in assimilating a large number of the Kubrawi believers, assuming the position of dominance in Central Asia that has persisted until today. Presently, it wields influence in the Fergana Valley, eastern and southern Turkmenistan, and Kyrgyzstan. Bennigsen has adequately outlined the underlying reasons for its sweeping success, of which the following is most relevant to the argument made here:

- The Naqshbandi has a unique ability to adapt to changing social and political conditions. An adept is not an ascetic: he remains "in the world" *(Khalwat dar anjoman*—solitary in the world"; *safar dar vatan* —"journeying toward God while remaining in the world"). Thus, as an individual, the Naqshbandi adept is required to adjust his social behavior to meet the requirements of everyday life: that is to say he must be socially flexible.
- The Naqshbandi is linguistically accessible to everyone. In Central Asia it has a Persian and Turkic character; in the Caucasus it assumes an Arabic character in addition to its Persian and Turkic forms.
- This order embodies what we might think of as doctrinal liberalism, in that it excludes fanaticism and radicalism. It is for this reason that Naqshbandi has been successful in superimposing itself on other brotherhoods, absorbing them without insisting on their elimination.[21]

Yet another significant characteristic of the Naqshbandi order is its highly decentralized structure, which has lead to the development of multiple centers of independent religious authority whose totality is held together only through common yet simplified Sufi rituals.

Second, the membership and leadership of the Sufi orders are exclusive rather than inclusive and in most instances are directly tied to the local clan structures. This particular attribute has historically prevented the development of large-scale Islamic coalitions capable of instigating radical political action. It must be indicated, however, that Sufi orders in the past have become politically active, leading various movements against Buddhists, Kalmyks, Russians, and even Communists. But, their politicization has been primarily geared toward staving off foreign enemies rather than challenging domestic political authority. The exclusive nature of membership in the Sufi orders has traditionally limited its recruitment activities, especially in places where clan structures define the scope of admission into the brotherhood. In Turkmenistan and Kyrgyzstan, for instance, recruitment is done almost entirely from within the clan population. Elsewhere, new members are carefully selected and observed before they are assimilated. While the process of selection is highly rigorous, initiation is devoid of complexity. Seen in this light, the active Sufi orders have helped bring about doctrinal fragmentation rather than consolidation in Central Asia. Although from a quantitative perspective brotherhoods on the whole have limited appeal, such decentralizing tendencies seem to work against the emergence of radical hegemonic ideologies that are most successful in religiously monolithic societies. As far as the leadership of the orders are concerned, the smaller centralized Sufi brotherhood such as the Qadiri have well-defined hierarchical structures, which have facilitated the preservation of the leadership lineage within the family of the founder, thus limiting its geographical expansion beyond the residence of the current leader.

Finally, some Sufi sects have exhibited religiously unorthodox tendencies such as admission of women, not only as members, but as leaders of their orders, which is yet another indication of its antifundamentalist character. Although the most popular order, the Naqshbandi, has been reluctant to allow women into their closed circles, some branches of Yasawi, the so-called Lachi and Hairy Ishans, have allowed the establishment of women Sufi groups with their own leaders. Admission of women into the Sufihood, Bennigsen pointed out, is in response to the fundamental role women play in the preservation of national and cultural heritage of Central Asia.

In addition to the dominant Hanafi doctrine and Sufi orders, the Shi'i sects have been represented in several Central Asian locations. The Ismaili Shi'ites of the Nizari rite are found in the Pamir mountainous region in southeastern Tajikistan, known as Gorno Badakhshan. The origin of the Ismaili Shi'ites of Pamir has been traced back to Hassan-e Sabbah who defected from the Fatimid Ismailis subsequent to the successful coup against Nizar, the designated successor of Caliph al-Mustansir, by al-Afdal ibn Badr al-Jamali in 1094. The defection lead to the development of a separate branch of Ismaili sect in Persia that later was reconnected with the Syrian Ismailis in 1374. Under the

Persian Safavids, one of the most influential Ismaili imams, Shah Tahir Huseini, was forced to leave Persia for India in 1522. Later, India became a refuge for the Ismaili imams who had to flee Persia for fear of religious persecution. According to Halm, the most recent Ismaili line of religious authority respected in Pamir is traced back to Imam Hassan Ali Shah Mahalati (Agha Khan) who fled to Afghanistan in 1842 and later to India, subsequent to a failed rebellion in Kirman during the reign of the Qajars. Ever since, the Ismailis of the Pamir region have maintained regular contact with their spiritual strongholds in India.[22] In conjunction with the activities of Agha Khan and his descendents in the Pamir area, other Ismaili *dais* had conducted missionary work in Transoxania as early as the first decade of the tenth century, under the direct guidance of Abu Hatim al-Razi, al-Nasafi, and Abu Ya'qub al-Sijistani.[23]

Apart from the Ismaili Shi'ites of Gorno Badakhshan, there are small communities of Twelver Shi'ism in Bukhara, Samarkand, and Tashkent. The origin of these communities goes back to the beginning of Abbasid rule in Central Asia. Although there are no historical records available as to the early establishment of these communities, the Shi'ites seem to have migrated from Khorasan to Bukhara and Merv and later to the other cities.[24] The Shi'ites as whole have sharp disagreements with the Sunnis over the question of succession after the departure of the Prophet Muhammad. The former submit to Ali ibn Abu Talib as the legitimate heir of the prophet, while the latter first follow Abu Bakr with Ali as the fourth legitimate ruler of the Muslim *umma*. This fundamental dispute has so far prevented the development of any meaningful religious coalition between the two sects. There are also irreconcilable differences between the Twelver and Ismaili Shi'ites over the issue of succession. Although both sects believe in Ali as the legitimate successor to Muhammad, the Ismailis consider Ismail, the eldest son of the sixth Shi'i imam, Ja'far Sadiq, as the true inheritor of the title Imamat. The Twelver Shi'ites, on the other hand, believe in Musa ibn Ja'far as the lawful successor in the line of the twelve imams.

While the general Islamic proclivity as outlined here, define one set of parameters of Islamization at the specific level, the organizational reach and mobilization capabilities of the Islamic forces operating in the region, defines the other set of parameters. Since the late 1980s, a number of Islamic parties, organizations, and movements with a variety of ideological orientations have entered into the public arena of the Central Asian republics. Driven by political objectives, these forces have presented a qualitatively different face of Central Asian Islam, which has been marked by fundamentalist features. Relatively limited in their appeal, such organizations have so far failed to alter the present course of Islamic revival in favor of a more comprehensively radical path desired by their leaders.

ISLAMIC ORGANIZATIONS AND MOVEMENTS

Two types of Islamic organizations have been active on the Central Asian political scene in recent years. The first are the republican parties that have so far exhibited weak to moderate organizational and mobilization capabilities, encompassing a wide range of ideological tendencies. The most radical of these organizations have either gone underground or have been absorbed by other organizations during the last two years. One such organization was Islam and Democracy of Uzbekistan, which held its founding congress in Alma-Ata (Almaty), the capital of Kazakhstan, on October, 28, 1988. Though at first it hoped to become an interrepublican party drawing support from all over Central Asia, it failed to reach beyond Uzbekistan's cities and rural areas. According to its chairman, Almaz Estekov, the basic objective of the organization was "the spiritual cleansing of people from immorality and preaching of the democratic principles of the Koran."[25] The organization was instrumental in forcing the removal of Mufti Babakhanov (Babakhan), in 1989 subsequent to a series of demonstrations on February 3. The leading members of the party, had apparently produced evidence attesting to the fact that Babakhan drank alcoholic beverages, womanized, and lacked the necessary religious credentials to remain as the mufti of the Muslim Religious Board of Central Asia and Kazakhstan. The membership of the party was estimated at 2,500 in 1989, of whom the overwhelming majority came from Uzbekistan's cities of Andijan, Bukhara, and Samarkand. It is not at all clear whether the organization is still active today; but as a fundamentalist party, Islam and Democracy may have been absorbed by larger organizations of the same ideological colorings in 1990.

The People's Front of Uzbekistan is also a radical organization operating out of Tashkent. Due to its clandestine nature, little has been publicized about its activities apart from the fact that it supports the establishment of an Islamic republic. Similarly, the Islamic Democratic Party has been advocating the creation of a theocracy modeled after the Islamic Republic of Iran. In a 1990 interview, one of the party leaders, Dadkhan Hassan, had openly praised the leader of the Islamic Republic of Iran, indicating that "Khomeini was very good for us." In its founding congress, the party called for veiling of women and the imposition of Islamic law on Uzbek society. Hassan, however, pointed out that "we will not attempt to seize power by force . . . our strategy first is to unite all our Muslims . . . and then to educate the new generation in the spirit of

Islam."[26] Furthermore, the party was to nominate candidates for local offices on an Islamic platform with the aim of replacing the secular Soviet law with Shariah law. But according to Doyle McManus, the party's objective was nothing short of a nonviolent Islamic revolution in the region. The proceedings of the party congress was broadcast live by a local radio station in Namangan without government interference. Yet, the scope of the party's activities has been limited to the city of Namangan in Uzbekistan.

In Kazakhstan, an Islamic party named Alash for the National Independence of Kazakhstan was established in April 1990. Headed by Aron Atabek and Rashid Yutoshev, the party had been pressing for the creation of an Islamic state in Kazakhstan. On December 13, 1991, the Alash party held a meeting during which a decision was adopted to remove the mufti of Kazakhstan, Nysanbai Uly Ratbek, who had been accused of violating the Islamic Shariah. Shortly thereafter, seven militant members of the Alash made their way into the muftiate in Almaty and demanded his resignation. Subsequently, a fight broke out during which the mufti was beaten and injured.[27] Also attacked was the bookkeeper of the muftiate. Nysanbai Uly was held hostage for two days and then released. The muftiate, however, remained under siege until the government militia stormed the building and captured the assailants whose numbers had grown to 200.[28] Forty-one members of Alash were detained by the government militia. According to the Kazakhstan's attorney general, Tukakbayev, this act was designed to raise the confidence of the fundamentalist forces within the republic and strengthen the Alash position in this regard. Some of the arrested were put on trial for their alleged "criminal activities" and sentenced to prison.

Faced with dwindling support, the party has moderated its position by dropping its demand for the establishment of an Islamic republic and the expulsion of all Russians from Kazakhstan. But Alash has maintained its pan-Turkic demand that calls for consolidation of the Turkic peoples of the former Soviet Union in a "peace-loving republic of Great Turkistan."[29] According to one government official, the party has a total of 85 members in Almaty.[30] Unconfirmed reports indicate a much larger following, most of whom operate out of Chimkent, bordering Uzbekistan. As an illegal party, its leaders have been forced into exile in Baku, and their newspaper, *Khak,* has been banned.[31] In the summer of 1993 the party moved its headquarters to Moscow in order to be able to conduct its affairs without fear of government reprisal.

The second type of Islamic organization emerged out of the interrepublican party of Islamic revival or Islamic renaissance—*Partiya Islamskovo Vozrozhdeniya.* It is this party that has commanded a relatively large following, particularly in Uzbekistan and Tajikistan, thus constituting the core of

Islamic activism in Central Asia. The Islamic Revival Party (IRP) held its founding congress in the city of Astrakhan in the Soviet part of the north Caucasus on June 10, 1990. Attended by 150 delegates from Dagestan (60 delegates), Abkhazia (2 delegates), Tajikistan (24 delegates), Azerbaijan (2 delegates), Tatarstan (1 delegate), and other Muslim republics, the party's initial goals revolved around "the revival of ideals of Islam."[32] But from the outset its objectives were political in nature. For instance, the party called for the establishment of Shariah courts and the teaching of Islam in secular schools. Although the creation of Islamic states was not explicitly addressed during the Astrakhan gathering, some members expressed their desire to move in that direction upon their return to their respective republics. Mullah Muhammad Abdullah (Mirsaidov) of Tajikistan, who later played a significant role as a local opposition leader to the Nabiyev government, had openly entertained such an idea in his sermons.[33]

The IRP has been campaigning through its newspaper *Al-Wahdah* since January 1991 in order to shed its negative reputation, unfortunately, its efforts have been hampered by financial problems in recent months. The participation in its annual congresses have also declined, which may be interpreted as a sign of its overall decline in the former Soviet Union. On April 12, 1992, only 40 delegates from Kazakhstan, Uzbekistan, Tajikistan, Belorussia, and elsewhere attended its third congress in Saratov.[34] Much of the discussion revolved around combating the party's declining popularity. At the leadership level, the IRP has been ideologically divided between those who wish to further radicalize the party's platform and those who would like to stress the educational and religious aspects of the organization. A member of the IRP council of ulema, Vali Ahmad Sadur, has been pressing for greater contact with Muslim nations to strengthen its financial arm. The party is known to have established relations with Sudan, Pakistan, Egypt, and Iran. Leaving aside the declining status of the central IRP in Moscow, the organizational reach and mobilization capacities of the IRP branches have been relatively more advanced in Tajikistan and Uzbekistan as compared to the rest of the Central Asian republics.

The IRP branch in Tajikistan was organized by two of the Tajik participants in the Astrakhan congress, Dawlat Usman and I. Gadoev, on October 6, 1990.[35] The party's request to hold its founding congress in the capital city Dushanbe was declined by the Communist Party first secretary, Ghahar Makhkamov, forcing the 300 participants of the constituent conference to convene a meeting in the village of Chortut outside the city.[36] A council of ulema with a membership of 27 was created. Abdussamad Himmatov was elected chairman.[37] Since its inception, the party has emphasized the primacy of electoral means for achieving its basic political objectives. For instance, the party secretary in charge of education and propaganda, Abdullah Dadkhuda, stated that: "The only way to advertize Islam is to do it through a parliamentary and democratic political system. . . . We are against forcing people to accept our path but we rely on any means to awaken them."[38] He further indicated that: "By an Islamic government, we mean that a government where the orders of God, the sacred Qur'an, the teaching and knowledge of the Prophet are the principal elements. We must have a parliament because the Qur'an encourages collective consultation. Future leaders should be chosen by the people and judged by their world view, their scholarly enlightenment and their knowledge of Islam."[39] The IRP received official recognition on October 26, 1991, and declared its independence from the all-Union IRP in December 1992 under the name of Nehzat-e Islami-ye Tajikistan. S. Tadjbakhsh has provided a summary of the basic objectives of the IRP as follows:

- a spiritual revival of the citizens of the republic;
- an independent economic and political system;
- a complete political and legal awakening with the aim of applying to the everyday life of Muslims of the republic the principles of Islam;
- the spread and advertising of Islamic thought among different nationalities of the republic.[40]

By 1991 the party had succeeded in developing an elaborate republican-wide organizational network, expanding its membership through active involvement in mosques and prayer houses whose numbers had expanded significantly since 1989. Quite expectedly, the bulk of its support came from four regions with strongest Islamic proclivity: Maschah and Ura Tepeh in Khojend oblast, Dushanbe and the surrounding areas, Gharm (Gharatakin), and Ghorghan Tepeh in Khatlon (Khatlan) oblast. Although the extent of the membership of the Tajik IRP has not been determined, a 1990 report in *Izvestia* put the figure at 10,000. In 1992 it was reported that some 30,000 members had joined the party.[41] The actual numbers may be as high as 40,000, not including the party sympathizers. The majority of the IRP members seem to be of rural socioeconomic background and much of its urban support comes from unemployed youth and elderly men and women. It must be indicated, however, that the IRP, at least publicly, has denied that it has been working toward the creation of an Islamic state. Its leaders, Muhammad Sharif Hematzoda and Dawlat Usman have frequently stated that the creation of an Islamic republic is an unattainable goal in the foreseeable future.[42]

Despite the party's united leadership stance, the Tajik IRP has been plagued by ideological factionalism, which has not yet affected its general political direction, but is bound to weaken its organizational strength in the long run. Three basic ideological tendencies may be identified within the IRP. The first faction has exhibited Wahhabi tendencies, such as those that condemn Muslim celebrations, feasting, and other costly rites such as *kalym,* or bride price, as well as the veneration of saints and deities. Mullah Abdullah (Mirsaidov) is a strong proponent of this condemnation, arguing that such activities have reduced the purity of the Islamic faith. The support for this view has recently been strengthened by exposure to Wahhabi literature smuggled through Uzbekistan and elsewhere into the republic.[43] This faction is also more adamant about the establishment of an Islamic republic in Tajikistan. The second faction is influenced by the ideology of the Muslim Brotherhood, which has a strong pan-Islamic orientation. This tendency has been strengthened by the introduction of the writings of Muhammad Seyyed Qutb (1906–66) of Egypt, Abdul Ala Ma'dudi (1903–79) of Pakistan, and other Brotherhood ideologists into Tajikistan during the past decade. The third faction is a moderate Islamic faction whose ideology is more or less in line with that of Kazi Ali Akbar Turajonzoda. This faction, which has been advocating the revival of Islam in Tajikistan, has been effectively absorbed by the IRP subsequent to the Communist takeover in the fall of 1992 that led to the removal of the kazi from his post.

The IRP in Uzbekistan was established on January 26, 1992, in Tashkent, provoking a similar reaction to that of the Tajikistan authorities that lead to the arrest of 400 participants and the expulsion of a member of the organizing committee from the republic. The party has been denied official recognition and its activities were banned under Uzbek law on Public Associations that went into effect in February of 1991. Ever since, the Party has been conducting its affairs underground. A review of the party's initial platform, which was made public on December 16, 1990, clearly demonstrates its comprehensively religious orientation and its similarities with the Tajikistan IRP:[44]

- To explain to the people the real meaning of the holy Koran and *hadith* and to call the people to live and act according to the Koran and *hadith.*
- To call to Islam by all means of mass media.
- To fight national and racial discrimination, impudence, crime, alcoholism, and all other things that are forbidden by Shariah through understanding and appeal.
- To educate young people on the principles of Islam and, for this purpose, to create instruction and training centers and *madrasehs.*
- To ensure that the rights of all Muslims are exercised according to the Koran.

- To strengthen Islamic brotherhood, to develop religious relations with the Muslim world, and to seek for a relationship of equal rights with representatives of other religions.
- To cooperate with other democratic parties and state organizations in all fields.
- To create philanthropic funds that will support anyone in need of help.
- To strengthen the family according to the principles of Islam and to ensure the rights of women and children.
- To ensure the principles of an Islamic economy and regaining ecological purity.
- To ensure the distribution of food according to the Shariah.
- To solve the problems of the people according to the holy Koran and *hadith.*

The party, however, has recently moderated its position and thus has eliminated any implicit or explicit reference to the idea of creating an Islamic republic. IRP leader Abdullah Uta has stressed on many occasions that although the government should remain secular in nature, Islam must play a significant role in the life of the Uzbek people.[45] In an interview published in April 1992, the first deputy of the party, Abdullah Yusuf, explained the party's vision of an Islamic democracy: "With our people, the notion democracy means no restrictions. . . . It would not be a one party state; the franchise would be universal; the rights of ethnic and religious minorities would be protected; and private property would be honored."[46]

The IRP stronghold in Uzbekistan is in the densely populated Fergana Valley, in particular the two cities of Namangan and Andijan. The party also enjoys substantial support among the rural Uzbek population. Due to the government crackdown, there are no verifiable sources of information on the membership of the IRP. But there may be as many as 40,000 to 50,000 members most of whom operate out of the Fergana region. There are also reports of the IRP activities in the Karakalpak region in the northwestern section of Uzbekistan. Both regions have had a long tradition in Islamic activism, containing the highest concentration of mosques in all of Central Asia. The organizational reach and mobilization capacity of the IRP have been severely hampered by the geographical isolation of the Fergana, which can become inaccessible during the winter months, by its predominantly rural constituency, and by its lack of financial resources. As such, the party has been less successful than its counterpart in Tajikistan in establishing local networks outside its sphere of influence in Fergana.

Contrary to Tajikistan and Uzbekistan, in Kyrgyzstan, Turkmenistan, and Kazakhstan, the IRP has had a considerably smaller following. Most of the

IRP activities in Kyrgyzstan are limited to the Osh and Jalalabad oblasts, particularly among those with Uzbek origin. In Turkmenistan, on the other hand there are no visible signs of the party. One Turkmen expert has stated that the Party has no organization in Turkmenistan.[47] The party, however, is represented by Qari Saeed, a well-known Muslim scholar. And although Kazakhstan was represented at the first all-Union IRP congress in Astrakhan, the members do not seem to have succeeded in instituting a nationwide party structure capable of mass mobilization. In November 1991, two Kazakh writers, Akim Tarazi and Zaryl-Kasem, proposed a plan for the establishment of an Islamic party that may have been the Kazakh IRP branch.[48] The plan did not materialize. However, there have been reports of Islamic activities in the Chimkent, Jambul, and Kyzyl Orda oblasts that are connected with the IRP. Apparently, the party has been officially registered with the city council in Jambul and Chimkent where several mosques have been opened by its members, independent of the Kazakhstan muftiate.[49] Abdul Jabbar has been referred to as the spiritual leader of the IRP. It is interesting to note that here too the most politically active Muslims in these regions are of Uzbek rather than Kazakh origin.

While the IRP branches have become increasingly independent, they share a number of functional and contextual characteristics. First, and most obvious, is the overriding objective of creating an Islamic republic sometime in the future. Although this objective has been dropped from the agendas of the IRP branches for tactical reasons, the party's principles can only be fully realized when such an Islamic state is established. Second, all parties have tried to capitalize on the deteriorating economic conditions, albeit with very limited success, to delegitimize the Central Asian governments.[50] In Uzbekistan, for instance, higher wages and lower food prices have been demanded by Muslim demonstrators in Fergana in 1992.[51] In Tajikistan, unemployment and housing shortages have been frequently brought up by Muslims but also by other political activists. Third, although militant tendencies exist among some IRP factions, the party as a whole does not seem to favor a militant approach to achieving its objectives. Rather, the electoral route to power or power-sharing has been declared the preferred method by the leadership. Finally, the IRP considers the present leaders of the republics as the old Communist elite with a new democratic facade. Moreover, they have been accused of political foot-dragging in carrying out reforms that would broaden the basis of participation and power-sharing, thus encompassing the opposition parties. In fact the record shows that except for the President of Kyrgyzstan the Central Asian presidents have been supportive of Communist policies in their republics and have assumed power either through the traditional Communist Party election procedures or by not facing genuine opposition.

Despite the similarities, the IRP branches have exhibited a fundamental difference in the past with regard to the party's willingness to compromise and cooperate with Central Asian governments. For instance, the party has adopted opposing views on the role and legitimacy of a state-supported religious establishment.

The IRP in Tajikistan, for example, was at first in support of the Muslim Religious Board (and its representative, Kazi Haji Akbar Turajonzoda), which had been known for its liberal attitude toward religion and politics.[52] This support, however, was removed subsequent to the outbreak of the Tajik civil war in the fall of 1992, when the Communists retook power and dissolved the coalition government that had been formed by the supporters of the former Communist Rahman Nabiyev and the democratic-Islamic opposition (see chapter 5). In contrast, the IRP in Uzbekistan had been opposing the board's authority. The party had been pressing for the dissolution of the board and its replacement by a new decentralized religious structure with more power vested in the regional and district organizations.[53] In an effort to assimilate the IRP religious leaders into the board's structure, on February 24, 1992, the former mufti of the board, Muhammad Sadiq Muhammad Yusuf, held a meeting with the IRP leaders, including Abdelaziz Mansur, the representative of IRP from Tashkent. The meeting was mediated by Uzbek presidential advisor Bakhtiyar Nazarov. According to the press service of the IRP, Muslim figures were offered posts of deputy muftis in return for their cooperation with the board, but to no avail.[54] In Kazakhstan and Kyrgyzstan no attempt at cooperation has been made and the governments have refused to allow the IRP leaders to enter into the mainstream politics of the country.

In addition to these Islamic parties, there is a growing Wahhabi movement in the Fergana Valley in Uzbekistan that has been slowly gaining influence among the Uzbeks of Osh and Jalalabad oblasts in Kyrgyzstan.[55] Known as the puritans of the Islamic faith, the Wahhabis believe in the establishment of a Muslim community similar to that which existed at the time of the Prophet Muhammad when Islam dominated every facet of the believer's life.

The Wahhabi movement was introduced to Central Asia from India in the early nineteenth century. But the origin of the sect is traced back to Muhammad ibn Abu al-Wahhab who was born in 1691 in Najd. He was instructed by his father in the tenets of the Muslim faith, according to the Hanbali teachings—the strictest of the four great schools of Islamic jurisprudence. Since his early adulthood, Abdul al-Wahhab was greatly disturbed by the laxities and superstitions of those who had stretched the rigid line of

Islam almost to the breaking point. To him, sacred shrines, richly ornamented tombs, the use of intoxicating drugs, and the silks and saints of the wealthy were blatant departures from the first principles of Islam, which he considered to be unwarrantable concessions to the luxury, idolatry, and decadence of the age. Having carefully studied the teachings of the Koran and hadith of the Prophet Muhammad, he thought he had learned to distinguish between the essential elements of Islam and its recent admixtures. He was thus determined to propagate nothing but the "pure faith" as laid down by the precepts and the practice of the Prophet Muhammad. By the time of his death in 1765, the Wahhabi movement had gained considerable acceptance in the Arabian peninsula and by 1830, a Wahhabi rule was established in eastern Arabia.[56]

The Wahhabi faith was introduced to India in 1822 by an Indian pilgrim to Mecca named Seyyed Ahmad, who subsequent to his return, began to spread the word in the northern part of the subcontinent. In 1826, he declared a *jihad* against the Sikhs in Peshawar that lasted for four years until his defeat and eventual death in 1830. Consequently, the movement suffered a temporary setback, but some of Ahmad's disciples continued to propagate the Wahhabi Islam in Herat and Balkh in Afghanistan and other cities in northern India. By the 1890s, many Central Asian Muslims had traveled to India to receive instructions from Wahhabi teachers, some of whom were invited to reside in Central Asian towns and villages for some time.

One of the contemporary Wahhabi leaders in Central Asia was Muhammad Haji Hindostani (d. 1991) who departed for India during the October Revolution where he received his education and subsequently returned to Andijan in Uzbekistan.[57] Although his teachings were based strictly on Wahhabi principles, he refused to politicize the faith, conducting what may be referred to as a defensive propagation of his beliefs. Disenchanted with his apolitical proselytizing, one of his disciples, Abdulwali Qari, began to criticize his acquiescence with regard to the destruction of Islam under Communist rule. Later, Abdulwali began to operate clandestine schools where they taught their version of political Islam. Another well-known Wahhabi leader was Rahmatollah, whose puritan Islamic views gathered a considerable following in Marghilan. He, too, began to politicize Wahhabism and conducted his teachings in secrecy with the aid of radical literature printed in small print houses set up by his followers.[58]

On December 8–9, 1991, the Wahhabis and members of other Islamic organizations, including the Uzbek IRP, Towba, and Adolat, participated in a demonstration in Namangan and captured a Communist Party building with the intention of establishing an Islamic center.[59] The protest was quickly transformed into a movement for Muslim self-government in Namangan, led by a twenty-four-year-old dropout from the Bukhara Technological Institute, Tahirjon Yuldashev, and others including the imams of the Wahhabi mosques in Namangan. The protesters demanded a constitutional provision in which Islam would be considered the state religion. They also demanded the reconstitution of the Shariah laws.[60] The genesis and the underlying cause of the establishment of a Muslim parallel government has been traced back to President Karimov's visit to Namangan during the presidential election campaign in December, during which representatives of the official clergy expressed support on behalf of all Muslims for Karimov's candidacy. This generated a storm of indignation among the people and resulted in a rally. The Muslim opposition leaders thus set up a parallel Islamic government in Namangan in defiance of the authorities. The movement was supported by as many as 50,000 people in January and February of 1991. The initial vigor of the movement forced Karimov to recognize Muslim self-government. But, on his orders, on January 26, an extraordinary oblast Soviet session was held behind closed doors to elect an official oblast head (hakim), again provoking a protest rally by the Muslims, which called for the resignation of the newly elected hakim, Burgut Rafikaliyev. Later, in a show of force, Karimov arrested 71 of the movement's organizers.[61] Although the demonstrations subsided and the self-government bodies were dissolved by the government, the Muslim activists succeeded in establishing an organization called Adolat whose cadres were to "monitor public morality and to punish theft and corruption."[62] Adolat is said to have cooperated with the Islam Lashkari (Army of Islam), a militant Islamic organization based in Fergana with alleged ties to the IRP and other radical Muslim organizations. The Adolat exercised considerable influence until the spring of 1992, by which time the government had managed to effectively restore its authority in the region.[63]

The Wahhabi movement has been receiving sizable financial support from the Saudi Arabian movement, Ahl-e Sunnah, for the construction of mosques and *madrasehs*. An estimated $1.3 million of Saudi money was to be spent for such purposes by the end of 1993.[64] A two-story Islamic complex at a cost of $127,000 is under construction in Namangan to provide Islamic education. It has been funded entirely by Ahl-e Sunnah. In Andijan, yet another Islamic complex has been built with the capacity for 100 students. In Marghilan, the headquarters of Ahl-e Sunnah, plans have been underway for the construction of an Islamic university with a student body of 5,000. Similar projects have been conceived for Kokand and Kuva with an estimated cost of 110 million rubles. The Saudis have also financed an Islamic center in Osh, a city in Kyrgyzstan, at a cost of 1 million rubles.[65]

The Wahhabis do not take into doctrinal consideration any opinions other than those expressed by the generation of the Prophet Muhammad. As such, they categorically repudiate the teachings of the four main schools of Sunni Islam, which are the Hanafi, the Maliki, the Shafi'i, and the Hanbali, although they have some common ground with the latter. Devoid of esotericism and mysticism, the movement rejects the idea of sainthood and condemns the building of shrines and holy places. The Koran and hadith are considered the only authoritative source by which the Islamic community may conduct its affairs.

The Wahhabi movement has subsequently reached the Osh and Jalalabad oblasts of Kyrgyzstan. It is reported that Abdulwali Qari has been active in these oblasts and that one of his colleagues, Mullah Abdul Khei, has been propagating Wahhabism in Kyrgyzstan. The movement is particularly strong in two villages of Bekabad and Suzak in Jalalabad, where the Wahhabi imams from Namangan and Andijan come to deliver sermons to the believers. As in Uzbekistan, in Kyrgyzstan the Wahhabis have managed to set up their own mosques, which according to one government official are well attended.[66] An overwhelming majority of the Wahhabis in Kyrgyzstan are of Uzbek origin.

For obvious ideological and political reasons, the Wahhabis have had limited cooperation with the IRP in Uzbekistan, which has restricted their sphere of influence. The Wahhabis have denounced the IRP leadership for its willingness to compromise with the Uzbek government in order to participate in parliamentary elections: a strategy that has been categorically condemned by the Wahhabi leaders. A leading Wahhabi clergy, Abdu Ahd, has publicly articulated the Wahhabi position in this regard: "the IRP wants to be in parliament. We have no desire to be in parliament. We want a revolution."[67] In addition to this radical political position, which will undoubtedly prevent the Wahhabi movement from assuming a meaningful political dimension, their puritanical views are not shared by the majority of the Muslims of Central Asia who adhere to the Hanafi school of Islam noted for its general liberal orientation and its emphasis on private opinion *(r'ay)* and public consensus *(jima),* in administration and interpretation of Islamic principles. The Wahhabis also condemn Sufism, which enjoys a sizable following in Central Asia, second only to Hanafi Islam. As such, it is unlikely that Wahhabism could gain a toehold in places other than the Fergana Valley.[68]

QUANTITATIVE DIMENSIONS OF ISLAMIC REVIVAL

While the political manifestations of Islam have so far remained relatively limited in scope, its unhindered religious presence has been slowly making a noticeable impact on the cultural landscape of Central Asia. Nearly eight decades ago, Islamic Turkistan was home to 26,279 mosques, 6,000 *maktabs,* 300 *madrasehs,* and 45,399 clergy. Today, this legacy remains a distant source of pride for Central Asian believers who wish to reconstitute the traditional chain that was violently broken by the imposition of the Communist rule in 1917. Quite expectedly, the Islamic revival in Central Asia follows closely the general pattern of Islamic proclivity that existed prior to the Communist takeover, with Uzbekistan and Tajikistan leading the process. Unfortunately, there is no comprehensive data to present a complete quantitative picture of Islamic revival in the region. The following is thus an attempt to piece together the available information in order to provide an understanding of the scope of the ongoing revival.

As of 1994, an estimated 7,800 mosques and prayer houses have been opened in Central Asia, of which nearly half are located in Uzbekistan.[69] An overwhelming number of these mosques are located in the Fergana and Karakalpak regions. Between 1989 and 1991, the Uzbek government returned a number of religious sites to the believers, including the Abu Issa al Termezi Mausoleum in the Republic's south, the Kalon mosque, the Ata Walikhai mosque in Namangan, the Imam al Bukhari mausoleum in Bukhara, and the Jami mosque in Kokand. In Tajikistan, 126 mosques and 2,870 prayer houses were established in the 1991–92 period.[70] And according to the kazi of Kyrgyzstan, Kimsanbay Ben Abdurahman, 1,000 mosques have been operating in the republic, more than 60 percent of which are located in the Osh and Jalalabad oblasts.[71] In Kazakhstan, 300 mosques have been officially registered by the Kazakh Religious Board, and as many as 200 were under construction in 1993. Here, too, the majority of mosques are located in the religiously strong Chimkent, Jambul, and Kyzyl Orda oblasts.[72] An estimated 80 mosques have been reopened in Turkmenistan, of which 20 are located in the capital city Ashkhabad (Ashgabat).[73] In 1994, the government reported that the construction of 180 mosques had been completed and that another 100 mosques were under construction. The most elaborate mosques under construction in the major cities in Central Asia have been financed by external funding from Saudi Arabia, Kuwait, Turkey, and other Gulf States, or donations by the people, as well as the government.

In conjunction with the opening of mosques, Islamic education has been gaining popularity among young Muslims who wish to make Islam into a career. An estimated 380 *madrasehs* have been operating in Uzbekistan since independence. The number of students enrolled in Barak Khan and Mir Arab, the two major *madrasehs,* has nearly tripled. In addition, other religious schools have been reopened, including the Kukledash *madraseh,* which has been under renovation but has been operating since 1991. The enrollment in Al Bukhari Higher Islamic Institute has doubled since independence. It is reported that as many as 5,000 students have been receiving Islamic education in various mosques throughout Uzbekistan. In 1990, the second largest Islamic institute for higher education was opened in Dushanbe. Although no verifiable data is available, an estimated 1,700 students have reportedly been involved in Islamic training. In Kyrgyzstan, the first *madraseh* was opened in October 1991, which was renamed the Hazarat-e Umar Islamic Institute the following year. The institute has two campuses, one in Bishkek and one in the village of Vostochni. A total of 760 students have been enrolled in the institute. There is also a *madraseh* in Kara Qol with a student body of 150, and in Osh a similar school, Ali'ah, has enrolled 200 students in 1993.[74] In Kazakhstan, a *madraseh* with the capacity of 60 students was opened in 1991 and plans are underway for the construction of an Islamic center containing a mosque, a university, a library, and dormitories.[75] In addition to these schools, several hundred students have been dispatched to various Middle Eastern countries to receive Islamic training. For instance, Kazakhstan has sent 100 students to Turkey, 40 to Egypt, and 40 to Pakistan. There are also 96 Kyrgyz students in Turkey and 26 students in Egypt. Turkmenistan has also sent some 200 students to Turkey to receive religious training in 1992.

The Central Asian Islamic school curriculums cover courses in Arabic, Shariah law, Fiqh, Islamic history and civilization, and Islamic culture. Due to the shortages of trained clergy, the length of schooling has been shortened to two years in Kazakhstan, but on average, five to seven years is required to graduate from Islamic schools. The most comprehensive training is offered by the Uzbek schools, where Arabic language and literature have been extensively taught. Besides Uzbekistan, shortages in Arabic instructors have been a serious problem in providing an in-depth Islamic education. In Kazakhstan, the mufti has recently translated the Koran into Kazakh, but most Central Asian clerics agree that the meaning of Islamic precepts can only be fully understood in Arabic.

Despite the availability of these institutions, the educational process has been severely hampered by an apparent lack of Islamic literature. In 1990, Saudi Arabia donated 1,000,000 copies of the Koran to the Religious Board in Uzbekistan for distribution. Egypt, Turkey, Pakistan, and Kuwait have also contributed literature, but the demand has far outstripped the supply. The most frequently mentioned problem is the expense involved in the printing of such materials; in particular the cost and scarcity of paper have prevented large scale production of Islamic literature in these republics. There is also a sizable quantity of illegal literature that has been smuggled into Central Asia by fundamentalist organizations, which clearly underscores the need to overcome this deficiency if the impact of such radical literature is to be counteracted. The problem is especially serious in Tajikistan and Uzbekistan's Fergana Valley.

The observance of Islamic rituals has also been steadily on the rise, and on the whole, it has followed the general regional and republican patterns of proclivity discussed earlier. It is interesting to note that of all Islamic practices, the most widely observed are the rituals of circumcision, marriage, and burial, which are in essence the most marginal and the least time-consuming aspects of Islamic conduct. Circumcision is observed almost invariably by all Central Asian Muslims. In a 1987 study, the marriage ceremonies, in particular *kalym* (bride price), was reported to be widely observed in the region, particularly in Tajikistan and Turkmenistan where substantial sums of money are offered by the groom's family to the bride's family. In this connection, Bennigsen has provided the following account:

> In the Andizhan region (the Uzbek part of the Fergana valley), the average price of *kalym* is 5,000 rubles. In the Khorezm region (Uzbekistan) it is 10,000 rubles. In Tajikistan and Turkmenistan it can reach 30,000 and even 40,000 rubles. *Turkmenskaia Iskra* gives several precise estimates of *kalyms* paid in 1987 in the Tejen oblast of the Turkmen SSR: in the first case, 14,000 rubles cash plus goods and cattle for 27,000 rubles was paid, which totalled 41,000 rubles. In the second case, 17,000 rubles in cash, plus 5268 rubles in goods and cattle was paid, which totalled 22,268 rubles.[76]

The postindependence economic decline has substantially reduced the financial ability of the brides' families to offer large sums of money. In most urban areas, however, goods, including clothing, housewares, and even family jewelry has replaced the ruble in marriage ceremonies. Muslim burials practices have also been practiced widely. The practice of placing the dead body in a traditional *yurt* for several days in a city street is no longer an unusual sight in Kazakhstan and Kyrgyzstan. Attendance at Muslim burial sites has shown a significant rise in recent years.

Participation in Friday prayers, one of the most significant acts of faith, has been on the rise in Uzbekistan and Tajikistan. In Kyrgyzstan, Kazakhstan, and Turkmenistan, however, mosque attendance has not increased in proportion to the numbers of mosques that have been opened since 1990. Here, too, the majority of those who attend Friday prayers are from those areas where the Uzbek population is present in significant numbers. It is noteworthy that in Turkmenistan the clergy have expressed disappointment with regard to low mosque attendance.[77]

Fasting during the holy month of Ramadan has made a significant come-back, especially in Uzbekistan where widespread observance has been reported in major cities in 1992. In 1991, the Uzbek president issued a decree whereby working Muslims were permitted to miss work on the first day of Ramadan. Most rural Uzbeks and Tajiks fast for the entire month of Ramadan. This practice, however, is often limited to three days to a week in urban areas where modern-day working schedules conflict with the rituals of fasting. Elaborate ceremonies marking the beginning of Ramadan are held annually in major mosques in Uzbekistan. In 1990 alone, an estimated 150 mosques participated in the ceremonies. In 1992, the numbers of participating mosques was reported to have reached 400 in major cities and towns.

Muslim pilgrimage from Central Asia to Mecca has increased steadily since 1990. In 1992, 40 pilgrims made the trip to Mecca from Kazakhstan and in 1993, 300 were sent directly to Saudi Arabia. The Kyrgyz religious author-ities arranged for the departure of 599 Muslims in 1991, 1,500 in 1992, and 1,000 in 1993. Some of the pilgrims were sent by buses via Uzbekistan, Turkmenistan, Iran, Turkey, Jordan, and Syria to Saudi Arabia.[78] The largest group of pilgrims from Central Asia belongs to Uzbekistan. In 1990, 500, in 1991, 1,250, in 1992, 4,000, and in 1993, 3,500 pilgrims paid a visit to Mecca.[79] There are no reliable statistics available for Tajikistan, but one report indicated that 500 Tajiks participated in the ceremony in 1993. The actual numbers of those who filed applications to travel to Saudi Arabia from the former Soviet Union is estimated at 10,000 to 12,000. The financial cost and the lack of orga-nization have been the underlying reasons for lower-than-expected participa-tion this year. The cost of the trip, on average, was estimated at $800, which is well beyond the financial ability of most Central Asian Muslims.[80] Contrary to previous years, the Saudi government did not subsidize the journey for Central Asian Muslims in 1993.

As to the observance of the Islamic dress code, no significant changes have taken place since 1990. Most city residents in Central Asia dress in Western clothing, and women do not cover their hair according to Islamic tradition. In the provincial parts of Uzbekistan and Kyrgyzstan women dress in traditional attire, which includes a headgear (*farangi*), in some regions. Only in the Fergana region of Uzbekistan, women are reported to follow the Islamic dress code, a tradition that has continued from the past. In Kyrgyzstan, there has been a rise in the number of men who wear a white Islamic hat, particularly when participating in public prayer sessions.

CHAPTER 4

The Democratic Drive

The fabrications that we have allegedly created some sort of a superstructure that will engulf its political rivals are far-fetched . . . if we look at the activity of any Kazakh political party, it is evident that none of them has grown to the level of a full-blown, organized party. Nonetheless, these parties . . . are making a positive contribution to laying the ground-work for democracy in Kazakhstan by putting continuing pressure on, and opposing, the authorities and government.

—MARAT TAJIN, DEPUTY CHAIR,
PEOPLE'S UNITY PARTY, KAZAKHSTAN

With all its negative consequences, the Communist domination of Central Asia brought about a rapid expansion of the intelligentsia whose modern secular outlook stood in sharp contrast to the traditional, and somewhat religious, worldview held by the majority of the population. Whereas most intellectuals remained dedicated to the principles of Marxist-Leninism, many other scientists, poets, and writers did so, not out of ideological conviction, but as a means of upward mobility in a rigid and highly centralized Soviet political structure. It was this latter segment of the Central Asian intelligentsia that considered Communism yet another expression of foreign colonial domination, thus later constituting the engine of the democratic drive in their respective republics. As an essentially imported ideology, however, democracy has a colossal task ahead, one that requires patience, perseverance, and above all, tenacity, if it is to become a permanent, or perhaps a dominant, feature of the Central Asian political landscape. Although in its formative stage and hence making it difficult to discern any significant lasting patterns of development, the following characteristics define the parameters of the democratic process within the larger Central Asian context.

First, the democratic organizations, quite expectedly, have not yet been fully institutionalized. As such, the personalities of individual leaders have largely been the source of organizational legitimacy. Consequently, competition for leadership has led to numerous splinter activities that have fragmented the democratic movement in Kazakhstan, Kyrgyzstan, and Uzbekistan. Second, with the exception of Turkmenistan, which has so far exhibited both weak Islamic and democratic tendencies, the democratic process has been most successful in those republics where the Islamic forces have had a considerably smaller following. This has placed Kazakhstan and Kyrgyzstan at the top of the list of the most likely republics to complete the transition to democracy. Third, the democratic parties in Uzbekistan and Tajikistan have been operating in an informal alliance with the Islamic forces, thus further legitimizing the governments' opposition to the former. Fourth, although the democratic parties have accepted a liberal democratic framework, they have considerable ideological differences, with some organizations advocating a nationalist platform with religious underpinnings. These ideological trends have led to the establishment of monoethnic parties with little or no prospects for their future success in the Central Asian multi-ethnic political environment. Fifth, a parallel democratic process has been initiated by the present republican leaders, which in the case of Uzbekistan, Tajikistan, and Turkmenistan, encompasses nothing more than the old Communist party structures and personnel under a new democratic facade. In Kazakhstan and Kyrgyzstan, where Presidents Nursultan Nazarbayev and Askar Akayev have distanced themselves from the old Communist parties, new presidential parties have been instituted to secure their political base of support. Sixth, with the exception of Kyrgyzstan, whose president has been supporting a genuine democratic process, the democratic forces have been working to achieve an electoral majority with the aim of removing the present republican governments. Finally, much like the Islamic organizations operating in the region, the democratic parties have so far demonstrated considerable differences in organizational reach, financial strength, and mobilization capacity that will, to a large extent, determine their fate in the highly fluid Central Asian political process.

FROM NATIONALISM TO DEMOCRACY

The drive toward democracy in Central Asia gathered considerable momentum in 1988-89 at the height of Gorbachev's campaign for restructuring the economic and political makeup of the Soviet Union. Ironically, those intellectuals who have now become the champions of democratic ideals were the least concerned about democracy in the initial stages of their political activities. Instead, it was nationalism with its various environmental, linguistic, cultural, and economic expressions that dominated the political agendas in the republics. The most vociferous of these early expressions that gathered a sizable following was the environmental movement in Kazakhstan whose organizational manifestation, Nevada-Semipalatinsk, received worldwide attention. Founded on February 28, 1989, the movement was concerned with such issues as the effects of nuclear testing, industrial pollution caused by the Kazakh chemical projects, and the degradation of agricultural land due to overintensive cultivation. The unsafe practices of nuclear testing at Semipalatinsk, in eastern Kazakhstan, had produced devastating health problems in the nearby towns and villages, causing definite dissatisfaction with the Communist government. To make matters worse, in mid-September 1990, an explosion in a nuclear-fuel factory in Ulba led to the radioactive contamination of a large area, including Ust-Kamenogorsk. An estimated 120,000 people were affected by the incident. Through organizing mass demonstrations, Nevada-Semipalatinsk played a significant role in forcing the government to place a ban on nuclear testing in 1991. The Uzbek intellectuals were also at the forefront of the battle against the environmental problems facing the republic. Of particular concern was the agricultural mismanagement that had caused both salination of the soil and the desiccation of the Aral Sea beyond repair. Linguistic grievances also played a major role in the politicization of the Tajik, Uzbek, Turkmen, and Kazakh populations, leading to the enactment of a series of legislation to promote the national languages of the Central Asian republics. Tajik, for instance, was declared the state language in 1989, and the teaching of Arabic script was temporarily reinstituted in the republic. A similar law went into effect in Kazakhstan in 1989, whereby the Kazakh language became the official language of the state, while Russian remained as the language of interethnic communication. In Kyrgyzstan, the first widespread expression of nationalism assumed an economic dimension. With the aim of alleviating housing shortages among the Kyrgyz nationals, the organization Ashar carried out housing construction on illegally confiscated land. A similar organization, Osh Aymaghi, pursued the same objective in Osh oblast, which contributed to the interethnic tension between the resident Uzbek and Kyrgyz populations, culminating in the violent clashes of the summer of 1990.

With the breakup of the Soviet Union imminent, the process of national revival gradually assumed significant political and organizational dimensions, encompassing issues that were intimately related to the substance and method of government. It was subsequent to this qualitative shift in orientation that democracy as an alternative ideological framework was seriously contemplated, giving birth to a multiplicity of democratic movements and currents in Central Asia. Interestingly enough, the overwhelming majority of political parties in Kazakhstan, Kyrgyzstan, Tajikistan, and Uzbekistan emerged out of similar movements for national independence and cultural revival. Later, however, personal rivalries and ideological discordance brought about a rapid polarization of these movements, giving rise to separate political entities.

The origin of a number of democratic parties in Kazakhstan is traced back to the Civil Movement of Kazakhstan, Azat, founded on July 1, 1990, by M. Shormanov, N. Nurbakhy, S. Aktayev (Aktaev), M. Esanaliyev, S. Shapagatov, N. Koishibekov, and U. Bibolkinov. As an essentially nationalist organization, Azat's objectives were geared toward the realization of Kazakh independence and sovereignty.[1] This issue dominated the activities of the movement in the fall of 1990 when some Russian inhabitants of Kazakhstan called for the annexation of a part of Kazakh territory by Russia. The problem was further exacerbated by the publication of Alexander Solzhenitsyn's proposal in September 1990, which justified such an action. Subsequently, the Azat movement organized demonstrations to counteract the growing threat of Russian nationalism within the Kazakh borders. The movement also targeted the Communist *nomenklatura* whose subservience to the Soviet central authority was claimed to have caused the destruction of the Kazakh cultural heritage. Azat, in essence, combined in a coherent whole various nationalist groupings in an effort to reassert Kazakh supremacy in the republic. The focus of the movement shifted somewhat in October 1990, when Kazakhstan formally declared its sovereignty, as emphasis was placed on other issues such as the economic status of the Kazakh population vis-à-vis Russians, Kazakh language, and culture. On the political front, the movement demanded the dissolution of the parliament and the creation of a coalitional government. On October 12, 1990, the first issue of the movement's newspaper, *Azat,* was published that carried criticisms of the government's Communist orientation and its inaction with regard to the socioeconomic problems of the Kazakh population who were characterized as second class citizens in their own republic. The general nationalist orientation of the Azat Civil Movement prevented the incorporation of other ethnic populations residing in Kazakhstan. As such, it has remained as a mono-ethnic organization, unable to expand its base of support in its struggle against the government.[2] The movement has been blamed for disturbing the delicate ethnic balance of the republic, hence contributing to the outbreak of small-scale interethnic violence in various regions in 1990.

Tajikistan's drive toward freedom and democracy was set in motion by a group of intellectuals in Moscow who wished to revive the Tajik national heritage. Their initiative was at first welcomed by the Communist Party Central Committee in 1989, as most other former Soviet republics had engaged in similar activities since 1987-88. Subsequently, an organization called Soghdian Association was established by Rajab Safar, Hakem Mohabat, Doost Muhammad Doost, and others to develop and pursue cultural programs designed to glorify Tajik national identity within the framework of what was essentially a student cultural society.[3] Since inception, however, the Communist Party kept a close watch on the activities of the organization with the objective of controlling its agenda. To the Central Committee's surprise, in a short period of time, the Soghdian Association attracted a large number of Tajik students and residents in Moscow, giving the organization a high degree of legitimacy and prestige. On January 9, 1989, Rajab Safar returned to Tajikistan to secure from the First Secretary of the Communist Party, Ghahar Makhkamov, a date for the official establishment of the Soghdian Association, and to discuss the agenda of the organization, which was to emphasize the need for extensive propaganda to reintroduce Tajikistan as a distinct national entity in a predominately Turkic Central Asia. Makhkamov agreed to convene a meeting on March 16, 1989, to discuss the association's operational plan, but no official permission was granted to hold a founding congress. Despite the Communist Party's reluctance to expedite the establishment of the organization, it was decided to hold a founding congress on February 28, 1989. The Communist Party's inability or unwillingness to contain the activities of the Association gave its leaders a sense of confidence, leading to the broadening of their agenda that included expressions of dissatisfaction with the existing socioeconomic and political conditions of the Tajik Republic. At the March 16 meeting with influential members of the Communist Party, the newly elected chairman of the Soghdian Association, Rajab Safar, and other founding members delivered a series of well-documented and highly critical speeches, blaming the Makhkamov government for the acute problems facing the republic. This historic meeting not only marked the beginning of public criticism of the Communist government in Tajikistan, but it also provided the impetus for other organizations to emerge within the republic soon after.

The first democratic organization in Tajikistan was established in September 1989 by an economist of the Tajik Academy of Sciences, Tohir Abdujabbor, under the name Rastokhez. Similar to its Kazakh counterpart, the Azat Civil Movement, Rastokhez was initially concerned with the question of Tajikistan's independence and sovereignty, and the revival of Tajik culture, in particular the Farsi language. In addition, the organization called for the renewal of the Islamic heritage and greater cultural autonomy for the Tajiks of Uzbekistan. Due to its nationalist agenda, the Rastokhez movement began to attract considerable followings shortly after its inception. The growth of the movement, however, was dealt a severe blow in mid-February 1990, when, during several days of public gatherings in the capital city Dushanbe, to protest the relocation of the Armenian refugees to Tajikistan, security forces killed nine and injured 15 protestors and bystanders.[4] It was reported that what had been initially a spontaneous peaceful demonstration against the Armenian resettlement, turned into an organized anti-government protest with a series of demands which included the resignation of the Communist Party leaders, jobs for the unemployed, improvements in housing shortages, return of all profits from the sale of cotton to the republic, and the closure of an unsafe aluminum plant.[5]

Rastokhez was blamed for the incitement of the public that resulted in arson fires that partially destroyed the Central Committee Building and the Ministry of Land Reclamation. Although Rastokhez publicly denied the government allegations, the public perception of the organization changed rather quickly, limiting its ability to maintain its rapidly expanding organizational structure. Despite its tarnished reputation, Rastokhez continued its activities, which by 1991 had assumed a more political orientation, calling for the establishment of a democratic rule in the republic and the dissolution of the parliament. Although supportive of a liberal democratic framework, in an interview conducted in 1992, Tohir Abdujabbor expressed his preference for a parliamentary rather than presidential form of government:

> Only the parliament and a prime minister should have the jurisdiction to rule. The new government may or may not have a president. Two years ago [1990], we needed a president, but I don't personally support a presidential system. Because in Tajikistan, democratic traditions are not solid and our people have been kept far from governing themselves, elections don't take place as they should. People don't know the candidate they are presented with and end up voting for the one who received the most advertising. . . . In Central Asia in general, conditions encourage the fostering of dictatorships under different veils, of communist, democratic or Islamic regimes. A parliamentary system is the only solution.[6]

For Rastokhez, however, Islam was considered a fact of life, one which was to be reckoned with, within the confines of its proposed democratic framework: "Our ideal is a democratic society where freedom and human rights of all citizens are assured . . . it is natural that in Tajikistan, the majority of people choose for Islam to play a great role in culture and lifestyle, as well as politics. One cannot say that Islam functions outside of politics. But government systems, the state organs and the prosecutor's office must not interfere with people's lives, nor have anything to do with ideology."[7]

The movement continued to play a significant, albeit diminished, role in post-independence Tajik politics until June 21, 1993, when the Supreme Court decided to ban all opposition organizations. However, much like other Central Asian nationalist organizations, Rastokhez failed to broaden its appeal among non-Tajik residents of the republic that accounted for nearly 35 percent of the population of 5.3 million. As such, the organization has remained as an essentially monoethnic entity with no real prospects for its further expansion, should the government lift the ban.

Similar to the Azat Civil Movement and the Rastokhez, the first sizable nationalist crusade in Uzbekistan was organized by the Birlik Movement for the Preservation of Uzbekistan's Natural, Material, and Spiritual Riches.[8] Birlik was established in February 1988 on the birthday of the famous Uzbek poet, Mir Ali Shir Navoi, by a number of intellectuals from the Uzbek Writers Union and the Academy of Sciences, among whom Muhammad Solih (Salih), Ibrahim Pulatov, Shokrat Ismatollayev, and Ahmad A'zam gained considerable popularity.[9] Birlik began to gather followers in the summer of 1988 when its leading members joined a protest rally organized in response to the construction of a factory in the Bostonlikski district, the site of which had been set aside for recreational purposes. The protest strengthened the resolve of the Uzbek population, paving the way for public criticisms of the Communist government on a number of cultural and socioeconomic issues that had not been expressed openly in recent decades. Birlik stood for the sovereignty and independence of Uzbekistan, lawful recognition of the Uzbek language as the official language of the republic, objective reexamination of Uzbek history, preservation of the natural environment, and economic diversification with the aim of supplanting the republic's cotton monoculture.

In March 1989, Birlik sponsored a mass demonstration calling for the official recognition of Uzbek as the state language. Similar demonstrations were held in October during which Ibrahim Pulatov and nearly 100 other demonstrators were arrested. In addition to the cultural and linguistic grievances, Birlik leaders voiced their dissatisfaction with the socioeconomic conditions of the Uzbek population. Solih, for instance, blamed the Communist government for the deteriorating economic conditions, rampant corruption, and the widespread health problems in the republic: "We have lost not only our lands and waters, we have forfeited the health of our people. The land is ailing and also the people who work on it. About eighty percent of Uzbeks live in *kishlaks,* traditional rural Uzbek settlements, where they work the cotton fields. This part of the population is basically in a state of ill health."[10] Also addressed frequently was the inferior economic status of the Uzbek population compared to the Russian residents of the republic. Most high-paying positions were traditionally filled by the Russians to the economic detriment of the Uzbeks many of whom were equally qualified to fill those positions. Much like Kazakhstan and Tajikistan, the nationalist vigor of the Birlik movement, at least in the initial stages of its activities, alienated the non-Uzbek population of the republic. Later, however, as the focus of the organization shifted away from Uzbek cultural glorification to the democratic struggle against the Communist regime, many Russians and other ethnic minorities joined the ranks of the movement.

In Kyrgyzstan, much like Tajikistan, the Communist Party undertook to control and dominate the activities of the newly emerging student and youth opposition in the 1987-88 period. In fact, the Communist Party hoped to rely on Komsomol as an institutional mechanism to define the nature and scope of the opposition activities. The Demos, Sovremennik, Pozitsia, and a host of other university clubs were created under Komsomol supervision to conduct open discussions with regard to the future political development of the Soviet Union.[11] The Communist Party plan, however, not only failed to define the agenda for the opposition, but also lost control over the organizational activities of the students, many of whom were fully aware of the government's ploy. In 1989, the leading members of the Demos created the Memorial, whose primary objective was to develop a systematic criticism of socialism to which much of the republic's political and economic ills were attributed. Much like the Soghdian Association, the Memorial played an instrumental role in the subsequent creation of a number of independent student organizations with clear nationalist and anti-Communist orientations. By the spring of 1989, the agenda of the opposition had been broadened to include the pressing socioeconomic problems of the Kyrgyz population, giving birth to Ashar, an organization which aimed at alleviating the housing shortages by confiscation of state-owned vacant land and construction of family dwellings for the Kyrgyz population.

On January 25-26, 1990, the leaders of Ashar and other informal associations organized a mass demonstration in front of the main government building on the central square to voice opposition to the Communist Party. Shortly thereafter, as a face-saving measure, the government agreed to issue registration permits for a number of small organizations to conduct their activities openly. The January demonstration marked the beginning of a new phase in the nationalist and democratic struggle against the Communist rule in Kyrgyzstan. Several new regional organizations were subsequently formed, pressing for a wide range of demands with clear nationalist underpinnings of which the Democratic Party of the City of Maily Sae and the Democratic League of Jalalabad enjoyed considerable support. However, the rapid expansion of these organizations began to decelerate and weaken the Kyrgyz anti-Communist movement. Subsequently, a decision was made to coordinate the activities of these organizations whose numbers had reached 24 by May 1990.

On May 26, 1990, with the initiative of Qazat Akhmatov, Jepar Jeksheyev, Tupchubek Turgunaliyev, Toulon Dihqanov, and Qadir Motqaziyev, an umbrella organization under the name of the Democratic Movement of Kyrgyzstan (DDK) was formed. Approximately a week later, a series of violent disturbances engulfed the Osh oblast during which a number of Kyrgyz were killed and injured by Uzbeks over land and housing disputes.[12] The discredited Masaliyev government, unable to bring the situation under control, sought the assistance of the DDK whose leaders enjoyed widespread support in the region. During the ensuing negotiations, the DDK played a substantial role in preventing further bloodshed. With its new-gained confidence, on September 7, 1990, DDK issued a statement that included the following demands:[13]

- Declaration of independence and the drafting of a new constitution;
- Socioeconomic improvement in the life of the Kyrgyz population of the republic;
- Freedom of choice in the adoption of a new political structure for Kyrgyzstan;
- Creation of a multiparty system;
- Freedom to secede from the Soviet Union;
- Transfer of political and economic powers of the republic from the Communist Party to the Parliament;
- Development of a market economy and the acceptance of all forms of property;
- Health and environmental guarantees;
- Kyrgyz citizenship for all residents of the republic;
- The right to represent the republic must be given only to the president and the parliament;
- Dismantling of the one party rule, and freedom of choice in party affiliation;
- Maintenance of the current borders and the republic's right to claim ownership of all that is within the territorial boundaries of Kyrgyzstan;[14]

- The adoption of the policy of noninterference by parties in government affairs;
- Conformity to the international laws and norms of behavior.

The DDK commanded approximately 300,000 followers, the majority of whom were the Kyrgyz nationals who continued to push for the dismantling of the Communist regime. In October 1990, during an extraordinary session of the Kyrgyz Supreme Soviet, and with the support of the DDK, Askar Akayev, the liberal-minded head of the Academy of Sciences, was elected the president of the republic, ushering in a new phase in the political development of the free Kyrgyzstan.

Unlike other Central Asian republics, the nationalist movement in Turkmenistan was severely hampered by the noticeable absence of an active intelligentsia. Nevertheless, in the late 1980s, a small group of Turkmen intellectuals who had been influenced by the events in other Soviet republics began to express concern over the status of Turkmen language, indigenous arts, and environmental and socioeconomic issues. Under the Communist rule, the republic had suffered from health and ecological problems associated with the extensive cultivation of cotton since the completion in 1953 of the Kara Kum canal, which diverted massive amounts of water from the Aral Sea into Turkmen grasslands. In addition, the chemical pollution caused by the overutilization of pesticides, coupled with the lack of medical and sanitary facilities, had given Turkmenistan the worst public health record of all the former Soviet republics. Issues of this nature dominated the agenda of the intellectuals who had been provided with a carefully monitored public forum in 1989.

The Communist Party, however, continued to dominate the politics of Turkmenistan, making only a few minor concessions to a largely ineffective nationalist movement. One such concession was the May 1990 language legislation that declared Turkmen the state language, but leaving Russian as the language of interethnic communication. As Rahim Esenov, a well-known Turkmen writer has indicated, the inability of the intellectuals to mobilize support of the magnitude experienced in other Central Asian republics has been due, in part, to their "envious and dogmatic" approach to politics.[15] Also significant, has been what the chief editor of the Turkmen literary newspaper *Edebiyat ve Sungat,* Tirkish Jumageldiyev, has referred to as a noticeable lack of "energetic commentators and writers whose speeches inspire the people." But more important, the movement has been the victim of tribal rivalries that has been more pervasive in Turkmenistan than any other Central Asian republic. It is interesting to note that President Saparmurt Niyazov enjoys the support of the tribe of his origin, Teke, which constitutes 40 percent of the Turkmen population. Niyazov's tribal association has been a significant force in preventing the emergence of a united Turkmen opposition capable of influencing the course of events in favor of more radical reforms in the republic. Yet, as will be discussed later, two small but growing democratic organizations have been pressing for wholesale liberalization of the republic, despite continuous crackdown and repression by the Turkmen government.

With the collapse of Communism and the declaration of independence by the Central Asian republics in 1991, the nationalist forces lost one of the most critical elements that had thus far provided the necessary organizational cohesion and the unity of purpose in their struggle against the vestiges of Soviet power. In the absence of a common adversary, the nature and scope of the nationalist movements began to assume new qualitative dimensions as group consensus and political accord gave way to personal rivalries and ideological dissension, the outcome of which was the emergence of a wide spectrum of political parties with overlapping agendas.

THE NATIONAL DEMOCRATIC PARTIES

The nationalist forces in Central Asia constitute the backbone of a multiplicity of parties and political organizations whose basic objective has been to promote the interests of a particular ethnic population in each republic. Several characteristics define the broad structural and functional parameters of these parties. First, there are considerable differences in the intensity of nationalist sentiments, with some parties advocating an uncompromising radical platform, while others are following a moderate course of action. Second, most parties suffer from organizational and financial weaknesses, which have so far limited their capacity to mobilize the substantial support necessary to capture a larger share of political power. Third, some organizations have incorporated Islam into their nationalist agenda, thus reducing the prospects for forging alliances with other nationalist parties that assign a considerably smaller role to religion. Finally, there is a positive correlation between the strength of nationalist movements and the ratio of the Russian population residing in each Central Asian republic. This has placed Kazakhstan and Kyrgyzstan at the top of the list of the republics whose future political stability may require a particular attention to the ethnic demands of such organizations.[16]

The Azat Party of Kazakhstan is one of the main nationalist organizations in the republic. The party held its founding congress on September 4, 1991, during which Sabetkazi Aktayev was elected its chairman. Since inception, Azat has advocated a nationalist platform, which, among other things, calls for Kazakh cultural and linguistic supremacy and a complete decolonization of the country. In short, the party has been moving against the political and economic interest of the Russians, whose population was only slightly smaller than its Kazakh counterpart. Due to its nationalist orientation as well as personality conflicts among its leaders, the party has splintered three times since 1991. The first division occurred almost immediately after the party held its constituent assembly, leading to the separation of Marat Shormanov and Nurbakhy Koishibekov; they discussed the creation of a centrist party with Uljas Suleimonov and Mukhtar Shakhanov who later became the founders of the People's Congress of Kazakhstan. The second split happened in October of 1992, four months after the party participated in peaceful rallies in front of the Parliament during which protestors demanded that "members of the opposition be given government posts."[17] It was reported that the June 14-24 rallies intensified the personality conflicts, which helped magnify the policy differences among the party leaders, causing the resignation of S. Aktayev, who later decided to support the government of President Nazarbayev after all. Aktayev has since created his own party, the Republican Party of Kazakhstan. The third splinter took place in October 1993, when the new chairman of Azat, Kamal Ormantay, established the National Democratic Party.[18] Details of the party's objectives have not yet been publicized, but Ormantay has reportedly adopted an environmental platform, reaching out to the non-Kazakh population in an effort to improve his chances in an electoral competition.

These developments have adversely affected the popularity of Azat as the main nationalist party in Kazakhstan.[19] The party has maintained its mono-ethnic character with limited prospects for its future parliamentary success. Although its present leaders claim to have a nationwide organizational network, the party maintains offices in nine oblasts. However, it is strongest in those oblasts where Kazakhs constitute the majority, that is in three out of 18 oblasts. These include south Kazakhstan (Chimkent), Jambul, Atyrau, Almaty (city), Alama-Ata, West Kazakhstan, Mangistau, and Taldykorgan. The party is particularly strong in the first three oblasts.

The Azat membership has been declining since October 1992 and it has been reported that a large portion of its estimated 30,000 to 40,000 members have defected to the Republican and National Democratic parties. Azat draws much of its support from urban areas. The bulk of its membership are high school graduates between the ages of thirty and forty. There is also some moderate support from among the more educated intellectuals concerned with the plight of the Kazakh population.[20] Though former members of the Communist Party, the majority of the members had been on the periphery of political power during the Soviet era. The party does not have adequate funding and thus its propaganda activities have been severely hampered. Its official news-paper, *Azat,* has a circulation of 40,000.

Azat has not yet developed an alternative policy platform to challenge the government, but it has formed strong views on a number of pertinent issues facing Kazakh society today. According to Batirhan Darimbet, the underlying demand of the party is "the restructuring of the political and economic makeup of Kazakhstan solely for the benefit of the Kazakh people." As such, the party has been critical of the government's cultural and economic policies, which have been designed to maintain the delicate ethnic balance of the republic:

> We have no objections to Russians living in Kazakhstan, but in Turkey which is a multiethnic society everyone speaks Turkish. We want the same for our republic. We were the victims of Russification for decades and although the situation is stable now, it can change rather quickly. We are worried that the Russians may reestablish their dominance in the region. Why should Russian be the language of interethnic communication when everywhere in the world English is the international language? The Russians began to learn Kazakh when we declared our language the state language, but when the Constitution gave Russian the status of interethnic communication, they stopped learning Kazakh. Given the government's policy, our youth will never learn their own language.[21]

Azat has also been critical of the ongoing privatization program, which is claimed to have benefited the Russians of the republic:

> Last year [1992] we offered a plan for economic privatization. We proposed to carry out a property distribution program on the basis of the labor of our ancestors who built our society. We suggested that preference be given in property distribution, to those who had lived in Kazakhstan since 1917 and who could document their residency. We do not believe that more recent immigrants should be given the same status for acquiring property. Our proposal was turned down by the government. But, six months later, Belarus adopted an iden-tical proposal to ours. According to the laws on privatization, all kinds of property can be sold to individuals who could afford them. This has led to the concentration of wealth in the hands of a few while the majority of Kazakhs have been left destitute.[22]

In light of the fact that most Russians have relocated in Kazakhstan much later than 1917, the Azat's privatization program effectively eliminates Russians from acquiring any property.

Leaving aside Azat's cultural and economic grievances, the party holds a moderate view on the role of Islam in the Kazakh society. Most members do not regularly follow Islamic precepts and do not encourage religious practices. The party leadership, however, does not support the head of the Kazakh Religious Board, Mufti Nysanbai Ratbek, who is claimed to have maintained good relations with the old Communists, many of whom hold prominent positions within the government of Nazarbayev. Azat has been supportive of Kazi Jaqob, the former head of the Kazakh Religious Board who was removed for his independent views. The kazi has been involved in the activities of the party since the beginning. Since his removal he has been preaching in the Kokchetav region in Northern Kazakhstan.

A more moderate nationalist party is the Republican Party of Kazakhstan whose chairman, S. Aktayev, and three regional leaders from Kokchetav, Turgai, and Kustanai splintered from Azat in October 1992. Two factors have been instrumental in the breakup of the Azat party. First, there seems to have been disagreement over the choice of party strategy with some advocating a more confrontational approach, while Aktayev favored a more conciliatory course of action. Second, personal rivalry over the question of party leadership had apparently forced Aktayev to leave Azat. Aktayev has since toned down his nationalist rhetoric but in essence has been advocating a watered-down version of the Azat nationalist views. Furthermore, the Republican party has chosen to support the policies of President Nazarbayev for the sake of stabilizing the potentially explosive ethnic situation in the republic.[23]

In addition to Azat, a small but highly active nationalist organization called Jeltoqsan has been pushing for Kazakh economic and cultural reassertion in the republic. The party began its activities as an interest group to help gain the release of those involved in the 1986 Alma-Ata riots, which broke out in response to the removal of the first secretary of the Kazakh Communist Party, Kunayev.[24] Jeltoqsan held its founding congress as a party in December 1988. More radical in orientation than Azat, Jeltoqsan has been pressing for the voluntary out-migration of Russians from Kazakhstan. In April 1992, the party drafted a ten-point proposal that symbolized the essence of its demands:

- Complete decolonization of Kazakhstan;
- Kazakh language to become the sole communication language of the republic;
- All foreign military bases to cease operations and come under Kazakh jurisdiction;
- Military conscription to be abolished and in its place a new professional army created;[25]

- Political and economic reforms should take into account the interest of the Kazakh people first;
- Kazakhstan's present boundaries should remain unaltered;
- The government should provide adequate incentives for all Kazakhs living outside the republic to facilitate their return;
- Parliament should be represented by all parties, according to free and fair elections;
- Greater cooperation between the Turkic republics must be established;
- The Islamic Shariah must become the law of the land.[26]

The party's emphasis on Islam has been one of the most significant obstacles to gaining approval of the Kazakh population, many of whom have not been in favor of the imposition of an Islamic legal framework in the republic. Given its illegal status, in April 1992, Jeltoqsan proposed to join forces with Azat in order to expand its sphere of influence. Disagreements over strategy and objectives, however, prevented the alliance from going forward. Nevertheless, the party has been active in staging small-scale demonstrations to voice its opposition to government policies. For instance, on September 15, 1993, Jeltoqsan, in collaboration with other nationalist organizations, staged a gathering during which they called for the resignation of the prime minister, Sergey Treshenko, and the reform of the government's privatization program.[27] Yet again, on October 12, 1993, Jeltoqsan joined Alash and Pokolenie, a pensioners' advocacy group, to demand higher social welfare expenditures to offset the rising cost of living in Kazakhstan. Despite its activities, however, Jeltoqsan has been faced with dwindling support and a shrinking budget. The party published the final issue of its newspaper in May 1993. The majority of its members are young high school graduates. Given its radical orientation and its unwillingness to compromise its anti-Russian stance, Jeltoqsan will remain as a minor player in Kazakhstan's political future.

If Azat and Jeltoqsan represent the organized expression of Kazakh nationalism, Yedinstvo and the Social Democratic Party symbolize the aspirations of the Russian residents of Kazakhstan. The co-chair of Yedinstvo, Yuri S. Startsev, has been engaged in lobbying the government to help preserve the generally privileged position of Russians in Kazakhstan. Its members have been more than sympathetic to the idea of annexation of parts of northern Kazakhstan by Russia. The Social Democratic Party was created in 1989 so as to counterbalance the Azat Civil Movement and to reduce its potential impact on the political process. Its chair and vice-chair also operate an independent radio and television station in the capital. The Social Democratic Party has espoused a more moderate political view than Yedinstvo, yet both parties have been pursuing the same basic objectives with regard to the political and economic status of the Russians. Quite expectedly, both parties in essence face the same predicament as the all-Kazakh nationalist parties with little hope for their future parliamentary success.[28]

The Party of National Revival (Asaba) and Erkin are the main national democratic parties in Kyrgyzstan that have been advocating a political platform similar to Azat, the Republican Party, and Jeltoqsan in Kazakhstan. Asaba first attracted attention as a movement during the May 1, 1990, parade when its members marched in a separate column carrying their own blue flag instead of the traditional Communist red banner. The movement was later organized as a party by Chupareshti Bazarbayev and Jepar Jeksheyev on October 20, 1990, attracting nationwide attention three days later when it organized a hunger strike to voice its opposition to the Communist government. Ever since, Asaba has been pressing for a program of reform that assigns priority to the cultural, political, and economic status of the Kyrgyz population in the republic. In 1992, the party presented two pieces of legislation concerning citizenship and immigration to the parliament in an effort to eliminate dual citizenship and force the non-Kyrgyz population to leave the republic. It was proposed that citizenship should be awarded to those who could provide proof of residency in Kyrgyzstan prior to 1916. This in essence excludes almost all non-Kyrgyz citizens from the legislation.[29] Asaba has been critical of government for its insensitivity to the plight of the Kyrgyz population whose standard of living is claimed to have been much lower than the other nationalities residing in Kyrgyzstan: "We insist that the interest of Kyrgyz people should be given priority. We are against materialism and believe in the significance of spiritual life. Since the main goal of our party is national revival, we believe that all aspects of Kyrgyz life should be revived including Islam, Kyrgyz language and culture."[30] In July 1992, Asaba made yet another legislative appeal to halt the privatization of the state sector since most shares have been purchased by the urban population, of which only 20 percent are Kyrgyz nationals. It also demanded a ban on the sale of land to the non-Kyrgyz population.[31]

Despite its continuing efforts, Asaba lacks a sufficient organizational network in the Issyk-Kul, Naryn, and Talas oblasts, which are predominantly inhabited by Russian residents. However, it commands a moderate following in the Bishkek, Osh, and Jalalabad oblasts. Due to its radical nationalist orientation the party has attracted a small following of about 2,000, most of whom lack higher education and seem to have come from a rural socio-economic background. The party's efforts to set up its own newspaper have been frustrated by financial problems, thus limiting its ability to expand its base of support through propaganda.

The second nationalist party, Erkin Kyrgyzstan, was organized on February 9, 1991, by Umarbek Tekebayev and Tupchubek Turgunaliyev. The latter's domineering personality and confrontational attitude has been instrumental in the disintegration of the Democratic Movement of Kyrgyzstan. Although the party has been advocating a policy of Kyrgyz national revival, since 1992 it has moderated its nationalist stance on various issues in order to increase its membership and enhance the party composition, which is currently monoethnic. Erkin, for instance, has abandoned the principle of "Kyrgyz interests only" in favor of "Kyrgyz interests first." It has also been advocating a secular system of government within which religious freedom must be ensured. As far as the party's political and economic platform is concerned, Turgunaliyev offered the following remarks:

> Politically we stand for the creation of a free and independent Kyrgyzstan. We believe in political pluralism and individual rights, and fight against any type of extremism or ethnic domination. We would like to implement these ideas for the benefit of the Kyrgyz nation. In terms of political procedures, we wish to compete in parliamentary elections and we categorically condemn violence as a method of achieving political power. Economically, we are in favor of all forms of property including state, private, and mixed, but we prefer private property. We also support individual economic initiative and freedom of economic activity.[32]

Erkin Kyrgyzstan was heavily involved in the constitutional debate in 1993 and reportedly had developed an alternative draft of the Constitution that was designed to promote Kyrgyz national interests. Although the government version of the Constitution was approved by the Parliament in May 1993, as a compromise with the nationalist opposition forces its implementation was postponed until 1995, when a new parliamentary election is scheduled to be held. Erkin has also been involved in drafting various pieces of legislation that have been submitted to the Parliament for consideration, among which the following have been widely publicized. The first bill entitled "Foreign Investment and Capital Export," was designed to provide incentives for foreign investments by allowing capital to move freely in and out of the republic. Under current regulations, the Kyrgyz government has placed restrictions on the outflow of capital. The second piece of legislation, on "Extension of Credit," obligated the government to provide financial opportunities for those who qualify to start their own business. The third bill called for a reduction in taxes so as to stimulate business investment. Finally, Erkin has proposed an election bill based on a secret ballot and multi-candidate principles. However, as of October 1993, none of the above proposals have been given serious consideration by the government of Askar Akayev.

In September 1992, an internal political rivalry between Tekebayev, who represented the liberal wing of the party, and Turgunaliyev, who commanded the radical wing, led to the defection of Tekebayev and an estimated 30 percent of the members of Erkin Kyrgyzstan, who later created a new liberal democratic party, Ata Meken.[33] Turgunaliyev, however, has been conducting an aggressive campaign to expand the party's organizational network. It has also been frequently opposing the government polices. For instance, on March 1, 1993, in a gathering of the democratic forces organized at the initiative of the President Akayev, Erkin Kyrgyzstan and Asaba presented an ultimatum, demanding the resignation of Prime Minister Tursunbek Chingishev.[34] Yet again, on July 30, 1993, Erkin mounted another attack on the government, criticizing its economic policies, in particular the premature introduction of the national currency in May 1993, which is claimed to have greatly contributed to the economic deterioration of the republic. Subsequently, the party called for the dissolution of the parliament and early presidential and parliamentary elections.[35]

The membership of the organization is estimated at about 7,000, mostly young high-school graduates and college students between the ages of eighteen and thirty. The party has been publishing a popular newspaper entitled *Erk,* which as of July 1993, was the only party newspaper in the republic. Although the financial status of the party has not been disclosed, Erkin seems to be solvent. Much like Asaba, Erkin's organizational reach is limited to those oblasts where the Kyrgyz population is large, as in Jalalabad and Osh, though party structures exist in the Russian-dominated oblasts Issyk-Kul and Talas.[36] Erkin has the potential to capture some parliamentary seats in the upcoming election, but will most likely remain as a marginal power player in the Kyrgyz political process in the near future.

THE LIBERAL DEMOCRATIC PARTIES

In conjunction with the nationalist parties, a host of liberal democratic parties have entered the Central Asian political stage since independence. Here, too, Kazakhstan and Kyrgyzstan have been most successful in establishing viable organizations with relatively well-developed party platforms capable of influencing the future political development of their respective republics. The People's Congress of Kazakhstan is the most popular of the liberal democratic parties. Organized by two well-known poets, Uljas Suleimonov and Mukhtar Shakhanov, the party held its founding congress on October 5, 1991. According to Shakhanov, the party was created to "prevent the socialist party from gathering strength and again emerging as the ruling party which could lead to totalitarianism once more."[37] Since inception, the party has been criticized by the nationalist forces for catering to the needs of the Russians to the detriment of Kazakhs. Clearly, the party leaders have shied away from the extremist views of "Kazakh supremacy" in the political and economic spheres espoused by the nationalist organizations. The People's Congress has been well aware of the highly sensitive ethnic situation in the republic, and accordingly has strived to develop a multiethnic organization, thus maximizing its chances of winning an electoral majority in the upcoming parliamentary elections. Nevertheless, the party has been faced with internal opposition by those who believe that Suleimonov has not been sensitive enough to the plight of the Kazakh people. It is reported that during its first congress, held on June 29, 1992, complaints were raised that the program and the charter of the party lacked adequate national basis, which prompted the following response by Suleimonov: "Forming a party on a national basis is easy, but it may lead only to division of the people. We have chosen the most difficult path forming a party of all people, and we will not deviate from it."[38] Suleimonov's stance in this regard is claimed to have caused the resignation of Shakhanov from his post as co-chair at that session, though he has retained his place in the central committee of the party. Recently, at the urging of Suleimonov, the People's Congress passed a resolution to create a Russian-Kazakh federation with the objective of establishing an interstate union with common banking, fiscal, and credit policies.[39] Quite expectedly, the resolution came under heavy criticism by the nationalist parties who accused Suleimonov of "selling out to the Russians." Leaving aside the party's positive orientation toward Russia and the Russian residents of Kazakhstan, its program presents a well-balanced liberal democratic framework with little room for meaningful criticism. It, for instance, calls for political pluralism, protection of individual rights, a mixed economy, and social welfare guarantees for those unable to earn a living due to age, health, or other justifiable reasons.[40]

The People's Congress has a well-developed organizational structure covering all 18 oblasts of Kazakhstan. Since 1992, Suleimonov has been traveling on a semi-regular basis to various regions to campaign on the party's behalf and to coordinate the activities of local leaders. Preparations for the 1995 parliamentary elections are already underway. On May 17, 1993, for instance, the Karaganda branch of the party held a meeting to devise campaign strategies and coordinate its activities with the local branch of the Nevada-Semipalatinsk in order to mobilize election support. In Suleimonov's presence, Dimkesh Mukhanov, the popular director of a local metal production factory, was elected the head of the party branch to organize its election efforts.[41]

Similar activities have also been reported in other regions of the republic. Although party structures exist in the Chimkent and Jambul oblasts, Suleimonov does not seem to enjoy the same popularity as in those regions where the Russian population is considerably larger.

Besides the president's party—the Union of People's Unity—the People's Congress is perhaps the only liberal democratic party that has adequate funding to support its expanding structural network. Over the past two years, Suleimonov has established a number of viable commercial ventures in connection with the Nevada-Semipalatinsk, making healthy profits from the sale of oil, metals, and granite rock. As a means of attracting support, the People's Congress has also been sponsoring small-scale economic projects that benefit the local communities. It is this financial strength that has made the party a potentially strong electoral contender. Although the members have denied the possibility of Suleimonov running for president, many believe that he is a likely candidate. The party has a weekly publication that is printed in Russian and Kazakh with a circulation of 40,000. Unlike Azat, the People's Congress has among its leadership and rank-and-file members many active former Communists who had held high positions during the Soviet era. Suleimonov, for instance, was a member of the Supreme Soviet of Kazakhstan. The party has been most popular among intellectuals, but has also been attracting a wide spectrum of the Kazakh citizens. According to the first vice-chair, Amanchy Gunashev, 15 nationalities are represented in the party with Russians constituting 40 percent of an estimated 40,000 to 50,000 total membership. Some observers, however, argue that the party has been organized around the charismatic personality of Suleimonov and will lose its appeal once he is no longer in charge.

In addition to the People's Congress, two smaller liberal democratic parties have been active in Kazakhstan. The Party of the Law-based Development of Kazakhstan was created in September 1993 by Vitali Voronov and Alexandr Peregrin. Both are currently serving as the deputy chairman and secretary of the Kazakh parliament's human rights committee respectively. The party; Peregrin pointed out, had been formed to stop Kazakhstan turning into a "state under tyranny," and to ensure the rule of law in the republic. Several hundred have so far joined the party, which is preparing for the upcoming elections. According to *Nezavisimaya Gazeta,* its chances of success are good, since the nationalist and liberal democratic parties in Kazakhstan have neither a broad base of support, nor clear goals and ideas.[42] The second party, National Democratic, was founded on October 3, 1993, by Kamal Ormantay, the former head of the Azat Party.[43] Apparently, Ormantay has abandoned his nationalist agenda in favor of a more moderate platform that "intends to contribute to the strengthening of inter-ethnic accord in the republic." The party has offered to cooperate with those political forces that are interested in creating a civilized and prosperous nation. Ormantay has announced that he will give priority to defending the rights of the citizens of the ecological disaster zones, where the native population mainly resides. He has also been reaching out to the non-Kazakh population of the republic in order to improve his chances in an electoral competition.[44]

Ata Meken, Republican People's Party, and Kyrgyz Democratic Movement —a party since 1993—present the liberal democratic wing of the newly created parties in Kyrgyzstan.[45] All three parties have been advocating the following platform to attract not only Kyrgyz, but also other ethnic minorities in the republic:

- Executive supremacy;
- Professional parliament;[46]
- Rule of law;
- Equity in privatization and freedom for all forms of property;
- Social welfare guarantees.

Ata Meken was instituted on December 16, 1992, subsequent to the defection of Kamila Kenenbayeva and Umarbek Tekebayev from Erkin Kyrgyzstan. The party's executive secretary, Apasov Resbek, provided the following explanation as to the underlying reason for the establishment of Ata Meken: "We wanted to create a centrist platform for those who were not in support of the parties on the left and on the right. For instance, Asaba and Erkin were too far to the left and the Party of the Communist people of Kyrgyzstan was too far to the right. Earlier there were demonstrations and strikes that were organized by the extreme parties which had a de-stabilizing effect on our society. We created our party to give voice to those who disapproved of the radical tendencies exhibited by the extremist parties."[47] The party stands for evolutionary change, national consolidation, and Kyrgyz national revival within the limitations imposed by the multiethnic reality of the republic. Although the party has not yet developed sound policy alternatives to that of the government of Askar Akayev, it has been critical of the government's monetary and economic policies, in particular the timing of the introduction of national currency (som), in May 1993, and agricultural privatization has been regarded as premature at best.[48] The party's sensitivity to the political and economic conditions of non-Kyrgyz has helped its position considerably. As of 1993, the party had an estimated 5,000 members, 30 percent of whom are non-Kyrgyz. The party has some support among the intellectuals and high school students, as well as government bureaucrats and workers.

The Republican People's Party was organized on March 7, 1992, and officially registered on September 5, 1992. According to its co-chair, Aripa Turdaliyeva, the party was formed to "fight against discrimination on ethnic, social, and religious grounds." Similar to Ata Meken, the party has been critical of the rapid pace of economic reform, but it has also been calling for a permanent and considerably larger economic role for the government, which seems to run against the present global economic trends. The party has been even less nationalist in orientation than Ata Meken, in particular on issues concerning language and religion. While Ata Meken has been pressing for the eventual introduction of the Kyrgyz language to replace Russian, the Republican People's Party has been indifferent to the choice of language. Similarly the party places no emphasis on religious revival. In fact, Turdaliyeva has indicated that "we should not give priority to Islam simply because most Kyrgyz are Muslims."[49] This view is not held by the Ata Meken leaders, who argue that Islam should be revived within the parameters of a secular state.

From the financial point of view, the Republican People's Party is in an excellent situation as it has managed to attract the members of the powerful union, Manas Ata, as well as the largest clothing factory, Ilbis. Also noteworthy, is the support given to the party by some parliament members and the old *nomenklatura,* many of whom have capitalized on the privatization drive by establishing profitable private ventures, which have translated into sizable contributions to the party. The overwhelming majority of the party's estimated 3,000 members are intellectuals and new entrepreneurs from the major cities in the republic. Although the party has established local chapters, it has essentially concentrated its activities in the capital city, Bishkek, and in the Issyk-Kul and Talas oblasts. Its membership is rapidly expanding and will perhaps surpass that of its rivals in the next two years.

The Democratic Movement of Kyrgyzstan (DDK), headed by Jepar Jeksheyev was registered as a party on July 20, 1993.[50] Although slightly more nationalist in orientation than Ata Meken and the Republican People's Party, the DDK has been supportive of the principles outlined earlier. The party, however, has been more critical of the government's economic policies than its counterparts, in particular in the area of implementation of the privatization, which is handled by the State Property Fund. Jeksheyev has been skeptical of the manner in which the above institution has conducted its affairs, arguing that more than 50 percent of the newly created joint stock companies have been purchased by a handful of people close to the center of political power. In September 1993, the local chapter of the party in the Naryn oblast organized a protest under the banner of "dissatisfaction with the social and economic policy of the government of Kyrgyz republic." The local chairman of the party,

Kadmambetov, pointed out that the rally was designed to remind the government of the poor economic conditions in Naryn and stated that "instead of concern for the people in the oblast, they [the government] have started building an as yet unnecessary trolley bus line, while in winter the townspeople will have nothing with which to heat their stoves. Young people and specialists are leaving their home areas, leaving old people in the villages."[51] The DDK has an estimated 2-3,000 members. Most are between the ages of twenty-five and thirty-five and approximately 50 percent have secondary and technical education.[52] The party lacks a nationwide organizational network, and seems to have moderate support in the Issyk-Kul and Chu oblasts, and the capital Bishkek, and a weak following in the Osh, Talas, and Jalalabad oblasts.

In Uzbekistan and Tajikistan the democratic process has been more limited in scope and less pluralistic in nature. The largest democratic organization, the Birlik Movement, was formed in November 1988 and was permitted to register as a movement in 1991. By January 1992, at the time of the visit of the United States Secretary of State James Baker, Birlik had gathered 10,000 signatures, almost three and a half times the limit set by the Ministry of Justice to be granted legal party status. Nevertheless, the application was turned down, forcing Birlik to operate illegally. According to Ibrahim Pulatov, the initial objectives of the party were the achievement of independence, the politicization of the masses, and the democratization of the Uzbek society.[53] Ever since the declaration of independence, Birlik has been pressing for a complete separation of powers, recognition of human rights, drafting of a new democratic constitution, and economic privatization in all spheres of economy, including land.[54]

Due to personal rivalries and differences in political strategy, some leading members of Birlik, most notably, Muhammad Solih and Ahmad A'zam, left the party and created Erk in 1990.[55] The main controversy revolved around two issues. First, some Birlik leaders were of the opinion that public demonstrations should be used as a method of political struggle against the government. Erk leaders, on the other hand, preferred a purely parliamentary means to realize their objectives. Second, Birlik was in favor of the dissolution of the parliament altogether, while Erk proposed to reform the existing parliament by replacing candidates who had Communist tendencies. The tolerant attitude of Erk helped secure an official recognition in September 1991, allowing Muhammad Solih to run as a presidential candidate against Karimov in the December 1991 elections, though he was handily defeated, receiving only 12 percent of the vote. It later became apparent that Karimov's lenient attitude toward Erk was part of a premeditated plan to create an image of a democratic election in order to influence public opinion in the West in his favor.[56]

In the absence of genuine democratic reforms, Muhammad Solih began to intensify his criticism of the government and, in an unexpected move, joined Birlik's call for public demonstrations on July 2, 1992.[57] Later that day Solih resigned his post as a deputy to the parliament when his request to speak to the floor was denied. In an interview with Interfax, he pointed out: "The Erk party has maintained stability in the republic by its silence for two years; however, this silence did not serve democratic reforms but was strengthening the old Communist system and dictatorship."[58] In response to Solih's growing condemnation of the government, orders were sent out to confiscate printing equipment, freeze bank accounts, and move the party offices to the suburbs of the Tashkent.[59] Thanks to Karimov's initial approval of Erk's activities, its membership expanded from 5,000 to 40,000 by 1992.[60]

The activities of Erk were severely curtailed as of September 1992, and later the organization was in effect banned.[61] Birlik, however, has been less successful in conducting its affairs freely and its leadership has been more frequently subjected to coercion than has the Erk leaders.[62] Birlik has also been discredited for its willingness to cooperate with the Uzbek IRP. Pulatov was among the participants in the founding congress of IRP in 1991 and had been marginally involved with their activities in Fergana. Pulatov, however, has justified the party's positive attitude toward the IRP by saying that the Islamic movement is in a better position to reach people through mosques than the democratic movement, which is essentially banned. Birlik's position in this regard has been based on tactical rather than philosophical considerations: "people who have already lost their faith in the Communist regime are afraid to join the democrats but not afraid to join the Islamic movement."[63] He has also indicated that it is better to be in contact with the IRP so as "to move Islam in a more progressive direction."[64]

Both Birlik and Erk are essentially urban oriented and enjoy the support of the intelligentsia. However, Birlik has been reaching out to the rural areas since 1992, using a variety of propaganda tactics to discredit Karimov for its unwillingness to privatize collective farms.[65] Birlik has also struck an alliance with the Business People's Movement, an organization created by the newly-emerging class of small entrepreneurs, to further expand its base of support. From an organizational point of view, Erk has been more successful in setting up a nationwide network.[66] Given its semi-legal status, Birlik, however, has been less successful in developing an organizational infrastructure. Both parties are essentially monoethnic, though Russians and other ethnic minorities have been incorporated. From a financial point of view, both parties have been experiencing difficulties, particularly since Karimov banned the financing of public organizations by sources outside the republic. In August 1992, Erk lost

192,000 rubles claimed to have been contributed to the party by a Russian sponsor in Moscow. This, coupled with constant government intervention, have prevented either party from publishing a newspaper on a regular basis, thus limiting their capacity to use propaganda to attract more followings. Since early 1992, Birlik has been publishing a newspaper in Russia, titled *The Independent Weekly,* that has been smuggled into Uzbekistan but with limited success. As to the membership of Birlik, there are no verifiable reports, but according to Pulatov, the party would not receive more than 20 to 25 percent of the vote in a presidential election.

In addition to Erk and Birlik, a host of other parties have been set up by individuals who support the policies of the President Karimov. One such party, Vatan Taraqiaty, was established on August 5, 1992, by Usman Azim, a politician and former deputy chairman of the Birlik Movement. The party has been officially recognized by the government and has so far attracted some 4,000 to 5,000 members, most of whom are scholars, writers, journalists, and businessmen. It essentially advocates slow reform and parliamentary methods of achieving power.[67] Another party, Social Progress, was founded on May 19, 1992. There are no reports as to the background of its leaders. The party has taken a reformist stance in favor of constructing a democratic state that guarantees individual rights for all citizens regardless of ethnic, religious, and national origin. Its structure is modeled after the Communist Party and the members are required to submit a written testimony that obligates them to follow the party's goals and guidelines, should they be elected to any legislative, executive, or judicial positions in future elections. Finally, there is the Party of the Heirs of Timur, organized by the well-known poet Olimjan Adilov. The party's objective is the rediscovery of the Uzbek heritage through the re-examination of history. It is also a reformist party in support of the present government. According to Cassandra Cavanaugh, the party has been set up to attract the members of Birlik.[68] The latest addition has been the Independence Path Party set up by Shadi Karimov, a former Birlik leader who has decided to cooperate with the government.

The Democratic Party of Tajikistan was organized on August 10, 1990, by Shodmon Yusuf in an effort to promote Western-style democratization and Tajik national revival. The party held its first congress in October of that year, during which a resolution was adopted, calling for the newly elected President Makhkamov to resign his post as first secretary of the Communist Party Central Committee and suspend his membership in the Communist Party altogether. In addition, it demanded that Makhkamov use his authority to dissolve the parliament and call for new elections to be conducted on a multiparty basis.[69] The Communist Party, however, remained in power, exercising tight control over the activities of the Tajik Democratic Party. According to the party's spokesman, Doost Muhammad Doost, the authorities prohibited the party from contacting workers and government bureaucrats, paralyzing its mobilization drive. In the absence of a cohesive organization and as a method of evading the Communist Party, the leadership decided to use the network of mosques to establish contact with the people in order to discuss the party's basic ideas and objectives. Subsequently, a strategic alliance was struck with the Tajik IRP whose members were also engaged in developing an organizational infrastructure to oppose Communist rule in the republic.[70]

The political platform of the Tajik Democratic Party has been almost identical to the other liberal democratic parties operating in Central Asia, as for instance, it has emphasized, a parliamentary method of government, the rule of law, and the protection of individual rights irrespective of race, religion, and culture. As for the role of Islam in the Tajik society, Yusuf presented the following explanation: "Islam must play a very big role in society and culture. Islam provides the necessary knowledge to teach about yesterday, today and tomorrow. Muslim parties and organizations must have their own representatives in the government to protect the Muslims' rights. The Democratic Party supports the freedom of religion of every member, and whether they pray or not is their choice."[71] As of 1992, the party had claimed to have 15,000 members. With the outbreak of the civil war in Tajikistan, which will be discussed in detail in chapter 5, the party has been practically paralyzed and its leaders have fled to Iran, Afghanistan, and Moscow in an effort to coordinate the armed struggle against the Communist regime in Dushanbe. On June 21, 1993, the Democratic Party of Tajikistan together with the IRP, Rastokhez, and other opposition organizations, were officially banned by the government.[72] In their place, a few government-sponsored parties have been established which has not yet developed adequate organizational strength. One such party is the People's Democratic Party that was set up in Khojend. Its declared objective has been the creation of "a united democratic, secular and law-based state." The party is headed by the Khojend local administrator Abduljalil Homidov. The Political and Economic Revolutionary Party, established in April 1994, has been another addition to the political process since the outbreak of the civil war. Its head Mukhtor Bobokhonov has been in favor of cooperation with the government of Rahmonov.[73]

The weakest link in the democratic chain in Central Asia is Turkmenistan. Two small democratic organizations have been active but with limited success. Agzi Birlik was organized on October 25, 1989, mainly by Nurberdy Nurmuhammadov (Nurmamedov). Its membership has been estimated at around 300, and consists of mostly intellectuals from the capital, Ashgabat. The party's registration was revoked on January 15, 1990, forcing the members to conduct their activities underground. The other organization, Democratic Party of Turkmenistan, was established in 1990 by Durdymurat Khojamuhammad but changed its name to Democratic Progressive Party in 1992 following the renaming of the old Communist Party of President Niyazov as the Democratic Party of Turkmenistan. With an estimated 600 members, this party also has a limited appeal. Nevertheless, both parties have been engaged in consciousness-raising in the republic since 1990. In August 1991, in an effort to strengthen the democratic drive, the two parties as well as the reformist faction of the old Communist Party, created the Union of Turkmenistan's Democratic Forces, Gengesh. In its first public statement on August 24, 1991, Gengesh called for the dissolution of the parliament, the establishment of a multiparty framework, freedom of the press, release of dissident political activists from jail, free distribution of land, and the improvement of the living standards of the Turkmen people. Notwithstanding the government's constant harassment and imprisonment of the democratic activists, Gengesh has not been able to expand its membership, and Agzi Birlik, the largest of these organizations, has frequently failed to gather the 1,000 required signatures to register as a legal organization.[74]

THE COMMUNIST AND PRESIDENTIAL PARTIES

In conjunction with the national and liberal democratic parties, a number of presidential and revamped Communist parties with new democratic facades have been operating in Central Asia. Largely staffed by the old Communist party members and leaders, these organizations, in essence, represent a parallel democratic process, one that is currently limited in scope but similar in objectives to the independent democratic drive discussed earlier. In Kazakhstan, two such parties have been established. The Union of People's Unity Party (movement) held its founding congress on February 6, 1993. Its basic objectives are almost identical to Uljas Suleimonov's People's Congress. The party was apparently masterminded by President Nazarbayev's friend and former advisor Serik Abdurahmanov subsequent to Suleimonov's decision not to support the president, presenting himself as a potential candidate for the upcoming election in 1995.[75]

People's Unity held its first congress on October 2, 1993, to outline once again its role in the future political development of Kazakhstan: "Such a union is objectively necessary on our republic's political scene and to counteract the national radicalism that, I'm not afraid to say, will inevitably exist in some form or another during the formation of a young, independent state. This Union must serve as a weighty counterbalance to all parties, public movements, and individuals, who seek to solve the problems of their own ethnic community at the expense of others, who fan up the inter-ethnic strife and act in contravention to the law."[76] Of the 230 participants in the congress, 35 percent were the leaders of industrial and agricultural enterprises, 7 percent were entrepreneurs, and the rest were mainly from the Kazakh intelligentsia. The union had an estimated 9,000 members in October 1993 and has been growing rapidly.[77] A report of the meeting appeared in the Russian newspaper *Nezavisimaya Gazeta,* indicating that "despite the generally 'pro-president' mood of the event, members of the organizing committee spent a lot of time dispelling suspicions among the press and many politicians that the Union had been tailor-made for the head of state."[78] Nazarbayev, however, has been quick to mention that People's Unity is not a party but an "association of all patriots of Kazakhstan irrespective of their nationality . . . it is above the parties and classes, and shares my views, my policy." It is noteworthy that the People's Unity draft rules have been formulated in a way in which the provisions related to the role of its leader are quite flexible, stressing that the leader is not an official of the organization and does not exercise administrative functions. This provision is apparently designed to stave off criticisms of Nazarbayev who made a pledge not to engage in party politics back in August 1991.

The Nazarbayev and Suleimonov rivalry has been brought out into the open in recent months with each one leveling harsh criticisms against the other: "I don't want to offend him [Suleimonov] by saying so, but just think about a man—a poet, musician and all that—who came to power on the crest of a wave of rallies, he'll only last two to three years. Politics is an immoral business. People do not spare one another when they strive for power."[79] Suleimonov, on the other hand, has indicated that he regards the union "as an attempt at, or a tool for, creating a system of monopartyism, which, as we know, leads to Bonapartism."[80] Nazarbayev, however, has extended an invitation to the People's Congress to join the union in an effort to reduce the possibility of political and ethnic strife. Moreover, the union has joined the roundtable discussions organized regularly by the parties and movements so as to stave of the oppositions' criticism regarding the creation of a one party rule in the republic.[81]

In addition to the Union of People's Unity, the Socialist Party of Kazakhstan has been advocating a democratic platform somewhat similar to the Scandinavian models, premised on comprehensive social welfare guarantees and mixed property ownership. In both structural makeup and membership composition, the party is in essence the post-independence successor to the Communist Party. Its first chairman, Anwar Alimjonov, enjoyed considerable power and prestige among the high-ranking officials of the Nazarbayev government, and the former Prime Minister, Sergey Treshenko, has been a member of the party. Alimjonov worked closely with the government to alleviate the economic problems facing the nation. Two anti-crisis programs adopted by the government in 1992 were in reality developed by the Socialist Party. The first, was designed to prevent the emerging economic disparities between the poor and the rich through the introduction of minimum welfare standards to assist the underprivileged population in the republic. The second measure concerned the privatization of agricultural land, which has been turned down by the government. Alimjonov was critical of the land privatization, arguing that only limited privatization based on Kazakh communal tradition is the most suitable model.[82]

The party has an estimated 50,000 members and enjoys multiethnic support. The majority of the members are between the ages of twenty and forty, many of whom have some college education. Recently, there has been an attempt to attract members of the newly created class of entrepreneurs into the party. This decision has helped the party's image and has strengthened its finances. Similar to the People's Congress, the Socialist Party has been carrying out small-scale construction projects sponsored by businessmen in Kokchetav and Semipalatinsk. Since October 1993, with the generous support of these entrepreneurs through the Asia joint stock company, the Council for Peace and Consent of the Republic of Kazakhstan, and Informmedi joint stock society, the party has also begun the publication of its newspaper, which is published in Russian under the name *Respublika* and in Kazakh under, *Kazakh Mamlekati*. It has a circulation of 50,000.[83]

Besides the Socialist Party, whose membership had been largely drawn from the old Communist Party, a separate Communist Party has been organized by Doosmuhammad Koishibekov and others on June 19, 1992, but the government refused to register it for nearly two and a half years until March 1994, when it finally joined the People's Congress, the Republican Party, the Union of People's Unity, and the Socialist Party as the only organizations that have been awarded legal status.[84] The Communist Party, which claims to have an estimated 55,000 members, has been advocating a Leninist course of action and the reconstitution of the Soviet Union. Two months after its establishment, the party's central committee addressed an open letter to the president complaining about the restrictions imposed on freedom of thought.[85] On February 16, 1993, the party made yet another unsuccessful attempt to register after failing twice in the past, this time pledging that their "application stresses that the party will take into account the concept of the new Kazakh Constitution in its activities." Koishibekov has also stated that "we emphasize human rights, social justice, and internationalism. We want to join the parliamentary election campaign and become a parliamentary party along with other public associations."[86]

In Kyrgyzstan, President Akayev has supported the Social Democratic Party, which was established on July 7, 1993.[87] The party held its founding congress in October of 1993. No details have yet been made available as to the status of the party. But it has been reported that the party has come under criticism because its membership is drawn primarily from among the present ruling *nomenklatura*. Akayev, however, has announced that the party strives for national reconciliation and hopes to solve the pressing socioeconomic problems of the republic. The declining popularity of Akayev and the growing criticism of his policies prompted him to call for a referendum on his presidency that was held on January 24, 1994. As expected, his mandate was renewed, securing his position until the upcoming general elections.

The Communist Party of Kyrgyzstan, renamed Party of the Communists of Kyrgyzstan held its founding congress in late June 1992 and was awarded legal status in November of that year.[88] The party has been critical of the ongoing privatization program, in particular the speed with which it has been carried out. In fact, its former chairman, Jumgalbek Amanbayev, had frequently declared "that the regime is doomed on the account of numerous mistakes in implementation of the reforms."[89] In addition, it has been calling for the reconstitution of the Soviet republic and the restoration of the Leninist principle of state ownership. The party has reestablished its nationwide network, cautiously awaiting the opportunity to reassert itself as the dominant party in the republic. On March 13, 1993, the party held its second congress in Bishkek during which Gorbachev and his aids were condemned for the breakup of the Soviet Union. Moreover, the members demanded that Akayev reevaluate his presidency and to subordinate his policies to the interest of the people. Given the fragmented nature of the democratic opposition, the 10,000-member strong Party of the Communists of Kyrgyzstan presents a formidable force, capable of winning an electoral majority in the near future.

In Uzbekistan, Tajikistan, and Turkmenistan the Communist parties have been reconstituted under new names. The People's Democratic Party of Uzbekistan, headed by the president Islam Karimov, was organized in the fall of 1991. Its membership has been estimated at 337,000. Based on a 1993 government report, the composition of the party is as follows: 59 percent are workers and peasants, 44 percent white-collar workers. 56 percent of members are between the ages of thirty-one and fifty, 18 percent are under thirty, and 25 percent are over fifty. Women constitute 21 percent of the total membership. Altogether 71 nationalities belong to the party, of which 79 percent are Uzbeks.[90] The party virtually controls the main organs of the government as well as the parliament. Quite expectedly it has the most extensive organizational network of all parties in the republic. Karimov has been quite explicit about the role of his party during the transition to a market economy, emphasizing the supremacy of economics over politics: "The undue politicization of society is to the detriment of the economy . . . people cannot be persuaded of anything unless they are . . . fed and provided for . . . the state should not let go of the reins in the transitional period."[91]

In Tajikistan the office of the presidency was temporarily abolished in November 1992 subsequent to the election of Imomali Rahmonov as the chairman of the Supreme Soviet of Tajikistan. Under his supervision, First Secretary of the Communist Party Shadi Shabdallov has been able to revitalize the party structure. And since May 1993, the Communist Party has stepped up its activities considerably, quickly reestablishing its pre-independence network that extended to every administrative division, factory, collective, and state farm. There has also been proposals to launch a purge of teachers, workers, and peasants who have supported the Islamic-democratic opposition in the past few years. The Communist Party is currently the only party allowed to conduct its activities, and much like its Uzbek counterpart has established control over all the major political and economic institutions in the republic.

Finally, the Communist Party of Turkmenistan was renamed the Democratic Party in December 1991. Headed by President Saparmurat Niyazov, the Democratic Party was "to serve as the 'mother party,' dominating all political activities in the republic."[92] The current membership of the party is estimated at 52,000, of which 4,000 have joined since 1991 who do not have any Communist affiliation. Niyazov has been against the development of independent parties in Turkmenistan but has encouraged a number of organizations and parties to develop an infrastructure under the supervision of his Democratic Party. One such organization, the Peasant Justice Party, headed by an intellectual named Bairamov, has been allowed to register. Niyazov has been arguing that his countrymen are not yet ready for a Western-style democracy.[93] It is interesting to note that Niyazov has been quite successful in keeping the political situation under control by implementing generous economic policies such as free gas and electricity and handsome pay raises for the salaried workers. For how long these policies can compensate for genuine democratic reforms is a matter to be decided by the people of Turkmenistan.

CONCLUSION

As this chapter has outlined, the democratic drive in Central Asia, much like the Islamic drive, has not been uniform in scope and intensity at the inter-republican level. Quite the opposite, republican proclivity towards democracy varies considerably, with Kazakhstan and Kyrgyzstan having the best opportunity to complete their transition to democracy and Uzbekistan, Tajikistan, and Turkmenistan lagging behind in their democratization efforts. In the final analysis, however, the future of democracy in Central Asia is not only dependent upon its ability to deliver greater political freedom, but also in its in capacity to bring about substantive economic change for the benefit of a wide cross-section of the population.

CHAPTER 5

Government and Politics

We should determine the rhythm and pace of our reform ourselves on the basis of local conditions, not according to the demands of some sort of classic, democratic formulas or perceptions worked out in some prosperous Western country.

—PRESIDENT SAPARMURAT NIYAZOV, TURKMENISTAN

The collapse of the Soviet Union in 1991 will perhaps be remembered as the most significant political event of the late-twentieth century, one that among other things, offered the promise of greater freedom and democracy through radical structural transformation of its component republics. Yet, at least in the case of Central Asia, the developments of the last three years have clearly demonstrated a marked reluctance on the part of those in power to pursue expeditious and meaningful democratic reform initiatives that would permit greater participation by all segments of the population. This has been most noticeable in Turkmenistan, Tajikistan, and Uzbekistan, and less apparent in Kazakhstan and Kyrgyzstan. The root of the problem lies in the fact that contrary to most postcolonial governments, the Central Asian independence did not alter, to any significant degree, the republican power structure, leaving intact a Communist personnel whose authority is being slowly challenged by the very nature of reforms they are obligated to undertake. From a political point of view, democratization in principle has presented a golden opportunity for various groups outside the old Communist network to compete for a greater share of power. In the zero-sum game of politics, it is easy to understand why in the republics of Turkmenistan, Tajikistan, and Uzbekistan political opposition has been actively or passively repressed since the independence. It is precisely this potentially threatening feature of reform that has prevented the implementation of a more comprehensive reform program in Central Asia. Consequently, the present governments have been faced with a crisis of legitimacy of various proportions, the most blatant manifestation of which has been the bloody civil war in Tajikistan.

The picture is, of course, more complex in that in places such as Kazakhstan and Kyrgyzstan where some degree of commitment to democratic reform has been exhibited by the republican presidents, the Communist-oriented parliaments have been hard at work to slow down or altogether emasculate the democratic reform initiatives.[1] Interestingly enough, the need for political stability has been the most frequently used official justification for the relatively slow pace of reform in a region whose complex ethnic makeup has often presented a potentially explosive situation. The democratic and Islamic opposition, however, have dismissed the above rationale, arguing that the majority of those in charge have been career Communists with little or no desire to bring about a qualitative change in either the political or economic spheres of life. While there is an element of truth to the former argument, recent history provides powerful evidence in favor of the latter, in particular when one considers the methods by which the present leaders have secured their power, their reaction to the coup of August 1991, and the manner in which the opposition has so far been treated. In the final analysis, what may determine the longevity of the present Central Asian governments and at the same time may prevent further politicization of the Islamic forces in the foreseeable future, is the willingness to institute an all-inclusive democratic framework within which all social forces, irrespective of their ideological orientation, could partake in a peaceful plural electoral competition.

THE COMMUNIST HERITAGE, 1989–1993

With the notable exception of Kyrgyzstan, the current Central Asian leaders have been veterans of Communist politics, well-versed in the lessons of totalitarianism. And most, if not all, were elected to office without affording the opposition a fair chance in a free and open electoral competition. The last pre-independence election to Kyrgyzstan's Supreme Soviet was held in February 1990, conducted in traditional Soviet style, with Communist candidates winning most seats unopposed. In April of that year the Supreme Soviet elected the First Secretary Absamat Masaliyev to the newly created post of chairman of the Supreme Soviet. Cognizant of the political changes taking place elsewhere in the Soviet Union, Masaliyev advocated the introduction of an executive presidency, hoping to become the first occupant of that office. The presidential election was to be conducted by the Supreme Soviet, whose members seemed at first to favor Masaliyev's candidacy. By October, however, when an extraordinary session of the Supreme Soviet was convened to elect the president, Masaliyev had been seriously discredited in the aftermath of the Osh disturbances where violent clashes between the Uzbek and Kyrgyz residents continued from June to August of 1990, leaving behind more than 600 dead and wounded.[2] Masaliyev's mishandling of the crisis on the one hand and the growing strength of the newly created Democratic Movement of Kyrgyzstan (DDK) on the other hand, brought about a political regrouping within the Supreme Soviet, seriously threatening Masaliyev's presidential bid. In the first round of voting, Masaliyev and two other career Communists, Chairman of the Council of Ministers Apas Jumagulov and Issyk-Kul oblast leader Jumgalbek Amanbayev, failed to secure the required percentage of votes to be elected president. Once again, in a second round of voting, Masaliyev fell short of the designated number of votes. Subsequently, his name was removed from the ballot,[3] paving the way for Askar Akayev, the president of the Kyrgyz Academy of Sciences, who was elected to the post in a further round of voting. Akayev quickly allied himself with the reformist politicians, economists, and the Democratic Movement of Kyrgyzstan, which had played a critical role in turning the public opinion against Masaliyev. Shortly after the election, in an effort to facilitate his reform agenda, Akayev established a 12-member presidential council, which included the co-chair of the Democratic Movement of Kyrgyzstan, Qazat Akhmatov.

In December 1990, Masaliyev resigned as chairman of the Supreme Soviet and was replaced by Medetkan Sherimkulov. A month later, Akayev introduced new government structures, replacing the conservative Council of Ministers with a small Cabinet of Ministers, and appointed a new government comprised mainly of young reformers. Despite opposition from the Kyrgyz Communist Party and Masaliyev, in mid-December 1990 the Supreme Soviet voted to change the name of the republic from Kirghiz SSR to Republic of Kyrgyzstan. Akayev's program of political and economic reform generated heavy criticism by the Communist Party and the security forces. Unable to change the reformist orientation of the Akayev government, Masaliyev handed in his second resignation as the first secretary of the party in April.[4] He was replaced by Jumgalbek Amanbayev. Although Amanbayev seemed to be more eager about Akayev's reform program than his predecessor, he too sided with the Communist Party and the Supreme Soviet in opposing Akayev's various proposals that, among other things, aimed at drastically reducing the role of the Communist Party in all spheres of Kyrgyz society.

On August 19, 1991, when the State Committee for the State of Emergency (SCSE) announced that it had assumed power in Moscow, there was an attempt to stage a coup against Akayev.[5] The Communist Party declared its support for the coup leaders, and the commander of Turkistan military district threatened to dispatch troops and tanks to the republic. To preempt military action against him, Akayev dismissed General Asasankulov, the chairman of the republican KGB, and ordered Interior Ministry troops to guard strategic buildings in Bishkek. Despite warnings from Vladimir Kriuchkov, chairman of the all-Union KGB and a member of the SCSE, Akayev established contact with Boris Yeltsin, president of the Russian Federation, and broadcast Yeltsin's opposition to the SCSE on republican television. On August 21, 1991, Akayev made a public appeal denouncing the coup: "The events of the past two days leave no doubt that an unconstitutional coup took place in the country on August 19. It is now obvious that the people who carried it out were motivated by one thing—a desire to preserve the state power and totalitarian regime that are slipping away from them."[6] Subsequently, he issued a decree prohibiting activity by any political party in government or state bodies. He also ordered all military units in the republic to remain on their bases. On August 26, after the coup had collapsed in Moscow, Akayev and Vice-President German Kuznetsov announced their resignation from the Communist Party. Following the coup, Akayev continued with his policy of seeking more independence for Kyrgyzstan and pressing for the implementation of ambitious economic reforms. On August 31, the Supreme Soviet of Kyrgyzstan voted to declare independence from the Soviet Union. With the Communist Party completely discredited, on October 12, 1991, Akayev was elected President with 95.3 percent of the votes cast; no other candidate was nominated.

A similar political process helped move Nursultan Nazarbayev to the apex of the power structure in Kazakhstan. Contrary to Akayev, however, Nazarbayev did not enjoy the support of the nascent democratic forces in the republic. Rather, it was the Communist Party that facilitated his political accession. Nazarbayev was the chairman of the Council of Ministers when Gorbachev decided to replace Kunayev as first secretary of the Kazakhstan Communist Party in 1986. The Kazakh Communists believed that Nazarbayev was the best choice for the post, but Moscow sent Genady Kolbin, a Russian, instead—an unfortunate choice that led to the first sizable outburst of ethnic violence in Central Asia in mid-December 1986, when young Kazakhs staged a series of protests against the appointment of a non-Kazakh to the post. Although Kolbin remained in his post for some time, the social unrest was to pave the way for his eventual removal.

Despite Gorbachev's directives to reform the political structure of the Soviet Union, the March 1989 elections to the Supreme Soviet of Kazakhstan were conducted in traditional single-candidate style with the Communists winning most of the seats. In June 1989, Kolbin was finally transferred to Moscow and Nursultan Nazarbayev was appointed First Secretary of the Communist Party. He quickly established himself as a prominent politician in republican and all-Union affairs who strongly supported economic reform while emphasizing the need for political stability. In September 1989, the political and administrative system in Kazakhstan was restructured with the objective of establishing a full-time Supreme Soviet and introducing a multi-candidate electoral design. Much like elsewhere in the Union, Kazakhstan also transferred the executive duties, which were the responsibility of the first secretary, to the office of chairman of the Supreme Soviet. Quite expectedly, in February 1990, Nazarbayev was elected to this post. Elections to the new Supreme Soviet took place in March 1990. Despite the introduction of multi-candidate electoral laws, most Communist deputies stood unopposed, and the old quota system for Communist Party-affiliated organizations was retained. The end result was the reestablishment of a Communist majority in the Supreme Soviet. In late April, Nazarbayev was elected to the newly created post of executive president by the Supreme Soviet.

On October 25, 1990, Kazakhstan declared its sovereignty, which underscored republican control over natural resources and the economy, yet emphasized the equality of all nationalities living in the republic. The declaration was considered too weak by the Kazakh nationalist organizations whose declared position on the issue was a complete "decolonization" of the republic. This was taken to mean, by some segments of Kazakh population, the expulsion of the Russians from the republic. The declaration of sovereignty also came under criticism by the Slavic population of Kazakhstan who wished to remain under the legal and political protection of the Slav-dominated Soviet Union. Consequently, Russian residents staged a series of demonstrations in Ust-Kamenogorsk and other Russian-dominated regions of Kazakhstan to express their reservations with regard to the republic's drive toward independence.

In line with other Central Asian republics, Kazakhstan was ready to sign Gorbachev's proposed Union Treaty on August 20, 1991, but the attempted coup in Moscow circumvented the event. Nazarbayev was initially cautious, advocating calm, without openly condemning the coup: "At this extremely critical hour for the country, I urge you to remain calm and show restraint . . . it is very important to set aside current differences and base your actions on common sense and a feeling of responsibility to the people, and to avoid confrontation."[7] On August 20, however, he issued a statement that denounced the SCSE as illegal and harmful to economic and political progress. Subsequent to the collapse of the coup, Nazarbayev resigned from the Politburo and Central Committee of the Communist Party. The same day the Communist Party was ordered to cease activities in state and government organs.

Kazakhstan was one of the last republics that had not declared its independence from the Soviet Union. This was in part due to Nazarbayev's decision to preserve the delicate interethnic balance between Russians and Kazakhs in the republic, preventing further discussion of the secession of Kazakhstan's border territories with Russia. But it was also due to his determination to retain many of the personnel and structures of the Kazakh Communist Party—renamed the Socialist Party of Kazakhstan—as the instrument of economic policy in the republic. Nazarbayev was of the opinion that economic reform should take precedence over political reform. Initially, there was little political opposition to his policies. He also managed to gain popularity by banning nuclear tests at the Semipalatinsk site after the failed coup. During the December 1, 1991 election, he was the only major candidate for president of Kazakhstan. Azat Civil Movement, however, accused the Nazarbayev camp of sabotaging its candidate's bid for the presidency by ransacking the movement's tent headquarters shortly before the election.[8] The chairman of Jeltoqsan, Hassan Kojakhmetov, also hoped to participate in the election, but his party failed to gather the required 100,000 signatures to qualify him for the ballot.[9] In the end, Nazarbayev received 98.8 percent of the votes cast. Some 87.4 percent of the electorate took part.

Although Nazarbayev has been as receptive to the ideas of reform as Akayev, he has clearly demonstrated a high degree of concern for stability in his political conduct over the past few years. Valery Chalidze has provided the following account of Nazarbayev's orientation and motives:

> When Nazarbayev was among the Communist leaders he did as they did; he supported Kunaev and Kolbin when they were in power and opposed them when the time came. He was like other Party leaders, but after becoming the "First Communist" of Kazakhstan, at a time when the authority and prestige of the Party were declining all across the Soviet Union, he departed from the path of many republican leaders—he did not opt for nationalist or populist slogans to gain popularity and neutralize the results of the falling prestige of his Party. Nor was he one of those who contributed to the collapse of the Soviet Union by pressuring Gorbachev's government. On the contrary, Nazarbayev supported the Union to the end.[10]

Whereas Nazarbayev has so far succeeded in maintaining his power, he has come under increasing criticism since the establishment of the Union of the People's Unity Movement (Party) in 1993, which he has openly supported as the party of his choice. According to the opposition parties, this has raised a justifiable suspicion about Nazarbayev's plan to slow down and perhaps even abandon democratic reforms in favor of establishing what may amount to a one-party rule in Kazakhstan.

In contrast to the Kyrgyz and Kazakh presidents who have at least publicly distanced themselves from their republics' Communist past and instituted some degree of political and economic reforms, in Turkmenistan, Uzbekistan, and Tajikistan, the Communist *nomenklatura* have openly supported the old power structures by giving them a new democratic facade. In Turkmenistan, as a result of the official animosity toward the nascent democratic movement, the Communist Party was the only party permitted to participate in elections to the Supreme Soviet and local soviets in the republic, which took place in January 1990, with Communist Party members winning most of the seats.[11] When the new Supreme Soviet convened Saparmurat Niyazov was elected chairman of the Supreme Soviet. On October 27, 1990, he was elected by direct ballot as president of Turkmenistan. He was unopposed in the election and received 98.3 percent of the votes cast.

There was little response in Turkmenistan to the attempted conservative coup of August 1991. President Niyazov made no public announcements either opposing or supporting the self-proclaimed State Committee for the State of Emergency in Moscow. Although Niyazov had promised to submit a written statement to the editors of the major newspapers in the republic expressing his views on the coup, no such statement was delivered, forcing the newspapers to publish reports from Moscow. The two small opposition groups, Agzi Birlik and the Democratic Progressive Party, publicly opposed the coup, but when democratic groups attempted to form a coalition against the coup, some opposition leaders were arrested. No punitive actions, however, were taken against the supporters of the coup, as for instance, when Bibi Palvanovna, a well-known conservative member of the Turkmen Academy of Sciences, publicly defended the coup: "Let the SCSE bring order to the country, and we will do the same here."[12]

Following the coup attempt, Niyazov held on to power and made a public announcement in which he ordered the Communist Party to remain as the ruling party, a blatant move indicative of Niyazov's true political orientation. Later, he provided the following justification for his decision: "The fact of the matter is that unlike other republics we did not destroy the old state apparatus and the top bodies of the Communist Party. Such a policy, unpopular at the time, had the purely pragmatic objective of avoiding anarchy and a power vacuum. Good or bad, the old structures were at the time the only force capable of ensuring order and stability."[13] However, in December 1991, in an effort to give the Communist Party a new face-lift, Niyazov changed its name to the Democratic Party of Turkmenistan, making himself its chairman. The party, according to its platform, was "to serve as the 'mother party,' dominating all political activity in the republic."[14] On October 26, 1991, a national referendum was held on the question of independence and 94.1 percent of the electorate voted in favor of its declaration. Niyazov was reelected to the office of president in June 1992, unopposed, subsequent to the ratification of a new Constitution that delegated a disproportionate amount of power to him. Niyazov is head of the state, head of the cabinet of ministers, he appoints the chairman of the Supreme Court, and the Supreme Economic Court, he can dissolve the parliament if it gives him two votes of no confidence in a period of eighteen months, he has the power to issue decrees, appoint and dismiss all judges, and choose the state prosecutor.[15]

Without a doubt, Niyazov is the most conservative leader in Central Asia who has made an ardent effort to minimize the local impact of the changes that have swept through the former Soviet Union over the past few years. It is interesting to note that Niyazov is heading a unique republic where the size of the intelligentsia is considerably small, Islam is relatively weak, and the population is largely apolitical. These factors, together with his iron-fist policy, has given him the opportunity to continue with his totalitarian rule in Turkmenistan with no prospects for its dismantling in the foreseeable future.[16]

The politics of power in Uzbekistan have followed, more or less, a similar pattern of development to that of Turkmenistan. On February 18, 1990, elections were held for the Uzbek Supreme Soviet. Quite expectedly, members of the Birlik Movement, the only viable opposition to the Communist government, were not permitted to participate in the elections, and consequently, many leading members of the Communist Party regained their seats unopposed, as had always been the case in previous Soviet-style elections. In some constituencies there were reports of isolated protests by the members of Birlik that were reportedly put down. The new Supreme Soviet convened in March 1990, and elected the First Secretary of the Communist Party, Islam Karimov, to the newly created post of executive president. Shokurollah Mirsaidov was elected chairman of the Council of Ministers. In November 1990, there was a reorganization of government. The Council of Ministers was abolished and replaced by a Cabinet of Ministers, headed by Karimov. The post of chairman of the Council of Ministers was eliminated, and Shokurollah Mirsaidov was appointed to the newly established post of vice-president.[17]

At the time of the August 1991, coup against Gorbachev, Karimov was caught off guard. On the evening of August 20, Tashkent television broadcast a speech by him, which merely called for discipline and order. Interestingly enough, Karimov neither spoke of the removal of Gorbachev nor did he approve or disapprove of the actions of the Emergency Committee: a clear indication of his political opportunism. He did, however, order the arrest of some opposition leaders in Uzbekistan who had issued a statement on August 19 condemning the coup. Once it became apparent that the coup had failed, Karimov declared invalid the directives of the coup leaders and expressed support for the course of Gorbachev's reforms.[18] On August 25, Karimov resigned from the Communist Party Central Committee on the grounds that the "orthodox section of the CPSU Central Committee leadership and its Politburo and Secretariat expressed no attitude to the anti-constitutional actions taken by the so-called State Committee for the State of Emergency."[19] Subsequently, the Supreme Soviet adopted the law of independence to be ratified by a public referendum at a later date. The 23rd Congress of the Communist Party was held in September during which it changed its name to the People's Democratic Party and elected Islam Karimov as its chairman.

On December 29, 1991, Karimov won the first direct presidential elections in Uzbekistan, receiving 86 percent of the total votes. His only opponent was Muhammad Solih, the leader of the Erk (freedom) opposition party, which had splintered from Birlik in 1990. He managed to gain 12 percent of the popular vote. Birlik itself was banned from contesting the election, as it had still not been granted official registration as a political party. Based on the law on presidential elections, only registered parties were allowed to introduce candidates for election. According to Bess Brown, Karimov won a fair and largely nonfraudulent election "albeit with considerable assistance from the intact power structures of the former Communist Party."[20] A referendum was held at the same time, in which 98.2 percent of the voters endorsed Uzbekistan's independence.

Ever since, Karimov has been relying on the old Communist Party personnel to conduct its political activities. Much like Niyazov of Turkmenistan, his office of president wields an unusually high level of power, which has given him the ability to become the sole policymaker in the republic. He has frequently justified his authoritarian rule as the only viable method of ensuring peace and order: "Strong executive power is necessary to prevent bloodshed and confrontation, and to preserve ethnic and civil concord, peace, and stability in our region. . . . My opponents would see Karimov as a dictator. I admit that my activities are somewhat authoritarian. But I have acted in this manner for the sake of economic progress and prosperity of our people."[21]

Tajikistan: The Roots of Catastrophe

While in Uzbekistan, Kazakhstan, Kyrgyzstan, and Turkmenistan the Communist *nomenklatura* has maintained some degree of credibility through the use of political repression and targeted economic incentives, in Tajikistan the Communist government has utterly failed to prevent the erosion of its legitimacy, which has led to the outbreak of a bloody civil war since 1992. The seeds of this conflict were sown, for the most part, by the late Rahman Nabiyev, a career Communist who was ousted by Gorbachev in 1985 but who managed to make a comeback a few years later.

Tajikistan's troubles began in 1990, when violence broke out in Dushanbe, after it was rumored that Armenian refugees from the Caucasus were to be relocated to the republic.[22] Given the severe housing shortages and high unemployment, many believed that the impending resettlement would further exacerbate the economic situation of the Tajiks. The first incident of violence occurred at a gathering of about 3,000 people when protestors rejected assurances by Communist Party First Secretary Ghahar Makhkamov that only 39 Armenian refugees—all staying with their relatives—were in Dushanbe.[23] The angry participants clashed with the security forces, overturned cars, and looted shops. Shortly thereafter, demonstrators broadened their demands, calling for political reforms, as well as more radical economic reforms. The worsening conditions forced Makhkamov to request military help from Moscow. A contingent of 5,000 troops from the Soviet Ministry of Internal Affairs were sent to Dushanbe. According to the members of the opposition parties, the troops put down the demonstrations at the cost of 22 deaths and 565 injured.[24]

The violence prompted some members of the Communist Party to side with the protestors, in particular the Rastokhez movement whose members were alleged to have been instrumental in inciting the public. In a sudden change of alliances, Deputy Chairman of the Council of Ministers Buri Karimov made a public demand for the resignation of the top Communist Party leaders, including the Council of Ministers and the Presidium of the Supreme Soviet. The increasing public pressure finally forced the First Secretary Makhkamov and Prime Minister Ezatolloh Khayeyev to tender their resignations on February 14, 1990. However, the Communist Party Central Committee did not honor their request to step down, and with the Communist Party regaining control over the streets of Dushanbe, Buri Karimov and the Minister of Culture Nur Tabarov were dismissed and expelled from the Communist Party for their clear involvement in antigovernment activities during the disturbances in Dushanbe. The events of February 1990 further strengthened the government's intolerance for the opposition, hence the continuation of the state of emergency throughout 1990. Quite expectedly, in the March elections to the

Supreme Soviet, the opposition politicians from Rastokhez and the Democratic Party of Tajikistan were refused permission to participate, and 94 percent of the elected deputies were members of the Communist Party. In November 1990, Makhkamov was elected to the new post of executive president of the republic by the Supreme Soviet. His only opponent was the former Communist Party First Secretary Rahman Nabiyev.

In response to the Communist Party's control of Tajik political life, the democratic opposition staged a series of hunger strikes prior, during, and after the election of Makhkamov to the post of president, forcing the government to grant an official permission to the Democratic Party of Tajikistan to hold its founding Congress less than a week after the presidential election. The Supreme Soviet, however, declined a similar request by the Tajik branch of the Islamic Revival Party, banning all religious organizations from participating in the political process. Later, as a show of solidarity with the all-Union Communists, Makhkamov delivered a speech to the Central Committee calling on his supporters "to resolutely repulse the destructive forces which . . . are placing in doubt the existence of the USSR, calling for a retreat from socialism, and sowing inter-ethnic strife."[25]

When the news of the August 19 coup against Gorbachev reached Dushanbe, Makhkamov exhibited a decidedly positive response to it, and a day later he told the head of the Tajik Journalists' Union that he was in fact supportive of the junta in principle. On the second day of the coup, Makhkamov flew to Moscow for consultations and to take part in the Communist Party Central Committee meeting.[26] To save his career, upon his return he made a public apology, stating that "This information about what I was doing during the failed coup in no way justifies my tardiness in defining my attitude to the well-known event . . . the problem was primarily the lack of information. I deeply regret this and am very upset about it."[27] On August 31, Makhkamov resigned as president. His resignation had been forced by a vote of no confidence from the Supreme Soviet and mass demonstrations organized by the Democratic Party of Tajikistan, Rastokhez, and the Islamic Revival Party. In the next few months the political battle between the two sides raged, with the Communists leaders resorting to a series of defensive and offensive strategies to maintain their hold on power.

On September 9, following the declarations of independence by neighboring Uzbekistan and Kyrgyzstan, the Tajik Supreme Soviet announced Tajikistan's independence. This, however, did not satisfy the demonstrators, who called for the dismantling of the Communist Party and the holding of new, multiparty elections. Consequently, the Chairman of the Supreme Soviet and acting President Ghadreddin Aslonov issued a decree that banned the Communist

Party and nationalized its assets.[28] Angry that the statue of Lenin had been toppled in Dushanbe, the Supreme Soviet imposed a state of emergency from September 24 to January 1, 1992, demanded Aslonov's resignation, and reinstated the Communist Party. Aslonov resigned and was replaced by the former Communist Party leader Rahman Nabiyev. His resignation prompted the democratic and Islamic opposition to stage a series of demonstrations calling once again for the dissolution of the Communist Party and new elections. In response to growing popular protest, the Supreme Soviet rescinded the state of emergency, suspended the Communist Party, legalized the Islamic Revival Party (IRP)—previously banned under legislation prohibiting the formation of religious parties—and agreed to hold new presidential elections. On October 6, 1991, Nabiyev resigned as acting president, in advance of the presidential election and was replaced by Akbarshah (Akbarsho) Eskandarov, who remained in that post until November.

Seven candidates participated in the presidential election that took place on November 24, 1991. The main contenders were Nabiyev and Dawlat Khodanazarov, the liberal chairman of the USSR Cinematographers' Union, who was supported by the main opposition parties. Mostly as a result of strong support from the heavily populated urban, industrial, and Russified northern region Khojend and the Kulab (Kulyab) region in the south, Nabiyev won 57 percent of the votes cast, compared with 39 percent for Khodanazarov. There was an 84.6 percent turnout. Khodanazarov claimed that there was widespread electoral malpractice, but the electoral commission found that only 3 percent of the ballot papers were invalid. Subsequently, Nabiyev took office in early December and Safarali Kenjoyev (Kenjayev) was appointed the chairman of the Supreme Soviet.[29] One month later a new prime minister, Akbar Mirzoyev, was appointed to head the government. As a precautionary measure and in line with the traditional Tajik rulers of the past, Nabiyev issued a decree to establish a 700-strong National Guard, directly subordinate to the president. Furthermore, the activity of the Communist Party was restored by him. In January 1992, the Communist Party held its first Congress after the presidential elections and reaffirmed its adherence to Marxist-Leninist ideology, renaming itself the Communist Party again.

March 22, 1992, marked the beginning of a new wave of antigovernment demonstrations that led to the outbreak of the civil war in Tajikistan. It all began when Nabiyev dismissed Muhammadayez Nowjavonov (Nojavanov), the minister of Internal Affairs, who was an influential Badakhshani (Pamiri) and a supporter of democratic reforms. Protests against his removal were led by Pamiris, many of whom were the members of La'l-e Badakhshan, a group that advocated greater autonomy for the Pamiri peoples of the Gorno-Badakhshan

Autonomous Region.[30] Soon the demonstrations assumed a wider political dimension as the Pamiris were joined by Rastokhez, the IRP, and the Democratic Party on March 26 subsequent to the arrest of Maksud Ikramov, the mayor of Dushanbe, an opposition sympathizer accused of abusing his authority. Demonstrators called for the resignation of the president and the Supreme Soviet, remaining in makeshift tents in Shahidon Square for nearly two months, while supporters of the president held rival demonstrations in the Ozodi Square.

In late April members of the opposition took 18 hostages—16 Supreme Soviet deputies and two ministers—in support of their demands for the resignation of the chairman of the Supreme Soviet, Safarali Kenjoyev, and for multiparty elections. To gain the release of the hostages and "to preserve the unity of the nation and avoid bloodshed," Kenjoyev agreed to resign.[31] On April 26, the pro-government demonstrators held a counter-rally on Ozodi Square demanding the return of Kenjoyev. The organizer of the gathering was Mullah Heidar of Kulyab, an ardent supporter of Nabiyev, who had been assimilated into the ranks of the government-controlled muftiate of Tajikistan under Rahmonov's regime. Despite the decision to refrain from holding public demonstrations, both sides continued their protests and on April 29, the flag of the Soviet Union was raised at the pro-government rally during which Abdullah Achilov, the rally organizer, made a speech blaming Yeltsin for the collapse of the Soviet Union.[32]

On April 30, 1992, in an unexpected move, a presidential rule for six months was introduced by the Supreme Soviet delegating absolute authority to Nabiyev to rule. Soon after, Nabiyev banned rallies and reappointed Kenjoyev to his previous post as the chairman of the Supreme Soviet. In early May, the newly formed national guard, loyal to President Nabiyev, opened fire on the demonstrators, killing at least eight people, leading to violent clashes between the anti- and pro-government protesters. For a brief period the Islamic-democratic opposition exercised control over the television station, the airport, the presidential palace, and most of the capital, forcing Nabiyev to begin negotiations with the opposition. During the overnight talks, on May 7, 1992, between the two sides, an agreement was reached that included the resignation of the Chairman of the Supreme Soviet Kenjoyev Vice-President Nasrolloh Dustov, Procurator-General Nurolloh Hoveidollohyev, and the chairman of the state radio and television, Atokhon Seifolloyev. It also called for the formation of a coalition government, lifting of the state of emergency, disbanding of the presidential guard, and an end to demonstrations in Dushanbe.[33] Unfortunately, the agreement did not immediately put an end to fighting. But four days later, the agreement on the formation of a coalition government brought peace to Dushanbe. The opposition was given 8 of the 24 cabinet posts including defense, education, and broadcasting.[34] Nabiyev was to remain president and Abdulmalik Abdulojonov as acting prime minister until December 6, 1992 when new presidential elections were to be held. The deputy chairman of the IRP, Dawlat Usman, was appointed deputy prime minister in charge of the republic's law enforcement.[35]

Although the agreement brought an end to demonstrations in Dushanbe, violent clashes continued in the Kulyab region in the south of the republic between pro-Communist Kulyabi forces who opposed the president's compromise with the opposition, and members of Islamic and democratic forces. As indicated earlier, the Kulyab region and the northern, industrial Khojend (Leninabad) region were the main bases of support for President Nabiyev, while most members of Islamic and democratic groups were from the southern Ghorghan Tepeh region and the Gharm Valley to the east of Dushanbe. The Communist opposition in Khojend went so far as to announce at their oblast meeting that if the president's decision was not revoked, Khojend would declare its autonomy.[36] In late May 1992, the conflict spread from the Kulyab region into the Ghorghan Tepeh region, where a Kulyabi militia, the Tajik People's Front (TPF) led by Sangak Safarov, attempted to suppress the local forces of the Islamic-democratic coalition. The Kulyabis alleged that their opponents were receiving arms and assistance from Islamic groups in Afghanistan, and there were reports that Gulbeddin Hekmatyar, the leader of the Afghan Mujahidin group, Hizb-e Islami, had established training camps in Afghanistan for Tajik fighters.

In late August 1992, several members of the DPT and La'l-e Badakhshan were killed by members of Kulyabi militia in the town of Ghorghan Tepeh. A violent conflict ensued in the town between local members of the opposition and Kulyabis, in which several hundred people were reported to have been killed.[37] Meanwhile, in Dushanbe, where there had been little violence since May, anti-government demonstrations resumed, and at the end of August demonstrators entered the presidential palace and took 30 officials hostage, although President Nabiyev succeeded in escaping and went into hiding.[38] On September 7, however, he was captured by opposition forces at the Dushanbe airport, and was forced to announced his resignation. Akbarshah Eskandarov, the chairman of the Supreme Soviet, temporarily assumed the responsibilities of head of state, while the coalition government remained in office.

Eskandarov's administration, which had the support of all the main Islamic and democratic groups, had little influence outside the capital, as much of the south of the country was under the control of Safarov's TPF militia, while the Communist leaders in Khojend, where there is a large Uzbek community, exercised control over the north in defiance of Eskandarov's government. In late October 1992, the government's rule in Dushanbe itself was threatened, when forces led by Safarali Kenjoyev, a Nabiyev supporter, entered the capital and attempted to seize power. Kenjoyev briefly proclaimed himself head of state, but his troops were forced to retreat outside the city by forces loyal to the government. During the ensuing two months, however, Kenjoyev's militia enforced a virtual economic blockade of the capital, resulting in shortages of foodstuffs and other goods in the city.[39]

On November 10, 1992, having failed to achieve any success in ending the civil war, acting president Eskandarov and the government resigned. Shortly thereafter, the Tajik Supreme Soviet convened in the town of Khojend to elect a new government and to negotiate a cease-fire. The legislature abolished the office of president and Imamali (Imomali) Sharifovich Rahmanov, a collective farm chairman from Kulyab region, was appointed chairman of the Supreme Soviet, a post now equivalent to head of state. The Supreme Soviet elected a new government in which Abdulmalik Abdulojonov retained the post of prime minister. However, all members of the opposition parties lost their portfolios, and the majority of the new ministers were Kulyabis, or identified as sympathetic to ex-president Nabiyev. The Supreme Soviet also voted to combine the Ghorghan Tepeh and Kulyab regions into one administrative region, Khatlon (Khatlan), apparently in an attempt to ensure control of the south of the republic by pro-Communist forces from Kulyab. The region has since been more or less cleansed of opposition supporters.[40]

In December 1992, forces loyal to the new government, mostly units of the TPF and militia from the Gissar district, captured Dushanbe, hitherto under the control of the Popular Democratic Army (PDA), a newly formed military coalition of Islamic and democratic groups. Hundreds of PDA fighters were reported to have been killed during the attack, and there were also reports of maltreatment of civilians. By the end of January 1993, the government and its allied militia claimed to be in control of most of the country, with the last remaining rebel formations having retreated into the mountainous areas to the east of Dushanbe, notably the Gharm valley and Gorno-Badakhshan. The government estimated that some 20,000 people had been killed during six months of civil war, while there were an estimated 600,000 refugees who had been displaced.

In December 1992 and January 1993, some 80,000 Tajiks fled to Afghanistan, after reports of reprisals against supporters of the democratic and Islamic forces, including executions of opposition members, and attacks on Tajiks from Gharm by Kulyabis. Such reports were denied by the government and Kulyabi military leaders. Among those reported to have fled were the chair and deputy chair of the IRP, Muhammad Sharif Hematzoda and Dawlat Usman, the head of the radical elements of the IRP, Mullah Abdullah Nureddin Mirsaidov, and the influential kazi of Tajikistan, Akbar Turajonzoda, the highest-ranking Muslim clergyman in the country, who was accused by the new government of attempting to establish an Islamic state in Tajikistan. In February 1993, he was replaced as spiritual leader of Tajikistan's Muslims by Fatollah Sharifov (Sharifzoda), who was given the title of mufti.

Armed opposition to the government continued in the mountainous areas to the east of Dushanbe, where popular support for the rebels was reported to be strong. In February 1993, the Gharm district declared itself an "autonomous Islamic republic," but government forces continued to disarm rebel groups in the area. Mullah Azam and field commander Rizvan, the organizers of the Islamic Republic, fled Gharm upon the arrival of the government forces.[41] In early March Communist government forces finally captured the Ramit gorge, which opposition forces had been defending for more than one month. During the first two weeks of March some 170 government troops were reported to have been killed during an offensive in the Gorno-Badakhshan region. In April the government claimed to have the region under control, although there were continued reports of sporadic raids on government positions by Islamic fighters, allegedly supported by Afghan Mujahidin. In late March the TPF leader, Sangak Safarov, was killed, apparently as a result of an altercation with one of his chief military commanders, Saidov, and in April former president Nabiyev died of a heart attack.[42]

Although the government of Imomali Rahmonov has managed to exercise control over much of the republic since the summer of 1993, the border clashes with the Afghan-backed Islamic-democratic forces have continued unabated. It must be noted that the Uzbek and Russian military assistance to Rahmanov has been instrumental not only in containing the scope of the war, but also in keeping him in power by guarding major military and political centers in Dushanbe. According to one report a large number of Rahmanov's fighting forces are of Uzbek origin. Many members of Safarov's Popular Front were also Uzbek, who had received their training in Uzbekistan near the city of Termez under the command of an Uzbek general.[43] The Uzbek air force has been involved in bombing of the Tajik opposition camps near the Afghan border. While the Uzbek involvement in Tajik affairs has not been widely publicized, the Russian involvement, particularly the role of the 201st division, has been the subject of frequent commentary by the opposition long before the political instability gave way to civil war.[44]

The developments in Tajikistan have raised a serious question as to the future stability of Central Asia as a whole. While some observers have argued that the civil war in Tajikistan could easily be repeated elsewhere in the region, others have pointed to the republic's unique characteristics, particularly its non-Turkic Iranian heritage, to disqualify such a possibility. The causal origin of the civil war has become the subject of intense debate among Central Asian scholars and policymakers since the spring of 1992, leading to the proliferation of a variety of explanations. The most plausible, however, fall into three categories.[45] The first and most frequently cited explanation places a heavy emphasis on the post-independence emergence of a sharp ideological division within the Tajik society between the Communists on the one hand and the democratic and Islamic fundamentalist forces on the other hand.[46] The Communists in power accused the Islamic fundamentalists of pressing for the establishment of a theocracy in the republic. The advocates of this view refer to the April-May demonstrations in Shahidon Square, where the demonstrators raised the green banner of Islam, chanted slogans in favor of an Islamic republic, and used the network of mosques to recruit supporters for their cause. But more important, they point to the background of the leading members of the IRP, such as Dawlat Usman, and Mullah Abdullah Nureddin Mirsaidov, and others who have had a documented record of advocating an Iranian-style Islamic republic.[47] Conversely, the Communists who attended the demonstrations in Ozodi Square condemned the breakup of the Soviet Union, raised the red banner, and called for the reinstatement of Communist leaders in the Supreme Soviet and other governing bodies. But more importantly, those who are now in power have been hard at work reconstituting the Communist Party all the way down to the factory and farm levels.

The second explanation focuses on the political nature of the conflict between the supporters of reform and the Communist *nomenklatura* wary of losing their hold on power. S. Tadjbakhsh has eloquently summarized the crux of this explanation as follows: "With the introduction of *glasnost,* two forces clashed in Tajikistan, each lacking political knowledge but both organized, ambitious and uncompromising: conservative forces, powerful and relatively experienced at ruling, albeit by taking direct orders from Moscow, and forces demanding change, a coalition of democrats, nationalists, Islamists, and inhabitants of regions seldom represented in the government."[48] According to this argument the reformers wished to gain access to the political process that had been monopolized by the Communist Party for decades. This, of course, encompassed demands that not only required the wholesale democratization of the society but also involved issues of independence and sovereignty that had been compromised by the Tajik Communists who wished to continue their symbiotic relationship with the Soviet Union and later the Russian Federation. It must be noted, however, the methods used by the reformers occasionally violated the very principles they hoped to establish in Tajikistan. These included the holding of hostages and a variety of extraconstitutional measures to achieve their objectives. What led to the civil war, according to this argument, was a clear lack of interest, particularly on the part of the Communist elite, to reach a compromise whereby some degree of power-sharing could be instituted.

Finally, there are those who stress the regional and interclan rivalries as the overarching cause of the crisis.[49] According to this thesis, the Soviet domination of Tajikistan helped polarize the society along geographic and clan lines, with the north, Khojend (Leninabad), exercising political and economic control over the south. Various studies during the Cold War era have clearly demonstrated the political impact of the Soviet cadre recruitment that had been primarily drawn from the north. Since 1943 until the breakup of the Soviet Union, Khojend was the only region that provided the first secretaries of the Communist Party.[50] The north also sponsored the bulk of the Tajik industrial development as, for instance, in 1991 an estimated 65 percent of the Tajik GNP was produced in Khojend. The picture is, of course, more complex in that in the 1950s whole villages from the Gharm and Badakhshan regions were subjected to forced resettlement to Kulyab and Ghorghan Tepeh to boost the latter's agricultural development. The south, however, remained considerably underdeveloped and impoverished as compared to the north. The catalyst for confrontation between the regions and clans was Gorbachev's policies of glasnost and perestroika: the south seeking to improve its economic conditions and expand its political influence challenged the north's political monopoly. It must be noted that the bulk of the southern backing for the Communist-dominated north in Kulyab came from the supporters of Nabiyev and other Khojendi officials who had been stationed in the south and who had managed to create a system of patronage among the Kulyabis.

In the final analysis, all three explanations hold an element of truth in them. What is interesting is that there are considerable overlaps among these explanations insofar as the supporters of the two sides are concerned. The south has traditionally exhibited stronger religious tendencies than the north. The south has also been historically left out of the political game in Tajikistan. And finally, the south has been economically agricultural and therefore more underdeveloped than the north. While these explanations address, quite accurately, the causes of the conflict, they fail to provide an answer to its continuation. What seems to have helped prolong the civil war is the clear involvement of Russia and Uzbekistan in the Tajik affair. Russia's intervention is said to have been motivated by its foreign policy objective of containing the spread of Islamic fundamentalism from Iran and Afghanistan into Tajikistan and Uzbekistan. Barylski has provided the following account:

The Russian Federation made the struggle against Islamic fundamentalism part of its general foreign policy and the foundation for
improved relations with the more conservative political elites of the
Middle East and the Persian Gulf. This strategy was announced at
a Ministry of Foreign Affairs press conference held on the eve of a
final push to place a reliable government in power in Tajikistan and
in a general statement on Middle East policy issued in January
1993. Official statements made a distinction between Islam as a positive force in societal renewal, and radical political Islam that promoted conflict.[51]

Russia has also expressed concern over the fate of the Russian population in
Central Asia, many of whom had become wary of the future political and economic uncertainties, and thus had chosen to return to Russia. But, Russia's
actual intentions in Tajikistan seems to be far broader than its stated objective
of struggle against Islamic fundamentalism, particularly when one takes into
account its direct and indirect intervention in the political affairs of other former Soviet Union republics, such as Georgia and Azerbaijan. It is, therefore,
safe to assume that Russia is still very much interested in exercising dominance over the newly independent republics.

Uzbekistan's involvement in Tajikistan is motivated by two objectives.
First, Uzbekistan is home to a large Tajik population in Samarkand and
Bukhara whose postindependence political activities, though effectively
suppressed, could destabilize the government of Karimov in the future, particularly in the light of the fact that the opposition organizations in Tajikistan
are rumored to have entertained the idea of reunification of Samarkand and
Bukhara with present-day Tajikistan in 1990 and 1991. As such, Karimov
found it necessary to side with the Communist government in Tajikistan and
provide support for their war efforts against the Islamic-democratic opposition. Second, Karimov had been wary of the Islamic fundamentalist influence in Uzbekistan, whose supporters had been gaining confidence by the
unfolding events in Tajikistan. The removal of the head mufti of Uzbekistan,
Muhammad Sadiq Muhammad Yusuf, was precipitated by his growing independence and his alleged secret ties to the former kazi of Tajikistan, Akbar
Turajonzoda, who has been wrongly accused of pressing for the establishment of an Islamic republic in Tajikistan. Given the support the government
of Imomali Rahmonov has been receiving from Russia and Uzbekistan, it is
unlikely that Tajikistan could reach a peaceful settlement with the opposition in the near future.[52]

DEVELOPMENTS SINCE 1994

While Tajikistan's political situation has changed very little since the collapse of the government of national reconciliation, a number of new initiatives have been taken in the other four republics that will undoubtedly play a critical role in defining the future political dynamics of the region. Although some of the initiatives have been clearly designed to strengthen the authoritarian rule in the region, others have the potential to accelerate the process of democratization and thus help offset further politicization of Islam in Central Asia.

The most significant political development involves Turkmenistan. On December 28, 1993, the Khalq Maslahaty, a super-legislative body, composed of Turkmen notables, convened a session to pass a proposal to extend President Niyazov's term of office for another five years, bypassing the formal election procedures. A day later, the Majlis (parliament) voted in favor of the plan.[53] The decision was to be submitted to a nationwide referendum on January 15, 1994. First publicized by Niyazov's Democratic (Communist) Party in early December—apparently with his recommendation—the news caught the nation by surprise. The official justification for this blatant breach of the Constitution has been Niyazov's desire to carry out his ten-year economic and political development program without unnecessary interruptions. In reality, however, the move has been interpreted as an attempt by the president to prevent the small but growing democratic opposition from having a meaningful chance at expressing its views or gaining a toehold in the government. Quite expectedly, in the January 15 referendum only 212 out of 1,959,637 eligible voters chose to vote against the proposal to exempt the president from the 1997 election. According to Niyazov's closest advisor, Valeri Ochertsov, the overwhelming support for this proposal would guarantee stability and the continuation of the economic reform in Turkmenistan.[54] It must be noted, however, that although Niyazov has considerable support from his own tribe, the Teke, which constitutes an estimated 40 percent of the population, the majority of Turkmens may have been reluctant to express their true opinions for the fear of reprisal by the government, which has been in full control of the Turkmen economy and politics. Yet, Niyazov has also been hard at work improving his image by offering a host of economic rewards to the population that has so far included free utilities. There are also plans underway to provide bread free of charge and three months summer vacation for all working Turkmens. As such, it is quite possible that the voters have manifested their satisfaction with the status quo in the referendum.

The political process in Kazakhstan has also been affected by several new proposals that could significantly change the balance of power in the republic.

It all began in late November 1993, when three influential members of the Parliament's steering committee, Orazali Sabdenov, Birganim Aytinov, and Bulat Janasayev, made a public appeal in *Kazakhstanskaya Pravda* to dissolve the present parliament and create a professional parliament that would be permanently in session to deal with ongoing socioeconomic changes.[55] The appeal called for the introduction of a bill on parliamentary and local elections to be passed before the end of the year. The decision to disband the parliament received overwhelming support by the opposition parties whose members had been demanding such an action for the last three years. On December 8 through 10, 1993, in a closed session, the parliament voted to dissolve itself, designating March 7, 1994, as the date for the new elections. Subsequently, 190 out of 360 deputies handed in their resignations, and 789 local and regional councils disbanded themselves. During the parliamentary session President Nazarbayev made a request to the deputies to support his call for the establishment of a "presidential quota" system in the new parliament: "In the Supreme Kenges (parliament) of the future there should be at least a group of deputies who support the president. If this president is legitimately elected by the whole nation and expresses the interest of the majority of the people in Kazakhstan . . . then why should parliament be in opposition or in confrontation with such a president." He further pointed out that the presidential nominees will have to go through the election process and be voted on by the electorate. According to his proposal, 30 percent of the deputies were to be presidential nominees, 30 percent from the political parties and 40 percent from the general population.[56] On December 15, 1993, the powers of the parliament were transferred to President Nazarbayev until the new elections to the parliament would be held.

A week later, Kazakhstan's Central Electoral Commission made an announcement that candidates for the local and parliamentary elections must be nominated between December 27 and January 25. All public organizations were given legal sanctity to introduce candidates who enjoy the support of the population at large. According to the commission, the estimated cost of the republic's election would be 17 million dollars to be financed entirely by the government.[57] In yet another public announcement the chairman of the commission, Karatay Turysov, outlined the rules and regulations governing the election campaign. It included, among other things, a provision for television and press election coverage based on equal access principle, a provision that prohibited candidates from seeking funding from any other sources, and a ban on dissemination of racial, national, and religious remarks that would undermine the stability of the republic. In addition, the candidates were barred from campaigning on issues that would call for changes in the existing Constitution or territorial integrity of Kazakhstan.[58]

Although the election reinvigorated the democratic process in the republic, the government was hard at work creating obstacles to prevent certain parties from entering into electoral competition. For instance, the electoral commission asked all political organizations to reregister in order to qualify for elections. Deliberate or otherwise, the registration permit of Jeltoqsan, a religious-nationalist party, and the Democratic Committee for Human Rights were lost by the Ministry of Justice, for which no satisfactory explanation was provided. Several independent newspapers and radio and television stations involved in the election process were also closed or subjected to harassment by the authorities. A frequently employed tactic was the use of the fire department to close the printing facilities on the day of publication of the newspapers for fire safety reasons. The privately owned radio and television station, Max, and the popular newspaper *Karavan* were the subject of such government actions, forcing the former to broadcast clandestinely, and the latter to move to Bishkek.[59] Furthermore, the government placed a three-week time limit on candidates' campaign activities to prevent the spread of ideas perceived to be detrimental to the reelection of the pro-government candidates, many of whom had the advantage of name recognition compared to the opposition candidates. The dominant theme of the campaign was the declining economy and the deterioration of living standards. Consequently, many candidates called for economic compensation and reestablishment of social welfare guarantees. A total of 756 registered candidates competed in the March parliamentary elections, of which 361 were self-nominated, 331 were nominees of public organizations, and 64 were endorsed by the president.

Despite bad weather, 73.8 percent of the eligible voters participated in the elections. The Election Commission also reported that in virtually all oblasts the turnout had surpassed the 50 percent mark required to validate the election. Unfortunately, foreign observers who had been sent to the republic to monitor the elections reported widespread irregularities. The Dutch parliamentarian, Jan Van Houwelingen, who headed a delegation to Kazakhstan told a news conference that "election procedures did not meet internationally accepted standards." In particular, he spoke of the arbitrary disqualification of candidates by local election commissions and the harassment of the media for criticizing election rules. He had also been critical of the presidential list of candidates who campaigned for 42 reserved parliamentary seats not available for general electoral competition. Yet another alarming development was reported by the CIS and Russian observers who had spoken of the "ethnocratization" of power in Kazakhstan, since an estimated 58 percent of the parliamentary seats have been occupied by the Kazakh nationals who constitute only 42 percent of the total population. Of the 176 parliamentary seats,

105 were won by the Kazakhs, 49 by the Russians, 10 by the Ukrainians, 3 by the Germans, and 3 seats won by a Korean, a Pole, and a Uigor.[60] While it is too early to determine the exact composition of the parliament and local councils, it is plausible to assume that most seats will be occupied by those who will follow Nazarbayev's directives. In fact, the new chairman of the parliament, Abish Kekilbayev, is a close friend of President Nazarbayev.

Yet another significant political development occurred in Kyrgyzstan, where President Akayev's government came under severe criticism by the Communist-dominated parliament for its failed economic reform initiatives, forcing Akayev to make a nationwide television announcement on November 29, 1993, calling for a referendum on his presidency to be held in January 1994. Subsequently, on December 13, 1993, Akayev received a vote of no confidence by the parliament. In a secret ballot 190 deputies expressed their dissatisfaction with the government's reform program, which has caused great economic hardship for the Kyrgyz population. The deputies were also angered by the lack of progress on the investigation of corruption charges leveled against the prime minister, Tursunbek Chingishev, who had been accused of smuggling large quantities of gold with the help of the Canadian firm Seabecco.[61] Although the vote fell short of the constitutionally designated two-third majority, Akayev dismissed the entire government.

The referendum on Akayev's presidency was held on January 30, 1994. An estimated 96.3 percent of the 2,176,000 eligible voters cast a vote of confidence in the president's ability to continue with his reform policies. According to the Central Electoral Commission, 95.9 percent of the electorate took part in the referendum.[62] Akayev's success has been seen as a devastating blow to the parliament, which has consistently created obstacles to his plan to expand the scope and increase the speed of economic reform in the republic. It is interesting to note that the majority of deputies have frequently refused to disband the parliament for fear of losing their privileged status. The most recent call for the dissolution of the parliament came on December 7, 1993, which was rejected. The parliament has also declined to hold new elections while maintaining the present legislative structure. With Akayev's decisive referendum victory, however, the expectations for the eventual dissolution of the parliament in the near future has been raised, a hopeful prospect that will undoubtedly prevent the radicalization of the opposition forces as it provides an opportunity for greater participation in mainstream politics in Kyrgyzstan.

The final development involves Uzbekistan's decision to hold parliamentary elections in 1994. This decision was reached by the republic's Supreme Soviet on December 28, 1993, subsequent to the recommendation of President Islam Karimov. The new parliament, Majlis, will have 250 deputies as designated by the Constitution. However, contrary to Kazakhstan and Kyrgyzstan, where the opposition has been given a chance to participate in the future parliamentary and presidential elections, Uzbekistan has systematically destroyed the opposition organizations, which leads one to believe that the upcoming elections will have very little impact on the power structure of the republic. The main opposition organizations, Birlik and Erk, and the banned Islamic Revival Party have been unable to gain access to the political process, and its leaders have either been jailed or live in exile in Turkey and elsewhere outside the country.

The unwillingness on the part of the Central Asian governments to expand the boundaries of political participation and to include the newly emerging democratic forces in the national dialogue has begun to produce signs of intragovernmental rifts with grave political consequences for the future. Quite predictably, such tendencies have so far manifested themselves in the two most authoritarian republics, Turkmenistan and Uzbekistan. The first signs of internal opposition in Turkmenistan became apparent when in late 1992 the foreign minister of Turkmenistan, Abdu Kuliyev, resigned his post in protest against President Niyazov's political and economic policies, which he considered to be detrimental to the interests of the Turkmen people. Kuliyev has been apparently critical of Niyazov's refusal to democratize the republic's politics. In an interview with Radio Liberty in early July 1993 Kuliyev expressed his desire to run as a presidential candidate in the 1997 election.[63] Reportedly, he has the support of the democratic opposition in Turkmenistan. Unfortunately, the January 1994 referendum to extend Niyazov's term of office has removed the prospects for the opposition to have a meaningful voice in the Turkmen political process. The problem, however, is far from resolution, since in December 1993, Kuliyev's successor, Khalikberdy Atayev, also resigned his post in protest to the parliament's proposal to make Niyazov president for life. According to the Russian newspaper *Segodnya,* Atayev has accused Niyazov of building up "more personal power than a medieval despot" and of destroying "the glimmer of democracy in the republic."[64]

In Uzbekistan, Shokurollah Mirsaidov, a close friend of Karimov and an influential member of the Mirsaidov family, was removed on alleged corruption charges and was given a three-year jail sentence that was later suspended. In reality, however, Mirsaidov had frequently expressed his disapproval of the manner in which Karimov had been conducting the republic's political affairs, in particular his reluctance to instigate democratic reform. Mirsaidov had been in contact with the opposition leader, Muhammad Solih of the Erk Party, and had participated in the democratic congress in 1992.[65] He has been gaining popularity in Uzbekistan for his independent and principled political orientation. As such, the government has been monitoring his behavior closely and has been reportedly using scare tactics to silence him. In August 1993, for instance, a car bomb was exploded near his house in Tashkent, allegedly by the secret police. The Uzbek government has denied any involvement.[66] To what extent the present political repression in Uzbekistan is capable of obstructing the inevitable path of political reform may be dependent upon the support that will be given to such political personalities with genuine interest in democracy.

OFFICIAL ISLAM: THE EMERGING PATTERNS

Despite the apparent nuances, the Central Asian leaders have publicly advocated a liberal stance toward religion, which has guaranteed freedom of conscience yet prohibited religious extremism.[67] As such, the establishment of Islamic states, as the ultimate expression of that extremism, has been vehemently opposed. The fear of an Islamic fundamentalist takeover in the region has been the subject of frequent commentaries by government officials who have effectively used it as an excuse to, in fact, perpetuate the religious policies of the Soviet era when the state-controlled Muslim Religious Board of Central Asia and Kazakhstan defined the nature and scope of religious activities for the believers, instituting what has been referred to as the "official Islam."[68] However, since the collapse of Communism, the governments' religious policies have become more reconciliatory in approach and accommodating in orientation, partly because there are no ideological justifications to impose restrictions of the sort that prevailed under the banner of Marxism, and partly because the process of national revival in Central Asia has a religious component that cannot be ignored by those in power. Nevertheless, the official Islam has continued to play a significant role in shaping the ongoing Islamic revival by keeping a close watch on the activities of those Muslims who have chosen to return to the traditional ways of life after nearly 80 years of involuntary interruption. It is interesting to note that the Central Asian governments have publicly denied any involvement in the religious affairs of their republics, yet there is ample evidence to document a link between the official religious structures and the high-ranking republican leaders. The reaction of independent political and religious organizations to the continuing government support for the official Islam has been far from uniform, but the overall attitude seems to be one of condemnation. Some segments of the general public have also been critical of the official Muslim clergy who have been accused of compromising the interests of Islam and the Muslim community by collaborating with the old Communist *nomenklatura,* who have no genuine religious conviction. Some government officials on the other hand, have argued, off the record, that any attempt at reducing control over the official religious structures will inevitably lead to the infiltration and eventual politicization of Islam by radical elements who wish to establish theocracies in the region.

Be it legitimate or not, concern over the spread of Islamic fundamentalism has prompted the Central Asian governments to adopt a series of policies that has so far produced mixed results. The first of these policies was initiated by President Nazarbayev, who severed Kazakhstan's religious ties with the Muslim Religious Board and created a separate muftiate in 1990, in an attempt to reduce the spillover effect of the perceived Islamic fundamentalist activities in neighboring Uzbekistan. The Mufti, Nysanbai Ratbek, however, has downplayed the political significance of this move and instead has emphasized the discriminatory financial policy of the Muslim Religious Board as the underlying cause of the decision:

> For forty-seven years until 1990 the central muftiate for Kazakhstan was in Tashkent. Kazakh Muslims contributed an estimated 250,000 rubles annually to Tashkent but in return we did not gain any benefits from our contributions. The Tashkent muftiate rarely visited us to see the conditions of mosques and not a single letter of inquiry was sent to us. Most Islamic literature were printed in Uzbek. But we are not Uzbeks. These are the reasons why we chose to establish our own muftiate.[69]

Tajikistan became the second Central Asian republic to create its own separate muftiate in the aftermath of the civil war in 1992 essentially to curtail the influence of Islamic forces operating within the Uzbek territory, in particular in the Fergana Valley, that were sympathetic to the Islamic Revival Party. Turkmenistan and Kyrgyzstan have yet to officially organize independent muftiates. The Kyrgyzstan's kazi, Kimsanbay Ben Abdurahman, has been an ardent supporter of the Tashkent Board and has refused to even entertain the idea of a separate muftiate. His excuse has been based on spiritual considerations, arguing that the Islamic *umma* (community) is a notion that transcends territorial boundaries and, as such, the creation of separate religious establishments runs counter to the very nature of Islam.[70] But apparently, Tashkent has been historically more generous in its dealings with the Kyrgyz Kaziat than its Kazakh counterpart. However, the nationalist organizations that are in opposition to the kazi, such as the Asaba and Erkin Kyrgyzstan, have argued that Kimsanbay is an Uzbek at heart. He has lived in Uzbekistan for more than 20 years where he married an Uzbek national. It is this ethnic proclivity that seems to have played a major role in his decision to remain attached to the Tashkent muftiate.[71]

The second government strategy has been legislation and constitutional provisions designed to define the parameters of religious activities, the violations of which would give the government legal sanctity to level criminal charges against individuals and religious organizations. In Uzbekistan, the law "On Freedom of Conscience and Religious Organizations" was put into effect on July 2, 1991. Under the law, the citizens are protected from harassment and coercion based on religious beliefs. Religious organizations have also been recognized as legal persons once their charters are registered. Moreover, the religious centers have been granted the right to establish religious educational institutions for training students and clergy subject to the approval of the Ministry of Justice. Similar laws and provisions have been put in place in other republics. Not withstanding their essentially positive character, such legal safeguards have been instituted primarily to control and monitor the organizational behavior of the Muslims, who are forced to gain prior approval from various government agencies to operate. However, in Uzbekistan, where religious revival has been strongest, the government has not been able to conduct a systematic monitoring of the ever-increasing numbers of religious schools and mosques established by the citizens in various parts of the republic. According to deputy mufti, Shamsuddin Babakhan, an estimated 5,000 unofficial religious schools have been operating in various regions of the republic, of which only a small fraction has been inspected by the government.[72] This problem is, of course, less acute in Turkmenistan, Kazakhstan, and Kyrgyzstan where religious revival has a considerably lower tempo.

The third policy to combat fundamentalism has taken the form of repression and a crackdown on the religious opposition that has been carried out systematically in Uzbekistan and Tajikistan, but also to some extent in Turkmenistan and Kazakhstan. At least 20 high-ranking members of the outlawed IRP in Uzbekistan, including its Chairman, Abdullah Utaev, have been jailed.[73] Members of Adolat who exercised considerable power in the Fergana Valley in 1992 have also been arrested and tried. In Tajikistan, criminal charges have been brought against the chair and deputy chair of the IRP as well as former kazi Turajonzoda and a leading IRP member, Mullah Abdullah Nuri (Mir Saidov). Since July 1993, a host of other IRP leaders including Ajik Aliyev have been tried and sentenced to death by the government of Imamali Rahmonov.[74] Several hundred sympathizers of the IRP have also been captured and executed without trial since 1992 in the Kulyab and elsewhere in southern Tajikistan. In Kazakhstan, members of the religious-nationalist party, Alash, have been tried and given jail sentences, forcing its leaders to go into exile. Quite expectedly, the repression has produced some negative results, which in the long term are bound to offset the short-term gains. Perhaps the most alarming consequence is that the Islamic forces have been forced to go underground, making it more difficult to determine the actual strength and scope of their activities, particularly in Uzbekistan but also in Tajikistan where the threat of execution has provided a powerful justification for concealed activities. The repression has also helped further legitimize the Islamic forces in the eyes of some Muslim believers who have been quietly questioning the rationale behind the government's strong-arm policy.

Finally, the Central Asian governments have resorted to the policies of assimilation of the Islamic forces and appeasement of the general public in an effort to stave off the perceived fundamentalist tendencies. In both Kazakhstan and Uzbekistan the official clerical structures have made numerous attempts to coopt the members of the Islamic opposition so as to prevent further radicalization of their activities. Mufti Ratbek, for instance, has extended an invitation to the unofficial clergy—particularly from Chimkent and Jambul—sympathetic to the IRP to join the official clerical establishment. In Uzbekistan, the former mufti, Muhammad Sadiq Muhammad Yusuf, had met with the IRP and unofficial clergy on numerous occasions to assimilate them into the muftiate but to no avail. One such meeting was publicized during the fifth Kurultay of the Muslim Religious Board of Central Asia on February 26, 1992. Reportedly, the Mufti Muhammad Yusuf, met with Islamic opposition representatives, including the Mufti of Tashkent, Abduaziz Mansur, an IRP supporter. The meeting was mediated by the Uzbek presidential advisor, Bakhtiyar Nazarov, during which the IRP members were offered posts of deputy muftis, but the muftiate's invitation was turned down.[75] The basic objection of the Islamic opposition has been the government's constant monitoring of, and interference with, the affairs of the religious establishment. The Central Asian governments have also been active in placating the public in an effort to reduce the appeal of Islamic opposition forces. This has included financial assistance for the construction and renovation of mosques, which has been done sometimes quietly and indirectly through the official clerical structures, or with fanfare and propaganda to boost the image of the republican leaders in Uzbekistan and Kazakhstan, as well as in Kyrgyzstan and Turkmenistan. Karimov, for instance, has organized and refurbished many Islamic holy sites including the Islamic complex at the shrine of the Sufi leader, Khoja Bahaudin Naqshband, near Bukhara and the tomb and Islamic complex of Abu Abdullah Muhammad Al-Bukhari outside Samarkand. In addition, local television and radio stations have incorporated limited Islamic and language programs designed to reach the more traditional segments of the population in Kazakhstan and Kyrgyzstan. On February 25, 1994, Tajikistan banned the broadcast of all programs "that might offend national traditions and generally-accepted moral standards."[76] The state media has also been prohibited from carrying advertisements for alcoholic beverages and tobacco products.

Despite concerted efforts to maintain control over official Islam, the Central Asian governments have been challenged on several occasions from within the clerical establishment. This has raised serious questions as to the political utility of a policy that has already been proven to be less than effective as the Islamic experience under the Soviet rule has clearly demonstrated. In fact, some observers have argued that in the more open religious environment of postindependence, such a close association between the official Islamic structures and the state has accelerated the growth of the so-called "un-official Islam" in many areas with strong religious proclivity, a trend that could help further deligitimize official Islam, which has historically received negative publicity for its subservience to the Communist governments in the region. Over the past few years, official Islam has exhibited three distinct patterns of response to the postindependence political and religious conditions. The first pattern, which may be characterized as radical, emerged in Tajikistan and Uzbekistan where Kazi Akbar Turajonzoda and Mufti Muhammad Sadiq Muhammad Yusuf chose to challenge the ever-increasing involvement of government in religious affairs.[77] Given the scarcity of information and government propaganda, it is rather difficult to discern the prime motive behind their actions. The official explanation has accused them of masterminding an Islamic fundamentalist conspiracy to establish theocracies in their respective republics. The two men, however, have argued that their objective has been to create independent religious structures with minimal government intervention. But it may well be true that Turajonzoda and Muhammad Yusuf were also interested in giving Islam a more powerful and meaningful voice in the political process, which until now has been dominated by the Communist elite. Whether one would interpret this as a drive toward fundamentalism or simply an introductory exercise in democratic politics is intimately related to one's ideological predilections.

Judged by their public speeches and interviews given over the past few years, neither clergy had made any implicit or explicit reference to a plan to set up theocracies in their republics. In fact, Turajonzoda had been critical of the establishment of the IRP in Tajikistan as was evidenced in his 1991 address to the Supreme Soviet when he strongly opposed the extension of a legal status to the party.[78] In one of his interviews during the spring of 1992, Turajonzoda once again reiterated his long-held view on the subject of Islamic fundamentalism as follows: "Only in a democratic society can religion develop normally in a non-violent way, by means of freedom of choice. So we do not make it our aim to create, to organize in Tajikistan a theocratic state, a religious state. We are all for a secular society." In the Fall of 1992, he repeated this view once again before he went into hiding: "Our hopes can come true when there is a veritable democratic, rule-of-law and, however strange one may find it, a secular state. As a Muslim leader, I certainly dream of living in a state governed by the laws of Islam, but, if one is realistic, one should realize that our society is not ready for this."[79] Turajonzoda had also demonstrated considerable statesmanship and the forthrightness to reject the IRP proposal to remove President Rahman Nabiyev from the government of national reconciliation, a decision that could hardly be considered belligerent or radical in orientation. It is very difficult to determine what factors contributed to the eventual assimilation of the kazi into the IRP camp, given that most Tajiks had an extremely positive view of him as a learned man with liberal political beliefs. Many independent Tajik journalists believe that the retaliatory policy of the Communist government of Rahmonov toward the opposition was the underlying cause of his decision to join the exiled IRP leaders in Afghanistan.[80] He has since made numerous appeals to the Dushanbe government to stop the bloodshed and agree to negotiate with the opposition forces. With his efforts an agreement was reached on March 9, 1994, to begin peace talks under Russian and UN supervision.[81]

Mufti Muhammad Sadiq Muhammad Yusuf has also denounced Islamic fundamentalism on frequent occasions arguing that involvement in politics runs counter to the basic principles of Islam. In an interview with Interfax news agency on January 27, 1993, the mufti was quick to express his disappointment with the events in Tajikistan indicating that he "repeatedly warned religious leaders in Tajikistan to keep out of the political struggle in the republic" and that the Muslim Religious Board in no way condones the actions of Kazi Turajonzoda.[82] Although opposed to fundamentalism, the mufti has been noted for his strong independent views ever since he took office in 1989 subsequent to the ouster of his predecessor, Shamsuddin Babakhan, on charges of ignorance of the Koran, blasphemous behavior, such as drinking and womanizing, and subservience to secular authorities. In one of his first public announcements the mufti made an unequivocal reference to perestroika as the instrument of change: "With the help of the all-merciful Allah, perestroika will bring about many changes, including in relations between religious organizations and the state."[83] His popularity and independent religious orientation triggered an expedited response by the Karimov government to first discredit and then remove him from his post. But unlike Tajikistan's government, which opted for a direct action against the kazi and other members of the religious opposition, the Uzbek government chose to orchestrate religious protests in Tashkent's main square against the mufti, pitting one group of Muslims against another. The first attempt to replace Muhammad Sadiq was carried out on August 30, 1990, nearly a year and a half after he was elected to the post. He was accused of embezzling $9 million donated by foreign countries to the board to be spent on renovation of mosques and Islamic education. The charge was later dropped as it could not be substantiated. A second attempt was carried out on July 6, 1991, when the Assembly of Muslim Communities in Tashkent voted unanimously to remove him. This time he was accused of ten offenses, including embezzlement of $20 million donated by Saudi Arabia, Pakistan, Yemen, and Syria, the illegal sale of donated Saudi Korans, and preferential treatment of his family members who had been appointed to important positions within the board. To demonstrate its impartiality, the government decided to set up a commission to investigate the charges under the chairmanship of the then Vice-President Mirsaidov. Once again the government plan failed as no evidence could be produced to demonstrate any wrongdoing. On January 8, 1992, yet another protest was organized during which the Muslims demanded the mufti's resignation.[84] The demonstration came after a two-week ultimatum had been given to Muhammad Yusuf to resign or face a removal by force. It is reported that sometime later his house came under attack by the protestors who used scare tactics to bring about his resignation. Subsequently, the pro-government religious leaders in Tashkent elected the ousted mufti, Shamsuddin Babakhan, to replace Muhammad Sadiq. However, he remained in power until April 1993 when he was forcibly removed from office, apparently after being beaten and hospitalized. The government-controlled media, however, announced that the mufti could no longer carry out his duties due to his poor health. It is more than likely that all the charges brought against him had been fabricated by the government, including his alleged collaboration with Kazi Turajonzoda who had reportedly taken refuge in Fergana for some time with the mufti's assistance. In fact, the phony charges brought against the mufti perfectly fit the pattern of charges leveled against those who have challenged Karimov's authority both from within and without the power structure. Muhammad Sadiq is believed to have moved from Saudi Arabia to Turkey.

The second pattern of response by official Islam that may be characterized as "moderate defection" occurred in Kyrgyzstan when Sadiqjan Kamalov was removed from his post as the kazi of the republic in 1991. Kamalov, who had also exhibited considerable independence and religious vigor, chose to abandon his religious affiliation with the Muslim Board in favor of establishing his own Islamic Center in Kyrgyzstan. While Kamalov has refused to press for a greater voice for Islam in politics, he has been very active in pushing his own religious agenda, which seems to be influenced by Saudi Arabia. Although a Sunni Hanafi, Kamalov has demonstrated Wahhabi tendencies, particularly in connection with Central Asian Muslim funeral and marriage traditions that he has denounced as extravagant, wasteful, and un-Islamic in nature. With the Saudi Arabian contributions, Kamalov has managed to gather a considerable following in Bishkek. His Islamic Center has been involved in a plan to employ two to three thousand Kyrgyz in Saudi Arabia.[85]

Besides the discussed two patterns of response, official Islam has continued to be subservient to the Communist authorities in all of the five republics. In Tajikistan, for instance, the new mufti, Fatollah Sharifzoda (Sharifov), was elected to office on February 12, 1993. Before assuming office, the fifty-eight-year old Sharifov worked for the irrigation network in Gissar, and since 1989 he had occupied the post of Imam Khatib of a mosque in his region. Shortly after his election, he delivered a speech in support of the government's policy of religious noninterference in politics, outlining a new plan for the muftiate that included the resumption of Islamic education, training of clergy, and publication and distribution of Islamic literature.[86] The new mufti of Uzbekistan, Mukhtarkhan Abdulayev, has also been apolitical in orientation and completely obedient to the Karimov's regime. He was the Imam of the Naqshbandi mosque near Bukhara. In fact, Abdulayev wields no power and has been elected for his Sufi background, an issue that has been capitalized by Karimov to boost his popularity since 1992. The mufti's appointments are literally controlled by his secretary who seems to be keeping him in near complete isolation. The real power was entrusted with Shamsuddin Babakhan—until his appointment as the ambassador to Egypt in the summer of 1994—whose past connection to the Communist authorities could hardly be contested. Most, if not all, of the mufti's decision-making authority was quietly transferred to him, even though he was officially functioning as a deputy to Abdulayev. In Turkmenistan a new official religious structure has been created by the President Niyazov to facilitate closer supervision of the state's religious affairs, hitherto under the jurisdiction of the Council for Religious Affairs.[87]

Given the general Islamic proclivity of Kazakhstan, Kyrgyzstan, and Turkmenistan, it is very unlikely that the official Islam in those republics would exhibit a radical pattern of behavior similar to the Tajik and the Uzbek muftiates. But, such behavior could be very easily repeated in the latter two republics if the present government policies of control and intervention continues.

CHAPTER 6

Islam and Ethnic Relations

An Uzbek may feel Uzbek, Muslim . . . or just part of his extended family, depending on the situation, the identity of the interlocutor, or just the mood of the moment. Facing a Kazakh he feels Uzbek, facing a Tatar he feels Turkistani, while confronting a Christian or a Jew he feels Muslim. A Russian makes him feel all three (Uzbek, Turkistani, Muslim) and awakens the latent resentment of a native against a settler.

—MICHAEL RYWKIN, PROFESSOR OF RUSSIAN STUDIES,
CITY COLLEGE OF NEW YORK

Much like Islam, the Turko-Iranian ethnic heritage has been an integral part of the native Central Asian psyche, forced to lie dormant under the ideological hegemony of Marxist-Leninism. With the collapse of that hegemony during the Gorbachev era, the ethnic factor has assumed a more prominent role in redefining the general political and ideological direction of the region. In fact, the republican governments have been directly involved in developing themes with strong ethnic and national overtones in order to accommodate the regeneration of pre-Communist national symbols. Leaving aside the governments' role in this regard, two ethnic currents of differing strengths have been at work in the region during the last few years, and particularly since the independence. The first is pan-Turkism, a progressive late-nineteenth century ideology conceived largely in response to foreign domination and rapid Western progress, toward which many Turkic intellectuals exhibited a great deal of sensitivity. Thus far, however, pan-Turkism has failed to secure a sizable political following or institute viable organizational structures. To what extent the growth of this ideology could facilitate the rise or decline of radical Islam in Central Asia is a subject of considerable controversy, as pan-Turkism could readily serve a double purpose. The second current may adequately be characterized as ethnic separatism. Reinforced by age-old regional, subregional, and local exclusivist tendencies, ethnic separatism will undoubtedly become a force to be reckoned with in the foreseeable future. It is this current that has the ingredient to significantly decelerate, and perhaps altogether arrest, the development of radical Islam which, similar to all other political ideologies, requires a high degree of national unity and popular support if it is to succeed in capturing power. This chapter will attempt to put into perspective the dynamics of ethnicity in an effort to assess its strengths vis-à-vis Islam in the region.

ETHNIC LINEAGE: THE OLD AND THE NEW

Far from monolithic, the Central Asian ethnic makeup has been a colorful mix of the Iranian, Turkic, and Mongol races who were joined by a host of other ethnic groups during the czarist and later the Communist era, of which the Slavs continue to play a prominent, yet potentially destabilizing role. The original inhabitants of ancient Turkistan and the southwestern Steppe region were of Iranian blood. In the fifth century A.D., the Ephthalites, also known as White Huns, subjugated the Iranians and founded a kingdom in the region of Oxus. The Ephthalites themselves were defeated in around 550 A.D. by Turkic tribes who succeeded in establishing a sizable nomadic empire.[1] The southern regions gradually came under Arab rule beginning in the eighth century, but retained much of their dual Turko-Iranian cultural attributes. The Persian and Turkic dynasties reclaimed much of the sedentary areas of Central Asia by the eleventh century, then occupied by a largely bilingual mix of Turkic and Iranian (Tajik) peoples whose culture and tradition had been heavily influenced by the spread of Islam from the Middle East proper. By the thirteenth century the Mongol tribes under the command of Chingiz (Genghis) Khan managed to exercise control over much of the region. Mongol rulers were also quickly Turkified and later converted to Islam at a very early phase subsequent to the establishment of their empire. The direct descendants of the Mongols, the Timurids, continued to be further acculturated by the local population whose cultural and intellectual achievements had elevated the status of the Central

Asian cities of Samarkand and Bukhara to new heights in the medieval world. In fact, Timur's grandson, Ulugh Beg, had exhibited extraordinary enthusiasm for the development of arts and sciences, to which the Timurid courtiers made substantial financial contributions.

The Central Asian political scene was altered again during the early sixteenth century by the invading Uzbek armies from the northeastern frontiers under the capable leadership of the Shaibani Khan.[2] Much of the Timurid possessions, stretching from Khorezm to the eastern reaches of Turkistan, were captured by the nomadic Uzbeks who also became fascinated and later willfully consumed by the Islamic and pre-Islamic cultures of the region. The year 1598 marked the dissolution of the Shaibanid dynasty when its last ruler, Abd al-Mu'men, passed away, leaving behind a kingdom without an heir. From then until the Russian advances, Central Asia remained unaffected by outside forces except for the brief Persian military expedition conducted under Nadir Shah Afshar's leadership in the mid-eighteenth century, which led to the temporary annexation of parts of the region by the Afsharids. Apart from this, the region largely escaped foreign domination, yet endured the frequent invasions carried out from within by the Turkmens in the west and Kazakhs in the north. The former were descendants of the 24 tribes of the Oghuz who moved into the Turkmen region from the northwest in the eleventh century; the latter were composed of various nomadic tribes who moved to the Kazakh Steppe between the tenth and sixteenth century, eventually establishing three tribal confederations of the Greater, Middle, and Smaller hordes.

By the end of the eighteenth century three principalities of Uzbek origin had managed to consolidate their reign over various parts of Turkistan. The Emirate of Bukhara founded by the Mangits covered a large territory between the Amu Darya and Syr Darya rivers south of the Aral Sea. The Khanate of Khiva, created by the Kungrats was located on both shores of the Amu Darya that ran through the middle of the Khanate. A third principality was carved out by the Fergana rulers who ruled the vast territories between the Syr Darya and the Sinkiang of China. In the absence of clearly demarcated borders, the three principalities remained in a constant state of hostility until the Russian expansion from the north brought them first into contact, and later under the protection of the czars.

Beginning in the 1860s the Central Asian towns and villages were systematically conquered by the Russians who began their expeditions along the Syr Darya river toward the Tian Shan mountain ranges. Between 1860 and 1865 Tokmak, Pishpek, Julek (Djulek), Yani-Kurgan, Chimkent, and Tashkent were seized. By 1868, Samarkand and Zervashan were captured, forcing the Emirate of Bukhara to accept the Russian protectorate. Khanate of Khiva and Kokand were brought under Russian dominion in 1873 and 1876 respectively. All three principalities managed to maintain some degree of internal economic and political autonomy. By 1884-85 almost the entire region of Turkistan was brought under direct czarist administrative control.[3] And despite widespread revolt and resistance, the Kazakhs of the Steppe were also subjected to the same fate between 1822 and 1854, as were the tribes of the Turkmen grasslands by 1886.

The czarist conquest led to a gradual colonization of Central Asia first by the Cossacks, and then by the Russian peasants who settled in Semirechie and northern Kyrgyzstan in around 1866-67. The number of Russian settlements in the former region rose from 20 in 1907 to 61 in 1914. The Russians had also established various settlements in the Osh region of Kyrgyzstan, the numbers of which were reported at 50 by 1915.[4] According to Barthold, the native inhabitants of this part of Central Asia were Tian Shan Kyrgyz who may have settled there during the Karakhanid period in the tenth century and later intermingled with the Mongol tribes, assuming their present genetic structure. As for the Kazakh Steppe, by the 1880s numerous Russian peasant colonies had been founded in Akmolinsk and Semipalatinsk in the eastern Steppe and Turgai and Uralsk in the western Steppe. An estimated 1,544,000 peasant settlers found their way into the Kazakh Steppe by 1911. The tempo of colonization in Turkistan, however, was noticeably slower than the Steppe. According to Wheeler, approximately 407,000 Russians settled there, most of whom lived outside the Khanates of Bukhara and Khiva. The Slavic migration to Turkistan was further facilitated by a treaty between Russia and the Khanate of Bukhara in 1888, allowing the settlement and deployment of troops along the newly constructed railway stations and river landing spots.[5]

Quite expectedly, internal political instability at the turn of the century, as well as the outbreak of World War I and the Bolshevik revolution, severely hampered the settlement activities until the 1920s, when the Marxists finally managed to consolidate their reign over the former czarist empire. In the ensuing years, the process of colonization was resumed in earnest, bringing about a fundamental change in the ethnic landscape of Central Asia, one that has continued to play a significant role in determining the overall political destiny of some republics, such as Kazakhstan and Kyrgyzstan where a sizable Slavic population still exists.[6] This development may be identified as one of the most important factors in realigning the parameters of the Central Asian ethnic identity, the ramifications of which have only become more evident since the collapse of the Soviet Union, particularly in two respects.[7]

First, the increasing presence of the Russians and later other groups exiled to the region, provided a sharp contrast against which the native Central Asians could better comprehend their own identity, as for instance, Christianity put Islam into a more meaningful perspective, or Slavic ethnicity helped further define the Turkic heritage. This was further reinforced by the fact that the majority of the outsiders had made their way into the region by way of coercion and without the consent of the native population, an issue that has been frequently raised since independence by some members of the nationalist parties who have implicitly, and at times quite openly, advocated decolonization of the region. The opening quotation by Michael Rywkin is perhaps the most obvious yet eloquent account of what is meant by Central Asian identity, emphasizing the critical role played by the settlers in its reinforcement. Second, ethnic and culturally related issues of language, education, citizenship, and so on have become highly political and contentious, as the republican governments attempt to gradually revive some aspects of their pre-Communist past. Consequently, the Slavic population, as will be discussed in more detail later, has resorted to a variety of strategies to minimize the impact of cultural de-Sovietization of Central Asia, including diplomatic pressure from the Russian Federation, legislative appeals where possible, and in some cases passive economic threats by those Russian technocrats who occupy key positions in the severely weakened economies of the region. Others, on the other hand, have chosen to migrate back to Russia instead of adapting to the changing situation.

National Territorial Delimitation

An equally profound change that has affected the Central Asian ethnic identity has been the breakup of Turkistan into distinct political entities under the so-called national-territorial delimitation program introduced by Stalin in the fall of 1924 and set in motion the following spring. While the territorial division did not completely separate the main ethnic groups from one another, it left a substantial majority to each territory as, for instance, 94.2 percent of all Turkmens were allocated to Turkmenistan, and 82.6 percent of all Uzbeks came under the Uzbekistan national jurisdiction at the time of implementation.[8]

The territorial division of the region introduced fundamental changes with respect to the political dimension of Central Asian identity, of which two rank prominently. First, national delimitation has brought about the emergence of separate political elites in each republic, thus providing leadership status to those ethnic groups, such as the Kazakhs and the Kyrgyz, who had historically been subordinate to Uzbek hegemony in Central Asia, perhaps as early as the sixteenth century. This development may be identified as one of the main factors offsetting the reunification of the region as each main ethnic group hopes to retain its political and economic autonomy. Second, the territorial division of Central Asia has augmented the feelings of ethnic exclusivity between the dominant and subordinate groups within each republic. This may be recognized as one of the main sources of ethnic conflict in recent years and could well develop into much larger confrontations than have been witnessed so far. Explanations abound as to the underlying reasons for the breakup of the Central Asian territory. Stalin, the architect of the national delimitation, provided the following justification for his policy: "I think the recent delimitation of national territories in Turkistan may be regarded as an excellent example of how the Soviets can be brought into closer contact with the masses. . . . In a pre-revolutionary era these countries were torn into fragments and were a convenient field for the exploitatory machinations of the powers that be. The time is now come when these scattered fragments can be reunited into independent states, so that the toiling masses can be welded with the organs of government."[9] Stalin's argument in this regard was based on the Marxist conviction that the prerequisite for a successful transition to socialism required an expeditious conversion of the tribal peoples of the region into modern nations. This was to be done in accordance with four principles enunciated by him as a part of his new nationalities policy: unity of territory, of language, of economy, and of culture.[10] Others, however, have argued that Stalin was primarily interested in establishing a tighter administrative control over a region that had more or less maintained its pre-Communist political structure under Lenin. He hoped to achieve his objective through the use of the "divide and rule" principle, skillfully applied under the guise of nation-building. Of course, the underlying motive for tighter administrative control was to further expand economic ties to Central Asia, a factor that M. Mikhailov has clearly underscored: "Care was taken in laying the frontiers in accordance with the national principle not to clash in any way with the economic divisions. Regions that were economic units were not broken up. Each irrigation system, for instance, was included as a rule in one state. The national principle was completed and corrected by the economic principle."[11] Stalin had also been disappointed by the false assimilation of native Central Asians into the Communist Party rank-and-file, many of whom remained faithful to the culture and tradition of the region.[12] Hence, in utter violation of Lenin's liberal nationalities policy, Stalin expanded the Soviet control over the region by creating some of the most unusual and meandering borders ever created by a colonial power.

Prior to September 1924 the Bolsheviks had only nominally altered the political structure of Central Asia, which had been under the jurisdiction of the governor general of Turkistan and governor general of the Steppes. In 1918, the Turkistan territory was merely renamed Turkistan Autonomous Soviet Socialist Republic and the Steppe region renamed Kyrgyz Autonomous Soviet

Socialist Republic. In addition to these two territories, the two principalities of Bukhara and Khiva were assigned new names: the Soviet People's Republic of Bukhara and the Soviet People's Republic of Khorezm in 1920. Both, however, were considered outside the Soviet Union, yet tied to it by treaties of alliance. In 1924 Stalin redrew the map of the region, eliminating the Republics of Turkistan, Bukhara, and Khorezm, and in their place creating the Soviet Socialist Republics of Uzbekistan and Turkmenistan, the Autonomous Region of the Kara Kyrgyz, and the Autonomous Republic of Tajikistan, formally within the boundaries of the Republic of Uzbekistan. The Steppe was renamed the Kazakh Autonomous Republic. The Autonomous Region of Kara Kyrgyz was yet again renamed the Kyrgyz Autonomous Region in 1925 and later in 1926 Kyrgyz Autonomous Republic, and finally it was converted into the Soviet Socialist Republic of Kyrgyzstan in 1936. The Autonomous Republic of Tajikistan was also transformed into the Soviet Socialist Republic in 1929 and was formally severed from Uzbekistan. In May 1925 the Autonomous Region of Karakalpaks was created only to be renamed an Autonomous Republic in 1932. And finally, the Kazakh Autonomous Republic became the fifth Soviet Socialist Republic in Central Asia. From an ethnic point of view, the Kyrgyz Republic and the Karakalpak Autonomous Republic were clearly artificial entities. The inhabitants of the former republic, for instance, were essentially indistinguishable from the Kazakhs, except for their lifestyle and minor linguistic differences, and the residents of the latter republic were a combination of Uzbek and Kazakh peoples who merely spoke a different Turkic dialect of the same name.

As the process of national delimitation divided the once seemingly united Central Asia into distinct political entities, Stalin further complicated the ethnic picture by his policy of deportation of the "politically unreliable" and the resettlement of minority groups to the region. This continued throughout much of his reign and included Volga Germans, Crimean Tatars, Chechens, Koreans, and a host of other Asian and European nationalities.[13] With the introduction of Khrushchev's "virgin land program" in the mid-1950s, more Russian, Ukrainian, Belarussian, and Latvian peoples were settled in the region. The number of Russians and Ukrainians alone was estimated at 7.3 million in 1959. Interestingly enough, the rates of natural population growth and migration by the Russians and other Europeans exceeded the growth rates of the indigenous population until the end of World War II. However, nearly two decades later this trend was reversed as some Russians out-migrated, health standards improved, and the average birth rate of the local population rapidly increased.

TABLE 6.1
Population of the Central Asian Republics

	1939	1959	1970	1979	1989	1992
Kazakhstan	6,094,000	9,310,000	13,008,726	14,684,000	16,464,000	17,104,000
Kyrgyzstan	1,458,000	2,066,000	2,932,805	3,523,000	4,258,000	4,568,000
Tajikistan	1,484,000	1,980,000	2,899,602	3,806,000	5,093,000	5,680,000
Turkmenistan	1,252,000	1,516,000	2,158,880	2,765,000	3,523,000	3,838,000
Uzbekistan	6,336,000	8,106,000	11,799,429	15,389,000	19,810,000	21,627,000
TOTAL	16,624,000	22,978,000	32,799,442	40,167,000	49,148,000	52,817,000

Source: Figures for the 1939 and 1959 census are from Edward Allworth, ed., *Central Asia: 120 Years of Russian Rule* (Durham: Duke University Press, 1989), p. 96. Figures for 1970 and 1979 are from Alexandre Bennigsen and S. Enders Wimbush, *Muslims of the Soviet Empire: A Guide* (Bloomington: Indiana University Press, 1986), p. 47. Figures for 1989 are from Lee Schwartz, "USSR Nationality Distribution by Republic," *Soviet Geography*, vol. XXXII, no. 4 (April 1991). Figures for 1992 are from several map layouts prepared by the Central Intelligence Agency and made available to the public in September 1992 under the title of *The States of the Former Soviet Union: An Updated Overview*.

DEMOGRAPHIC AND ETHNOGRAPHIC DATA

According to mid-1992 estimates, the combined population of the Central Asian republics was reported at 52,817,000, 40 percent of whom belong to Uzbekistan. Between 1959 and 1979 the republics' population nearly doubled, registering one of the highest growth rates in the former Soviet Union and perhaps the world. The growth estimates for 1992 have placed Tajikistan at the top of the list with 3.0 percent, followed by Uzbekistan at 2.4 percent,

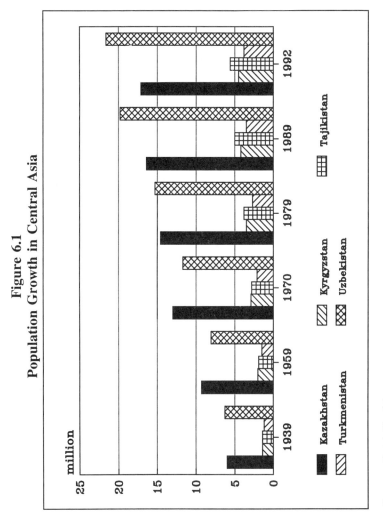

Figure 6.1
Population Growth in Central Asia

Source: See table 6.1.

Turkmenistan at 2.4 percent, Kyrgyzstan at 1.9 percent, and Kazakhstan at 1.0 percent. Table 6.1 and Figure 6.1 put into perspective the population size of each republic as well as the republican growth trends.

Several demographic trends may have a significant bearing on the future political development of the Central Asian republics. First, and perhaps the most obvious, is the rapid increase in the Muslim population since the 1950s. Figures 6.2 and 6.3 provide a breakdown of Muslim versus non-Muslim populations. Whereas in 1959 the non-Muslim population accounted for 40 percent of the total population, in 1992 it had dropped to only 23 percent. Quite

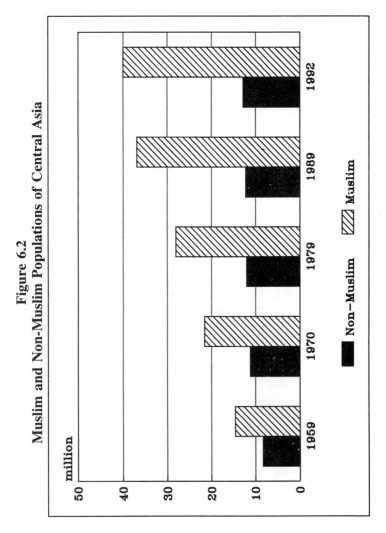

Figure 6.2
Muslim and Non-Muslim Populations of Central Asia

Source: See table 6.1. Figures have been retabulated for this figure.

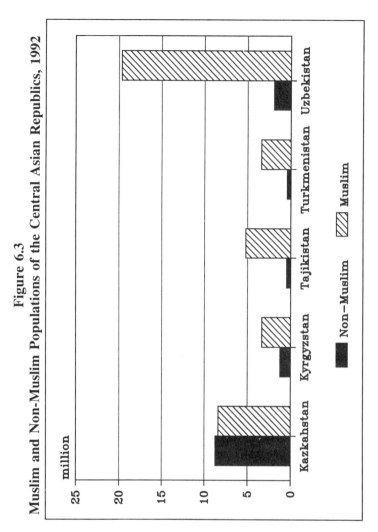

Figure 6.3

Muslim and Non-Muslim Populations of the Central Asian Republics, 1992

Source: See table 6.1. The Y axis figures are based on estimates derived from the 1992 source.

predictably, the long-term ramification of this trend is that the Slavs will play an increasingly smaller political and economic role in Central Asia. But, given its size in Kazakhstan, the Slavic influence will most likely last much longer than the other republics.[14]

In the short term, however, the Slavic population, and in particular the Russian population, will continue to play a critical role in the region, partly because of the Russian Federation's diplomatic pressure to safeguard their interests, and partly because a large number of Russians occupy key technocratic positions without whom the already weakened economies could further falter.[15] In his tour of Central Asia in November 1993 and in later visits, the Russian foreign minister, Andrey Kozyrev, exerted considerable pressure on the republican leaders to agree to extend dual citizenship to the Russians so as to preserve their privileged status.[16] President Nazarbayev, however, has skillfully repudiated this demand by arguing that the Russians are free to choose the country in which they would like to reside, but once that decision is made it is only natural to assume the citizenship of that country. To end all disputes, Kazakhstan drafted an immigration legislation that was publicized in August 1992 and subsequently simplified by a presidential decree the following December. The decree extended the deadline for acquiring citizenship until March 1, 1995. It also reduced the residency requirement from ten to five years to expedite the process. In addition, Nazarbayev has instituted a stringent legal framework to severely punish both Kazakhs and Russians who stir up interethnic enmities. The Russian Federation, however, has not ceased to pursue this matter despite Kazakhstan's clear policy position. On May 24, 1994, the chairman of the Commission on Issues of Citizenship, Abdulat Mikitayev, arrived in Almaty to further study the problems of migration and citizenship and examine the procedures by which Russians in Kazakhstan could receive citizenship.[17] It must be noted that Nazarbayev's firm position, and the future economic uncertainties have prompted many Russians to leave Kazakhstan as the last resort. An estimated 247,000 Russians returned home in 1993. Figures for 1992, 1990, and 1989 were reported at 369,000, 306,000, and 53,000 respectively.[18] In Kyrgyzstan, too, there has been an intense debate over the issue with President Akayev looking favorably toward an extension of dual citizenship. The Kyrgyz parliament rejected the idea in 1993 during the constitutional debate, yet Akayev has been wary of the departure of Russians and Germans whose technical expertise are needed to help the Kyrgyz economy readjust to the changing domestic situation. As a compromise, however, on June 14, 1994, Akayev issued a decree whereby Russian will be considered the state language in those regions where Russians constitute a majority.[19] The leader of Erkin Kyrgyzstan, Tupchubek Turgunaliyev, has frequently criticized Akayev for his stance on citizenship, accusing him of "bowing to the pressure of Russia's imperialist forces."[20] An estimated 144,000 Kyrgyz residents left the republic in 1993, of which 70 percent were Russians, of whom 50,000 have migrated from the Chu Valley to Russia, Ukraine, Belarussia, Kazakhstan, and Uzbekistan.[21] As for Turkmenistan, President Niyazov has accepted the only dual citizenship arrangement in Central Asia, covering an estimated 400,000 Russians.[22] An estimated 5 to 7 percent of Russians in Uzbekistan have also expressed willingness to leave that republic. It was reported that the

Uzbek authorities had been annoyed by the repeated Russian Federation request to reconsider dual citizenship.[23] And in Tajikistan an estimated 350,000 have left the republic since independence.

The second major demographic trend involves the ethnic Uzbeks who are present in relatively large numbers in all of the other Central Asian republics. The Uzbek population of Tajikistan and Kyrgyzstan amount to 1,360,000 and 590,000 respectively. Most are concentrated near the Uzbek-Tajik and Uzbek-Kyrgyz borders. It is noteworthy that since independence, the Uzbeks of these republics have exhibited separatist tendencies with the objective of creating autonomous regions and perhaps eventual unification with Uzbekistan. There is also an estimated 382,000 and 356,000 Uzbeks in Turkmenistan and Kazakhstan respectively, most of whom reside near the borders in the Tashauz and Chimkent regions. Given the subtle yet growing resurgence of Uzbek chauvinism that is being implicitly legitimized, on the one hand, by the present size of its population and its vast resources, and on the other hand, by its past claims to leadership in the region, the Uzbek factor may indeed play a destabilizing role in the future of Central Asia.[24]

Finally, in each republic there exists substantial numbers of ethnic groups other than Russian, a factor that should concern the republican leaders when charting the future course of political development. Nearly 17 percent of Turkmenistan's population, 21 percent of Uzbekistan's population, 30 percent of Tajikistan's population, 27 percent of Kyrgyzstan's population, and 21 percent of Kazakhstan's population are other than the dominant ethnic or the Russian groups in each republic. Any attempt at successful democratization must take into account the ethnic diversity of present-day Central Asia. In this transitional period, however, the problems of language and cultural assimilation must be handled with great care and determination if stability is to be ensured. Figures 6.4 through 6.8 and tables 6.2 through 6.6 (following the end of this chapter, pages 202-206) provide a picture of the ethnic composition and complexity in Central Asia.

In addition to the complex ethnic makeup of the Central Asian republics, there are considerable subethnic and tribal divisions and differences that further complicate the ethnographic picture. Kazakhs, for instance, are the descendants of several tribes that moved to the Steppe between the tenth and the sixteenth centuries.[25] The Usun, Kypchak, and Karluk appeared in the region in the tenth and eleventh centuries. The Mongol tribe of Kara Kitay arrived in the thirteenth century followed by other Mongol tribes of Naiman, Ming, Mangyt, Tangut and Dulat in the thirteenth century. In the fifteenth and sixteenth centuries yet other Turkified Mongol tribes of Kangly and Argyn appeared on the scene. With the death of Qasim Khan, who had managed to unify a number of these tribes including Kypchak, Naiman, Usun, and Dulat by the end of the fifteenth century, the Kazakhs regrouped to create three separate confederations, each claiming a part of the Steppe territory. The Greater Horde, *Ulu Juz,* which occupied the eastern and southeastern Kazakhstan was composed of twelve tribes: Kangly, Sary Usun, Shanshkyly, Ysty, Dulat, Jalair, Alban, Suan, Bes-Tangbaly, Oshakty, Sizgeli, and Shaparashty. The most numerous and politically significant tribes of the *Ulu Juz* are Dulat and Jalair. The Middle Horde, *Orta Juz,* controlled central, southern, and northern Kazakhstan. The largest of the three Hordes, it was divided into five major tribes of Argyn, Naiman, Kypchak, Kungrat, and Kerey. The Smaller Horde, *Kishi Juz,* inhabited western Kazakhstan and was made up of three tribes: Bay Uly, Yet Ru, and Alim Uly. These tribes were divided into clans and subclans whose sociopolitical weight has continued to play a major role in defining the power structure in modern Central Asia.

Much like the Kazakhs, the Kyrgyz have been divided into federations: The Otuz Uul and the Ich Kilik. The former is further divided into two formations; the Ong Kanat have traditionally occupied the northern, southern, and western Kyrgyzstan and the Sol Kanat occupied the central and western regions. The Ich Kilik tribes have historically inhabited the southern region and eastern Pamir mountains. The Ong Kanat of the north who are residents of the present-day Issyk-Kul oblast and eastern Naryn oblast include the politically powerful Tagay tribe, which is also the most populous of tribes in Kyrgyzstan. The political, military, bureaucratic, and intellectual elites have been predominantly drawn from the Tagays who are divided into thirteen clans: Bugu, Sary Bagysh, Bagysh, Mongoldor, Tynym Seyit, Sayak, Salto, Azyk, Cherkir Sayak, Sun Nurun, Cherik, Jetiger, and Baaryn. The southern and western Ong Kanat federation who inhabit the Osh and parts of the Fergana and Naryn oblasts include Adigine and the Mungush tribes with the former divided into six small clans and the latter divided into two. The Sol Kanat of the western and central Kyrgyzstan are composed of the following clans: Kushchu, Saruu, Munduz, Jetigen, Ktay, Basyz, and Ching Bagysh. The Ich Kilik tribal federation that has occupied southern Kyrgyzstan and eastern Pamir mountains include the Kypchak, Naiman, Teyyit, Kesek, Ihoo Kesek, Kandy, Boston, and Noygut.[26]

While tribal and clan affiliation and loyalty are very much alive in modern Kazakh and Kyrgyz societies, the sedentary Tajiks have lost their tribal attributes and instead rely on extended family or village, and region as a primary sources of their ethnic identity. Despite their sedentary orientation, however, the Tajiks have their own distinct ethnic groups. First are the Pamiris who occupy the western part of the Gorno Badakhshan Autonomous Region. They speak a distinct Iranian dialect and belong to the Ismaili sect. Second are the mountain Tajiks who occupy the high mountain ranges. They too have a distinct dialect and culture that sets them apart from the other Tajiks. Third are the small community of Yagnubis who inhabit the Yagnub Valley of Fan Darya in Zeravshan, as well as Varzob. They speak a Soghdian dialect incomprehensible to other Tajiks. Finally, there are the Chagatais who are of Turko-Mongol origin and who have adopted the Tajik language and culture, though some speak Uzbek. They primarily reside in Ghorghan Tepeh in Tajikistan and Surkhan Darya of Uzbekistan.

Of the remaining two major ethnic groups in Central Asia, the Turkmens and the Uzbeks, the former have preserved much of their social, political, and psychological ties to tribalism. Tribal loyalties continue to play a defining role in extension of political appointments and promotions. Such tribal bonds have been traditionally reinforced by territorial and dialectal exclusivity that has persisted until today. There are an estimated thirty Turkmen tribes, of which seven are considered numerically significant. The most politically powerful and influential tribe is the Teke tribe that occupies the Murghab and Tejen valleys and constitutes 40 percent of the population. The Ersary tribe inhabits the Amu Darya Valley south of Charjow and northwest of Afghanistan. The Yomuds of western Turkmenistan reside near the Caspian seashore south of Mangyshlak and the western region of the Khorasan oasis. The Guklen tribe inhabits the Kara-Kala district, Sumbar, and Chandyr valleys, as well as northern Iran. The Salor, Saryk, and Chowdor tribes live in various eastern, southern, and northern regions of Turkmenistan. In addition to these, a number of smaller tribes with distinct identities live on the Turkmen territory and include the following: Bayat, Chandyr, Karadashly, Nokhurli, Emreli, Sayat, Mukry, Alam, Marchaly, Ata, Hoja, Seyyed, and Shikh. Similar to the Kazakh and Kyrgyz, the Turkmen tribes are also divided into clans and subclans with clear social and economic divisions. Superimposed on these divisions are three pre-Soviet class distinctions that have persisted until today. They include: nobles *(iq)*, former slaves *(kul)*, and a class in the middle of the two referred to as *yarim*.

Finally, the largest of the Central Asian ethnic groups, the Uzbeks, are divided into subethnic categories. Although predominantly sedentary, most Uzbeks have retained some of their distant tribal and linguistic peculiarities. Bennigsen has identified three ethnic layers from which the Uzbeks are descended. The first are the urban Uzbeks, the oldest of the three ethnic strata, most of whom have been categorized as Turkified Iranians. The second layer are the descendants of the pre-Shaibanid Turkic and Mongol tribes that inhabited present-day Uzbekistan between the eleventh and fifteenth centuries. Some have been identified as Turks and others as Chagatais. The most influential tribes of this layer are the Karluks, Kypchaks, Turks of Samarkand,

Jalair, Barlas, Orlat, Kanchin, and Mughul. Third are the Shaibanid Uzbeks, the last Turkic tribes to set foot on Central Asian land in the early sixteenth century. More thoroughly Mongolized than the other Uzbeks, this ethnic layer is closer to the Kazakhs than to the sedentary Uzbeks also known as Sart Uzbeks. These tribes have maintained their identity and continue to distinguish their members from other tribal orders. The most prominent of these are Kungrat, Mangyt, Kiyat, Ktay, Kangly, Keneges, Ming, Kirk, Yuz, Saray, Kusheht, and Durman. These first four tribes are common to other ethnic groups such as the Kazakhs, Kyrgyz, and Karakalpaks.[27]

The Central Asian ethnic design on the one hand, and its precolonial and colonial history on the other hand, have given birth to two ideological currents: pan-Turkism and ethnic separatism. Though not fully developed as a framework to guide collective action or to help formulate policy, both currents have produced identifiable patterns of behavior by the masses as well as the elite in recent years. As stated at the outset, the particular interplay of these two currents influence the nature and scope of Islamization in the region. It is thus necessary to examine the parameters of this interaction first in connection to pan-Turkism and then in the context of ethnic separatism.

PAN-TURKISM

As a late-nineteenth century ideology, pan-Turkism came to symbolize the true aspirations of the Turkic peoples, whose small but vigorous intelligentsia, having witnessed the rapid progress of the European civilization and its colonizing strengths, hoped to defend and revitalize its heritage by fostering ethnic unity and solidarity. While the objective of pan-Turkism was hardly contested, Turkic intellectuals who espoused such an ideology exhibited considerable philosophical differences as to how to reach that goal. It may not be an exaggeration to argue that Ismael Gasprinski (Gaspirali), the spiritual father of pan-Turkism, relied primarily on the power of passion rather than reason in his treatment of the subject, and as such left behind a recipe whose ingredients had not been accurately defined. It was he who popularized the phrase, *Dilde, fikirde, ishte birlik,* meaning unity of language, of thought and of action.[28] His newspaper, *Tarjuman,* was used as a pan-Turkic platform to campaign for the solidarity of the Turks from Volga to Kashgar. As idealistic and abstract as his ideas were, Gasprinski did offer a concrete proposal that aimed at the creation of a single comprehensible language, cleansed of all its Persian and Arabic impurities, to be used by all Turkic peoples. And indeed, he developed such a language, which became the literary instrument of his newspaper. His linguistic success, however, can hardly be commended since the average Central Asian reader could not fully understand the text of his paper.[29] In this connection, Rorlich has made the following remark: ". . . by choosing to develop and promote their own dialect instead of adopting an all-Turkic language, the Volga Tatars exhibited boldness and confidence in their ability to assume the cultural leadership of Russian Muslims."[30] This somewhat elitist attitude of the Tatars has weakened their ethnic tie to the Central Asian peoples over the past two centuries, producing a less-than-desirable atmosphere for the growth of pan-Turkic feelings.

While Gasprinski stopped short of advocating a political union of the Turkic peoples, Yusuf Akhchura a Ph.D. graduate from Sorbonne, made such a proposition the cornerstone of his pan-Turkic activities. As a Jadidist with more than adequate Western intellectual training, Akhchura had recognized the significance of developing a common political space if pan-Turkism was to succeed. His Istanbul-based newspaper, *Turk Yurdu* (the Turkish Homeland), played a similar role as Gasprinski's *Tarjuman* in pushing for pan-Turkism. In achieving this objective, he went so far as to express a willingness to strike an alliance with the liberal Russian intellectuals who seemed to have understood the dilemmas of the Turks under the shackles of colonialism. Akhchura's view in this regard, however, was not shared by Gasprinski, and others, who found any collaboration with Russians detrimental to the interest of the Turks. Leaving aside this issue, for many Turkic intellectuals the inevitable by-product of cultural pan-Turkism, devoid of an encompassing political framework, was the further Russian resettlement and exploitation of Turkistan.[31] Such philosophical disagreements among the Turkic intellectuals did much to distract them from the very mission they had set out to accomplish for their own generation.[32] The idea of political union, nevertheless, was given a military expression under Enver Pasha, whose failed attempt at rescuing the political future of Turkistan left a lasting scar on the psyche of the proud Central Asians in the early 1920s.[33] It was hoped that political pan-Turkism could be quietly salvaged later by Sultan Galiyev, who also believed in the necessity of having an all-Turkic military to give further meaning to the movement. With Galiyev's removal and brutal death in the hands of Stalin, the idea of pan-Turkism was dealt a severe blow. In the ensuing decades, however, some segments within the Turkic intelligentsia remained cognizant, and tacitly supportive of the ideals it symbolized.

The era of glasnost reinvigorated the debate over pan-Turkism among the Central Asians, many of whom had maintained a more objective view of the Turkistan colonial history despite Soviet efforts at a Marxist reinterpretation. The first organized manifestation of pan-Turkism came to light in Moscow in 1990 under the name of the Assembly of the Turkic Peoples. One of its main organizers was the famous Kazakh poet and politician, Uljas Suleimonov. There have also been some unconfirmed reports that in 1991 a number of branch organizations with the name of the Turkistan Party—much like the Islamic Revival Party—were established in all of the Central Asian republics with the exception of Tajikistan. It is not at all clear whether there has been a connection between the first all-Turkic meeting in Moscow and these quasi-party organizations. Based on Western news information, however, none of these branch organizations have yet made any attempt to legally register. The Turkistan Party seems to have a clandestine organization in Uzbekistan, claiming a total interrepublican membership of 100,000. According to the Interfax Agency, on July 1, 1992, legal proceedings were set in motion against one of the main leaders of the Turkistan party, Bahram Goeb, who had been fictitiously charged with assaulting a law-enforcement official. Goeb, however, has indicated that his arrest was due to his call for the resignation of President Karimov during a student rally in January 1992.[34] Goeb is reportedly serving a jail sentence in Uzbekistan.

Leaving aside the Turkistan Party, which has been advocating the unification of Central Asia, many members of the nationalist parties in Kazakhstan and Kyrgyzstan have advocated these same idea. Some high-ranking members of the Azat Party of Kazakhstan, for instance, have openly expressed their support for pan-Turkism. The co-chair of the party, Batirhan Darimbet, has been publishing a newspaper entitled, *Turk Birligi* (Unity of the Turks), with a circulation of 20,000. The paper has been clearly addressing, among other things, pan-Turkic ideas.[35] Similar views have been expressed by the Kyrgyz nationalist party members, in particular Erkin Kyrgyzstan and Erk leaders of Uzbekistan.[36] It is interesting to note that the leaders of the Central Asian intelligentsia have been in semiregular contact with one another over the past few years. Most such gatherings have revolved around the issues of human rights and democracy, though pan-Turkic ideas have been given an open platform for expression in private conversations around the main meetings. Apart from these activities, pan-Turkism has so far been largely neglected by the bulk of the Central Asian population.

Several factors may be identified as the reasons for this rather apparent lack of organizational strength and popular support for pan-Turkism. First, over the past several decades, little has changed with respect to the debate over what constitutes the main pillars of pan-Turkic ideology. Interestingly enough, similar lines of division that separated Gasprinski and Akhchura have persisted until now, making it ever more difficult to arrive at a substantive philosophical consensus. Therefore, in the absence of a coherent ideological framework and concomitant strategy for action, pan-Turkism will most likely remain as an intellectual token of the past. Second, pan-Turkism has been in essence a phenomenon developed and sponsored by Tatars without regard for the cultural specificities of the Central Asians. This, coupled with the fact that Tatars have never bought into the idea of Turkic co-equalship, has prevented the strengthening of pan-Turkism in the region. Third, pan-Turkism received its fullest expression when the Young Turks of the Ottoman empire captured the seat of power in 1908 and hoped to use such an ideology as a defensive instrument against colonial penetration. That symbolic support of the once powerful Ottomans played a critical role in the spread of pan-Turkic sentiments in the rest of the Turkic regions. In stark contrast, however, present-day Turkey seems less interested in harboring such a philosophy, thus denying the pan-Turkic current in Central Asia the push-start it desperately needs to become a viable political framework. Turkey's official position in this regard was expressed by the late Turgut Ozal in a television appearance in Ankara on April 2, 1993:

> Fantasies of pan-Turkism are totally out of the question, especially in today's world. What do we have instead? These republics are all separate states. They are equal and brotherly states. We can form a community with them. For example . . . we can work as a group at the United Nations, and we are together in ECO [Economic Cooperation Organization]. In time we can become a community of Turkish states, just like the Arabs, but we must regard all of them as independent states. Let no one even think of a big brother role.[37]

What seems to prevent Turkey from entering into a pan-Turkic equation in Central Asia is intimately related, among other things, to its own precarious economic and political situation. Turkey does not have the type of financial and technical resources needed to legitimize its leadership position in Central Asia, a factor that could help provide a sound forum for pan-Turkism. But more important, Turkey has been plagued by a number of crises in recent years that will continue to consume its political energy. These include the Kurdish problem and the rise of Islamic fundamentalism. The former problem has been threatening Turkey's territorial integrity and the latter, its political structure. Also significant has been Turkey's westward orientation, which has been an integral part of its diplomatic strategy for decades. Turkey's desire to be fully incorporated into the new European economic structure is perhaps the most pressing foreign policy issue, far more critical than any other, including its role in Central Asia.[38]

The fourth factor responsible for the less-than-enthusiastic response to political pan-Turkism in Central Asia has been Stalin's national-territorial delimitation. This program without a doubt contributed to the development of separate republican elites whose political interests are clearly at stake if the idea of pan-Turkism is promoted. For better or worse, each republic in Central Asia has, over the years, developed a fully functioning political and administrative machinery with vested interests in maintaining the current territorial arrangements at any cost. What is interesting, however, is that while each republic has an independent political structure capable of maintaining itself, none has a viable economic structure strong enough to withstand the economic shocks of transition to a market economy. This has prompted the Central Asian leaders to promote economic union, which may be identified as a form of pan-Turkic drive.

The first serious attempt at working out a detailed plan for economic integration of Central Asia was made shortly before the disintegration of the Soviet Union in September 1991.[39] The meeting placed heavy emphasis on setting up a "single economic zone for the development of the market" based on common price indices, national currencies, uniform tax codes, and privatization schemes.[40] Also discussed and approved, was the establishment of a Consultative Council to coordinate the interrepublican activities for economic integration. Less than a year later, a meeting of the heads of the Central Asian republics took place in Bishkek during which earlier decisions were discussed and debated. But due to Turkmenistan's objection, the signing of the draft agreements on various economic issues was postponed. It was reported at the time that Niyazov had been reluctant to step out of the Russian Federation's economic sphere of influence for fear of further economic decline. Also noteworthy has been the frequent reference by Turkmen, Kyrgyz, and Tajik officials to the real possibility of Uzbekistan dominating any future Central Asian economic space to the detriment of the other four republics.[41] On January 3 and 4, 1993, yet another meeting was held in Tashkent to hammer out differences of opinion concerning the economic union. Very little, however, was accomplished in terms of the stated objectives of the meeting except for the formal adoption of the term "Central Asia" to be used in reference to the region. Also agreed upon was the creation of a single information area, a council of economic experts, joint commissions on oil, electricity, and cotton, and an international foundation for the protection of the Aral Sea.[42]

The apparent lack of progress on the economic front prompted the Uzbek president—the most outspoken supporter of Central Asian integration—to propose a bilateral economic cooperation agreement with Kazakhstan in November of 1993. A treaty was formally signed on January 10, 1994, which included strengthening of ties in the fields of culture, tourism, health, sciences, and education. But the most significant aspect of the treaty was the removal of customs on all common borders between the two countries.[43] A week later, Kyrgyzstan joined Uzbekistan and Kazakhstan by agreeing to create a common economic space by lowering tariffs and coordinating fiscal and monetary policies. To what extent Uzbekistan's efforts to unify Central Asia, at least economically, will succeed in the near future is first and foremost dependent upon the economic success of this tripartite agreement and secondly on the willingness of Turkmenistan to reevaluate its economic ties with the Russian Federation, which seems to maintain a strong grip on the republic.

In addition to attempts at fostering economic unity and cooperation that could, if successful, bring these republics closer to one another, the Turkic republics have agreed to adopt Latin script as their written language of communication.[44] This decision, if carried through, will undoubtedly help facilitate the integration of the region and will bring Central Asia closer to Turkey, whose bold move to abandon Arabic script in favor of Latin, under the reign of Kemal Ata Turk, radically changed the country's orientation. Until 1923-24 Kazakhstan, Kyrgyzstan, Uzbekistan, and Turkmenistan used the Arabic alphabet. The Soviet authorities introduced a modified Arabic script between 1923-24 and 1928-30. From then until 1940 several revised forms of the Latin alphabet were introduced in the Central Asian republics; in some cases such as Uzbekistan and Kazakhstan two forms of the Latin alphabet were introduced. As for the Iranian-speaking Tajikistan, the Arabic alphabet was used until 1930. From 1930 to 1940 Latin was used. The Cyrillic alphabet replaced Latin in 1940 in all republics with the justification that it could better accommodate Turkish and Persian sounds. The Uzbek language, for instance, has 38 sounds that the Latin alphabet could accommodate with only 26 letters, whereas Cyrillic offered 32 letters. The real motive, however, was nothing more than a comprehensive attempt at cultural domination of the region.[45]

Despite such efforts on the economic and cultural fronts, pan-Turkism will most likely remain as a weak ideology unable to influence the course of events in Central Asia any time soon. Nonetheless, from a theoretical point of view, should pan-Turkism gain substantial support among the masses and the elite, it has the ingredients to either strengthen or weaken the radical Islamic currents depending on how it will be interpreted. It can strengthen those currents, if the anticolonial parameters of pan-Turkism are accentuated. As such, it indeed could further legitimize the anticolonial drive of Islamic fundamentalism in Central Asia. On the other hand, it could weaken radical Islamic tide if its reformist and secular aspects are emphasized. Pan-Turkism, as it was originally conceived, had much in common with the Jadid movement, which in essence strived for a restructuring of Islamic education through the introduction of secular and scientific subjects in religious school curricula. Such secular tendencies, run counter to radical fundamentalist views, predicated on the strict adherence to the age-old principles of Islam. Seen in this light, pan-Turkism can become an effective ideological weapon against radical Islam in Central Asia. One must also bear in mind that such theoretical possibilities are not applicable to Tajikistan with its Iranian cultural tradition.

ETHNIC SEPARATISM

While pan-Turkism has yet to make a significant ideological imprint on the social fabric of post-independence Central Asia, ethnic separatism as a relatively pervasive current has left behind ample clues with which to offer a preliminary assessment of what may lie ahead. It is this centrifugal current that may certainly be considered an obstacle to the politicization of Islam, since it invariably weakens large-scale consensus building, a critical ingredient for the success of any populist movement, including that of radical Islam. Although less philosophically sophisticated than pan-Turkism, ethnic separatist tendencies have been historically compounded by regional, subregional, and tribal exclusivist sentiments, thus further accentuating the differences rather than the similarities within and between ethnic groups. It should be indicated that ethnic discord has always been a major feature of the Central Asian landscape, symbolized most frequently by the now dormant antipathies between the nomadic Kazakhs and Turkmens and the sedentary Uzbeks and Tajiks. As far as Turkistan was concerned, what preserved the delicate ethnic balance and prevented continued bloodshed in the pre-Communist past was the de facto acceptance of the ethnic pecking order in which the Uzbeks generally dominated or claimed a substantial portion of political power, with the Tajiks, Kazakhs, Kyrgyz and Turkmens commonly assuming subordinate roles with respect to the Uzbeks. And although the Uzbeks fought amongst themselves over territorial claims, the other ethnic groups rarely challenged their leadership status. This arrangement was replaced under Communism by the Soviet central authority whose local representatives resorted to a host of coercive and ideological measures to ensure ethnic stability, nurture the growth of independent political elites in each republic, and to guarantee the safety of the large Slavic settlements in Central Asia. The inevitable consequence of the penultimate policy was a drastic reorganization of the traditional power structure in the region with subordinate ethnic groups—the Kazakh, Kyrgyz, Tajik, and Turkmen—becoming more resolute in emphasizing their supremacy over the numerically smaller groups in their own republics. The post-independence politics has thus been dominated by two trends that are each capable of having a qualitative impact on the regional power structure. First, the Uzbeks have begun a subtle campaign to regain their traditional leadership status in Central Asia.[46] Second, each republic is hoping to maintain its own political integrity and ethnic superiority both with respect to the Uzbeks and the Russian settlers. Seen as such, ethnic separatist tendencies may be broadly organized into two categories: Muslims versus non-Muslims and Muslims versus Muslims. The former has received its most widespread expression in Kazakhstan with its very large Slavic population, but it has also been evident in Kyrgyzstan, Tajikistan, and Uzbekistan where it has exhibited considerable vigor. The latter category has had both inter- and intraethnic manifestations. Quite expectedly, the Uzbeks have been party to the majority of Muslim interethnic conflicts in the region.

Muslims Versus Non-Muslims

Much has been written about the general attitude of the Russians vis-à-vis Central Asians and vice versa. Most if not all point to the colonial factor in the assessment of the relations between the two groups.[47] Governed by the basic principles of colonialism, the Russians were no different than their British, French, and Spanish counterparts in projecting the image of superiority over their subjects. This attitude, as is well known, was given its fullest expression in the Steppe where the czars and later the commissars forcefully redefined the fragmented sociopolitical and economic environments of the Kazakh nation. The painful process of transformation, which included forced tribal settlement, collectivization, and the loss of land, left behind tragic memories with which the Kazakhs judged their "Russian elder brothers."[48] Not surprisingly, the overall perception with regard to the colonial masters was more or less the same elsewhere in Central Asia. The Russian settlers, of course, did much to reinforce such a negative attitude as they perpetuated a largely segregated existence, occupied the most prominent scientific, technical, political, and economic positions, and wilfully disregarded the local customs and cultures of the region.

Decades of Kazakh frustration finally manifested itself in the capital, Almaty (Alma-Ata), on December 17-18, 1986, when violent civil disturbances targeted against the Russians engulfed the city, leaving behind a trail of death and destruction. The riots were apparently triggered by the removal of the first secretary of the Kazakh Communist Party, Dinmuhammad Kunayev, an ethnic Kazakh, and his replacement thereof by Genady Kolbin, a Russian. Ordered by Gorbachev as a policy step to combat administrative corruption everywhere in the Soviet Union, Kunayev's departure was interpreted by the Kazakhs as yet another act of Russian chauvinism that could no longer be tolerated. While Kunayev may have been corrupt, he was quite popular among the Kazakhs for whom he had regularly bent administrative rules to rechannel funds for the improvement of the socio-economic conditions of Kazakhs since the 1960. The Almaty incident had several noteworthy features that set it apart from other cases that followed. First, it was clearly planned and premeditated. Second, it required a large security force to regain control of the city. Third, though the bulk of the demonstrators were young students, the incident attracted a wide range of Kazakhs. Fourth, demonstrators had clearly ethnic motives as were evident in their slogans: "Kazakhstan for Kazakhs," "Russians Go Back to Russia," "Kolbin Go Back to Russia," and "America Is With Us."[49] Finally, the incident drew into the discourse of ethnic discontent several high-ranking officials who lost their party positions for their outspoken views regarding the replacement of Kunayev and the harsh treatment of those who participated in the disturbances. One such individual was the first secretary of the Kazakh Komsomol, Serik Abdurahmanov, who later became an advisor to President Nazarbayev and is currently the Chairman of the president's party, the Union of the People's Unity.

The riots began in various parts of the city, leading eventually to the Almaty stadium. An estimated 20,000 to 25,000 demonstrators took part in nearly 36 hours of seemingly uninterrupted protests. In one incident, several young students broke into two prisons and freed Kazakh detainees. Conditions deteriorated considerably by December 18, prompting the government to request security forces from the outside, the numbers of which had reached 70,000 by the following day.[50] At least 30 were killed and 200 were injured during the two-day unrest. Gorbachev's immediate solution was more repression as scores of participants were given jail sentences of four to fifteen years duration. An estimated 2,000 students were also expelled from various academic and technical schools.[51] In the ensuing months, until his replacement in 1989, Kolbin conducted an anticorruption campaign that targeted Kazakhs in all walks of life. In Almaty, for instance, 600 Kazakh families were accused of nepotism in obtaining their apartments and were thus evicted, and many party officials were demoted for alleged misappropriation of funds.

The eventual departure of Kolbin, however, did little to normalize the republic's sociopolitical scene. With the introduction of Kazakh as the official language in 1989, the Russian nationalist organization, Yedinstvo, began to publicly voice its support for annexation of the northern regions of Kazakhstan by the Russian Federation. The situation was made worse when in September 1990 Alexander Solzhenitsyn publicly supported that proposition, which led to a series of demonstrations by the Kazakh nationalists who called for the preservation of current territorial boundaries. Ever since, the city of Ust-Kamenogorsk, in northeastern Kazakhstan, has become the site of highly emotional Russian nationalist activities. In 1990, for instance, the City Council threatened the authorities with secession if more autonomy was not granted to the Russian-dominated region. Ethnic expressions of a similar nature continued to capture the headlines in Kazakhstan, particularly since independence.

Conscious of the delicate situation, only four days after the declaration of independence on December 16, 1991, Nazarbayev made an appeal to both Russians and Kazakhs, to help prevent the ethnic polarization of the republic that could lead to violence and separatist tendencies.[52] The problems, however, continued to surface from time to time in various parts of the republic. In February 1992, ethnic violence broke out in Baikonur Cosmodrome where Kazakh officers and soldiers staged a protest to demand the resignation of several Russian officers who had humiliated junior Kazakh personnel. Three soldiers were killed, four barracks were set on fire, and 17 cars were stolen.[53] A similar incident occurred on June 3-4, 1993, when 500 Kazakhs from the military construction division at Baikonur looted warehouses. While the ethnic nature of both incidents had been played down by the government, it has been reported that the Kazakhs on the Cosmodrome are considerably less paid than their Russian counterparts and are often mistreated by them.

President Nazarbayev has also been working vigorously to avert the emergence of large-scale separatist movements instigated by the Russians in Kazakhstan. To this end, on August 10, 1993, he met with the heads of the Russian oblasts of Samara, Saratov, and Orenburg, bordering his republic to direct their attention to the interrepublican treaties that had been signed with the Russian Federation on the inviolability of borders.[54] The Cossacks have so far been the most outspoken advocates of border revisions and the territorial annexation of northern Kazakhstan. As such, the Kazakh government has been keeping a close watch on their activities since September 1991, when in a widely publicized event, the Cossacks of Uralsk called for the creation of a separate republic. The Union of Cossacks, which is in essence a nationalist organization, has been denied registration on several occasions for their pronounced separatist platform.[55]

Since the parliamentary elections in March 1994, which gave the lion's share of the seats to the Kazakh nationals, the Russians and Cossacks have somewhat stepped up their agitational activities. On April 7, 1994, for instance, it was reported that the Cossacks in the Taldykorgan region north of Almaty declared two of their villages, Pokatilovka and Topolevka, border outposts, provoking a near violent reaction by the resident Kazakhs. Consequently, six Cossacks were arrested and communications to the villages were temporarily severed to prevent further escalation of hostilities. The Cossacks have denied these reports, arguing instead that the Kazakh nationalists have destroyed the house of a Cossack leader in one of the villages.[56] A week later, and perhaps related, the journalist and spokesperson for the Russian Community in Kazakhstan, Boris Suprunyuk, was arrested in Petropavlovsk for having announced that an 800-strong Cossack army had been set up to protect the interests of the Russians. Accused of violating Article 60 of the Criminal Code, the Kazakh Supreme Court has been preparing a case to prosecute Suprunyuk, while another Cossack leader, Victor Ochkasov, was also given a severe warning not to interfere in state affairs.[57] The Cossacks have since made several appeals for his release and made numerous announcements as to the nonseparatist and peaceful nature of their demands, which have not been given due attention. The rising tension between the Kazakhs and the Russians in the north has prompted Nazarbayev to renew his earlier proposal to move the capital from Almaty to Akmola in the north-central part of the country as a signal to those Russians who have espoused secessionary ideas. It is also a message to the Russian Federation that Kazakhstan is determined to hold onto its northern territories.[58]

Admittedly, the Nazarbayev government has been engaged in a slow but deliberate campaign of Kazakhization of the republic. Many high-ranking Russians in key economic and political positions have been replaced by ethnic Kazakhs. In addition, since the adoption of the Constitution on January 28, 1992, fluency in the Kazakh language has become a requirement for those who hold or seek government jobs, and by 1995 non-Kazakhs must determine their citizenship if they wish to legally remain in Kazakhstan. Russians, however, still occupy some major technical posts and control the wheat production in the north without which the republic would face further decline. Despite all this, according to Melvin the Russian Embassy in Almaty, which has been specifically charged with gathering evidence of discontent, has registered only a few serious complaints.[59] It is interesting to note that many Russians who had left Kazakhstan over the past few years have begun to return as they have not been welcomed back in Russia. Nevertheless, President Yeltsin has been campaigning hard to ensure the socioeconomic safety and security of the Russians in Kazakhstan, hoping that Nazarbayev will eventually accept the dual citizenship arrangement for his republic. The Russian nationalist organization, Lad, has been working for that objective not only in Kazakhstan but also in other republics with large Russian populations. The organization's chairman, Valery Galeyeko, has pointed out that "we need dual citizenship to restore the destroyed Soviet Union and combat Kazakh discrimination."[60]

Though much less pronounced than in Kazakhstan, separatist sentiments between Muslims and non-Muslims, particularly Russians, have been witnessed in Kyrgyzstan, Tajikistan, and Uzbekistan. President Askar Akayev has been faced with a similar upsurge of Kyrgyz nationalist sentiments against the Russians, expressed frequently, yet less fervently, by the nationalist parties, Asaba and Erkin Kyrgyzstan. Akayev, however, has been economically and politically more vulnerable to the Russian Federation, which has been playing identical diplomatic cards to Kazakhstan to help maintain its citizens' privileged status in the republic. In response, measures have been taken to decelerate the Russian out-migration, which has been accelerating since 1991. Akayev has also officially opened a Slavonic University on September 9, 1993, in Bishkek to ensure that the Russians will have a good future in Kyrgyzstan.[61] The Society of Kyrgyz-Russian Friendship has also been involved in a campaign to promote better interethnic relations. Despite all the above, Kyrgyzstan began its linguistic transition on April 15, 1992, in those organizations that employed more than 70 to 80 percent Kyrgyz. According to the government timetable, the shift to the Kyrgyz language must be completed by 1997. Such policies, have significantly contributed to the growing animosity between the two ethnic groups.[62]

In Tajikistan, the interethnic relations have been strained more severely, in some respects, as compared to the other republics because of the Russian military involvement in the civil war. A systematic campaign of murder and assassination of Russian citizens involved with the 201st Motorized Rifle Division has been underway since December 1993. A January 4, 1994, report, for instance, indicated that nine Russian Baptists and a Russian Orthodox priest had been murdered in Dushanbe, subsequent to a religious service conducted for the members of the division. In addition, a lieutenant-colonel of the Russian border troops was assassinated in May 1994.[63] The government of Imomali Rahmonov has been hard at work restoring stability in the republic even at the expense of reducing Tajikistan to a Russian protectorate. The trade-off has been the preservation of the status of the Russians in Tajikistan that has been cemented with a number of bilateral economic and political agreements since 1992. According to one estimate, fewer than 100,000 Russians out of a total of 454,000 have remained in Tajikistan.[64]

Tajikistan has also been the site of an anti-Armenian ethnic incident that occurred February 12-13, 1990, when scores of Tajiks voiced their opposition to the planned resettlement of dislodged Armenians from the conflict in Nagorno-Karabakh. The most detailed account of the incident was produced by the Helsinki Watch in 1991.[65] Suffice it to say that the disenchanted protestors criticized the government's insensitivity to the plight of the Tajiks whose economic conditions would have been adversely affected by the presumably impending influx of Armenians. The protests claimed many lives and caused considerable damage to government property.

While Uzbekistan has been less eventful with respect to the friction between the Muslims and non-Muslims, many Uzbeks have expressed rather bluntly that the Russian population must some day return to Russia and leave Uzbekistan to the Uzbeks. Under President Islam Karimov's directives the Russians are kept out of high government positions. Karimov, however, has downplayed its ethnocentric orientation when dealing with the Russian Federation. But the ongoing departure of the Russians over the last two years has not escaped the attention of Kozyrev, who recently complained about the high numbers of immigration applications filed on a daily basis at the Russian Embassy in Tashkent.[66] Uzbekistan, however, will not submit to the Russian Federation pressures to restore preindependence privileges for Russian citizens. Much like Nazarbayev, Karimov has refused to reconsider dual citizenship, and is vigorously pursuing what may be referred to as the cultural, political, and economic de-Sovietization of Uzbekistan.

Muslims Versus Muslims

Another equally significant dimension of ethnic separatism involves only the Muslims. Admittedly, Islam has played a pivotal role in defining the overall makeup of the Central Asian identity. But even in places where it has had a convincing impact, such as Uzbekistan and Tajikistan, ethnic, regional, and sub-regional components of Central Asian identity have, on numerous occasions, exercised a more powerful influence on the minds of the politically active segments of the society. This, combined with the rise of Uzbek chauvinism, have produced a number of Muslim interethnic conflicts that could easily be repeated in the region in the near future. As indicated earlier, the Uzbeks have been a major player in most such cases.

One of the first, and perhaps most brutal, incidents of ethnic violence concerned the Uzbeks and the Meskhetian Turks.[67] The latter were relocated from southern Georgia to Central Asia by Stalin in 1944 for their alleged cooperation with the Turkish intelligence during the war. Of an estimated 100,000, 60 percent were resettled in various communities in Uzbekistan, of which an estimated 10,000 to 15,000 resided in the Fergana region. According to *Pravda*, the violence was provoked on May 23, 1989, by a Meskhetian Turk who overturned the strawberry stall of an Uzbek women in protest to her inflated prices. An altercation ensued, drawing a large crowd into the conflict. As a result, one person was killed and 60 were wounded. Ethnic clashes continued for another day in the city of Kussavi in Fergana, assuming a more violent character on June 3, 1989, in Tashlak where 200 Uzbeks carried out more assaults on the Meskhetian Turks. Reportedly, metal objects, knives, firearms, and firebombs were used to destroy people and property. On that day, 56 were announced killed, of which 43 were Meskhetian.[68] By June 4, an estimated 9,000 security forces from the Ministry of Internal Affairs had been dispatched to the Fergana Valley to restore order. Yet, violence and disorder went on in Marghilan, Bakatin, and Kokand, claiming more lives and causing more destruction to property. The city of Kokand was the scene of more violence on June 8, bringing the death toll to 80. In all of Fergana, more than 800 received bodily injuries, 550 buildings were set on fire, and 300 vehicles were destroyed. The disturbances continued on June 9 when the rampaging Uzbeks assaulted the Meskhetian Turks and the security forces in charge of their protection. The brutality with which the Uzbeks carried out their attacks prompted the security forces to evacuate the Meskhetian Turks as soon as possible. By June 11, the disturbances had claimed 100 lives and created an estimated 14,500 Meskhetian refugees who were housed in military barracks outside the Fergana Valley under the watchful eyes of the government.[69] It was not until June 15 that some semblance of order began to emerge in the troubled areas.

What led to this act of ethnic violence was the existing economic disparity between the relatively better-off Meskhetians and the economically deprived Uzbeks of Fergana. According to the Soviet authorities, an estimated 30,000 unemployed Uzbeks resided in the valley at the time of the incident while most Meskhetian Turks were economically secure.[70] Many Uzbeks involved in the violence were convinced that the Meskhetians' departure from the region would inevitably help improve the socioeconomic conditions for the natives. It is interesting to note that Birlik and other predominately Uzbek organizations lent their emotional and political support to the perpetrators of these violent acts.[71] The gross overreaction of the Uzbeks in this regard could only be rationalized if one took into account the centuries-old Uzbek sense of supremacy that had been profoundly frustrated by the presence of the Meskhetian Turks who enjoyed a relatively higher economic status in Fergana. This frustration was vented in 1989 with a vengeance, shattering the myths about the gathering strengths of pan-Turkism or pan-Islamism in the region. Once again, ethnic identity had superseded Islam as the final emotional arbiter of human conflict. Caused by a similar attitude toward other native Muslim Central Asians, the Uzbeks were involved in yet another bloody outbreak of ethnic violence against the native Kyrgyz in the Osh oblast of Kyrgyzstan. But this time, the Kyrgyz were also interested in testing their own sovereignty and resolve vis-à-vis the Uzbeks.

In the final analysis, two factors seem to have been responsible for one of the largest Central Asian ethnic conflicts in the post-Brezhnev era. The first was the establishment in Osh of an Uzbek organization named Adolat in late

1989.[72] According to one of its leaders, Rustam Mirahmedov, the hasty implementation of the Kyrgyz language law, introduced on August 24, 1989, was a major factor in the decision to organize Adolat. Yet, what was in reality an organized protest against the Kyrgyz language soon transformed itself into an autonomy-seeking political organization with an estimated membership of more than 400,000. As a group nearly half a million strong, most of whom reside in the Osh and Jalalabad oblasts, the Uzbeks never considered themselves a part of the Kyrgyz republic. However, with the borders relatively open and Soviet intelligence hard at work, the Osh Uzbeks never took their ideas of autonomy as far as they did before 1989 when Adolat was founded. For the Kyrgyz authorities, the demands of the autonomy-seeking Uzbeks of Osh were clearly in violation of the republican laws even though the oblast had a sizable Uzbek population. The second factor that fueled the fire of discontent was the establishment in May 1990 of Osh Aymaghi, a Kyrgyz nationalist organization led by Kambarali Bektemirov, whose declared objective was the distribution of land and housing among the economically deprived Kyrgyz of Osh. In retrospect, Osh Aymaghi played a critical role in exacerbating an already politically tense situation created by Adolat.

The trouble in Osh began at the end of May when Osh Aymaghi demanded that land belonging to an Uzbek collective farm be reallocated for the construction of housing for the Kyrgyz residents.[73] This led to the outbreak of violence between the two ethnic groups, drawing into conflict an estimated 10,000 Uzbeks and 2,000 Kyrgyz who continued to incite violence for nearly two months. By June 4, 1990, seven people had died and an estimated 200 were injured. Most deaths and injuries occurred when the security forces opened fire on protestors who had gathered to storm a police building. A state of emergency was declared in Osh and surrounding areas by the Kyrgyz authorities, and the border between Uzbekistan and Kyrgyzstan was closed to prevent further escalation of the conflict. Following three days of violence, the death toll reached 48, despite the arrival of 3,000 security guards and several tanks to patrol the streets of the city of Osh. It was reported that as a gesture of goodwill, the Kyrgyz authorities in Osh permitted 15,000 Uzbeks who had gathered in the Hajiabad district of Uzbekistan to cross the border in order to demonstrate that the Kyrgyz government had been forthright in its announcements regarding the safeguarding of the Uzbek residents of Osh—those injured, as well as those detained.[74] The violence was most pronounced in Uzgen where even children were murdered.

News about the slaughter of the Kyrgyz in Osh reached the capital Bishkek, prompting the newly established Democratic Movement of Kyrgyzstan to organize protests in favor of sending armed militia to defend the interest of the

Kyrgyz residents. By August the violence had subsided, but the state of emergency remained intact until November 21, 1990. Shortly thereafter, the first secretary of the Osh oblast, Usen Sydikov, was dismissed for incompetence in handling the interethnic issues before and during the disturbances. Both Osh Aymaghi and Adolat denied any direct involvement in the summer disturbances that, in the end, claimed an estimated 300 to as many as 1,000 lives. The Kyrgyz authorities blamed the Osh incident on the economic conditions of the region where high unemployment, and housing shortages had taken a toll on the Kyrgyz residents of the oblast. Uzbekistan's First Deputy Minister of Internal Affairs, V. G. Gusov, on the other hand, had offered an essentially political explanation for the inter-ethnic violence, intimately related to the question of power: "One often hears that hundreds of thousands of Uzbeks live in Kyrgyzstan. They are especially numerous in the districts bordering on Uzbekistan. However, one finds almost no Uzbek among the leadership of provinces, districts and farms. It is quite possible that this led to discontent, tension, and eventual confrontation between the Kyrgyz and Uzbek residents in Osh."[75] Whatever the immediate or the long-term causes of the violence, Uzbek-Kyrgyz relations have been clearly strained by the Osh incident, and many Kyrgyz politicians and intellectuals have since warned us about the possibility of its reoccurrence.[76] Again, in this case, Islam was definitely a lesser factor than ethnicity in determining the boundaries of consensus and conflict in the region.

Nowhere is the expression of Uzbek supremacy more pronounced than in Uzbekistan, where the Tajiks have been subjected to the same treatment that most Uzbeks in other republics have frequently complained about. Although less publicized than other instances of interethnic discontent, the Uzbek-Tajik antipathy constituted one of the oldest parameters of ethnic dynamics in the region. This, too, had been suppressed by Communism for nearly 70 years, only to reenter the public discourse at a time when most other Soviet republics had already started their ethnic and linguistic crusades in the late 1980s. The Tajiks of Uzbekistan, most of whom had been the residents of Samarkand and Bukhara, had struggled to maintain their cultural identity in an Uzbek environment that, at best, exhibited a weak to moderate tolerance. Interestingly enough, Tajikistan was an autonomous part of Uzbekistan prior to its delimitation as a Soviet Socialist Republic in 1929. The cities of Samarkand and Bukhara, however, remained within the political jurisdiction of Uzbekistan, leaving the fate of two major Tajik enclaves in the hand of the Uzbeks. Notwithstanding the government's cultural propaganda, the Tajiks were essentially given two choices at that time: either to willfully assume an Uzbek identity—many had indeed chosen this alternative in the past—or to leave for Tajikistan. It was thus apparent that the Tajiks will not be accommodated in maintaining their cultural independence, a dire fact that most Tajiks resentfully accepted.

When glasnost changed the political chemistry of the Soviet Union, the Tajik intellectuals of Samarkand found the courage to publicly press for their cultural revival. To this end, an organization with the name of Socio-Cultural Association of the Tajiks of Samarkand was founded by Uktum Bekmuhammadov and others in March 1989.[77] Its visibly growing strength forced the Communist Party to hold a joint meeting with the intention of establishing a dialogue to address the problems of the Tajik community. Three demands were expressed at the meeting. The first was the extension of the right to choose one's citizenship, an issue that had been contested by the Tajiks in the past. It must be indicated that those Tajiks who were born after the 1920s in Uzbekistan were given an Uzbek birth certificate, even though both parents were Tajik by ethnic origin.[78] This strategy helped the Uzbek government to understate the actual number of Tajiks residing in Uzbekistan in an attempt to downplay their significance as an ethnic minority. According to the official statistics in 1992, an estimated 1 million Tajiks live in Uzbekistan. Yet the actual number may be three to four times higher. Given the largely arbitrary nature of national delimitation, most Tajiks felt that they should be given a chance to freely express their cultural identity. Second, the organization demanded that the Tajik language become the second language of the republic. In the light of the fact that most residents of the Central Asian oases were fluent in both Tajik and Uzbek in the past, it seemed only reasonable to ask for a reconsideration of the status of the Tajik language.[79] Finally, it called for the freedom of Tajik educational and cultural activities, for which the Uzbek government was asked to provide a legal status. Of particular importance was the freedom to produce and broadcast television programs and publish newspapers. Interestingly enough, the third secretary of the Uzbek Communist Party, Jahangir Hamidov, told the representatives of the organization that their demands were mostly legitimate. With the enactment of an all-Union nationality legislation in September of 1989, the Tajik leaders gained more confidence in their pursuit of their demands. Shortly thereafter, the organization called for yet another meeting with Uzbek Communist Party officials. The request was promptly denied under the pretense that many of the demands could be met without further meetings. None of the demands, however, were met as promised. Nevertheless, the Tajiks in Samarkand continued their activities and further grew in strength. In October 1989, a Tajik-language conference and later a founding congress to formally inaugurate the organization were held.

Threatened by the grassroots support of the organization, the Uzbek government began a campaign to restrict and control what was in essence a Tajik movement for cultural revival in Uzbekistan. According to party officials, however, the movement had gone far beyond cultural demands, assuming political dimensions.[80] The organization had also established working relations with opposition groups such as Birlik, whose leaders temporarily supported the Tajik cause. At first, the Uzbek authorities hoped to dominate the organization by selecting its leaders from the Tajik community loyal to the government. One such attempt was made on June 23, 1990, when, having approved the creation of a Tajik Cultural Center in Samarkand, the government asked Nasereddin Ghamarzoda (Ghamarov), an apolitical and cooperative Tajik, to chair the center, despite the overwhelming disapproval of the Tajiks. Next, unable to curb the organization's activities, the government resorted to repression and violence beginning in June 1991, when the leading members of the organization were beaten, temporarily jailed, or forced to leave Samarkand. Bekmuhammadov was beaten and jailed for nearly a year. In 1992, the government accused the organization of separatist tendencies and allowed the Cultural Center in Samarkand to operate only under strict Uzbek supervision. Although, the Uzbek-Tajik affair has so far been kept under control, the continuing repression will undoubtedly strengthen the Tajik resolve in the long run, moving the interethnic discord in a more violent direction.

In addition to the Uzbek-Kyrgyz and the Uzbek-Tajik ethnic strife, there was also a limited Tajik-Kyrgyz conflict in 1989.[81] The incident began on June 6, as a water and land dispute in the Isfara district of Tajikistan and the adjacent Baktin district in Kyrgyzstan. Over the next few weeks it turned into a series of violent interethnic clashes. In 1958, a collective farm in Isfara had been given a 144-hectare tract of cultivable land to an abutting collective farm in Kyrgyzstan. During the next 30 years, the rapid population growth quickly exhausted the available land, causing great economic hardship on the Tajiks who were in need of private plots to make ends meet, hence the call to retake the 144 hectares from the Kyrgyz. The decision drew into dispute the villages of October in Tajikistan and Uch-Doba in Kyrgyzstan and other nearby villages. The dispute entered its violent phase on July 13, 1989, when one person was killed and 19 wounded in clashes on the border. The governments on both sides set up investigative commissions to determine the exact border so as to settle the land dispute.[82]

The interethnic discord is not the only centrifugal force that pulls the region apart; there are also strong intraethnic exclusivist tendencies at the regional, subregional, local, and tribal levels that further complicate Central Asian ethnic politics. Four characteristics, among others, both clarify the nature and underscore the significance of intraethnic continuum in the distribution of power in each republic. First, regional and tribal exclusivism in most instances imbricate each other and thus strengthen and intensify the patterns of intraethnic discord. This is clearly evident in Kazakhstan, and Kyrgyzstan, and to some extent, in Turkmenistan. Second, the most pronounced expression of intraethnic regional conflict has so far been produced in Tajikistan, but Kyrgyzstan and Uzbekistan have also exhibited regional factionalism, which may move the two republics closer to a full-scale conflict of the sort that engulfed Tajikistan. Third, with the exception of Tajikistan where intraethnic conflict has been supported by relatively well-developed organizational structures, most regional, subregional, local, and tribal discords have been subtle and nonconfrontational in orientation. Finally, there seems to be a strong economic component to the intraethnic discord, as the more deprived regions, subregions, or tribes challenge their better-off counterparts. This has been most obvious in Kyrgyzstan and Tajikistan where the north has been more affluent than the south.

Nowhere has the intraethnic conflict been so clear-cut than in Tajikistan. A brief account of the causes and consequences of the ethnic and regional rivalry was presented in chapter 5. It is, however, necessary to highlight the intra-ethnic parameters of the conflict. The well-known Orientalist, Rady Fish, has succinctly summarized the essence of the Tajik situation:

> To understand what is going on, one has to be aware of the Tajik peo-
> ple's psychology and its stronger and weaker sides. One of the
> weaker sides . . . is that the institute of association of people from the
> same area, a remnant of feudal order, is very widely spread. This
> problem has always been dealt with very carefully in Tajikistan,
> trying to preserve the balance even in small organizations. In the
> Writers' Association, for instance, the deceased Mirzo Tursunzade,
> its former head, paid much attention to the balance among different
> ethnic groups. If the secretary came from Darvoz, the Sadoi Shark
> journal was being edited by a poet from Penjikent . . . Though all
> main posts were occupied by the Hudzhand [Khojend] people, mem-
> bers of other ethnic formations got their share too. The result of this
> is evident: the [Khojend] clan exploited the rest of Tajikistan and the
> southern regions . . . received a hundred-fold less than the northern
> ones, in the social and economic aspects.[83]

The northern region of Khojend, where a high concentration of Uzbeks reside, has traditionally been in close contact with the Uzbek Communist Party and receptive to their policy preferences in Tajikistan. The Khojend power elite has managed to exercise control over much of the south through its alliance with the Kulabis (Kulabis) and some loyal elements in Gissar. This alliance had been strengthened during the late Rahman Nabiyev's tenure in Kulyab prior to his appointment as the first secretary of the party. Less united than the north, southern Tajikistan came together in the early 1990s to form the brunt of the opposition to the status quo, under the organizational banner of the Islamic Revival Party, the Democratic Party, Rastokhez, and La'l-e Badakhshan. For a brief period in the summer of 1992, the south managed to enter into a power-sharing agreement with the north, subsequent to the establishment of the Government of National Reconciliation. With the outbreak of the civil war, which was in essence the manifestation of regional discord, the north once again regained some of its lost power, receiving critical help from the militant Kulyabis under the leadership of Sangak Safarov and his allies in the Gissar Valley. Owing much of its initial success to the armed factions in Kulyab and Gissar, the Khojendi elite had been forced to offer several important portfolios to its southern allies in order to prevent infighting. The appointment of the chairman of Gissar rayon, Jamoliddin Mansurov, to the post of the mayor of Dushanbe on April 12, 1993, was but an attempt to diffuse a potentially threatening situation to the government. Mansurov was the organizer of the second largest armed grouping out of the Gissar Valley and a rival to Sangak Safarov who headed the largest militia organization. When Safarov was killed in the spring of 1993, Mansurov began to push for a greater share of power for his region.[84] Far from settled, the regional jockeying for power has continued unabated. The defeated south has also been hard at work to expand its base of support in the north through frequent radio appeals calling on the people to join in the struggle to topple the government of Imomali Rahmonov.[85]

A similar scenario is being developed slowly in Kyrgyzstan where the south and the north have been involved in a struggle for political power and economic gain. Here, too, the north has historically captured a larger share of power to the detriment of the southern regions of Osh and Jalalabad. The Issyk-Kul region has been the undisputed political power base, with Naryn and Talas making occasional high-level contributions to the government in the last three decades. Quite expectedly, the expressions of regional rivalry have become more frequent and deliberate since the independence, creating a potentially destabilizing situation for President Akayev, who has been less than successful in striking a balance with regard to the regional distribution of power.[86] On October 25, 1992, for instance, spontaneous demonstrations broke out in Jalalabad during which the supporters of the head administrator, Bekmamat Usmonov, renounced a call for his resignation demanded by the government. Usmonov was accused of violating the principles of local self-government, and other legislative acts. He and his seven brothers head a powerful southern clan that has been quite explicit in its opposition to the north's disproportionate share of power. Akayev appointed a close friend, Abdygany Erkebayev, to head the Osh oblast, which has not been free from criticism in the south. Public opinion polls conducted in the towns of Osh and Jalalabad in 1992 and 1993 have reaffirmed the continuing conflict between the north and the south with no prospects for its disappearance in the near future.[87] The polls also show a general pattern of disapproval in the way in which the government has so far handled the socioeconomic problems in the republic. It must be noted, however, that the south has not established organizational structures of the sort that were witnessed in Tajikistan, though nationalist and liberal democratic parties have been involved in the north-south debate on power. As such, the prospects for large-scale outbreaks of intraethnic violence are considerably lower than in Tajikistan.

In Kazakhstan and Turkmenistan, on the other hand, though tribal rivalries have geographic parameters, they do not fit the Kyrgyz and Tajik generally bipolar pattern of regionalism. Instead, the republic has three zones that roughly correspond to the traditional territories occupied by the Greater, Middle, and Smaller Hordes, with the former dominating the south, the penultimate controlling the central region, and the latter active in the north. The political power, however, has been in the hands of the Greater Horde and the Middle Horde. Each of the three Hordes maintained a qualitatively different relationship with the czars and the Communists as, for instance, the Smaller Horde was more receptive to Russian rule and was more systematically Russified. The Middle Horde exercised more independence and the Greater Horde was coopted by being allowed to remain the main power broker in the republic. Here, too, the collapse of the central authority has intensified tribal conflict, which has been subtle in nature. A member of the Greater Horde, President Nazarbayev, has been accused of favoritism and tribal discrimination. The inevitable by-product of this policy has been the emergence of quasi alliances between the Kazakhs and non-Kazakhs, particularly in the north, where in the spring of 1993, the members of the Russified Smaller Horde joined the Russians in defense of the ousted head of Kazakh television who was replaced by a member of the Greater Horde.[88] In Turkmenistan, the Teke, which has been the tribe of the president and most of the high-ranking members of the government, has dominated the political scene for decades. The extent of tribal antagonism has not been fully explored in that republic, but its seems to be less pronounced than in the other Central Asian republics.

Finally, Uzbekistan has been dominated by families and regional alliances. The first secretaries of the Communist Party and many high- ranking members of the government in the republic have come from Samarkand. According to some observers, the political and economic life of Tashkent has been dominated by six families. Family rivalries reached a critical point in 1993 when, the former Vice President, Shokurollah Mirsaidov—also a member of an influential family—was put on trial for an alleged embezzlement of funds. It has been reported, however, that his growing popularity in the country and his association with the democratic opposition, Birlik, were the underlying causes of his removal from the political scene.[89] In Uzbekistan, and also in other republics, the traditional clan structures have been preserved in the collective farms and neighborhood concentrations (*mahalah*), further accentuating rather than minimizing the differences among the peoples.

CONCLUSION

Quite clearly, diversity has and will continue to play a cardinal role in shaping the dynamics of ethnicity in Central Asia. This chapter was an attempt to demonstrate the breadth and depth of ethnic diversity as a factor that could inherently curb the growth of radical Islam in the region. The recent episodes of ethnic violence committed by Muslims against Muslims at both inter- and intrarepublican levels simply underscore the vitality of nonreligious components of Central Asian culture in determining the parameters of social accord. In the postindependence environment of political and economic uncertainties, the likelihood for the outbreak of similar, or perhaps more widespread, incidents of ethnic discord must be viewed as relatively high. Two factors may exacerbate ethnic problems and thus contribute to the ethnic instability of the region. The first is that of the presence of a large Russian population that has become increasingly agitated by the slow but systematic de-Sovietization of Kazakhstan. Ethnic discord could engulf the republic and draw the Russian Federation into a situation with no substantive short-term solution. The second is that of the subtle but significant rise in what has been referred to as Uzbek chauvinism in Central Asia. This, too, could seriously raise the possibility of ethnic violence in the near future as the Uzbeks move to reclaim their traditional right to Central Asian leadership.

Figure 6.4
Ethnic Composition of Kazakhstan, 1993

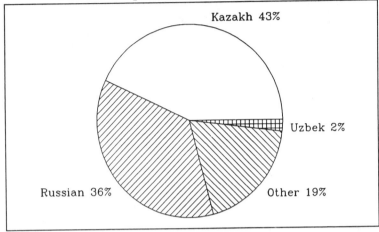

Source: British Broadcasting Corporation, *Summary of World Broadcasts* (January 25, 1993), SU/1724, B/6.

TABLE 6.2
Ethnic Trends in Kazakhstan (in thousands)

	1959	1970	1979	1989	1992
Kazakhs	2,795	4,234	5,289	6,535	7,073
Russians	3,974 ·	5,522	5,991	6,228	6,275
Ukranians	762	934	898	896	890
Germans	660	858	900	958	786
Uzbkeks	137	216	263	332	356
Tatars	192	288	313	328	337
Belarussians	107	198	181	183	n/a
Uighurs	60	121	148	185	n/a
Koreans	74	82	92	103	n/a
Azerbaijanis	38	58	73	90	n/a
Poles	52	61.1	61.4	60	n/a
Bashkirs	9	21	32	43	n/a
Others	435	416	464.8	524.5	n/a

Source: See table 6.1. Figures for 1992 are from British Broadcasting Corporation, *Summary of World Broadcasts*, (August 28, 1992), SU/1471, B/6.

Figure 6.5
Ethnic Composition of Kyrgyzstan, 1992

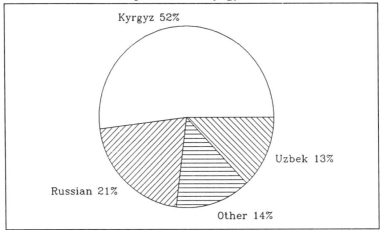

Kyrgyz 52%

Uzbek 13%

Russian 21%

Other 14%

Source: See table 6.1.

TABLE 6.3
Ethnic Trends in Kyrgyzstan (in thousands)

	1959	1970	1979	1989	1992
Kyrgyz	837	1,285	1687	2,230	2,317
Russians	624	865	912	917	959
Uzbeks	219	333	426	550	593
Ukranians	137	120	109	108	n/a
Germans	49	90	101	101	n/a
Tatars	56	69	72	70	n/a
Uighurs	14	25	30	37	n/a
Kazakhs	20	22	27	37	n/a
Tajiks	15	22	23	34	n/a
Others	104	111	136	174	n/a

Source: See table 6.1.

Figure 6.6
Ethnic Composition of Tajikistan, 1992

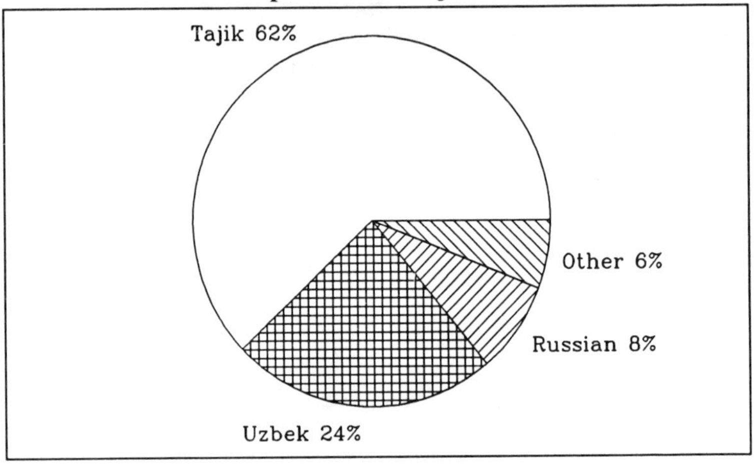

Source: See table 6.1.

TABLE 6.4
Ethnic Trends in Tajikistan (in thousands)

	1959	1970	1979	1989	1992
Tajiks	1,051	1,630	2,237	3,172	3,521
Uzbeks	454	666	873	1,198	1,363
Russians*	263	344	395	388	454
Tatars	57	71	78	72	n/a
Kyrgyz	26	36	48	64	n/a
Germans+	33	38	39	33	n/a
Ukranians	27	32	36	41	n/a
Turkmens	7	11	14	20	n/a
Others	63	74	86.4	105.2	n/a

Source: See table 6.1.

* The outbreak of the civil war in 1992 has reduced the size of the Russian population as many have out-migrated. Unconfirmed estimates put the figure as high as 300,000.

+ Many Germans have also returned to Germany since 1989, and more so since the independence.

Figure 6.7
Ethnic Composition of Turkmenistan, 1993

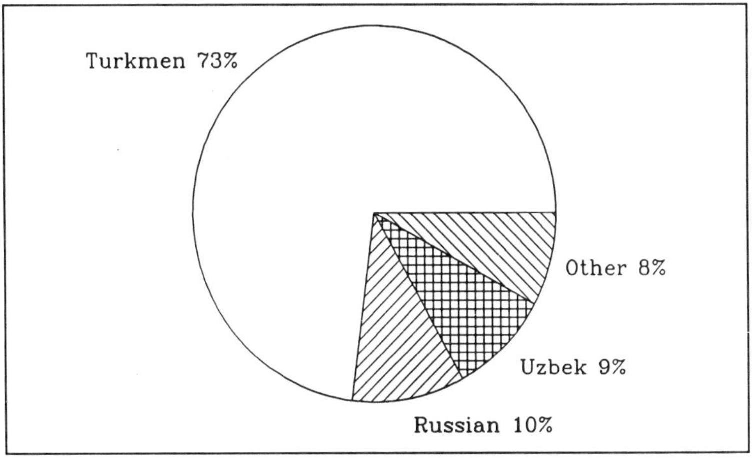

Turkmen 73%

Other 8%

Uzbek 9%

Russian 10%

Source: British Broadcasting Corporation, *Summary of World Broadcasts* (March 20, 1993), SU/1462, B/14.

TABLE 6.5
Ethnic Trends in Turkmenistan (in thousands)

	1959	1970	1979	1989	1993
Turkmens	924	1,417	1,892	2,537	3,118
Russians	263	313	349	334	419
Uzbeks	125	180	234	317	382
Kazakhs	70	69	80	88	87
Tatars	30	37	40	39	39
Ukranians	21	35	37	36	34
Azerbaijanis	13	17	24	33	32
Armenians	20	23	27	32	32
Others	50	68	82	107	109

Source: See table 6.1. Figures for 1993 are from British Broadcasting Corporation, *Summary of World Broadcasts* (March 23, 1993), SU/1642, B/14.

Figure 6.8
Ethnic Composition of Uzbekistan, 1992

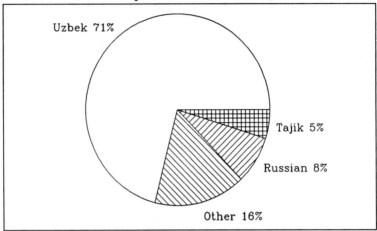

Uzbek 71%

Tajik 5%

Russian 8%

Other 16%

Source: See table 6.1.

TABLE 6.6
Ethnic Trends in Uzbekistan (in thousands)

	1959	1970	1979	1989	1992
Uzbeks	5,038	7,724	10,569	14,142	15,355
Russians	1,091	1,474	1,666	1,653	1,730
Tajiks	311	449	595	934	1,081
Tatars	445	574	531	468	n/a
Kazakhs	335	476	620	808	n/a
Koreans	138	148	163	183	n/a
Kyrgyz	93	111	142	153	n/a
Turkmens	55	71	92	122	n/a
Azerbaijanis	41	39	60	44	n/a
Others	404	503	574	680	n/a

Source: See table 6.1.

CHAPTER 7

Conclusion

If our supporters grew militant, they did so in reaction to the government repression, discrimination, violence, and double-talk.

—AKBAR TURAJONZODA, FORMER KAZI KALON, TAJIKISTAN

The newly independent Central Asian republics have been faced with the difficult and potentially destabilizing task of political and economic restructuring, most urgently needed to cope with the post-Communist domestic and international environments. This process, quite expectedly, has unleashed new social and political forces with a wide range of objectives, potentially capable of having a definite qualitative impact on the structural nature and functional scope of the post-Communist governments. This book has endeavored to study Islam as one of the contending forces in the region in an effort to assess its likely influence on the future course of political developments. So far, however, the Islamic revival has clearly exhibited a moderate character. It has been moderate because the active Islamic forces have, at least in principle, ruled out violence as a method of capturing power, and no widespread anti-Western sentiments have been expressed by these forces. This can be attributed first and foremost to the general Islamic proclivity of Central Asia discussed earlier in some detail. While the overall propensity toward Islam has been characterized as moderate in comparison to the Middle East, there are considerable variations at both inter- and intrarepublican levels. In the case of the former, the sedentary/tribal dichotomy presented in this study offers the most valuable classification to evaluate Islamic proclivity in Central Asia. This places Uzbekistan and Tajikistan at the top of the list followed by Kyrgyzstan, Kazakhstan, and Turkmenistan. The last three constitute the tribal societies of the region that were exposed to Islam less thoroughly than the first two. At the intrarepublican level, the propensity toward Islam seems to have its center in the Fergana Valley, which has been divided between the three republics of Uzbekistan, Tajikistan, and Kyrgyzstan. There are, of course, other regions with a somewhat similar Islamic orientation to Fergana, such as Karakalpak, parts of eastern Turkmenistan bordering Uzbekistan, and several regions in Tajikistan. With its rich Islamic legacy, the Fergana Valley will continue to set standards for Islamic activism in Central Asia. Yet its geographic remoteness will diminish its capacity to sensitize the public beyond its immediate vicinity. The valley has the highest population concentration in Central Asia and one of the lowest economic standards. Any positive economic change could help prevent radical Islam from capitalizing on poverty as a mobilizing anchor. The most significant pattern in all this, is that the Uzbeks are found in large numbers in most, but not all, places with a stronger Islamic propensity. As anticipated, the organizational strength and mobilization capacity of Islamic forces have been more advanced in Uzbekistan and Tajikistan as compared to the other republics.

The Islamic proclivity has been only one of the four parameters influencing the nature, scope, intensity, and speed of Islamic revival in Central Asia. The others being the strengths and weaknesses of the democratic drive, the governments' policies toward Islam and their willingness to institute socially inclusive political reforms, and the ethnic orientation and makeup of each republic. Of these, the penultimate has the potential to move Islam in a sharply radical direction. Two factors support this assumption. The first, has been the governments' use of repression to deal with Islamic forces. This policy has been carried out to the extreme in Uzbekistan and Tajikistan where Islamic parties and organizations have been banned and their leaders have been jailed, given death sentences, or forced to go into exile for advocating a particular set of ideas. The governments, however, have simply driven the Islamic forces underground, which will make it extremely difficult to study their overall strength and influence in the years to come. This is particularly true of the Fergana Valley where Muslim forces have kept the Uzbek government in the dark since 1992 as to the scope of their activities.[1] The continuing repression is bound to strengthen the resolve of the Islamic forces and further radicalize their agenda as has indeed been the case in Algeria and Egypt.

Repression has been a less frequently used method of political control in Kazakhstan and Turkmenistan, and almost never employed in Kyrgyzstan, which has given that republic a much better chance of averting the radical-ization of Islam in the future. The second factor that must be mentioned has to do with the banning of Islamic parties and movements. Experience has shown that such authoritarian policies, almost invariably, strengthen the legit-imacy of such organizations while at the same time adversely affecting the legitimacy of the government, with devastating long term consequences. This has been the case in Egypt, Algeria, Tunisia, and Morocco; Central Asia may not be much different. Based on the republican proclivity toward Islam and governments' harsh treatment of the Islamic forces, Uzbekistan and Tajikistan present the worst possible cases, as both score high on these two parameters while the other three republics present a less threatening picture of Islamic development. Interestingly enough, to offset their negative image, the Uzbek and Tajik governments have taken an active role in the promotion of Islam by sponsoring a variety of projects that are designed to underscore the govern-ments' enthusiasm for the ongoing religious and cultural revival.

While the governments' policies toward Islam have the potential to alter the moderate character of the Islamic revival in some republics, the democratic drive in Central Asia could, if given a fighting chance, weaken radical ten-dencies of Islam, for it offers an ideological paradigm with popular political objectives. Much like the Islamic drive, however, the democratic drive has not been a monolithic phenomenon with uniform interrepublican patterns. To the contrary, republican propensity toward democracy varies considerably from republic to republic with Kyrgyzstan and Kazakhstan having the strongest and Uzbekistan, Tajikistan, and Turkmenistan having the weakest tendencies. Here again, Kyrgyzstan has been the most successful republic in allowing democracy to grow relatively unhindered. The government of Askar Akayev has deliberately refrained from the use of force to curtail the activities of the secular political parties. The most inclusive of all democratic movements, the Kyrgyz democracy has also embraced the Communists in a system that may some day resemble that of the multiparty European models. Kazakhstan offers the second most successful experiment with procedural democracy. But President Nazarbayev has set a more stringent limit as to what organizations are allowed to compete for power. Both extremist Kazakh and Russian orga-nizations have been carefully kept out of the political process for their appar-ent destabilizing effect on the fragile multiethnic environment of Kazakhstan. Nazarbayev's ethnic dilemma is very real and must be dealt with intelligently and decisively if he is to prevent Kazakhstan from plunging into instability, and even civil war in the near future. In Uzbekistan and Tajikistan the demo-cratic forces have been faced with the same predicament as the Islamic forces, with their organizations banned and leaders brutalized or exiled. Despite the government crackdown, the Islamic and democratic forces in both republics have managed to maintain a working relationship that has so far survived, not so much because of an ideological consensus, but because of the presence of a common adversary: the Communist *nomenklatura*. Accused of perpetuating the dominance of the old Communist system under a democratic facade, the forces of democracy have asked for the dissolution of the government and holding of multiparty elections; demands that are considered detrimental to the stability of the republics. In Turkmenistan, which could be labeled as the weakest link in the democratic chain, the combination of a small intelligentsia and a politically apathetic public has severely retarded the growth of democratic principles and institutions, denying the republic a powerful instrument to combat the possible advances of radical Islam.

Finally, the ethnic makeup and orientation of the Central Asian republics influence the process under study. Given its mild Islamic proclivity and unique ethnic composition, Islam will play a secondary role in Kazakhstan in the foreseeable future. This is in part due to the presence of a large non-Muslim population, which almost equals its Muslim population. The ethnic composition has slightly changed in recent years because of the departure of Russians and higher birth rates of the Kazakh population. But the rate of change is not enough to fundamentally alter the present ethnic picture. This is to some extent true in Kyrgyzstan where the Slavic population is sizable, making the success of radical Islamic forces a less likely possibility. On the other hand, the picture is substantially different in Uzbekistan and Tajikistan were the ratio of non-Muslim population to that of the Muslim population is substantially smaller. Given the Islamic proclivity, the extent of government repression, and the relative weaknesses of the democratic drive, both republics have a much more conducive environments for the growth of radical Islam.

Ethnic makeup as a factor, however, is counterpoised by the ongoing ethnic current that has been labeled in this study as ethnic separatism. Reinforced by tribal, regional, subregional, and local exclusivist tendencies, ethnic separatism has been on the rise in the region, offering a centrifugal force with considerable power. One need not wander too far to witness the relevance of this force in shaping the future political development of these republics as has been the case in Tajikistan.[2] The most potentially threatening of these ethnic separatist currents is that which defines the Russian-Kazakh relations in Kazakhstan. Since the March 1994 elections the Russian political influence in the republic has been on the decline as more Kazakhs have been elected to the parliament. This, combined with the Kazakh cultural and linguistic revival, has prompted the Russian nationalist forces to organize tirelessly so as to slow the process of "Kazakhization" of the republic. Secessionary ideas have also been circulating in the north among the Russians and Cossacks who feel threatened by ongoing political developments. President Nazarbayev's renewed call to relocate the capital to Akmola is but a sign of the sensitive ethnic situation in that republic. The second threat has its roots in the subtle revival of Uzbek chauvinism, which has so far manifested itself in confrontations with the Kyrgyz, the Tajiks, and the Meskhetian Turks. This tendency could pose a threat to the security of the region if it is coupled with an arms buildup by the Uzbek government.

While it is unlikely that any of the five Central Asian republics would follow the path Iran pursued in 1979, Uzbekistan and Tajikistan have the ingredients to experience political turmoil with religious dimensions. But, the broad outlines of regional stability will be determined not so much by the Islamic but by the ethnic and subethnic parameters. It is this dimension of Central Asian politics that will in the short term define its evolution. And one can largely blame Soviet nationality policies for the ethnic contradictions of present-day Central Asia.

Michael Mandelbaum once wrote, "the region is peripheral in the political and economic calculations of the West." While from the point of view of real politics this statement can hardly be contested, the new world order, if it is to maintain global peace and stability, must consider Central Asia as an opportunity to test and redefine its operational principles. It must be emphasized that in the absence of Communism, the leadership of the West, and in particular of the United States, will ultimately be questioned if these and other former Soviet republics fail to develop viable political and economic systems in the future. It is, therefore, imperative to foster democratic movements in the region even if it means substantive power-sharing with the Islamic forces. So long as democratic electoral methods are chosen, and democratic principles respected, the Islamic forces should be permitted to participate in constructing the political future of their region. The West's implicit or explicit support for those Central Asian regimes that have resorted to repression and violence will undoubtedly produce an adverse effect on the perception of not only the Islamic but also the nascent democratic forces in these republics.

NOTES

Introduction

1. Comprised of Kazakhstan, Kyrgyzstan, Tajikistan, Turkmenistan, and Uzbekistan, the Central Asian region is surrounded by Russia and China in the north and east, Iran and Afghanistan in the south, and the Caspian Sea in the west.
2. Radical or fundamentalist Islam is understood, here and elsewhere in the book, not so much as a creed that coerces the society to preach and practice a particular version of Islam, but rather in terms of the anti-Western tenets they sponsor and their principle objective of gaining political power.
3. Graham Fuller has frequently stressed the relationship between economic conditions and the rise of radical Islam in Central Asia. For more information see, G. Fuller, "Russia and Central Asia: Federation or Fault Line?" in *Central Asia and the World,* ed. Michael Mandelbaum (New York: Council on Foreign Relations Press, 1994), 118. See also, G. Fuller, "Central Asia: The Quest for Identity," *Current History,* vol. 93, no. 582 (April 1994): 147.
4. For more information see, Mehrdad Haghayeghi, "Islam and Democratic Politics in Central Asia," *World Affairs,* vol. 156, no. 4 (Spring 1994): 196.
5. The most outspoken advocate of this view is Allen Hetmanek, who has emphasized Iran's role in shaping the events that led to the bloody conflict in Tajikistan. Ahmed Rashid has also documented Iran's and Afghanistan's involvement in Tajik affairs. For a detailed account of Hetmanek's view on the subject, see, A. Hetmanek, "Islamic Revolution Comes to the Former Soviet Central Asia: The Case of Tajikistan," *Central Asian Survey,* vol. 12, no. 3 (1993): 365–378, and "The Political Face of Islam in Tajikistan," *Central Asian Survey,* vol. 9, no. 3 (1990):99–111. See also, A. Rashid, *The Resurgence of Central Asia: Islam or Nationalism?* (London: Zed Press, 1994).
6. Although a number of Middle Eastern countries have established ties to Central Asia, most have been largely interested in commercial and economic interactions. Thus far, only three Middle Eastern actors have been directly involved in the religious and cultural affairs of the region: Turkey, Iran, and Saudi Arabia. From an ideological perspective, however, only two forces have been at work. First, the force of radical Islam, which has combined elements of fundamentalism and anti-Western imperialism in its approach to politics and society. This, as is well known, has been synonymous with the name of Iran, though to a lesser degree since the death of Ayatollah Khomeini in 1989. Second, the force of conservative Islam with no anti-Western tenets, which is represented by the Saudi Arabian-style of fundamentalism on the one hand and the Turkish secular version on the other. For an overview of the involvement of these countries in Central Asia see, Oles M. Smolansky, "Turkish and Iranian Policies in Central Asia," and Carol R. Saivetz, "Central Asia: Emerging Relations with the Arab States," in *Central*

Asia: Its Strategic Importance and Future Prospects, ed. Hafeez Malik (New York: St. Martin's Press, 1994),283–310 and 311–325; Mehrdad Haghayeghi, "Islamic Revival in the Central Asian Republics," *Central Asian Survey,* vol. 13, no. 2 (1994):249–266; Peri Pamir, "Turkey, the Transcaucasus and Central Asia," *Security Dialogue,* vol. 24, no. 1 (March 1993):49–54; Alexei Vasiliev, "Turkey and Iran in Transcaucasia and Central Asia," paper presented at the symposium on The Gulf and the Central Asian Republics, July 12–14, 1993, University of Exeter, England.

7. Both Barthold and Wheeler have provided evidence in support of this thesis. For more information see, V. V. Barthold, *Four Studies on the History of Central Asia* (Netherlands: E.J. Berill, 1962), vol. 1, 14 and 19; Geoffery Wheeler, *The Modern History of Central Asia,* (New York: Frederick A. Praeger Publishers, 1964), 22.

8. British Broadcasting Corporation, *The Summary of the World Broadcasts* (hereafter *SWB*), (January 25, 1993), SU/1724, B/6.

Chapter 1

1. For an excellent summary of the Kazakh tribal lifestyle see, Elizabeth E. Bacon, *Central Asians Under Russian Rule: A Study in Cultural Change* (New York: Cornell University Press, 1966), ch. II. See also, Martha Brill Olcott, *The Kazakhs* (Stanford: Hoover Institution Press, 1987), 13.

2. In 1906 an estimated 5.3 million people occupied the Turkistan region, the majority of whom led an agricultural life.

3. Richard A. Pierce, *Russian Central Asia, 1867–1917* (Berkeley: University of California Press, 1960), 143.

4. Ibid., 146–47.

5. For a brilliant account of the conquest of Tashkent by Cherniyev see, David MacKenzie, *The Lion of Tashkent: The Career of General M. G. Cherniaev* (Athens: University of Georgia Press, 1974).

6. Hugh Seton-Watson, *The Decline of Imperial Russia, 1855–1914* (New York: Frederick A. Praeger Publishers, 1962), 86–87.

7. Pierce (1960), 47–50.

8. Ibid., 164–65.

9. Ibid., 165–66. See also, Michael Rywkin, *Moscow's Muslim Challenge: Soviet Central Asia* (New York: M.E. Sharpe Inc., 1982), 15.

10. Pierce (1960), 172–173; 176.

11. Ibid., 190–99. See also, Olcott (1987), 86–89.

12. Seymour Becker, *Russia's Protectorates in Central Asia: Bukhara and Khiva, 1865–1924* (Cambridge: Harvard University Press, 1968), 22.

13. Ian Murray Matley, "Industrialization," in *Central Asia: 120 Years of Russian Rule,* ed. Edward Allworth (Durham: Duke University Press, 1989), 321–22.

14. Pierce (1960), 70.

15. Geoffrey Wheeler, *The Modern History of the Soviet Central Asia* (New York: Frederick A. Praeger Publishers, 1964), 187.

16. Pierce (1960), 214.

17. Alexandre Bennigsen and Chantal Lemercier-Quelquejay, *Islam in the Soviet Union* (New York: Frederick A. Praeger Publishers, 1967), 12–14. Frederick Starr, "Tsarist Government: The Imperial Dimension," in *Soviet Nationality*

Policies and Practices, ed. Jeremy R. Azrael (New York: Frederick A. Praeger Publisher, 1978), 17.

18. Serge A. Zenkovsky, *Pan-Turkism and Islam in Russia* (Cambridge: Harvard University Press, 1967), 76.

19. For an in-depth study of Ilminski's philosophy of education in Central Asia see, Isabella Teitz Kreindler, "Educational Policies Toward the Eastern Nationalities," Ph.D. Dissertation, Columbia University, 1969.

20. Zenkovsky (1967), 78.

21. Seton-Watson (1962), 164.

22. By 1911, an estimated 1.5 million Russian had settled in the Kazakh Steppe and approximately 400,000 resided in Turkistan. For details see, Geoffrey Wheeler, "Russian Conquest and Colonization of Central Asia," in *Russian Imperialism from Ivan the Great to the Revolution,* ed. Taras Hunczak (New Jersey: Rutgers University Press, 1974), 281. See also' George J. Demko, *The Russian Colonization of Kazakhstan, 1896–1916* (Bloomington: Indiana University Press, 1969).

23. The uprising against the Russians was led by Muhammad Ali Ihsan and supported by former officials of the emir who had lost their privileges and had been driven to bankruptcy subsequent to the Russian conquest of Turkistan. For details see, Pierce (1960), 226–233.

24. Pierce (1960), 250–53.

25. The Central Asian population remained generally apathetic before 1905. But the revolutionary events of that year gradually politicized the region, culminating in a multiplicity of local parties and programs. For details see, Zenkovsky (1967), ch. IV.

26. It has also been argued that the Russian authorities helped preserve the most traditional Islamic cultural variants in an effort to retard the sociocultural progress of the Turkistani people. For example see, Alexandre Bennigsen, "Soviet Minority Nationalism in Historical Perspective," in *The Last Empire: Nationality and the Soviet Future,* ed. Robert Conquest (Stanford: Hoover Institution Press, 1986), 135.

27. Karl Marx, "Contribution to the critique of Hegel's Philosophy of Law," in Karl Marx and Frederick Engels, *Collected Works,* vol. 3 (Moscow: Progress Publishers, 1975), opening sentence of introduction. For an interpretive discussion of Marx's philosophical connection to Hegel and Feuerbach see, James Thrower, *Marxist-Leninist 'Scientific Atheism' and the Study of Religion and Atheism in the USSR* (Berlin: Mouton Publisher, 1983).

28. Frederick Engels, "Ludwig Feuerbach and the End of Classical German Philosophy," in Karl Marx and Frederick Engels, *Selected Works,* vol. 3 (Moscow: Progress Publishers, 1976), 372.

29. Frederick Engels, *Anti-Duhring* (Moscow: Progress Publishers, 1978), 382.

30. Marx and Engels (1975), vol. 3, 175.

31. N. S. Timasheff, *Religion in the Soviet Union* (Westport: Greenwood Press, 1942), 21–23.

32. George E. Kline, *Religion and Anti-Religious Thought in Russia* (Chicago: University of Chicago Press, 1968), 119.

33. Ibid., 122.

34. V. I. Lenin, "Socialism and Religion," *Collected Works,* vol. 10 (Moscow: Progress Publishers, 1978), 83–84.

35. For a brief discussion of Plekhanov's ideas on religion, in particular his belief about the animistic roots of all religions see, Georgi Plekhanov, *Selected Philosophical Works,* vol. 5 (Moscow: Progress Publishers, 1976), 333–34.
36. Lenin (1978), vol. 10, 86.
37. Ibid., vol. 15, 405–06.
38. For a different periodization of the Soviet antireligious policies, see, N. S. Timasheff (1942); Robert Conquest, *Religion in the U.S.S.R.* (New York: Frederick A. Praeger Publishers, 1968); Dimitry V. Pospielovsky, *A History of Marxist-Leninist Atheism and Soviet Anti-Religious Policies* (New York: St. Martin's Press, 1987). Most scholars of Soviet politics seem to have borrowed their periodization of the Soviet religious policies from I. Vorontsov study entitled *Leninskaia programma ateisticheskogo vospitaniia v deistvii (1917–1937 gg)* (Leningrad: Izdatel'stvo LGU, 1973).
39. Richard Pipes, *The Formation of the Soviet Union: Communism and Nationalism, 1917–1923* (Cambridge: Harvard University Press, 1955), 155.
40. The first postrevolutionary all-Russian Muslim Congress was held in May 1917 and was attended by 900 Muslims from all regions of Russia. Quite predictably, the debate over territorial issues dominated the session, creating from the outset two broad divisions, one in favor of a federalist system in which political autonomy ranked prominently, the other in favor of a centralist position in which only cultural autonomy was sanctified. Except for the Tatars, who had gradually established a working relationship with the Bolsheviks, the rest of the Muslim delegates supported the plan for the political autonomy of their respective regions. By a vote of 446 to 271, the federalist camp won the debate. Although a decisive victory, the federalists lost their winning edge when during the Second Muslim Congress—held in July 1917—the Tatars who had now openly sided with the socialists, scrapped the resolution of the First Congress in favor of only national cultural autonomy for which a coordinating "National Muslim Board" was established in Ufa. For more information on the history and function of Muslim organizations and parties during this period see, Alexandre Bennigsen and S. Enders Wimbush, *Muslim National Communism in the Soviet Union* (Chicago: The University of Chicago Press, 1979). See also, Zenkovsky (1967).
41. The Ulema Jama'ati splintered from the Shora-i Islami-ya in mid-March 1917.
42. Fazal-Ul-Rahim Kahn Marwat, *The Basmachi Movement in Soviet Central Asia: A Study in Political Development* (Peshawar: Emjay Books International, 1985), 27.
43. Robert C. Tucker, *Stalin in Power: The Revolution From Above, 1928–1941* (New York: W.W. Norton & Company, 1990), 489–90.
44. Marie Broxup, "The Basmachi," *Central Asian Survey,* vol. 2, no. 1 (1983): 57. For more detail on the underlying causes of the revolt and the history of the military operations by the warring parties see, Marwat (1985); Alexander G. Park, *Bolshevism in Turkistan* (New York: Columbia University Press, 1957); Seymour Becker, *Russia's Protectorate in Central Asia: Bukhara, and Khiva, 1865–1924* (Cambridge: Harvard University Press, 1968).
45. Marwat (1985), 11.
46. Galiyev, who had joined the Bolsheviks in 1917, was a firm believer that the Communist Party could be used as the vehicle for Muslim emancipation in the Soviet Union. As a brilliant tactician with influence among the Russians and Muslims, Stalin saw in him an opportunity to make substantial inroads into the

Muslim territories. He was, therefore, chosen as one of the three members of the inner circle in the Commissariat of the Nationality Affairs. He was also the editor of *Zhizn Natsionalnostey*, which he relied upon to influence Soviet policies toward Islam. Galiyev frequently urged that the antireligious propaganda be postponed, arguing that with educational improvements, the expansion of Communist Party activities, and the administrative and economic empowerment of the Muslims, Islam would loose its hold on society. For more information on Galiyev's life and personality see, Alexandre Bennigsen, "Sultan Galiyev: The USSR and the Colonial Revolution," in *The Middle East in Transition*, ed. Walter Laqueur (New York: Frederick A. Praeger Publishers, 1958).

47. Bennigsen and Wimbush (1979), 27–28.
48. Bennigsen and Lemercier-Quelquejay (1967), 108.
49. Walter Kolarz, *Religion in the Soviet Union* (New York: St. Martin's Press, 1961), 410–11.
50. Thomas Fitzsimmons, Peter Malof, John C. Fiske, *USSR: Its People, Its Society, Its Culture* (Westport: Greenwood Press, 1974), 90.
51. The groundwork for this was laid down in two decrees issued on December 18, 1917, neither of which were applied to Central Asia. For more information see, Robert Conquest (1968), 70.
52. For a discussion of the origin, evolution, and main provisions of the law see, Aleksei Barmenkov, *Freedom of Conscious in the USSR* (Moscow: Progress Publishers, 1983), ch. 2.
53. Bennigsen and Lemercier-Quelquejay (1967), 148–49. For a discussion of the origin and development of the Soviet secular education in Uzbekistan see, Dinora Azimova, *Youth and the Cultural Revolution in Soviet Central Asian Republics*, (Moscow: Central Department of Oriental Literature, 1988), ch. 1.
54. In the early 1920s, the old theoretical arguments espoused by Plekhanov and Lunacharski gave way to real controversies over the proper course of antireligious action between Yaroslavski and M. M. Kostelovski. The former advocated a Plekhanov-style scientific education. The latter, on the other hand, supported a harsh and aggressive attack on religion and the believers. By 1926, Yaroslavski had won a decisive victory against Kostelovski. For more information on the debates, strategies, evolution, and instruments of antireligious propaganda in the Soviet Union see, Joan Delaney, "The Origins of Soviet Anti-Religious Organization," in *Aspects of Religion in the Soviet Union, 1917–1967*, ed. Richard H. Marshal, Jr. (Chicago: University of Chicago Press, 1971); Fanny Bryan, "Anti-Islamic Propaganda: *Bezbozhnik*, 1925–1935," *Central Asian Survey*, vol. 5, no. 1 (1986):29–47; Martie Sapiets, "Anti-Religious Propaganda and Education," in *Candle in the Wind: Religion in the Soviet Union*, ed. Eugene B. Shirley, Jr., and Michael Rowe (Washington D.C.: Ethics and Public Policy Center, 1989), 91–116; Shoshana Keller, "Islam in Soviet Central Asia, 1917–1930: The Soviet Policy and the Struggle for Control," *Central Asian Survey*, vol. 11, no. 1 (1992):25–50.
55. Anonymous, *Religion in the USSR* (Munich: Institute for the Study of USSR, 1960), series 1, no. 59, 145.
56. Georg von Stackelberg, "The Tenacity of Islam in Soviet Central Asia," in *Religion and the Search for New Ideals in the USSR*, eds. William C. Fletcher and Anthony J. Strover (New York: Frederick A. Praeger Publishers, 1967), 95.
57. *Religion in the USSR* (1960), 163.

58. For a more detailed account of the law on religious associations see, Joshua Rothenberg, "The Legal Status of Religion in the Soviet Union," in *Aspects of Religion in the Soviet Union, 1917–1967,* ed. Richard H. Marshal, Jr. (Chicago: University of Chicago Press, 1971), 72–82.
59. Erich W. Bethmann, *The Fate of Muslims Under Soviet Rule* (New York: American Friends of the Middle East, Inc., 1958), 17–20.
60. Bennigsen and Lemercier-Quelquejay (1967), 150.
61. For an account of executions carried during the Stalin's rule see, Anonymous, "The Muslim Republics and the XXIInd Party Congress: Reactions to the Personality Cult and Anti-Party Group," *Central Asian Review,* vol. X, no. 2 (1962):125–28.
62. The exact date of the opening of Mir Arab is not known. Bennigsen, Conquest, and Rywkin provide the following years respectively: 1952, 1948, and 1945–46.
63. Bernard Wilhelm, "Moslems in the Soviet Union, 1948–1954," in *Aspects of Religion in the Soviet Union, 1917–1967,* ed. Richard H. Marshall, Jr. (Chicago: University of Chicago Press, 1971), 268.
64. Carrene d'Encausse, "Islam in the USSR," *Central Asian Review,* vol. IX, no. 4 (1960): 339.
65. Kolarz (1961), 423.
66. Bennigsen and Lemercier-Quelquejay (1967), 176.
67. David E. Powell, *Antireligious Propaganda in the Soviet Union: A Study of Mass Persuasion* (Cambridge: MIT Press, 1975), 50.
68. Joan Delaney Grossman, "Khrushchev's Anti-Religious Policy and the Campaign of 1954," *Soviet Studies,* vol. XXXIV, no. 3 (January 1973): 375.
69. Anonymous, "The Peoples of Central Asia: The Survival of Religion," *Central Asian Review,* vol. VII, no. 2 (1959): 112.
70. Grossman (1973), 379.
71. For an extensive view of Yaroslavski on religion see, Emilian Yaroslavski, *Religion in the U.S.S.R.* (London: Modern Books Ltd., 1932).
72. For more information on this method see, Powell (1975), ch. 7.
73. Harry Willetts, "The War Against Religion," *Problems of Communism,* vol. 14, no. 6 (1964): 37.
74. However, in 1959 Khrushchev did order the removal of the first party secretaries of Uzbekistan and Turkmenistan. The latter was accused of nationalist tendencies. For details see, Anonymous, "Nationalism in the Soviet Muslim Republics," *Central Asian Review,* vol. VII, no. 4 (1959): 75–83.
75. For a brief discussion of the formation of new rituals in Central Asia see, Anonymous, "Wedding Rites in the Uzbek SSR," *Central Asian Review,* vol. XV, no. 4 (1967): 290–291.
76. Yaroslavski (1960), 212.
77. For a brief discussion of Khrushchev and early Brezhnev religious policies see, Michael Bourdeaux, "Reform and Schism," *Problems of Communism,* vol. XVI (September–October 1967): 108–18.
78. Bohdan R. Bociurkiw, "Religion in the USSR After Khrushchev," in *The Soviet Union Under Brezhnev and Kosygin: The Transition Years,* ed. John W. Strong (New York: Van Nostrand Reinhold Company, 1971), 139.
79. Joshua Rothenberg, "Status of Cults," *Problems of Communism,* vol. XVI (September–October 1967): 121–23.

80. For a discussion of the nature and impact of the 1975 amendments see, Paul D. Steeves, "Amendment of the Soviet Law Concerning Religious Groups," *Journal of Church and State,* vol. 19, no. 1 (1977): 37–51. For the text of the amendments see, Pospielovsky (1987), 138–146.

81. Although Brezhnev's legal and constitutional measures as well as his emphasis on law-enforcement aspects of religion brought about some degree of stability and predictability to the church-state relations, there was an overall increase in the quantity of atheistic material published by the government during the 1970s. The number of books, for instance, was increased from an estimated 2,250,000 in 1970 to 7,000,000 in 1979. The circulation of related periodicals also saw an upward trend during the same period.

82. For an insightful discussion of the Soviet Muslim dilemma in the aftermath of the Islamic revolution and the invasion of Afghanistan, see, Yaccov Ro'i, "The Impact of the Islamic Fundamentalist Revival of the Late 1970's on the Soviet View of Islam," in *The USSR and the Muslim World: Issues in Domestic and Foreign Policy,* ed. Yaccov Ro'i (London: George Allen & Unwin, 1984), 149–77.

83. Jan-Ake Dellenbrant, "The Central Asian Challenge: Soviet Decision Making on Regional Stability Under Brezhnev and Gorbachev," *The Journal of Communist Studies,* vol. 4, no. 1 (March 1988): 65.

84. For details see, Helene Carrere d'Encausse, *Decline of an Empire: The Soviet Socialist Republic in Revolt,* trans. by Martin Sokolinsky and Henry A. La Farge (New York: Harper Colophon Books, 1979), 228–30.

85. As early as the 1920s, the Soviet authorities had resorted to the strategy of dismantling the traditional family structure in Central Asia by pitting women against men. But such strategies did not break the traditional cultural cycles of Central Asian families. For more information see, Gregory J. Massell, *The Surrogate Proletariat: Moslem Women and Revolutionary Strategies in Soviet Central Asia, 1919–1929* (New Jersey: Princeton University Press, 1974).

Chapter 2

1. For a similar interpretation of Brezhnev's neopatrimonial style of management, see, Linda J. Cook, "Brezhnev 'Social Contract' and Gorbachev's Reforms," *Soviet Studies,* vol. 44, no. 1 (1992): 37–38.

2. Stephen White, *Gorbachev and After,* (Cambridge: Cambridge University Press, 1991), 1.

3. Lerner and Treadgold indicate that the growth rate was approaching zero by the beginning of the 1980s. Lawrence W. Lerner, and Donald W. Treadgold, eds., *Gorbachev and the Soviet Future* (Boulder: Westview Press, 1988), 5. For an excellent summary of the economic contradictions of the Soviet society, see, Ernest Mandel, *Beyond Perestroika: The Future of Gorbachev's USSR* (London: Verso, 1989), ch. 1.

4. Marshal I. Goldman, *What Went Wrong With Perestroika* (New York: W.W. Norton, 1991), 63; 79. For related information see, Karl-Eugen Wadekin, "Agriculture," in *Gorbachev and Perestroika,* ed. Martin McCauley (New York: St. Martin's Press, 1990).

5. For a brief discussion of the stagnant nature of the Soviet economy and society see, Vladimir Shlapentokh, *Soviet Ideologies in the Period of Glasnost* (New York: Praeger Publishers, 1988), 61–65; see also, Hillel Ticktin, "The Contradictions of Gorbachev," *The Journal of Communist Studies,* vol. 4, no. 4 (December, 1988): 84–88.

6. *Radio Liberty Daily Report* (February 21, 1983) and *Pravda* (December 28, 1982).

7. As quoted in Francoise Thom, *The Gorbachev Phenomenon* (London: Printer Publishers, 1989), 18.

8. Kristian Gerner and Stefan Hedlund, *Ideology and Rationality in the Soviet Model: A Legacy for Gorbachev* (London: Routledge, 1989), 347–48.

9. For an interesting biography of Gorbachev see, Gail Sheehy, *The Man Who Changed the World: The Lives of Mikhail S. Gorbachev* (New York: Harper Collins Publishers, 1990); see also, Thos. G. Butson, *Gorbachev: A Biography* (New York: Stein and Day Publishers, 1985).

10. The Ipatovo projects were large-scale state-operated mechanized farms of the sort that Brezhnev had envisioned. The Stavropol projects, on the other hand, incorporated limited privatization as a method to raise production.

11. For a detailed background on Andropov's relationship with Gorbachev, see, Dusko Doder and Louise Branson, *Gorbachev: Heretic in the Kremlin* (New York: Penguin Group, 1990), 35–40.

12. *Current Digest of the Soviet Press,* vol. XXXVII, no. 1 (1986): 6; and vol. XXXVI, no. 43 (1983): 1.

13. Gromyko staged a publicity campaign for Gorbachev in February 1985 to enhance his image at home and abroad. Gromyko praised Gorbachev as a man "fully versed in Party affairs." He further stated that "The Politburo has pointed out that he is a man of principle, with strong convictions . . . He can grasp entirely and immediately the essence of the changes that occur outside our country on the international stage." Gromyko, however, was pushed aside by Gorbachev shortly after the assumption of power. For more information see, Michel Tatu, *Mikhail Gorbachev: The Origins of Perestroika* (New York: Colombia University Press, 1991), 67–70.

14. For more information on the nature and scope of Gorbachev's Party shakeup see, White (1991), 18–20. See also, Richard Sakwa, *Gorbachev and His Reforms, 1985–1990* (New York: Prentice Hall, 1990), 12–14.

15. For an example of Gorbachev's basic ideas see his keynote speech on ideological matters in: *Current Digest of the Soviet Press,* vol. XXXVI, no. 50 (1985): 1–6.

16. Seweryn Bialer, "The Domestic and International Sources of Gorbachev's Reforms," *Journal of International Affairs,* vol. 42, no. 2 (Spring 1989): 283–84.

17. *Current Digest of the Soviet Press,* vol. XXXVIII, no. 8 (1986): 11.

18. For the text of Gorbachev's speech at the January Plenum see, *Pravda,* (January 28, 1987). See also, Mikhail Gorbachev, *Perestroika: New Thinking for Our Country and the World* (New York: Harper & Row Publishers, 1987), 33–35.

19. For more information on the genesis, anatomy and implementation of perestroika see, Neil Robinson, "Gorbachev and the Place of the Party in Soviet Reform, 1985–91," *Soviet Studies,* vol. 44, no. 3 (1992): 423–43; Sakwa (1990), ch. 7; Moshe Lewin, "*Perestroika*: A New Historical Stage," *Journal of International Affairs,* vol. 42, no. 2 (Spring 1989): 299–315.

20. For a well-rounded discussion of the economic objectives of perestroika see, Richard E. Ericson, "Soviet Economic Reforms: The Motivation and Content of *Perestroika*," *Journal of International Affairs,* vol. 42, no. 2 (Spring 1989): 317–331.

21. Mikhail Gorbachev (1987), 75–78. For more information on the general impact and underlying purpose of *glasnost* see, Andrei Melville and Gail Lapidus, *The Glasnost Papers* (Boulder: Westview Press, 1990); Nick Lampert, "The Dilemmas of *Glasnost,*" in *Gorbachev and Gorbachevism,* eds. Hillel Ticktin and Stephen White (London: Frank Cass, 1989); Ben Eklof, *Soviet Briefing: Gorbachev and the Reform Period* (Boulder: Westview Press, 1989), ch. 3; Natalie Gross, "*Glasnost*: Roots and Practice," *Problems of Communism,* vol. XXXVI, (November– December 1987): 69–80.

22. *Current digest of the Soviet Press,* vol. XXXVI, no. 25 (1984): 17; vol. XXXVI, no. 26 (1984): 1–6; vol. XXXVI, no. 33 (1984): 9–12; vol. XXXVII, no. 3 (1985): 16.

23. *Current Digest of the Soviet Press,* vol. XXXVVI, no. 16 (1985): 10–14; vol. XXXII, no. 44 (1985): 18.

24. *Current Digest of the Soviet Press,* vol. XXXVII, no. 8 (1986): 33–34.

25. For instance, the first secretary of Tajikistan, Ghahar Makhkamov, who replaced Nabiyev after Gorbachev became general secretary stated: "We believe that the interrepublican exchange of cadres persuasively described by Ligachev, Secretary of the CPSU Central Committee, is introducing a new businesslike approach to the party committees' activity." For details see, Baruch A. Hazan, *Gorbachev and His Enemies* (Boulder: Westview Press, 1990), ch. 1.

26. James Critchlow, "Prelude to 'Independence': How Uzbek Party Apparatus Broke Moscow's Grip on Elite Recruitment," in *Soviet Central Asia: The Failed Transformation,* ed. William Fierman (Boulder: Westview Press, 1991), 136.

27. For an excellent account of the cotton scandal see, Gregory Gleason, "Nationalism or Organized Crime? The Case of the Cotton Scandal in the USSR," *Corruption and Reform,* vol. 5, no. 2 (1990):87–108. See also James Critchlow, *Nationalism in Uzbekistan: A Soviet Republic's Road to Sovereignty* (Boulder: Westview Press, 1991).

28. As quoted in Gleason (1990), 94.

29. As quoted in Boris Z. Rumer, *Soviet Central Asia: A Tragic Experiment* (Boston: Unwin Hyman, 1989), 151–52.

30. As quoted in Thom (1989), 17.

31. James Critchlow, "'Corruption', Nationalism, and Native Elites in Soviet Central Asia," *The Journal of Communist Studies,* vol. 4, no. 2 (June 1988): 149.

32. Bess Brown, "The Progress of Restructuring in Uzbekistan," *Radio Liberty Research Report* (June 25, 1987).

33. The post-Brezhnev ideological campaign and antireligious agenda was given a boost in June 1983 when the Communist Party Central Committee held a two-day session during which a resolution entitled "Critical Questions of Ideological and Mass Political Work of the Party" was passed. The resolution called for an intensification of atheistic and antireligious propaganda. The campaign was apparently spearheaded by Chernenko—the party Secretary in charge of ideological affairs—in an attempt to strengthen his position within the ruling elite at a time when the Andropov faction appeared to have gained an upper hand within the Central Committee. A month later the Soviet newspapers began to reflect the

general recommendation of the July meeting. Dr. F. M. Rudinsky, a professor of law at the Ministry of Internal Affairs, for instance, proposed to introduce a new legislation that would strengthen article 52 of the 1977 Constitution, which addressed the Leninist principle of the separation of church from state and school from the church. Rudinsky demanded the imposition of further restrictions on religious activities and tighter implementation and monitoring of religious cults across the board. For more information, see, *Current Digest of the Soviet Press,* vol. XXXV, no. 35 (1983): 13–14. See also, Paul Steeves, "The June 1983 Plenum and the Post-Brezhnev Anti-Religious Campaign," *Journal of Church and State,* vol. 26, no. 2 (1986): 349–57.

34. Michael Bourdeaux, *Gorbachev, Glasnost and the Gospel* (London: Hodder and Stoughton, 1990), 36.

35. Ibid., 37.

36. Martha B. Olcott, ed., *The Soviet Multinational State: Readings and Documents* (New York: M.E. Sharpe Inc., 1990), 375.

37. His remarks were apparently so insulting to Islam that the full text of his speech was not published. *Soviet Muslims Brief,* vol. 2, no. 4 (November– December 1986): 4.

38. For a brief overview of the local party perceptions on ideological and anti-religious activities see, Marie Broxup, "Islam in Central Asia Since Gorbachev," *Asian Affairs,* vol. XVIII, pt. III (October 1987): 283–84. See also, Joseph Seagram, "The Status of Islam in the USSR as Reflected in Speeches at the Republican Party Congresses," *Radio Research Liberty Report* (March 7, 1986) and "Uzbek Believer Recants and Denounces 'False Mullahs'," *Radio Liberty Research Report* (September 24, 1985).

39. *Current Digest of the Soviet Press,* vol. XXXVIII, no. 16 (1986): 21–22. *Soviet Muslims Brief,* vol. 2, no. 4 (November–December 1986): 5, and vol. 4, no. 2 (July–August 1988): 5–6.

40. Alex Alexiev, "Gorbachev's Muslim Dilemma," *Rand Corporation Report* (January 1987).

41. For details see, *Soviet Muslims Brief,* vol. 3, no. 3 (September–October 1987): 7–8. See also, *Religious Prisoners in the USSR* (Kent: Greenfire Books, 1987), 136–38, and Timur Kocaoglu, "An 'Unofficial' Mullah Sentenced in Uzbekistan," *Radio Liberty Report* (June 5, 1985).

42. Bess Brown, "Tajik Survey Reveals Extent of Religious Belief Among Young People," *Radio Liberty Research Report* (March 31, 1988); Bess Brown "Religion in Tajikistan—A Tough Nut to Crack," *Radio liberty Research Report* (December 28, 1987). See also, *Soviet Muslims Brief,* vol. 2, no. 5 (January– February 1987): 6–7.

43. Bess Brown, "Religion in Tajikistan—A Tough Nut to Crack," *Radio Liberty Research Report* (December 28, 1987): 1.

44. Yegor Ligachev was born in November 1920, almost a year earlier than Gorbachev. He graduated from the Ordzhonikidze Institute of Aircraft Construction in 1943. For the first 20 years of his career he was involved in various capacities with the administration of Novosibirsk oblast. He broke out of his provincial mold in 1961 when he became deputy chief of the Communist Party Central Committee Department of Agitation and Propaganda. Ligachev was finally promoted to the Central Committee Secretariat with Andropov's help. Later Gorbachev secured his position as a Politburo member. A combination of

two factors gave Ligachev his political clout and thus the legitimacy to become a credible opponent of Gorbachev. First was his association with Andropov, who had also given Gorbachev his chance to become a major power player. As such, Ligachev saw himself as a co-equal of Gorbachev. Second, Ligachev possessed impeccable political credentials. He was known as an incorruptible and devoted servant of the party. Lacking any weaknesses in this regard, Gorbachev was left with little room for criticism of his personality or career.

45. For an excellent account of the developments in the spring of 1988 that led to the defeat of Ligachev faction see, Doder and Branson (1990), ch. 16; Hazan (1990), ch. 7.

46. The focus of Gorbachev's reforms during the historic conference was on five areas: decentralization of political power; creation of a new 2,250-member national assembly; downsizing of the Soviet bureaucratic and administrative machinery; electoral reform; including secret ballots and competitive elections; and legal reform with the objective of developing a more independent judicial system. Despite heated debates and downright disagreements the conference supported much of what Gorbachev had in mind in the form of seven resolutions on: democratization; struggle against bureaucracy; interethnic relations; legal reform; glasnost; progress of the implementation of the 27th CPSU Congress; Certain Urgent Measures for the Practical Implementation of the Reform of the Country's Political System. For a brilliant discussion of the events at the conference, see, Hazan (1990), ch. 6.

47. Alexander Yakovlev, "Redefining Socialism at Home and Abroad," *Journal of International Affairs,* vol. 42, no. 2 (Spring 1989): 334.

48. *Current Digest of the Soviet Press,* vol. XXXVIII, no. 52 (1986): 2–4.

49. *Current Digest of the Soviet Press,* vol. XXXVIII, no. 47 (1986): 4–5. For a brief description of *Plakha* see, Gary L. Browning and Thomas F. Rogers, "Chingiz Aitmatov's *The Executioner's Block*: Through Dreams a Confrontation with Existential Good and Evil," *The Russian Review,*vol. 51, no. 1 (January 1992): 72–83. For an excellent survey of the literature on early discussions on religion and concomitant official criticisms see, Melville and Lapidus (1990), ch. 3. See also, Alec Nove, *Glasnost in Action: Cultural Renaissance in Russia* (Boston: Unwin Hyman, 1989), ch. 5.

50. Melville and Lapidus (1990), 129.

51. Bourdeaux (1990), 42.

52. Ibid., 44, and Paul Steeves, *Keeping the Faiths: Religion and Ideology in the Soviet Union* (New York: Holmes & Meier, 1989), 184.

53. *Soviet Muslim Brief,* vol. 4, no. 1 (May–June 1988): 3.

54. Steeves (1989), 172.

55. Karachev was appointed by Chernenko to his post in 1985. Raised in Gorky, he was educated as an engineer. Prior to his appointment to the council, he was the Ambassador Extraordinary and Plenipotentiary to the Cooperative Republic of Guyana.

56. As early as 1986, there were hints by Karachev that "religious policies were being rethought on highest levels in keeping with the themes of Gorbachev program." Steeves (1989), 173.

57. Later in September 1990 Deputy Muhammad Sadiq Muhammad Yusef, the head of the Muslim Religious Board of Central Asia and Kazakhstan, was included in the debate of the Supreme Soviet on the subject. For a brief description of

religious responses to the draft law, see, Jim Frost, *Free at Last? The Impact of Perestroika on Religious Life in the Soviet Union* (London: Darton, Longman and Todd, 1990), 202–203.

58. For a comprehensive discussion of the drafting of the law on Freedom of Conscience see, Albert Boiter, "Drafting a Freedom of Conscience Law," *Columbia Journal of Transnational Law*, no. 28 (1990): 157–187.

59. Ibid., 164–65.

60. *Current Digest of the Soviet Press*, vol. XLI, no. 16 (1989): 27.

61. *Current Digest of the Soviet Press*, vol. XLII, no. 40 (1990): 6–8; 32. See also: Igor Troyanovsky, *Religion in the Soviet Republics: A Guide to Christianity, Judaism, Islam, Buddhism, and Other Religions* (New York: Harper San Francisco, 1991), 19–39.

62. Perdo Ramet, "Gorbachev's Reforms and Religion," in *Candle in the Wind: Religion in the Soviet Union*, eds. Eugene B. Shirley, and Jr. and Michael Rowe (Washington, D.C.: Ethics and Public Policy Center, 1989), 280.

63. Critchlow (1991), 176.

64. *The New York Times* (February 6, and 8, 1989). See also, Annette Bohr, Background to Demonstration of Soviet Muslims in Tashkent," *Radio Liberty Research Report* (March 17, 1989).

65. *Current Digest of the Soviet Press*, vol. XLI, no. 8 (1989): 23–4. See also, Azade-Ayse Rorlich, "Islam and Atheism: Dynamic Tension in Soviet Central Asia," in *Soviet Central Asia: The Failed Transformation*, ed. William Fierman (Boulder: Westview Press, 1991), 208–09.

66. Moonis Ahmar, "Implications of Perestroika for the Soviet Asian Republics," *Central Asia*, no. 29 (Winter 1991): 36.

67. As quoted in Critchlow (1991), 179.

68. For more information on these statistics see, *The Current Digest of the Soviet Press*, vol. XLII, no. 36 (1990): 31, *Soviet Muslims Brief*, vol. 6, no. 4 (November– December 1990): 4–5.

69. Yaacov Ro'i, "The Islamic Influence on Nationalism in Soviet Central Asia," *Problems of Communism*, vol. XXXIX, (July–August 1990): 51.

Chapter 3

1. For a detailed account of the Arab conquest of Central Asia see, H.A.R. Gibb, *The Arab Conquests in Central Asia* (London: The Royal Asiatic Society, 1923), and W. Barthold, *Turkistan down to the Mongol Invasion* (London: Lowe and Brydone Lt.D., 1968). See also, Diloram Ibrahim, *The Islamization of Central Asia: A Case Study of Uzbekistan* (London: The Islamic Institute, 1993).

2. Gibb (1923), 17.

3. Ibid., 17.

4. Ibid., 32–54.

5. Ibid., 56.

6. Richard N. Frye, *Bukhara: The Medieval Achievement* (Norman: University of Oklohoma Press, 1965), 16.

7. Geoffery Wheeler, *The Modern History of Central Asia* (New York: Frederick A. Praeger Publishers, 1964), 22.

8. V. V. Barthold, *Four Studies on the History of Central Asia* (Netherlands: E.J. Berill, 1962), vol. 1, 14 and 19.
9. Ira M. Lapidus, *A History of the Islamic Societies* (New York: Cambridge University Press, 1989), 152–61.
10. Alexandre Bennigsen and S. Enders Wimbush, *Muslims of the Soviet Empire: A Guide* (Bloomington: Indiana University Press, 1986), 57–105.
11. Ibid., 70. See also, Martha Brill Olcott, *The Kazakhs* (Stanford: Hoover Institution Press, 1987), 105.
12. Alexandre Bennigsen and S. Enders Wimbush, *Mystics and Commissars: Sufism in the Soviet Union* (Berkeley: University of California Press, 1985), 7–8.
13. Bennigsen and Wimbush (1986), 105.
14. Richard Dobson conducted a public opinion survey in 1993 to measure Islamic proclivity in Uzbekistan, Kazakhstan, and Kyrgyzstan. According to his findings Kyrgyzstan has a stronger Islamic proclivity than Uzbekistan. Given the generally repressive political climate in Uzbekistan, public opinion surveys often do not reflect the reality, as had been the case with Soviet era surveys of religion. For more information on the survey see, Richard B. Dobson, "Islam in Central Asia: Findings From National Surveys," *Central Asia Monitor*, no. 2, (1994): 17–22.
15. Barthold (1962), vol. 1, 15–16.
16. It has also been stated that Abu Hanifah's father was a slave from Kabul who was sold to a woman of the Bani Taim-Allah tribe. He was later set free after serving her for a while. This has been the preferred theory of Abu Hanifah's origins used by his opponents to tarnish his reputation. For more information see, Allamah Shibli Nu'mani's Sirat-i-Nu'man, *Imam Abu Hanifah: Life and Work* (Lahore: Institute of Islamic Culture, 1977), 3–4.
17. Sirat-i Nu'man (1977), 101–102.
18. Ibid., 188.
19. For a full description of the basic principles of Hanafi school see, A. J. Wensinck, *The Muslim Creed: Its Genesis and Historical Development* (London: Frank Cass & Co. Ltd., 1965), ch. 6.
20. For a more detailed account of Sufi brotherhood in Central Asia see, Bennigsen and Wimbush (1986), 31–36. For a discussion of the Sufi revival in Tajikistan and Uzbekistan see, *Far Eastern Economic Review* (December 17, 1992).
21. Bennigsen and Wimbush (1985), 8–9.
22. Alexandre Bennigsen and Marie Broxup, *The Islamic Threat to the Soviet State* (New York: St. Martin's Press, 1983), 110. For more information on the genealogy of the Ismaili sect see, Heinz Halm, *Shiism* (Edinburgh: Edinburgh University Press, 1991).
23. For a detailed account of the activities of these *dais* in Central Asia see, S. M. Stern, *Studies in Early Ismailism* (Jerusalem: Magnes Press, 1983).
24. For more information see, Barthold (1968), 187–192; and 254–56; Fry (1965), 22–33.
25. Annette Bohr, "Background to Demonstrations of Soviet Muslims in Tashkent," *Radio Liberty Research Report* (February 24, 1989).
26. *Los Angeles Times*, August 6, 1990.
27. *The Current Digest of the Soviet Press*, vol. XLIV, no. 26 (1992): 29. For details of the incident see, Vitaly Naumkin, "Islam in the States of the Former Soviet Union," *Annals*, vol. 524 (November 1992): 140.

28. *SWB* (October 8, 1992), SU/1506, B/4.
29. *The Current Digest of the Soviet Press,* vol. XLIV, no. 26 (1992): 29.
30. Interview, Zhounisbek K. Soultanmuratov, Press-service Consultant to the President of the Republic of Kazakhstan, June 7, 1993.
31. *SWB* (August 27, 1992), SU/1470, C2/2.
32. *Soviet Muslims Brief,* vol. 6, no. 3 (September–October 1990): 4–5. See also, Mavlon Makhamov, "Islam and Politics in Tajikistan After 1985," in *Central Asia: Its Strategic Importance and Future Prospects,* ed, Hafeez Malik (New York: St. Martin's Press, 1994), 201.
33. According to Allen Hetmanek, Mullah Abdullah has been involved in clandestine activities since early 1983, when he began advocating the creation of an Islamic state. By 1986 he publicized his views in this regard, asking his followers to petition the 27th Congress of the USSR Communist Party to permit the formation of such a republic. When his request was denied, he called for a *jihad,* or holy war, against the authorities, leading to his arrest and a six-year jail sentence. He was, however, released in 1989, subsequent to Gorbachev's reorientation of the Soviet religious policies. For more information see, Allen Hetmanek, "Islamic Revolution Comes to the Former Soviet Central Asia: The Case of Tajikistan," *Central Asian Survey,* vol.12, no.3 (1993): 370–71.
34. *Central Asia Brief,* no. 3 (1992): 9–10.
35. The spokesman for the Democratic Party of Tajikistan has pointed out that a clandestine Islamic party had been operating in Tajikistan since 1977 with unofficial clergy conducting underground training of the young. Interview, Moscow, July 4, 1993. See also, Ahmed Rashid, "Tajikistan: State of Anarchy," *Karachi Herald* (November 1992): 68.
36. Bess Brown, "The Islamic Renaissance Party in Central Asia," *Radio Liberty Research Report* (April 26, 1991): 13.
37. Mavlon Makhamov, "Islam and the Political Development after 1985," in *Central Asia: Its Strategic Importance and Future Prospects,* ed. Hafeez Malik (New York: St. Martin's Press, 1994), 202.
38. Shahrbanou Tadjbakhsh, "The Tajik Spring of 1992," *Central Asia Monitor,* no. 2 (1993): 25.
39. Ibid.
40. Ibid.
41. *Radio Liberty Daily Report* (November 23, 1990); *The Economist,* December 19, 1992.
42. Muriel Atkin, "Islamic Assertiveness and the Waning of the Old Soviet Order," *The Nationalities Papers,* vol. 20, no.1 (Spring 1992): 64.
43. Allen Hetmanek, "The Political Face of Islam in Tajikistan," *Central Asian Survey,* vol. 9, no. 3 (1990): 106.
44. For a complete list of the items on the platform see, Abdujabar Abduvkhitov, "Islamic Revivalism in Uzbekistan," in *Russia's Muslim Frontiers,* ed. Dale Eickelman (Bloomington: Indiana University Press, 1993), 96–97.
45. Cassandra Cavanaugh, "Crackdown on the Opposition," *Radio Liberty Research Report* (July 31, 1992): 20.
46. Robin Right, "Report From Turkistan," *The New Yorker* (April 6, 1992): 57.
47. Interview, M. Zarif Nazar, Director of Turkmen Service, Radio Liberty, July 16, 1993.
48. *SWB* (November 20, 1991), SU/1234, B/9.

49. *Central Asia Brief,* no. 2 (1992): 6.
50. For an overview of the economic conditions in Central Asia see, William Fierman, ed., *Soviet Central: The Failed Transformation* (Boulder: Westview Press, 1991).
51. *SWB* (May 22, 1992), SU/1387, B/11.
52. *SWB* (May 12, 1992), SU/1376, C1/4. Kazi Turajonzoda sided with the IRP in the aftermath of the civil war and is now in exile in Tehran.
53. *SWB* (February 28, 1992), SU/1316, B/6.
54. *SWB* (February 28, 1992), SU/1316, B/6. Apparently, the IRP had called for an investigation of the finances of the board that they claimed to have involved embezzlement of funds by Mufti Muhammad Sadiq Muhammad Yusuf.
55. The term Wahhabi has been loosely used by the authorities in Uzbekistan and Tajikistan in reference to all fundamentalist Muslims who wish to create an Islamic state, causing confusion in journalistic reports covering the activities of the Muslim forces in Central Asia. The term, however, was first used in this connection by Soviet authorities in the late 1980s.
56. For a detailed account of the Wahhabi domination of the Arabian peninsula see, H. St. John B. Philby, *Saudi Arabia* (New York: Arno Press, 1972), and the same author's *Arabia of the Wahhabis* (New York: Arno Press, 1973).
57. Interview, Kimsanbay Ben Abdurahman, Kazi of the Krygyzstan branch of the Religious Board of Central Asia, June 17, 1993.
58. Abdujabar Abduvakhitov (1993), 83.
59. The organization Towba splintered from the Wahhabi group in Namangan in 1991 over the issues of strategy, in particular methods of struggle to broaden the scope of Islam in society. The Towba was in essence a militant organization that has since gone underground. Its membership is reported to be no more than a few hundred Muslims.
60. Abdujabar Abduvakhitov, "Independent Uzbekistan: A Muslim Community in Development," Meros Academy, Tashkent, 10.
61. Interview, Jamil Burna Asefi, BBC Monitor, July 13, 1993. See also, *SWB* (March 30, 1992), SU/1342, B/2.
62. *Foreign Report,* June 4, 1992, 4–5.
63. In September 1993 five members of Adolat were arrested by the Uzbek authorities and sentenced to labor camp terms of between 10 to 15 years. *Radio Liberty Daily Report* (September 27, 1993).
64. Another report has put the estimate at $1.5 million. For more information see, *Foreign Report,* February 11, 1993, 4–5.
65. *Far Eastern Economic Review* (November 19, 1992): 23–4.
66. Interview, Iman Dospayev, Vice-Chair, Public Relations of the President's Office and Government Specialist on Islam, July 18, 1993.
67. *Far Eastern Economic Review* (November 19, 1992): 26.
68. For a different interpretation of factors that affect the radical tendencies of Islamic forces in Central Asia see, Shireen Hunter, "The Muslim Republics of the Former Soviet Union: Policy Challenges for the United States," *Washington Quarterly,* vol. 15, no. 3 (Summer 1992): 57–71.
69. According to the deputy mufti, Shamsuddin Babakhan, an estimated 5,000 mosques and prayer houses have been opened in recent years. The numbers, however, seem to be exaggerated.
70. *Far Eastern Economic Review* (January 9, 1992). See also, *SWB* (October 26, 1991), SU/1213, B/15.

71. Interview, Kimsanbay Ben Abdurahman, Kazi of the Religious Board of Kyrgyzstan, June 18, 1993.
72. Interview, Nysanbai Uly Ratbek, President, Clerical Administration of Kazakhstan Muslims, June 6, 1993.
73. Interview, Nazar Zarif, Director, Turkmen Service, Radio Liberty, July 16, 1993.
74. Interview, Kimsanbay ben Abdurahman, Kazi of the Religious Board of Kyrgyzstan, June 18, 1993.
75. Interview, Nysanbai Uly Ratbek, President of Clerical Administration of Kazakhstan Muslims, June 6, 1993. See also, *SWB* (August 13, 1993), SU/1766, B/4.
76. Alexandre Bennigsen, "Islam in Retrospect," *Central Asian Survey,* vol. 8, no. 1 (1989): 95.
77. Interview, M. Zarif Nazar, Director of Turkmen Service, Radio Liberty, July 16, 1993.
78. Interview, Kimsanbay ben Abdurahman, Kazi of the Religious Board of Kyrgyzstan, June 18, 1993.
79. Interview, Shamsuddin Babakhan, deputy mufti, December 24, 1993.
80. *Central Asia Brief,* no. 4 (1993): 9.

Chapter 4

1. Interview, Batirhan Bozkurt Darimbet, Co-Chair, Azat Party, June 14, 1993.
2. *The Current Digest of the Soviet Press,* vol. XLIV, no. 25 (1992): 24-5.
3. Interview, Hakem Mohabat, former chair, Soghdian Association, July 4, 1993.
4. For a detailed account of the February 1990 demonstrations see, Saidkasym Djalolov, "February Riot," *Express Chronicle,* no. 6 (February 2-8, 1993): 5. According to another estimate 26 protestors were killed and more than 100 injured.
5. Nadia Diuk and Adrian Karatnycky, *The Hidden Nations: The People Challenge the Soviet Union* (New York: William Morrow and Company, 1992), 192-93.
6. For more information on the Rastokhez's background, aims, and objectives see, Shahrbanou Tadjbakhsh, "The Tajik Spring of 1992," *Central Asia Monitor,* no. 2 (1993): 22-3.
7. Ibid., 23.
8. For a brief background information on Birlik see, Roger D. Kangas, "The Challenge of Nationalism to the Gorbachev Reform Agenda," *The Current World Leaders,* vol. 34, no. 2 (April 1991): 235-254. See also, Yaacov Ro'i, "The Soviet and Russian Context of the Development of Nationalism," *Cahiers Du Monde Russe et Sovietique,* vol. 32, no. 1 (March 1991): 132.
9. Interview, Mikhail Ardzinov, Co-Chair, Human Rights Organization of Uzbekistan, Member of the Birlik Party, June 13, 1993.
10. Diuk and Karatnycky (1991), 174.
11. Interview, Iman Dospayev, Vice-Chair, Public Relations of the Office of the President, June 17, 1993.
12. For a full account of the inter-ethnic disturbances in Osh see chapter 6.
13. Interview, Jepar Jeksheyev, Chair, Democratic Movement of Kyrgyzstan, June 18, 1993. The movement has been registered as a party as of July 20, 1993.
14. This was included to preempt any future Soviet claims to Kyrgyz factories and other facilities built during the Soviet era.

15. Annette Bohr, "Turkmenistan Under *Perestroika,*" *Radio Liberty Research Report* (March 30, 1990): 21.
16. According to the 1993 statistics, Kazakhstan has the largest Russian population relative to the total population of the republic. This is followed by Kyrgyzstan, Turkmenistan, Uzbekistan, and Tajikistan.
17. Bess Brown, "Kazakhstan and Kyrgyzstan on the Road to Democracy," *Radio Liberty Research Report* (December 4, 1992): 21.
18. *Radio Liberty Daily Report* (on line), no. 193 (October 7, 1993). Subsequent to the departure of Ormantay, Khasen Koja-Ahmet was selected as the new chair of Azat.
19. The Azat central committee is composed of Khasen Koja-Ahmet, Casaral Kuanisali, Batirhan Darimbet, Atabay Kylyshaby, Aisulu Kadyrbai, and Amanjol Zeinullin.
20. Interview, Batirhan Darimbet, Co-Chair, Azat Party, June 14, 1993.
21. Ibid.
22. Ibid.
23. There are no details available on the Republican Party's platform other than the fact that its a moderate nationalist party with similar positions to that of the Azat. Its membership is estimated at 10,000 to 15,000. The party lacks a nationwide organization and had not been successful in expanding its base of support since it splintered from Azat.
24. For more information on the Alma-Ata riots see chapter 6.
25. The aim here is to remove the Russians from the Kazakh army. Under the present system both Russians and Kazakh my be inducted into military service.
26. Interview, Boron Bai Uly Juma Bai, First Secretary, Jeltoqsan, June 15, 1993.
27. British Broadcasting Corporation, *Monitoring Briefs: Kazakhstan,* issue 37 (September 1993): 1.
28. In addition to these all-Russian parties, Birlesu, an independent trade union organization, has been active in protecting the rights of the Russians. It, too, has been somewhat sympathetic to the revision of the present Kazakh borders so as to include sections of northern Kazakhstan in Russia. Birlesu has adopted a nonviolent yet confrontational strategy against the government, which has provoked harsh responses by the authorities. In July 1992, the trade union published a statement calling for the revival of the Leninist socialist structure and an immediate disbanding of the existing structures of power and administration. For more information see, *SWB,* (July 24, 1992), SU/1441 B/8; Bess Brown, "Kazakhstan and Kyrgyzstan on the Road to Democracy," *Radio Liberty Research Report,*(December 4, 1992): 21-2, and James Critchlow, "Democratization in Kazakhstan," *Radio Liberty Research Report,* (July 24, 1992): 12-13.
29. Interview, Chupareshti Bazarbayev, Chairman, National Revival Party (Asaba), June 28, 1993.
30. Ibid.
31. *Foreign Broadcast Information Service* (hereafter *FBIS*), SOV-92-143 (July 24, 1992): 60.
32. Interview, Tupchubek Turgunaliyev, Chairman, Erkin Kyrgyzstan, June 18, 1993.
33. *FBIS* (November 10, 1992), SOV-92-218, 64.
34. *SWB* (March 6, 1993), SU/1630, B/7.
35. *SWB* (August 4, 1993), SU/1758, B/5.

36. At its congress on December 14, 1991, Erkin members adopted a resolution to allow local Russian social democrats to join the party as a faction. But the resolution does not seem to have attracted the Russians into the party. For more information on the congress see, *SWB* (December 20, 1991), SU/1260, B/7.
37. James Critchlow, "Kazakhstan and Nazarbaev: Political prospects," *Radio Liberty Research Report,* (January 17, 1992): 34.
38. *SWB* (July 2, 1992), SU/1422, B/6.
39. *SWB* (July 17, 1993), SU/1743, B/5.
40. Interview, Amanchy Gunashev, First Vice-Chair, People's Congress of Kazakhstan, June 10, 1993.
41. *SWB* (May 19, 1993), SU/1692, B/16.
42. British Broadcasting Corporation, *Monitoring Briefs: Kazakhstan,* issue 35 (September 1993): 2.
43. *SWB* (October 13, 1993), SU/1818, G/1.
44. As of October 1993, 14 parties and organizations have been recognized by the government as legal entities. A number of these organizations have included environmental issues to their agendas as a tool of expanding their popular base of support. In some cases, the parties have been solely concerned with ecological issues, such as Tabigat (Nature), which was established on May 19, 1993.
45. There are also quasi democratic parties that have a limited objective, such as the Agrarian Party, established in December 1993 to protect the interest of the farmers in Kyrgyzstan. For more information see, *SWB* (December 9, 1993), SU/1867, G/2.
46. According to party leaders, the current parliament was elected on the basis of the old Communist quota system without regard to the level of knowledge and expertise of those elected to serve.
47. Interview, Apasov Resbek, Executive Secretary, Ata Meken, June 19, 1993.
48. Ibid.
49. Interview, Aripa Turdaliyeva, Co-Chair, Republican People's Party, June 14, 1993.
50. *SWB* (July 29, 1993), SU/1753, B/2.
51. *SWB* (September 15, 1993), SU/1794, G/1.
52. Jepar Jeksheyev, Chairman, Democratic Movement of Kyrgyzstan, June 18, 1993.
53. Interview, Ibrahim Pulatov, Co-Chair Birlik, April 15, 1993.
54. Interview, Mikhail Ardzinov, Co-Chair Human Rights Society of Uzbekistan, member of the Birlik, June 13, 1993.
55. For an excellent account of the Erk's early activities see, William Fierman, "The Communist Party, 'Erk' and the Changing Uzbek Political Environment," *Central Asian Survey,* vol. 10, no. 3 (1991): 54-72.
56. Ibid.
57. Cassandra Cavanaugh, "Crackdown on the Opposition in Uzbekistan," *Radio Liberty Research Report,* (July 31, 1992): 23.
58. *SWB* (July 8, 1992), SU/1427, B/2.
59. *SWB* (August 5, 1992), SU/1451, B/5.
60. *The Independent,* March 28, 1992.
61. In April 1993, the government moved the offices of the Erk to the outskirts of Tashkent in an effort to slow down its activities. In retrospect this event marked the beginning of the end for Erk as a legally registered party.

62. Ibrahim Pulatov, as well as many other Birlik leaders, has been frequently beaten, jailed, and threatened by the authorities. Pulatov was hospitalized for compound fractures of the skull caused by a severe beating on July 1, 1992. Ever since, incidents of beatings and arrests have been reported on a routine basis not only in Uzbekistan, but also in Moscow. On November 5, 1993, for instance, six armed people burst into a Moscow apartment where some Uzbek political refugees were residing and started beating Yadgar Obid, a famous poet, and others. For more information see, *SWB* (November 13, 1993), SU/ 1845, G/5. For similar accounts of this nature see, *SWB* (July 8, 1992), SU/1427, B/2; *SWB* (July 24, 1992), SU/1441, B/8; *SWB* (August 19, 1992), SU/1463, B/4; *The Current Digest of the Soviet Press,* vol. XLIV, no. 49 (1992): 26; *SWB* (January 29, 1993), SU/1599, B/6. Though less frequently, the members of Erk have also been subjected to the same type of treatment.

63. *The Christian Science Monitor,* October 16, 1992.

64. Interview, Ibrahim Pulatov, April 15, 1995.

65. Interview, Mikhail Ardzinov, Co-Chair, Human Rights Society of Uzbekistan, member of Birlik, June 13, 1993.

66. For more information on party politics in Uzbekistan see, Roger Kangas, "Recent Developments With Uzbek Political Parties," *Central Asia Monitor,* no. 4 (1992): 22-27.

67. *SWB* (August 15, 1992), SU/1460, B/9.

68. C. Cavanaugh, (1992): 24; *SWB* (May 22, 1992), SU/1387, B/11.

69. *The Current Digest of the Soviet Press,* vol. XLII, no. 48 (1990): 28-9.

70. Interview, Doost Muhammad Doost, Spokesman, Democratic Party of Tajikistan, July 5, 1993.

71. Tadjbakhsh, (1992), 24.

72. *SWB* (June 22, 1993), SU/1721, I.

73. *SWB* (December 4, 1993), SU/1863, G/3. See also, *FBIS* (April 12, 1994), SOV-94-070, 44.

74. Interview, Zarif Nazar, Director, Turkmen Service, Radio Liberty, July 15, 1993. It must be indicated, however, that the inability to collect the required signatures may be due to the fear of reprisal by the government, rather than a lack of genuine support on the part of the Turkmen people.

75. Suleimonov was at first supportive of the president. In fact, Nazarbayev was invited to the constituent assembly of the People's Congress in 1991, during which he delivered a speech and answered questions from the audience. By October 1992 the relationship between Nazarbayev and Suleimonov had soured, forcing the former to conceive of the idea of a new party to secure his electoral base of support. On October 22, 1992, Nazarbayev finally announced his intention of creating such a political entity. Two explanations have been set forth as to the reason why the two men drifted apart. First, implicit reference has been made to the fact that Suleimonov has been too pro-Russian in orientation, forcing Nazarbayev to distance himself from his party. Second, it has been pointed out that Suleimonov had been disillusioned about the sincerity of Nazarbayev's democratization drive.

76. *The Current Digest of the Soviet Press,* vol. XLV, no. 6 (1993): 21.

77. *SWB* (February 12, 1993), SU/1611, B/5. Interview, Serik Abdurahmanov, Chairman, Union of People's Unity, June 7, 1993.

78. British Broadcasting Corporation, *Monitoring Briefs: Kazakhstan,* issue 6, (February 1993): 1.

79. Ibid., issue 24 (June 1993): 2.
80. *The Current Digest of the Soviet Press,* vol. XLV, no. 7 (1993): 22.
81. *SWB* (May 14, 1993), SU/1688, B/5. Nazarbayev has also created a council to coordinate the republic's efforts "to work out scientifically substantiated conceptual guidelines for the social and political reform of society and the formation of a democratic mentality among the population." The 34-member council includes cultural, literary, and political figures such as Anwar Alimjonov, Mikhail Isinaliyev, Vladmir Grigoryev, Yerik Asanbayev, Marat Tajin, and many other well-known public figures. For more information see, *SWB* (June 15, 1993), SU/1715, B/6.
82. Interview, Anwar Alimjonov, Chairman, Socialist Party of Kazakhstan, June 15, 1993.
83. Ibid.
84. The Communist Party selected L. Korolkov as its chairman. For more information see, *FBIS* (March 24, 1994), SOV-94-057, 40.
85. *SWB* (August 5, 1992), SU/1451, B/4.
86. *SWB* (February 18, 1993), SU/1616, B/5. See also, *FBIS* (April 1, 1993), USR-93-041, 56-7.
87. *SWB* (July 17, 1993), SU/1743, B/4.
88. *SWB* (July 2, 1992), SU/1422, B/7.
89. *FBIS* (April 1, 1993), USR-93-041, 60-1.
90. *SWB* (April 16, 19930, SU/1664, B/16.
91. *SWB* (January 12, 1993), SU/1713, B/9.
92. Christopher J. Panico, "Neo-Stalinism in Ashgabat," Radio Liberty Draft Research Paper (January 13, 1993): 1.
93. *The Christian Science Monitor,* April 8, 1993.

Chapter 5

1. The most bitter disputes between the executive and legislative branches in Kazakhstan have occurred over the drafting of the constitution, the Constitutional Court, and the design of the administrative and territorial power structure. Reportedly, the former speaker of the Parliament, Serikbolsin Abdildin (Abdeddin), had made several attempts to increase his control over the parliament and to seize legislative initiatives that had been delegated under the Constitution to the deputies, the president, and the Cabinet of Ministers. Similar debates over the distribution of power in the Kyrgyz Constitution had been reported in 1993. The Kyrgyz Parliament has frequently altered Akayev's reform initiatives and refused to institute parliamentary reforms that call for a reduction in size and composition of the legislative branch, thus drastically reducing the power of the deputies. For more information on the Kazakh case see: *The Current Digest of the Soviet Press,* vol. XLV, no. 5 (1993): 8-10.
2. For details on the Osh disturbances see chapter 6.
3. According to a newly enacted legislation on presidential elections, new names were to be submitted if the second round of voting did not produce a clear majority. Masaliyev urged the deputies to rewrite the law in order for him to be qualified to be renominated, but his request was declined. For more information see, Bess Brown, "The Fall of Masaliyev: 'Silk Revolution' Advances," *Radio Liberty Research Report* (April 19, 1991): 12-15.

4. Bess Brown, "Central Asia Emerges on the World Stage," *Radio Liberty Research Report* (January 3, 1992): 54.
5. Kyrgyzstan was the only republic besides Russia that experienced a coup against the government. For more information see, "The Silk Revolution," *Economist* (October 19, 1991): 57.
6. *The Current Digest of the Soviet Press,* vol. XLIII, no. 33 (1991): 25-26.
7. Ibid., 25.
8. Interview, Batirhan Darimbet, Co-Chair, Azat Party, June 14, 1993.
9. B. Brown (January 3, 1991), 53.
10. Valery Chalidze, "President Nursultan Nazarbaev," *Central Asia Monitor,* no. 2 (1992): 13.
11. For a discussion of the undemocratic nature of the January 1990 elections in Turkmenistan, see, Bess Brown, "Democratization in Turkmenistan," *Radio Liberty Research Report* (June 1, 1990): 13.
12. *The Current Digest of the Soviet Press,* vol. XLIII, no. 33 (1991): 26.
13. *SWB* (May 18, 1993), SU/1691, B/14.
14. Christopher J. Panico, "Neo-Stalinism in Ashghabat," Draft Research Paper, *Radio Liberty Research Report* (January 13, 1993): 1.
15. *SWB* (May 22, 1992) SU/1387, B/9.
16. For more information on the anatomy of Niyazov's rule in Turkmenistan see, Bess Brown, "Turkmenistan Asserts Itself," *Radio Liberty Research Report* (October 1992): 27-29.
17. In early January 1992, the post of vice-president was abolished and Mirsaidov was appointed State Secretary under the president while the post of prime minister was reestablished.
18. *The Current Digest of the Soviet Press,* vol. XLIII, no. 33 (1991): 26.
19. British Broadcasting Corporation, *Monitoring Briefs: Uzbekistan,* issue 1 (December 1992): 2.
20. Bess Brown, "Presidential Election in Uzbekistan," *Radio Liberty Research Report* (January 24, 1992): 23.
21. *SWB* (February 18, 1993), SU/1616, B/4.
22. For a detailed study of the February 1990 events in Tajikistan see, "Conflict in the Soviet Union: Tajikistan," *A Helsinki Watch Report* (August 1991).
23. Interview, Iskandar Khatlani, Free lance Tajik Journalist, July 4, 1993.
24. *Helsinki Watch* (August 1991): 39-47.
25. Tass News Agency, February 18, 1991.
26. *Nezavisimaya Gazeta,* August 22, 1991.
27. *Kommunist Tajikistana,* August 30, 1991.
28. Earlier in September, the Communist Party had reorganized as the Socialist Party of Tajikistan, but the original name was reinstated in January 1992.
29. Kenjoyev was brought up in the family of Kazi Kalon Turajonzoda. He was a candidate of Sciences who began his career as a transportation prosecutor. He was Nabiyev's campaign manager during the presidential elections in 1991.
30. La'l-e Badakhshan was headed by Attobek Amirbekov, a professor at the Pedagogical Institute in Dushanbe. The organization's broader goal was the establishment of a law-based democratic system in Tajikistan. It advocated a parliamentary system of government.
31. On April 24, 1992, an agreement was reached that included the resignation of Kenjoyev, the nullification of the Tajik law on rallies, holding of new elections

to the Supreme Soviet, and the expansion of the Constitutional Commission by five members to facilitate the inclusion of the political parties and organizations. For more information on this agreement and Kenjoyev's resignation see, *SWB* (April 23, 1992), SU/1362, I; *SWB* (April 24, 1992), SU/1363, B/2.

32. The Current Digest of the Soviet Press, vol. XLIV, no. 17 (1992): 22.

33. The agreement also included a ban on the use of weapons in dealing with demonstrations, a policy of political noninterference on the part of the kaziat, and a policy of government nonintervention in the affairs of the kaziat. For the text of the agreement see, *SWB* (May 9, 1992), SU/1376, C1/1.

34. For a list of the appointments to the "government of national reconciliation" see, *SWB* (May 13, 1992), SU/1379 C1/1.

35. Although the opposition leaders, including the head of the IRP Muhammad Sharif Hematzoda and the head of the kaziat, Akbar Turajonzoda, did not call for the resignation of the president, the radical elements within the IRP continued to press for the resignation of the government in its entirety. It was this lack of unity on the part of the opposition that contributed to failure of the coalition government and the subsequent outbreak of the civil war. For more information see, *SWB* (May 12, 1992), SU/1378, C1/1.

36. *SWB* (May 11, 1992), SU/1377, C1/4. The Communist leaders of Khojend and Kulyab oblasts stressed that the formation of the coalition government was in violation of the republican Constitution. To further underscore their conviction in this regard, both oblasts threatened to halt the delivery of food and industrial products to the other regions of the republic.

37. For an overview of fighting in Kulab and Ghorghan Tepeh in August and September of 1992 see, *The Current Digest of the Soviet Press*, vol. XLIV, no. 38 (1992): 16.

38. Interview, Seyyed Ghasem Jalal, Tajik journalist, July 4, 1993.

39. For more information on the Kenjoyev-Safarov cooperation to regain control of the capital see, *The Current Digest of the Soviet Press*, vol. XLIV, no. 50 (1992): 24-5.

40. *New Times International*, February, 1993, 13.

41. *Express Chronicle*, March 9-16, 1993.

42. For a brief background on Safarov and Nabiyev see, *Central Asia Brief*, no. 1 (1993): 3; *The Daily Telegraph*, April 12, 1993.

43. *New Times International*, February, 1993, 11-12.

44. For an in-depth study of the Soviet and Uzbek involvement in the Tajik civil war see, Keith Martin, "Tajikistan: Civil War Without End?," *Radio Liberty Research Report* (August 20, 1993): 18-29.

45. For a provocative discussion of causes of the civil war in Tajikistan see, Shahrbanou Tadjbakhsh, "The Bloody Path of Change: The Case of Post-Soviet Tajikistan," *The Harriman Institute Forum*, vol. 6, no. 11 (July, 1993): 1-16.

46. For a reference to this argument see, Robert E. Barylski, "The Caucasus, Central Asia and the Near-Abroad Syndrome," *Central Asia Monitor*, no. 5 (1993): 24.

47. For more information see, Allen Hetmanek, "Islamic Revolution Comes to the former Soviet Central Asia: The Case of Tajikistan," *Central Asian Survey*, vol. 12, no. 3 (1993): 365-378.

48. S. Tadjbakhsh, (July 1993), 4.

49. For an in-depth account of the nature of clan rivalry and its significant contribution to the outbreak of the civil war see, Shahrbanou Tadjbakhsh, "Causes and

Consequence of the Civil War," *Central Asia Monitor,* no. 1 (1993): 10-14. See also, *The Financial Times,* September 7, 1992, and *The Guardian,* October 3, 1993.

50. For more information on cadre recruitment during the Soviet era see, Teresa Rakowska-Harmstone, *Russia and Nationalism in Central Asia,* (Baltimore: Johns Hopkins Press, 1970), ch. 4. See also, *Megapolis-Express,* September 16, 1992, 20.

51. R. Barylski, (1993), 27. For an account of Russian arms delivery to the Communist Nabiyev government see, *The Current Digest of the Soviet Press,* vol. XLIV, no. 38 (1992): 17.

52. For an excellent discussion of the causes of the civil war, and the Russian and Uzbek involvement see Alexander Bogolyubov's interview with Rady Fish in *Express Chronicle,* March 9-16, 1992, 3. Since the Spring of 1994 the Tajik government has been involved in negotiations with the opposition. But as of July 1994, no substantive breakthroughs have been announced. For more information see, *Radio Liberty Daily Report* (on line), no. 54 (March 18, 1994); no. 75 (April 20, 1994); no. 91 (May 13, 1994). See also, British Broadcasting Corporation, *Inside Central Asia,* issue 13 (April 1994): 4.

53. *Inside Central Asia,* issue 1 (January 1994): 1.

54. *Radio Liberty Daily Report* (on line), no. 10 (January 17, 1994).

55. *SWB* (December 4, 1993), SU/1863, G/3.

56. *SWB* (December 14, 1993), SU/1871, G/1.

57. *SWB* (January 1, 1994), SU/1884, G/1.

58. *SWB* (January 5, 1994), SU/1887, G/1.

59. *Radio Liberty Daily Report* (on line), no. 35 (February 21, 1994).

60. For more information on elections see, *FBIS* (March 7, 1994), SOV-94-044, 49; (March 18, 1994), SOV-94-053, 43, and *Radio Liberty Daily Report* (on Line), no. 46 (March 8, 1994); no. 48 (March 10, 1994); and no. 50, (March 14, 1994).

61. *SWB* (December 15, 1993), SU/1872, G/3.

62. *FBIS* (February 7, 1994), SOV-94-025, 57.

63. Interview, Zarif Nazar, Director, Turkmen Service, Radio Liberty, July 15, 1993.

64. *SWB* (December 4, 1993), SU/1863, G/3.

65. Interview, Mikhail Ardzinov, Co-Chair, Human Rights Organization of Uzbekistan, June 13, 1993.

66. *Radio Liberty Daily Report* (on Line), no. 163 (August 26, 1993).

67. For an early overview of the Central Asian governments views on the role of Islam as a domestic and foreign policy issue see, Martha Brill Olcott, "Central Asia's Catapult to Independence," *Foreign Affairs,* vol. 71, no. 3, (Summer 1992): 108-130.

68. For some background information on official Islam see, Alexandre Bennigsen and S. Enders Wimbush, *Muslims of the Soviet Empire: A Guide* (Bloomington: Indiana University Press, 1986).

69. Interview, Nysanbai Uly Ratbek, President of Clerical Administration of Kazakhstan Muslims, June 7, 1993.

70. Interview, Kimsanbay Ben Abdurahman, Kazi of Kyrgyzstan, June 22, 1993.

71. Interview, Chupareshti Bazarbayev, Chairman, National Revival Party, June 28, 1993.

72. Interview, Shamsuddin Babakhan, Deputy Mufti for Public Relations, December 22, 1993.

73. *The New York Times,* February 13, 1993.

74. *SWB* (July 29, 1993), SU/1753, B/3.
75. *SWB* (February 28, 1992), SU/1316, B/6.
76. *Radio Liberty Daily Report* (on line), no. 40 (February 28, 1994).
77. For a biographical background on Turajonzoda see, Sergei Gretsky, "Qadi Akbar Turajonzoda," *Central Asia Monitor,* no. 1 (1994): 16-24.
78. Interview, Eskandar Khatlani, Free lance Tajik Reporter, July 4, 1993. See also, *SWB* (May 12, 1992), SU/1376, C1/4.
79. *SWB* (May 12, 1992), SU/1378, C1/4 and *SWB* (September 19, 1992), SU/1490, B/5.
80. Ahmed Rashid has claimed that "the Qazi is lavishly funded by Iran, and foreign diplomats claim that he has also been receiving contributions from Saudi Arabia, Pakistan, and Turkey. His militia fought alongside the IRP in Kurgan Tyube [Ghorghan Tepeh], and he can claim the support of a large section of the IRP itself." For more information, see, Ahmed Rashid, "Tajikistan: State of Anarchy," *The Karachi Herald,* November, 1992, 69.
81. *FBIS* (March 10, 1994), SOV-94-047, 26-27.
82. *SWB* (January 29, 1993), SU/1599, B/6.
83. Interview conducted by Tass News Agency, March 24, 1989.
84. *SWB* (January, 13, 1992), SU/1276, B/8.
85. K. Warikoo and Dawa Norbu, *Ethnicity and Politics in Central Asia* (New Dehli: South Asian Publishers, 1992), 67.
86. *Express Chronicle,* February 22-March 2, 1993, 3.
87. *FBIS* (May 4, 1994), SOV-94-086, 57.

Chapter 6

1. I am greatly indebted to the late Alexandre Bennigsen, Geoffrey Wheeler, and Shirin Akiner for the bulk of ethnographic data utilized in this chapter. For more extensive detail see, Alexandre Bennigsen and S. Enders Wimbush, *Muslims of the Soviet Empire: A Guide* (Bloomington: Indiana University Press, 1986), Shirin Akiner, *Islamic Peoples of the Soviet Union* (London: KPI Publishers, 1986), and Geoffrey Wheeler, *The Modern History of Soviet Central Asia* (New York: Frederick A. Praeger Publishers, 1964).
2. According to Allworth, the Uzbek tribal sphere of activity in the fourteenth century was located in an area stretching from the Aral Sea north to Tura, east to lake Tengiz, and west to the river Yaik feeding the Caspian Sea. Allworth, *The Modern Uzbek: From the Fourteenth Century to the Present* (Stanford: Hoover Institution Press, 1990), 7.
3. For more information on the Russian incorporation of Central Asia see chapter 1.
4. Walter Kolarz, *Russia and Her Colonies* (New York: Archon Books, 1967), 270-71.
5. Wheeler (1964), 77.
6. By 1936, an estimated 1,700,000 new settlers had migrated to Central Asia, of which nearly 786,000 lived in Uzbekistan, 156,000 lived in Turkmenistan, 290,000 in Kyrgyzstan, and 202,000 in Tajikistan. For more information see, Michael Rywkin, *Russian Central Asia* (New York: Collier-Macmillan, 1963), 75-84.

7. For an excellent discussion on the main parameters of Central Asian identity see, Jo-Ann Gross, ed., *Muslims in Central Asia: Expressions of Identity and Change* (Durham: Duke University Press, 1992), 1-23; 46-72. See also, Alexandre Bennigsen and Marie Broxup, *The Islamic Threat to the Soviet State* (New York: St. Martin's Press, 1985), 135-40.

8. W. Kolarz (1967), 257.

9. As quoted in Olaf Caroe, *Soviet Empire: The Turks of Central Asia and Stalinism* (London: Macmillan, 1967), p. 146. Caroe seems to have modified the passage after its translation to English. For a different translation see, W. P. and Zelda K. Coates, *Soviets in Central Asia* (New York: Greenwood Press, 1951), 89.

10. Alexandre Bennigsen and Chantal Lemercier-Quelquejay, *Islam in the Soviet Union* (New York: Frederick A. Praeger Publishers, 1967), 125-26. For a more detailed account of the evolution of Stalin's Nationalities policy see, J. Stalin, *On the National Question* (London: Lawrence and Wishart, 1942).

11. As quoted in W. P. and Zelda K. Coates (1951), 88.

12. For a similar explanation see, James Critchlow, *Nationalism in Uzbekistan: A Soviet Republic's Road to Sovereignty* (Boulder: Westview Press, 1991), 11-12.

13. For an eye-opening account of the Soviet deportation policies see, Robert Conquest, *The Nation Killers: The Soviet Deportation of Nationalities* (London: Macmillan Company, 1970).

14. For an in-depth study of Kazakhstan ethnic complexity see, Philip S. Gillette, "Ethnic Balance and Imbalance in Kazakhstan's Regions," *Central Asia Monitor,* no. 3 (1993): 17-23.

15. For an interesting review of the status of Russians in various former Soviet republics see, Chauncy D. Harris, "The New Russian Minorities: A Statistical Overview," *Post-Soviet Geography,* vol. 34, no. 1 (1993): 1-27.

16. British Broadcasting Company, Monitoring Briefs: Kazakhstan, issue 45, (November 1993), 1. During the first quarter of 1994, an estimated 356,000 Russians had left Central Asia for the Russian Federation. For more information see, *Inside Central Asia,* issue 12 (April 1994): 1.

17. Foreign Broadcast Information Service, *FBIS* (May 25, 1994) SOV-94-101, 57. On April 19, 1994, Presidents Yeltsin and Nazarbayev signed a memorandum on the citizenship status of the Russians in Kazakhstan. It outlined the rights of the citizens of both countries with respect to employment, travel, residency, and so forth. For more information see, *FBIS* (April 20, 1994), SOV-94-076.

18. There are no reliable longitudinal data on the Russian out-migration. But the estimates put the figure as high as 1,000,000 for the 1990-93 period. *Inside Central Asia,* issue 20 (May 1994): 2. Ethnic Germans have also left Kazakhstan in sizable numbers. According to government statistics, during the 1990-93 period more than 300,000 Germans have returned home. *SWB* (March 5, 1993), SU/1629, B/11.

19. *FBIS* (June 15, 1994), SOV-94-115, 53. Akayev has also founded a Slavonic university in Bishkek to demonstrate his resolve to accommodate the Russians in Kyrgyzstan.

20. *Inside Central Asia,* issue 2 (January 1994): 4.

21. During the first half of the 1993 an estimated 13,000 Germans have also left the republic, and another 80,000 are planning to leave in the near future. *SWB* (July 29, 1993), SU/1753, B/2, and *SWB* (December 23, 1993), SU/1879, G/2.

22. For more information on Kazakhstan immigration law and Turkmenistan dual citizenship see, *SWB* (August 28, 1992) SU/1471, B/5; *SWB* (December 30, 1993),

SU/1882, G/2: *The Financial Times,* December 24, 1993. For more information on the ethnic problems and the vulnerability of the Russians in Central Asia see, "Panel on Social Dimensions of Interdependence in the States of the Former Soviet Union," *Soviet Geography,* vol. 34, no. 1 (1993): 28-51.

23. British Broadcasting Corporation, *Monitoring Briefs,* issue 47 (December 1993): 2. See also, *SWB* (March 5, 1993), SU/1629, B/11.

24. The significance of the rise of Uzbek chauvinism has been evidenced in a private conversation conducted between Presidents Karimov and Akayev in the aftermath of the Osh disturbances in June-August 1990, in which Karimov made an assertive remark to Akayev regarding the need for the unification of the two countries. It is reported that in response Akayev remained quiet, refusing to express any opinion. Interview, Tupchubek Turgunaliyev, Chair, Erkin Kyrgyzstan, June 18, 1993.

25. For a detailed account of the Kazakh tribal history see, Martha Brill Olcott, *The Kazakhs* (Stanford: Hoover Institution Press, 1987).

26. Some of these tribes and clans also enter into the composition of Uzbeks and Kazakhs in the region.

27. There are also several group of nomads that belong to this layer but have characteristics of both Uzbeks and Kazakhs with their own distinct language and ethnic identity, such as Kuramas.

28. For more information on Gasprinski's views see, Serge A. Zenkovski, *Pan-Turkism and Islam in Russia* (Cambridge: Harvard University Press, 1960).

29. Tadeusz Swietochowski, "Islam and Nationality in Tsarist Russia and the Soviet Union," in *Soviet Nationality Policies: Ruling Ethnic Groups in the USSR,* ed. Henry R. Huttenbach (London: Mansell Publishing Limited, 1990), 224.

30. Azade-Ayse Rorlich, *The Volga Tatars: A profile in National Resilience* (Stanford: Hoover Institution Press, 1986), 179.

31. Ibid., 129.

32. Mehmed Ziya, also known as Gukalp Ziya, was also an active participant in the pan-Turkic discourse of the early twentieth century. His views on the issue, however, changed over time as he limited the scope of his pan-Turkic ideology to include only the Ottoman Turks.

33. For an interesting account of the pan-Turkic movement subsequent to the death of Enver Pasha see, Glenda A. Fraser, "Haji Sami and Turkestan Federation, 1922-3," *Asian Affairs,* vol. XVIII, no. 1 (February 1987): 11-21.

34. *SWB* (July 17, 1992), SU/1435, B/12.

35. In an interview with the author on June 14, 1993, Darimbet was quick to mention that he was a Kazakh first, a pan-Turk second, and a pan-Islamic third.

36. For more information on pan-Turkic views of the chairman of the Erk, Muhammad Solih see, *The independent,* March 28, 1992.

37. *SWB* (April 5, 1993), ME/1655, C/4.

38. For more information on Turkey's Kurdish Problem see, Graham Fuller, "The Fate of the Kurds," *Foreign Affairs,* vol. 72, no. 2 (Spring 1993): 108-121. The rise of Islamic fundamentalism has so far manifested itself in the form of several electoral victories at the mayoral level during the March 1994, elections. For more information see, *Iran Times,* April 1, 1994. For a brief discussion of the erosion of Kemalist secularism and the rise of Islam see, Philip Robins, *Turkey and the Middle East* (London: Royal Institute of International Affairs, 1991). See also, Philip Robins, "Between Sentiment and Self-Interest: Turkey's Policy Toward

Azerbaijan and the Central Asian States," *Middle East Journal,* vol. 47, no. 4 (Autumn 1993): 593-610.

39. For an interesting interpretation of the Central Asian republics' lack of unity see, Martha Brill Olcott, "Ceremony and Substance: The Illusion of Unity in Central Asia," in *Central Asia and the World,* ed. Michael Mandelbaum (New York:Council on Foreign Relations Press, 1994).

40. *SWB* (October 17, 1991), SU/1205, B/11.

41. A similar reference to this point has been made by Bess Brown in "Central Asia 1992," Draft Research Paper, *Radio Liberty Research Report,* (December 16, 1992): 1.

42. Perhaps the only potentially promising result of the meeting was the establishment of an Aral Sea fund to help save the dying and polluted body of water. *The Independent,* February 27, 1993. See also, *Monitoring Briefs,* issue 2 (January 1993): 1.

43. Kyrgyzstan was formally admitted as a member of the new economic union during a summit in Issyk-Kul city of Cholpon Ata on April 29, 1994. *Radio Liberty Daily Report* (on line), no. 211 (November 3, 1993), and no. 22 (February 2, 1994). See also, *SWB* (January 15, 1994), SU/1896, G/1.

44. Despite timetable variations, the shift to the Latin alphabet will be gradual in all Turkic republics to be completed by the year 2000.

45. For a more detailed account of the Soviet-language policies and Central Asian linguistic characteristics see, Shirin Akiner (1986), 280-84; 297-300; 310-13; 322-25; 335-37.

46. For a similar line of argument regarding the rise of Uzbek chauvinism see, Christopher R. Kedzie, "Religion and Ethnicity in Central Asia," *Central Asia Monitor,* no. 3 (1992): 14-19.

47. One of the most recent documentation was conducted by Ronald Wixman in 1985. For more information see, Ronald Wixman, "Ethnic Attitudes and Relations in Modern Uzbek Cities," in *Central Asia: The failed Transformation,* ed. William Fierman (Boulder: Westview Press, 1991).

48. For an in-depth overview of the Russian colonial attitude under the imperial and Communist Russia see, Nadia Diuk and Adrian Karatnycky, *The Hidden Nations: The People Challenge the Soviet Union* (New York: William Morrow and Company, 1990), 194-225.

49. For a more detailed analysis of the causes of the Almaty riots see, S. Enders Wimbush, "The Muslim Ferment in Soviet Central Asia," *Global Affairs,* vol. 12, no. 3 (Summer 1987): 105-118.

50. *The Guardian,* December 30, 1986.

51. According to a 1990 government estimate, 1,700 were injured and 8,500 were detained. The authorities also tied the incident to the "antidemocratic methods used in replacing the first secretary of the republic Communist Party Central Committee." For more information see, *The Current Digest of the Soviet Press,* vol. XLII, no. 39 (1990): 33. See also, Ludmilla Alexeyeva, "Ethnic Unrest in the Soviet Union," *Washington Quarterly,* vol. 13, no. 1 (Winter 1990): 68.

52. *SWB* (December 21, 1991), SU/1261, B/9.

53. *SWB* (February 28, 1992), SU/1316, B/7.

54. *Radio Liberty Daily Report* (on line), no. 152 (August 11, 1993).

55. Of Scythian ancestry, the Cossacks had occupied the Black Sea Basin for centuries. Since the fourteenth century, they had been organized into self-sufficient

fishing and farming communities supported by a well-disciplined militia. Subject of frequent attacks by the Tatars, the Poles, and the Russians, Cossacks entered into a mutual agreement with czarist Russia in the mid-seventeenth century in which Russian sovereignty was accepted in return for internal autonomy. Cossacks thus helped defend the Russian frontiers. Later, the Turkish wars and the Cossack expeditions to Siberia scattered their settlements from the Black Sea to the banks of the Ussuri in the Far East. In 1992, President Yeltsin issued a decree, allowing the Cossacks to return to their old self-governing political system. Justifiably, this has caused considerable alarm among the Kazakh officials who believe that the treaty has raised the confidence of the Cossacks to pursue similar demands for autonomy in Kazakhstan.

56. *Radio Liberty Daily Report* (on line), no. 67 (April 8, 1994); *FBIS* (April 14, 1994), SOV-94-072, 51.

57. *Inside Central Asia,* issue 2 (January 1994): 5.

58. *Radio Liberty Report* (on line), no. 109 (June 10, 1994).

59. Neil Melvin, "Russia and the Ethno-Politics of Kazakhstan," *The World Today,* vol. 49, no. 11 (November 1993): 209.

60. *Far Eastern Economic Review* (February 24, 1994). The organization Lad was founded in 1992. It has since been denied registration and the government has given it the same type of negative treatment it has been giving the Kazakh nationalist organizations, such as Jeltoqsan.

61. *Radio Liberty Report* (on line), no. 174 (September 10, 1993).

62. *SWB* (February 9, 1993), SU/1608, B/6.

63. *Radio Liberty Report* (on line), no. 3 (January 5, 1994); no. 103 (June 1, 1994). Other killings have also been reported in June. The Tajik opposition in exile has denied responsibility and instead blamed the assassinations on "intrigues by forces which are not interested in resolving the conflict peacefully." For more information see, *Radio Liberty Report* (on line), no. 106 (June 7, 1994); no. 104 (June 3, 1994).

64. *Inside Central Asia,* issue 16 (May 1994): 4. For an overview of the Russian Federation's role in Tajikistan see, Shahrbanou Tadjbakhsh, "Tajikistan: From Freedom to War," *Current History,* vol. 93, no. 582 (April 1994): 173-177.

65. "Conflict in the Soviet Union," *A Helsinki Watch Report* (August 1991): 1-79.

66. In the summer of 1993, an estimated 700 applications were being filed on a daily basis by the Russian residents of Uzbekistan.

67. In June 1989, a similar incident in Novy Uzen of Kazakhstan caused five deaths and 118 injuries, when following a brawl at a dance hall, several thousand Kazakhs attacked the resident Lezgins and Chechens in several days of violent confrontation. An estimated 3,500 Caucasians were forced to flee the region. For more information see, Alexeyeva (Winter 1990): 65-6.

68. *The Current Digest of the Soviet Press,* vol. XLI, no. 23 (1989): 16.

69. Ibid., 19.

70. *The Current Digest of the Soviet Press,* vol. XLI, no. 24 (1989): 5-6.

71. Diuk and Karatnycky (1990), 179-80.

72. It is not at all clear that the Kyrgyz-based Adolat is tied to the Uzbek-based organization of the same name that exercised influence in the Fergana region until 1992.

73. *The Current Digest of the Soviet Press,* vol. XLII, no. 31 (1990): 29.

74. For more information on the Osh incident see, *The Current Digest of the Soviet Press,* vol. XLII, no. 23 (1990): 1-5.

75. *The Current Digest of the Soviet Press,* vol. XLII, no. 28 (1990): 19.

76. Kyrgyz relations with the Uzbek was the most frequent subject, second only to the declining economic conditions, which was brought up by those with whom the author conducted interviews in the summer of 1993.

77. Much of the discussion here is based on the author's extended interviews with the organization's executive secretary, Uktum Bekmuhammadov, and the committee chair for Makateb and Ma'aref, Amineh Sharafeddin, conducted on July 4 and 5, 1993.

78. *International Herald Tribune,* February 16, 1993.

79. For a discussion of the suppression of the Tajik language and culture see, *The Current Digest of the Soviet Press,* vol. XL, no. 25 (1988): 9-10.

80. In one instance, the Tajik leaders called for warehouse inspections with the hope of uncovering economic discrimination or corruption.

81. Within Tajikistan, there has also been separatist tendencies expressed by the Pamir people of Gorno-Badakhshan who wish to create a separate republic. To pursue this objective, an organization called the La'l-e Badakhshan was set up in the late 1980s under the banner of protection of the rights of the Pamiris. In December 1991, following several days of rallies, the oblast Soviet, many of whose members also belonged to La'l-e Badakhshan, passed a resolution on independence of the region. Later, the La'l-e Badakhshan joined the political struggle against the status quo, hoping that success would guarantee Pamiris their long-awaited independence. The organization was dealt a severe blow in June 1993, when it, together with the Islamic Revival Party, Rastokhez, and the Democratic Party of Tajikistan, was banned by the Rahmonov government. For a brief information on the La'l-e Badakhshan see, Shahrbanau Tadjbakhsh, "The Tajik Spring of 1992," *Central Asia Monitor,* no. 2 (1993): 27-8. See also, *SWB* (December 7, 1993), SU/1865, G/5.

82. For more information see, *The Current Digest of the Soviet Press,* vol. XLI, no. 28 (1989): 25-6.

83. *Express Chronicle* (March 9-16, 1993): 3.

84. *SWB* (April 21, 1993), SU/1668, B/15.

85. *Inside Central Asia,* issue 1 (January 1994): 5.

86. For a brief discussion of the ethnic and regional factor in the distribution of power in Central Asia see, Martha Brill Olcott, "Central Asia on Its Own," *Journal of Democracy,* vol. 4, no. 1 (January 1993): 101-2.

87. *SWB* (November 13, 1993), SU/1845, G/3. See also, *The Current Digest of the Soviet Press,* vol. XIV, no. 10 (1992): 5.

88. Neil Melvin, "Russia and the Ethno-Politics of Kazakhstan," *The World Today,* vol. 49, no. 11 (November 1993): 210.

89. *SWB* (June 12, 1993), SU/1713, B/11.

Chapter 7

1. It is reported, for instance, that some Namangan Uzbeks, sympathetic to the Islamic forces in Tajikistan, have been crossing the border to fight the Tajik government. *Central Asia Brief,* vol. 10, no. 6 (June 1994): 13.

2. For an engaging view of this and other factors influencing the Tajik affairs see: Barnett Rubin, "The fragmentation of Tajikistan," *Survival,* no. 35 (Winter 1993-4): 71-91.

SELECTED BIBLIOGRAPHY

BOOKS

Akiner, Shirin. *Political and Economic Trends in Central Asia.* London: British Academic Press 1994.
————. *Islamic Peoples of the Soviet Union.* London: KPI Publishers, 1986.
Allworth, Edward. *The Modern Uzbek: From the Fourteenth Century to the Present.* Stanford: Hoover Institution Press, 1990.
————. *Central Asia: 120 Years of Russian Rule.* Durham: Duke University Press, 1989.
Anonymous. *Religion in the USSR.* Munich: Institute for the Study of USSR, 1960 , series 1, no. 59.
Azimova, Dinora. *Youth and the Cultural Revolution in Soviet Central Asian Republics.* Moscow: Central Department of Oriental Literature, 1988.
Azrael, Jeremy R. ed. *Soviet Nationality Policies and Practices.* New York: Praeger Publishers, 1978.
Bacon, Elizabeth E. *Central Asians Under Russian Rule: A Study in Cultural Change.* New York: Cornell University Press, 1966.
Barmenkov. *Freedom of Conscience in the USSR.* Moscow: Progress Publishers, 1983.
Barthold, V. V. *Turkistan down to the Mongol Invasion.* London: Lowe and Brydone Lt.D., 1968.
————. *Four Studies on the History of Central Asia.* Netherlands: E. J. Berill, 1962, vol. 1.
Becker, Seymour. *Russia's Protectorates in Central Asia: Bukhara and Khiva, 1865-1924.* Cambridge: Harvard University Press, 1968.
Bennigsen, Alexandre and S. Enders Wimbush. *Muslim National Communism in the Soviet Union.* Chicago: The University of Chicago Press, 1979.
————. *Muslims of the Soviet Empire: A Guide.* Bloomington: Indiana University Press, 1986.
————. *Mystics and Commissars: Sufism in the Soviet Union* Berkeley: University of California Press, 1985.
Bennigsen, Alexandre and Marie Broxup. *The Islamic Threat to the Soviet State.* New York: St. Martin's Press, 1983.
Bennigsen, Alexandre and Chantal Lemercier-Quelquejay. *Islam in the Soviet Union.* New York: Frederick A. Praeger Publishers, 1967.
Bethmann, Erich W. *The Fate of Muslims Under Soviet Rule.* New York: American Friends of the Middle East, Inc., 1958.
Bourdeaux, Michael. *Gorbachev, Glasnost and the Gospel.* London: Hodder and Stoughton, 1990.
Butson, Thomas G. *Gorbachev: A Biography.* New York: Stein and Day Publishers, 1985.

Caroe, Olaf. *Soviet Empire: The Turks of Central Asia and Stalinism*. London: Macmillan, 1967.

Coates, W. P. and K. Zelda. *Soviets in Central Asia*. New York: Greenwood Press, 1951.

Conquest, Robert. *The Nation Killers: The Soviet Deportation of Nationalities*. London: Macmillan Company, 1970.

————. *Religion in the U.S.S.R.*. New York: Frederick A. Praeger Publishers, 1968.

Critchlow, James. *Nationalism in Uzbekistan: A Soviet Republic's Road to Sovereignty*. Boulder: Westview Press, 1991.

Demko, George J. *The Russian Colonization of Kazakhstan, 1896-1916*. Bloomington: Indiana University Press, 1969.

d'Encausse, Helene Carrere. *Decline of an Empire: The Soviet Socialist Republic in Revolt*. trans. by Martin Sokolinsky and Henry A. La Farge. New York: Harper Colophon Books, 1979.

Diuk, Nadia and Adrian Karatnycky. *The Hidden Nations: The People Challenge the Soviet Union*. New York: William Morrow and Company, 1992.

Doder, Dusko and Louise Branson. *Gorbachev: Heretic in the Kremlin*. New York: Penguin Group, 1990.

Eklof, Ben. *Soviet Briefing: Gorbachev and the Reform Period*. Boulder: Westview Press, 1989.

Fierman, William, ed. *Soviet Central: The Failed Transformation*. Boulder: Westview Press, 1991.

Fitzsimmons, Thomas, Malof, Peter and John C. Fiske. *USSR: Its People, Its Society, Its Culture*. Westport: Greenwood Press Publishers, 1974.

Fletcher, William and Anthony J. Strover. *Religion and the Search for New Ideals in the USSR*. New York: Frederick A. Praeger Publishers, 1967.

Frost, Jim. *Free at Last? The Impact of Peristroika on Religious Life in the Soviet Union*. London: Darton, Longman and Todd, 1990.

Frye, Richard N. *Bukhara: The Medieval Achievement*. Norman: University of Oklahoma Press, 1965.

Gerner, Kristian, and Hedlund, Stefan. *Ideology and Rationality in the Soviet Model: A Legacy for Gorbachev*. London: Routledge, 1989.

Gibb, H. A. R. *The Arab Conquests in Central Asia*. London: The Royal Asiatic Society, 1923.

Goldman, Marshal I. *What Went Wrong With Perestroika*. New York: W. W. Norton, 1991.

Gorbachev, Mikhail. *Perestroika: New Thinking for Our Country and the World*. New York: Harper & Row Publishers, 1987.

Gross, Jo-Ann, ed. *Muslims in Central Asia: Expressions of Identity and Change*. Durham: Duke University Press, 1992.

Halm, Heinz. *Shiism* Edinburgh: Edinburgh University Press, 1991.

Hazan, Baruch A. *Gorbachev and His Enemies*. Boulder: Westview Press, 1990.

Hiro, Dilip. *Between Marx and Muhammad: The Changing Face of Central Asia*. London: Harper Collins, 1994.

Hunczak, Taras. ed. *Russian Imperialism from Ivon the Great to the Revolution*. New Jersey: Rutgers University Press, 1974.

Huttenbach, Henry R. ed. *Soviet Nationality Policies: Ruling Ethnic Groups in the USSR*. London: Mansell Publishing Limited, 1990.

Kline, George E. *Religion and Anti-Religious Thought in Russia*. Chicago: University of Chicago Press, 1968.

Kolarz, Walter. *Religion in the Soviet Union* New York: St. Martin's Press, 1961.
———. *Russia and Her Colonies*. New York: Archon Books, 1967.
Krader, Lawrence. *Peoples of Central Asia*. Bloomington: Indiana University Press, 1963.
Lapidus, Ira M. *A History of the Islamic Societies*. New York: Cambridge University Press, 1989.
Lenin, V. I. *Collected Works*. Moscow: Progress Publishers, 1978.
Lerner, Lawrence W. and Donald W. Treadgold, eds. *Gorbachev and the Soviet Future*. Boulder: Westview Press, 1988.
McCauley, Martin. ed. *Gorbachev and Perestroika*. New York: St. Martin's Press, 1990.
Mackenzie, David. *The Lion of Tashkent: the Career of General M. G. Cherniaev*. Athens: University of Georgia Press, 1974.
Malik, Hafeez, ed. *Central Asia: Its Strategic Significance and Future Prospects*. New York: St. Martin's Press, 1994.
Mandel, Ernest. *Beyond Perestroika: The Future of Gorbachev's USSR*. London: Verso, 1989.
Mandelbaum, Michael, ed. *Central Asia and the World*. New York: Council on Foreign Relations Press, 1994.
Marshal, Richard Jr., ed. *Aspects of Religion in the Soviet Union, 1917-1967*. Chicago: University of Chicago Press, 1971.
Marwat, Fazal-Ul-Rahim Kahn. *The Basmachi Movement in Soviet Central Asia: A Study in Political Development*. Peshawar: Emjay Books International, 1985.
Massell, Gregory J. *The Surrogate Proletariat: Moslem Women and Revolutionary Strategies in Soviet Central Asia, 1919-1929*. New Jersey: Princeton University Press, 1974.
Melville, Andrei, and Lapidus, Gail. *The Glasnost Papers*. Boulder: Westview Press, 1990.
Nove, Alec. *Glasnost in Action: Cultural Renaissance in Russia*. Boston: Unwin Hyman, 1989.
Olcott, Martha Brill, ed. *The Kazakhs*. Stanford: Hoover Istitution Press, 1987.
———. *The Soviet Multinational State: Readings and Documents*. New York: M. E. Sharpe, 1990.
Paksoy, H. B., ed. *Central Asia Reader: The Rediscovery of History*. New York: M. E. Sharpe, 1994.
Park, Alexander G. *Bolshevism in Turkistan*. New York: Columbia University Press, 1957.
Philby, H. St. John B. *Arabia of the Wahhabis*. New York: Arno Press, 1973.
Pierce, Richard A. *Russian Central Asia, 1867-1917*. Berkeley: University of California Press, 1960.
Pipes, Richard. *The Formation of the Soviet Union: Communism and Nationalism, 1917-1923*. Cambridge: Harvard University Press, 1955.
Pospielovsky, Dimitry V. *A History of Marxist-Leninist Atheism and Soviet Anti-Religious Policies*. New York: St. Martin's Press, 1987.
Powell, David E. *Antireligious Propaganda in the Soviet Union: A Study of Mass Persuasion*. Cambridge: MIT Press, 1975.
Rashid, Ahmed. *The Resurgence of Central Asia: Islam or Nationalism?* London: Zed Press, 1994.
Ro'i, Yaccov, ed. *The USSR and the Muslim World: Issues in Domestic and Foreign Policy*. London: George Allen & Unwin, 1984.

Rokowska-Harmstone, Teresa. *Russia and Nationalism in Central Asia*. Baltimore: Johns Hopkins Press, 1970.

Rorlich, Azade-Ayse. *The Volga Tatars: A Profile in National Resilience*. Stanford: Hoover Institution Press, 1986.

Rumer, Boris Z. *Soviet Central Asia: A Tragic Experiment*. Boston: Unwin Hyman, 1989.

Rywkin, Michael. *Moscow's Muslim Challenge: Soviet Central Asia*. New York: M. E. Sharpe, 1982.

―――. *Russian Central Asia*. New York: Collier Macmillan, 1963.

Sakwa, Richard. *Gorbachev and His Reforms, 1985-1990*. New York: Prentice Hall, 1990.

Seton-Watson, Hugh. *The Decline of Imperial Russia, 1855-1914*. New York: Frederick A. Praeger Publishers, 1962.

Shirley, Eugene B., and Rowe, Michael, eds. *Candle in the Wind: Religion in the Soviet Union*. Washington, D.C.: Ethics and Public Policy Center, 1989.

Shlapentokh, Vladimir. *Soviet Ideologies in the Period of Glasnost*. New York: Praeger Publishers, 1988.

Sirat-i-Nu'man, Allamah Shibli Nu'mani's. *Imam Abu Hanifah: Life and Work*. Lahore: Institute of Islamic Culture, 1977.

Stalin, Joesph. *On the National Question*. London: Lawrence and Wishart, 1942.

Steeves, Paul. *Keeping the Faiths: Religion and Ideology in the Soviet Union*. New York: Holmes & Meier, 1989.

Stern, S. M. *Studies in Early Ismailism*. Jerusalem: Magnes Press, 1983.

Strong, John W., ed. *The Soviet Union Under Brezhnev and Kosygin: The Transition Years*. New York: Van Nostrand Reinhold Company, 1971.

Taheri, Amir. *Crescent in a Red Sky: The Future of Islam in the Soviet Union*. London: Hutchinson, 1989.

Tatu, Michel. *Mikhail Gorbachev: The Origins of Perestroika*. New York: Columbia University Press, 1991.

Thrower, James. *Marxist-Leninist "Scientific Atheism" and the Study of Religion and Atheism in the USSR*. Berlin: Mouton Publisher, 1984.

Timasheff, N. S. *Religion in the Soviet Union*. Westport: Greenwood Press, 1942.

Troyanosky, Igor. *Religion in the Soviet Republics: A Guide to Christianity, Judaism, Islam, Buddhism, and Other Religions*. New York: Harper San Francisco, 1991.

Tucker, Robert C. *Stalin in Power: The Revolution From Above, 1928-1941*. New York: W.W. Norton & Company, 1990.

Warikoo, K. and Norbu Dawa. *Ethnicity and Politics in Central Asia*. New Dehli: South Asian Publishers, 1992.

Wensinck, A. J. *The Muslim Creed: Its Genesis and Historical Development*. London: Frank Cass, 1965.

Wheeler, Geoffrey. *The Modern History of the Soviet Central Asia*. New York: Frederick A. Praeger Publishers, 1964.

―――. *The Peoples of Soviet Central Asia*. London: Dufour Editions, 1966.

White, Stephen. *Gorbachev and After*. Cambridge: Cambridge University Press, 1991.

Yaroslavski, Emilian. *Religion in the U.S.S.R.* London: Modern Books Ltd., 1932.

Zenkovsky, Serge A. *Pan-Turkism and Islam in Russia*. Cambridge: Harvard University Press, 1967.

JOURNAL ARTICLES

Alexeyeva, Ludmilla. "Ethnic Unrest in the Soviet Union," *Washington Quarterly*, vol. 13, no. 1 (Winter 1990): 63-77.

Anonymous. "The Muslim Republics and the XXIInd Party Congress: Reactions to the Personality Cult and Anti-Party Group," *Central Asian Review*, vol. X, no. 2 (1962): 125-128.

————. "The Peoples of Central Asia: The Survival of Religion," *Central Asian Review*, vol. VII, no. 2 (1959): 109-116.

————. "Wedding Rites in the Uzbek SSR," *Central Asian Review*, vol. XV, no. 4 (1967): 290-299.

Atkin, Muriel. "Islamic Assertiveness and the Waning of the Old Soviet Order," *The Nationalities Papers*, vol. 20, no. 1 (Spring 1992): 55-74.

Barylski, Robert E. "The Caucasus, Central Asia and the Near-Abroad Syndrome," *Central Asia Monitor*, no. 5 (1993): 21-28.

Bennigsen, Alexandre. "Islam in Retrospect," *Central Asian Survey*, vol. 8, no. 1 (1989): 89-109.

————. "Several Nations or One People? Ethnic Consciousness Among Soviet Central Asian Muslims," *Survey*, vol. 24, no. 3 (Summer 1979): 51-64.

Bialer, Seweryn. "The Domestic and International Sources of Gorbachev's Reforms," *Journal of International Affairs*, vol. 42, no. 2 (Spring 1989): 283-298.

Boiter, Albert. "Drafting a Freedom of Conscience Law," *Columbia Journal of Transnational Law*, vol. 28, no. 157 (1990): 157-187.

Bohr, Annette. "Turkmenistan Under Perestroika," *Radio Liberty Research Report*, vol. 2, no. 12 (March 23, 1990): 20-30.

————. "Background to Demonstrations of Soviet Muslims in Tashkent," *Radio Liberty Research Report*, vol. 1, no. 11 (February 24, 1989): 18-19.

Brown, Bess. "Turkmenistan Asserts Itself," *Radio Liberty Research Report*, vol. 1, no. 43 (October 30, 1992): 27-31.

————. "Presidential Election in Uzbekistan," *Radio Liberty Research Report*, vol. 1, no. 4 (January 24, 1992): 23-25.

————. "Central Asia Emerges on the World Stage," *Radio Liberty Research Report*, vol. 1, no. 1 (January 3, 1992): 51-56.

————. "Kazakhstan and Krygystan on the Road to Democracy," *Radio Liberty Research Report*, vol. 1, no. 48 (December 4, 1992): 20-22.

————. "The Islamic Renaissance Party in Central Asia," *Radio Liberty Research Report*, (May 10, 1991): 12-14.

————. "Tajik Survey Reveals Extent of Religious Belief Among Young People," *Radio Liberty Research Report*, (March 31, 1988): 1-3.

————. "Religion in Tajikistan—A Tough Nut to Crack," *Radio Liberty Report*, vol. 7, no. 88 (December 28, 1987): 23-26.

Broxup, Marie. "The Basmachi," *Central Asian Survey*, vol. 2, no. 1 (1983): 57- 81.

Cavanaugh, Cassandra, "Crackdown on the Opposition in Uzbekistan," *Radio Liberty Research Report*, vol. 1, no. 31 (July 31, 1992): 20-24.

Chalidze, Valery. "President Nursultan Nazarabaev," *Central Asia Monitor*, no. 2 (1992): 12-14.

Chavin, James. "Independent Central Asia: A Primer," *Current History*, vol. 93, no. 582 (April 1994): 160-163.

Chukin, Almas. "Free Kyrgyzstan: Problems and Solutions," *Current History*, vol. 93, no. 582 (April 1994): 169-172.

Conway, Patrick. "Kazakhstan: Land of Opportunity," *Current History*, vol. 93, no. 582 (April 1994): 164-168.

Cook, Linda J. "Brezhnev's 'Social Contract' and Gorbachev's Reforms," *Soviet Studies*, vol. 44, no. 1 (1992): 37-56.

Critchlow, James. "Democratization in Kazakhstan," *Radio Liberty Research Report*, vol. 1, no. 30 (July 24, 1992): 12-14.

————. "Kazakhstan and Nazarbaev: Political Prospects," *Radio Liberty Research Report*, vol. 1, no. 3 (January 17, 1992): 31-34.

Dellenbrant, Jan-Ake. "The Central Asian Challenge: Soviet Decision Making on Regional Stability Under Brezhnev and Gorbachev," *The Journal of Communist Studies*, vol.4, no.1 (March 1988): 54-77.

d'Encausse, Carrene. "Islam in the USSR," *Central Asian Review*, vol. IX, no. 4 (1961): 335-351.

Djalolov, Saidqasym. "February Riot," *Express Chronicle*, no. 6 (February 2-8, 1993): 6.

Ericson, Richard E. "Soviet Economic Reforms: The Motivation and Content of Perestroika," *Journal of International Affairs*, vol. 42, no. 2 (Spring 1989): 317-332.

Fraser, Glenda A. "Haji Sami and Turkestan Federation, 1922-3," *Asian Affairs*, vol. XVIII, no. 1 (February 1987): 11-21.

Fuller, Graham. "Central Asia: The Quest for Identity," *Current History*, vol. 93, no. 582 (April 1994): 145-149.

Gillette, Philip S. "Ethnic Balance and Imbalance in Kazakhstan's Regions," no.3 (1993), *Central Asia Monitor.*

Gretsky, Segei. "Qadi Akbar Turajonzoda," *Central Asia Monitor*, no. 1 (1994): 17-23.

Gross, Natalie. "Glasnost: Roots and Practice," *Problems of Communism*, vol. XXXVI (November-December 1987): 69-80.

Grossman, Joan Delaney. "Khrushchev's Anti-Religious Policy and the Campaign of 1954," *Soviet Studies*, vol. XXXIV, no. 3 (January 1973): 74-89 .

Haghayeghi, Mehrdad. "Islamic Revival in the Central Asian Republics," *Central Asian Survey,* vol. 13, no. 2 (1994): 249-266.

————. "Islam and Democratic Politics in Central Asia," *World Affairs*, vol. 156, no. 4 (Spring 1994):186-198.

Harris, Chauncy D. "The New Russian Minorities: A Statistical Overview," *Post Soviet Geography*, vol. 34, no. 1 (1993): 1-27.

Helsinki Watch Report, "Conflict in the Soviet Union: Tajikistan," (August 1991): 1-76.

Hetmanek, Allen. "Islamic Revolution Comes to the Former Soviet Central Asia: The Case of Tajikistan," *Central Asian Survey*, vol. 12, no. 3 (1993): 365-378.

————. "The Political Face of Islam in Tajikistan," *Central Asian Survey*, vol. 9, no. 3 (1990): 99-111.

Hunter, Shireen. "The Muslim Republics of the Former Soviet Union: Policy Challenges for the United States," *Washington Quarterly*, vol. 15, no. 3 (Summer 1992): 57-71.

Islam, Shafiqul. "Capitalism on the Silk Road," *Current History*, vol. 93, no. 582 (April 1994): 155-159.

Kangas, Roger D. "Uzbekistan: Evolving Authoritarianism," *Current History*, vol. 93, no. 582 (April 1994):178-182.

————. "Recent Developments With Uzbek Political Parties," *Central Asia Monitor*, no. 4 (1992): 22-27.

————. "The Challenge of Nationalism to the Gorbachev Reform Agenda," *The Current World Leaders*, vol. 34, no. 2 (April 1991): 235-254.

Kedzie, Christopher R. "Religion and Ethnicity in Central Asia," *Central Asia Monitor*, no. 3 (1992): 14-19.

Lewin, Moshe. "Perestroika: A New Historical Stage," *Journal of International Affairs*, vol. 42, no. 2 (Spring 1989): 18-29.

Martin, Keith. "Tajikistan: Civil War Without End?" *Radio Liberty Research Report*, vol. 2, no. 33, (August 20, 1993): 18-29.

Melvin, Neil. "Russia and the Ethno-Politics of Kazakhstan," *The World Today*, vol. 49, no. 11 (Novemeber 1993): 5-6.

Naumkin, Vitaly. "Islam in the States of the Former Soviet Union," *Annals*, vol. 524 (November 1992): 131-142.

Nissman, David. "Turkmenistan (Un)transformed," *Current History*, vol. 93, no. 582 (April 1994): 183-186.

Olcott, Martha Brill. "Central Asia's Catapult to Independence," *Foreign Affairs*, vol. 71, no. 3 (Summer 1992): 108-130.

————. "Central Asia on Its Own," *Journal of Democracy*, vol. 4, no. 1 (January 1993): 92-103.

————. "Central Asia's Islamic Awakening," *Current History*, vol. 93, no. 582 (April 1994): 150-154.

Panico, Christopher J. "Neo-Stalinism in Ashgabat," *Radio Liberty Draft Research Paper*, (January 13, 1993): 1-10.

Ro'i, Yaacov. "The Soviet and Russian Context of the Development of Nationalism," *Cahiers Du Monde Russe et Sovietique*, vol. 32, no. 1 (March 1991): 123-142.

————. "Central Asian Riots and Disturbances, 1989-1990: Causes and Context," *Central Asian Survey*, vol. 10, no. 3 (1991): 21-54.

Robins, Philip. "Between Sentiment and Self-Interest: Turkey's Policy Toward Azerbaijan and the Central Asian States," *Middle East Journal*, vol. 47, no. 4 (Autumn 1993): 593-610.

Steeves, Paul D. "Amendment of the Soviet Law Concerning Religious Groups," *Journal of Church and State*, vol. 19, no. 1 (1977): 36-52.

Tadjbakhsh, Shahrbanou. "Tajikistan: From Freedom to War," *Current History*, vol. 93, no. 582 (April 1994): 173-177.

————. "The Tajik Spring of 1992," *Central Asia Monitor*, no. 2 (1993): 21-29.

————. "Causes and Consequence of the Civil War," *Central Asia Monitor*, no. 1 (1993): 10-14.

————. "The Bloody Path of Change: The Case of Post-Soviet Tajikistan," *The Harriman Institute Forum*, vol. 6, no. 11 (July 1993): 1-16.

Ticktin, Hillel. "The Contradictions of Gorbachev," *The Journal of Communist Studies*, vol. 4, no. 4 (December 1988): 83-99.

Willets, Harry. "The War Against Religion," *Problems of Communism*, vol. 14, no. 6 (1964): 18-24.

Wimbush, S. Enders. "The Muslim Ferment in Soviet Central Asia," *Global Affairs*, vol. 12, no. 3 (Summer 1987): 106-118.

PARTIAL LIST OF JOURNALS, NEWSPAPERS, AND MAGAZINES

Journals

Annals
Asian Affairs
Central Asia Monitor
Central Asia Brief
Central Asiatic Journal
Central Asian Survey
Central Asian Review
Current History
Foreign Affairs
Global Affairs
Inside Central Asia
Journal of Communist Studies
Journal of Democracy
Journal of International Affairs
Nationalities Papers
Post Soviet Geography
Problems of Communism
Russian Review
Security Dialogue
Soviet Studies
Survey
The World Today
Washington Quarterly
World Affairs

Newspapers and Magazines

Christian Science Monitor
Daily Telegraph
Economist
Express Chronicle
Far Eastern Economic Review
Financial Times
The Guardian
The Independent
Iran Times
Karachi Herald
London Times
Los Angeles Times
Megapolis Express
New Times International
The New Yorker
New York Times

INDEX